MOVIE
MEMORABILIA

THE **OFFICIAL**

IDENTIFICATION AND PRICE GUIDE TO

MOVIE

MEMORABILIA

Richard De Thuin

FIRST EDITION

HOUSE OF COLLECTIBLES · NEW YORK

This is a registered trademark of Random House, Inc.

Cover photo by Don Banks

©1990 by Richard De Thuin

Published by: The House of Collectibles
201 East 50th Street
New York, New York 10022

Distributed by Ballantine Books, a division of Random House, Inc., New York, and simultaneously in Canada by Random House of Canada Limited, Toronto.

Manufactured in the United States of America

ISBN: 0-876-37788-6

First Edition: August 1990

10 9 8 7 6 5 4 3 2 1

For D. Cook,
who always knew that someday
I would trade in the Volkswagen

TABLE OF
CONTENTS

ACKNOWLEDGMENTS

Researching and writing this price guide on movie memorabilia has been a whirlwind courtship between the author and the collectibles marketplace. When I signed my contract in the Spring of 1988, I never dreamt that working on a price guide would be quite so detailed and time consuming as it eventually became. That there were sources to check, collectors to speak to, and auctions and collectibles shows to attend made my research infinitely more enjoyable, especially when there was a friendly ear to listen and a human voice to offer encouragement. I have always been a hard worker but I don't ever remember working so hard on anything else in my life.

Beginning at the top, I want to thank my agent Dorothy Crouch for her guidance and compassion through the last fourteen months, and also for opening the right doors for me to pass through in winning the opportunity to write this book. Special thanks go to Dorothy Harris, my editor at House of Collectibles, for giving me the green light to proceed with the price guide, for giving me her support, and for taking a chance on an unpublished author. Thanks also to Barbara Goldstein, Phil Scharper, and Cindy Berman at House of Collectibles for their invaluable help.

To professional photographers Edna McNabney and Jim Barthman, I extend my sincere appreciation for offering valuable tips on how, and how not, to take photographs for the book, and to Betty Gallagher of Betty Gallagher Antiques in Westfield, New Jersey, for her dealer and publicity referrals; friends like her don't come along too often in the collectibles world. Lee Anne Fahey at Christie's East was wonderful to give me photographs of important costume items sold at auction, and I'm grateful to Maryalice Adams at William Doyle Galleries for mailing a particularly interesting photograph of W.C. Fields in record time. Appreciation is also extended to the sales staff at Phillips and Sotheby's for all their help.

I was somewhat intimidated when I visited the Alexander Gallery on New York's Madison Avenue, having heard that its owner, Alexander Acevedo ("the Donald Trump of toys"), might be unapproachable; however, his staff couldn't have been more pleasant and willing to loan me a valuable photograph for my book—my thanks to the gallery, and, staying on the auction route, I would also like to thank Jesse Bien at Greenwich Auction Room and his staff members for answering questions the day I stopped by to photograph memorabilia at the "Not Just Puppets II" auction in June 1989.

Appreciation goes out to Jerry Granat and Herman Darvick for placing my name on their mailing list for autograph catalogs, and especially to Mr. Darvick for sending me autograph auction catalogs free of charge for an entire year, for allowing me to photograph select autographs at several of his previews, and, of course, for just being available to answer any questions I had.

I want to thank Malcolm Willets of Collectors Bookstore in Hollywood for allowing me to photograph auction items in his store, and also for the free catalogs he sent to me; Ken Bullock of Limelight Bookstore in San Francisco, who was kind enough to let me take lengthy notes of his film book titles (and photograph a few, too); the folks at Cinemonde for allowing me to rifle through their posters and lobby cards (without buying any), and to the proprietor at Memory Shop West, also in San Francisco, for her valuable tips concerning photographs and stills.

My very special gratitude to Melissa Vilkin at Camden House Auctioneers in Los Angeles for sending me nineteen photographs of movie memorabilia sold at the May 1989 auction (all free of charge), to the press department at Christie's South Kensington Auction Gallery in London for answering my fax, to Schoyer's Books in Pennsylvania for their sheet music catalogs, and to Lewis Rosen for allowing me the opportunity of viewing his extensive collection of movie music. Thanks also to Wayland Bunnell of Manchester, New Hampshire, a professional sheet music dealer who opened my eyes to a few facts concerning sheet music I was unaware of, and also for sending me copies of his lists; special thanks to John Aaron of Music Between the Sheets in Seattle for allowing me to refer to his sheet music catalogs and for referring me to Wayland Bunnell.

My gratitude to John Manley for helping me to alphabetize my price guide index cards (a very boring task)—he saved me from ripping my hair out—and thanks to friends and acquaintances who had the good taste not to call and fill my ear with small talk as my deadline approached. Appreciation to all the dealers, particularly Bob Gallagher, Lew Weinstein, and W.M. Nussbaum, at the Paper Collectables & Memorabilia Shows, to the women at The Attic who are always a pleasure to visit and where I picked up some inexpensive sheet music, and also to Sheldon Halper of Cobweb Collectables for allowing me to rummage through his movie memorabilia and ask questions.

Constance Nadig of Philadelphia, who exhibits at the Annex Arts & Antiques Flea Market, was especially generous in bringing up her collection of glass lantern slides for me to look at and photograph. Thanks also to Pepper & Stern in Santa Barbara; John C. Van Doren of Hopewell, New Jersey; Roger's Comics in New York; the Mouse Man Ink; Disneymania of Greensboro, North Carolina, for sending me their catalogs and lists of movie memorabilia for reference materials; C.E. Guarino of Denmark, Maine, for mailing me photocopies of stills from one of their 1988 auctions; and to all the other dealers and auction houses who were so generous in helping me with the price guide.

In closing I want to particularly thank Elaine and R. Neil Reynolds at Poster Mail Auction Co. in Waterford, Virginia, for taking the time out from their busy schedule to write the realized bids from the February 1989 poster auction, and also for their leniency in extending me credit for a personal purchase I made— I'm very grateful—and to Ted Hake at Hake's Americana & Collectibles for sending me unpublished prices on movie memorabilia sold at several mail/phone order auctions in 1988 and 1989, and for all the negatives he sent which look great in the book. Hake's Americana & Collectibles has specialized in character and personality collectibles along with all artifacts of popular culture for over 20 years. To receive a catalog of their next 3,000-item mail/phone bid auction, send $3 to Hake's Americana, P.O. Box 1444M, York, Pennsylvania 17405.

Thank you one and all. Without your help this price guide would never have become a reality. As a postscript, I'll be writing a second edition in the near future. Just enough time to catch your breath.

PROLOGUE

WHO IS THIS BOOK FOR?

I have seen him now at two major auctions held at Guernsey's, a New York auction house specializing in movie posters and lobby cards. At both auctions he had a copy of a movie memorabilia price guide in his lap.

He is a frequent bidder and very eclectic in his choice of movie paper. He doesn't appear to specialize in any particular genre of movie posters or lobby cards, for example, Disney, film noir, musicals, westerns or a special movie star, but spreads his bids over a wide range of movie subjects. He does tend, however, to bid on movie paper in as close to mint condition as possible, leaving the creased, excessively pinholed, taped, soiled, water-damaged or otherwise inferior movie paper to other bidders.

During an intermission at one auction we struck up a conversation. I learned that he was an out-of-state dealer who specialized exclusively in movie posters and lobby cards. When I asked him about the price guide, he told me that there were many instances of a movie poster or lobby card being overpriced, and sometimes, too, an outright bargain—having the book saved him from making costly mistakes.

His motto was to bid on the best and at the right price. Because of inferior movie paper appearing at auctions he wanted to be absolutely sure he received the best quality for the best price.

He also believed, and rightly so, that demand always supersedes supply, and that collectors and dealers can never be quite certain when a poster or lobby card of good quality or rarity will appear again on the market.

This dealer added, however, that he did make an exception for rare movie paper in questionable condition, provided that it wasn't beyond repair (too much fading, trimming, chunks missing), and could be fixed with professional restoration. Given that condition, beauty of graphics and design, and star names were all present, a poster or lobby card of an important Humphrey Bogart movie such as *Casablanca, To Have and Have Not,* or *The Maltese Falcon,* or perhaps a poster from one of the early Laurel and Hardy comedies such as *Babes in Toyland,* could be very desirable. He also liked movie paper of any of the Disney animation films, Greta Garbo, the Marx Brothers, and any of the films Marlene Dietrich made with the director Josef Von Sternberg before 1936. As movie paper of these stars seldom appeared on the market, it was logical for him to buy when they did. He could always find a buyer for less than perfect posters or lobby cards of these celebrities.

* * *

At the same auction, I also happened to speak with a young man who didn't have a price guide or even an auction catalog. When he raised his paddle to bid, it was usually for movie paper that began around $20 or $30, and rarely went higher than $80. Each time he would lose the final bid. When he lost out on two early 1950s, film noir one-sheets that were combined in the same lot, he looked visibly shaken. He had stopped bidding at $100 because after that amount bidding accelerated to $25 increments and he couldn't afford to go any higher.

"Did you see that," he said, "I almost had them, but that lady and her friend jumped in at the last minute. They've been buying up half the posters, too. What do you think they do with them all?"

"Probably decorate their bathroom," I said, half-jokingly. He didn't look amused.

"If it will make you feel any better," I continued, "I've been to many auctions and watched lots that I've wanted go to someone else because the price was too high. It happens to everyone."

He didn't seem to hear me.

"Yeah, but I almost had them," he reiterated despondently. "They could have left something for me!"

We both laughed and sat down. I didn't have the heart to tell him that the people who had won the bid were frequent customers at movie memorabilia auctions around town and that they were usually successful in their bids. Money didn't seem to be much of an object that bothered them. I also remembered hearing from a dealer that they liked to collect anything related to movies and New York, particularly if there was something hav-ing to do with transportation on the object. One of the one-sheets had a subway on it and I guessed that's why they bid so high (it finally sold for $150, much more than it was worth). But they had made a serious mistake. They hadn't done their homework. Although they both appeared to be knowledgeable collectors, what they didn't take the time to find out was that the subway pictured in the poster was actually a Chicago subway because that was where the film had been shot.

Before I return to my conversation with the young man, I want to mention here that even among supposedly "knowledge-able" collectors there is room for error. At auctions, there are lots of indiscriminate greedy-all-for-me-at-whatever-cost-type-bidding, and this is a situation ripe for a total breakdown of the auction-going process. Such greediness has long been a staple of antiques auctions and has recently crossed over into the movie collectible auction field as well. But more on this later.

When we were seated, the young man mentioned that he per-haps lost his bid because he was just a novice collector who really didn't know very much about posters, only that he knew what he liked. He was also vague on poster sizes, not really knowing the difference between a one-sheet versus a half-sheet, or a win-dow card from a title card. More importantly, he didn't know how to go about assembling a collection for his pleasure and investment despite his being an ardent movie buff. He didn't know what posters were worth or how much he should pay for one. I told him knowing what he liked was a sound criterion for beginning a collection, however small it might be.

That was okay with him, only he wasn't too sure that he even wanted to specialize in movie posters. He also liked movie mag-azines, autographs, stills, and sheet music. Unfortunately, he had no real expertise in any of these collecting areas.

When I suggested that he refer to a price guide for movie memorabilia, he told me that he had read a few books and found their prices too generalized. They were just a list of prices with-out any real descriptive advice. How could he be sure if he were paying too much for an item that was worth much less? Most of the time he didn't buy anything at all. I could understand his predicament because I had once been in his shoes.

Both of the men I have described are on the opposite ends of the movie collector's ladder. They are similar only in that each knows what he likes and is fascinated with the movies. The dealer, however, has the knowledge and experience to specialize in a particular area of movie memorabilia, while the young man has very little knowledge and is not sure how to go about acquiring it. This book is designed for both types of collectors.

**TAKE 1
INTRODUCTION**

WHY ONE COLLECTOR'S HUMPHREY BOGART IS WORTH MORE THAN ANOTHER COLLECTOR'S GARY COOPER

Why is a signed movie portrait or still of Greta Garbo more expensive than a signed movie portrait or still of Joan Crawford? What makes an autographed letter of Humphrey Bogart more valuable than an autographed letter of Gary Cooper?

The answer depends partly on a collector's point of view. One collector might like Greta Garbo or Humphrey Bogart, while another collector prefers Joan Crawford or Gary Cooper. Then too, it is a case of supply and demand. Signatures of Greta Garbo are extremely rare as the actress didn't like to sign anything that might fall into the hands of a collector (she shared this trait with Katharine Hepburn who to this day refuses to sign photos). Even in Garbo's correspondence it has been discovered that she used pseudonyms to sign her name in an effort to protect her identity.

It was a rare day in Hollywood that Garbo dipped a pen in ink. But for a movie star such as Joan Crawford, and she was the quintessential "star," there exists a myriad of autographed material. Crawford's passion for publicity was legendary and bordered on an obsession to keep her name in lights.

Movie memorabilia of Joan Crawford, who signed hundreds of stills, is more likely to be found in collections than stills signed by Greta Garbo. So when an autographed portrait, still, or letter that was signed by Garbo turns up in the marketplace, there is

7

bound to be more than a rudimentary interest by collectors.

Movie memorabilia of stars who have become legends, or who retain a certain "mystique," are usually more sought after and more scarce than stars who have not achieved a legendary status. Movie stars who died young, preferably through tragic circumstances, or who were considered "ahead of their times" and therefore have attained a kind of "cult" popularity are also very much in demand where it concerns anything associated with them that can be collected. James Dean is a perfect example. Not only has he attained a cult status but he died young and tragically, too. Other stars who fit into one or more of the above categories include Marilyn Monroe, Jean Harlow, Errol Flynn, Judy Garland, Maria Montez, Rudolph Valentino, Vivien Leigh, and, to a certain extent, Rock Hudson (primarily because of his tragic death from AIDS).

Collectors of movie memorabilia like tragedy. They enjoy melodrama and worship legends. They like hard-luck stories and even more, hard-luck lives. They want the memorabilia of stars who lived on the edge, indulged in bawdy pastimes, took too many drugs, drank too much booze, and had their careers "put on hold" as a result. This axiom applies to all areas of movie memorabilia. In a nutshell, the more tragic or legendary the star, the more desirable the memorabilia of that star.

Also commanding collector attention and achieving stellar prices in the marketplace are the real troupers of Hollywood, such as James Cagney, Claudette Colbert, Sean Connery, Bette Davis, Cary Grant, Katharine Hepburn, Tom Mix, Laurel and Hardy, Frank Sinatra, and Orson Welles. The childhood memorabilia of Shirley Temple is also heavily collected, and to some extent, so is the memorabilia of child actress Margaret O'Brien. Without going into a psychiatric evaluation of male collectors of movie memorabilia, who are in the majority, there is a diehard fascination with nubile young lasses of the silver screen. Hence, both Temple's and O'Brien's attraction.

On the whole, collectors of movie memorabilia are a finicky group who collect by stars more than by any other category. What they buy and how much they pay often determines who is in and who is out in the marketplace. All the stars previously mentioned are very much in, and, since their deaths in early 1988, the memorabilia of both Lucille Ball and Laurence Olivier has begun to pick up steam. Ms. Ball was always popular with collectors for her work in television, but now it's her Hollywood career that's stirring up collector interest. It's unlikely, however, that her memorabilia will ever reach the monetary heights of Marilyn Monroe or Judy Garland. She died too late in life and from heart failure.

Jayne Mansfield memorabilia has also become very fashionable. Prices for material from her career have been rising in price at a steady clip for the last couple of years. Interestingly, she also died under tragic circumstances.

Of all the stars who made their mark in Hollywood, the most universally appealing star is Humphrey Bogart. Unlike Gary Cooper, who, by current standards, is considered something of a wimp and who has not attained legendary status, Bogart has not only become a legend but has the capacity to charm almost everyone who watches him on the screen. Collectors are attracted to his memorabilia like bees to honey.

Bogart (Bogey or Bogie) is a 20th-century phenomenon among movie stars. Ever since the Brattle Theater, a small revival house in Cambridge, Massachusetts, began showing Bogart's old movies during the mid-1950s, Bogey has become the idol of millions. He was the best of the hard-boiled, cynical, gravel-voiced heroes that Hollywood promoted in the 1940s and early 1950s. Bogart was a loner who reacted to life with a smirk on his lips and a bottle in his hand.

The audience of college students and intellectuals watching Bogart in *Beat the Devil* way back in 1956 (a movie that had been released only two years earlier), sensed something tangible in this actor, something about his persona, long before the Bogart "mystique" was born. In essence, these young men and women gave the world Humphrey Bogart. And depending on the collector's viewpoint, this gift can be considered lucky or unlucky. Lucky because we have the actor's movies and memorabilia to enjoy, and unlucky because that same memorabilia has become so expensive that it is out of reach of many collectors.

THE BEST WAY
TO USE THIS BOOK

This is a movie memorabilia price guide that lists the prices for movie collectibles that have sold at auctions and through dealers in the thirteen-month period between June 1988 and June 1989. It also lists where and when the item was sold, and for how much. This three-tier pricing system will give the reader an accurate picture of what has sold recently in the collectibles marketplace.

Such a system gives the reader a successful means of collecting movie memorabilia. It provides an understanding of the way prices are set in the marketplace, for today's prices will not be the same tomorrow. Value comes down to what a particular buyer is willing to pay on a particular day, which is why prices collapse or escalate at auction, and why dealers and collectors can charge what the market will bear.

This book is not a seller's guide and it is not a buyer's guide. If any reader has a valuable piece of movie memorabilia similar or identical to any of the items listed in this price guide, they would be advised to have it appraised or to consign it to an auction house. Even talking about it with another collector can be profitable, if not in payment, then in knowledge. Just don't take your prize movie memorabilia to a dealer and expect to receive the same price you see in this book. The odds are heavily against you. (For readers who are interested in consigning material to an auction house, there is a reference chapter at the end of the book that lists major auction houses, as well as dealers and important collectible shows that specialize in movie memorabilia.)

With these thoughts in mind, both the novice and experienced collector can reap sufficient rewards in collecting movie memorabilia. Possessed of a strong fascination or obsession and plenty of knowledge, collectors can assemble a collection of movie memorabilia that will make an excellent investment for the future while providing innumerable pleasure in the present.

Welcome to the fascinating world of movie memorabilia and good luck on your journey.

SOME IMPORTANT
TIPS FOR COLLECTORS

1. Beware of fellow auction goers who bid to beat other auction goers out of a desirable piece of movie memorabilia.
2. At auctions, stick to a set price range for an item you would like to own. Don't let "auction fever" make you bid more than you can afford.
3. Bidding at auctions requires knowledge, skill, and good judgment.
4. Some auction houses offer a "sliding scale" commission rate. This rate is added to the 10% buyer's premium charged to consignors and can equal as much as 30% on an item(s) that sells for under a certain price. If you are consigning memorabilia to an auction house, ask questions before signing any papers.
5. Old auction catalogs are great reference materials. Hold on to them as they contain information left out of collectible books . . . and price guides.
6. Don't be foolish. If you aren't a millionaire or someone who enjoys throwing away money, use your head when bidding at auctions and buying from dealers. Don't do what a crazy bidder did in December of 1988 at Christie's South Kensington Auction Gallery in London. He paid £2860 for a poster of Marilyn Monroe in *Some Like It Hot* (1959, United Artists) that was estimated at between £50–100.
7. Never assume that auctions are brimming with cheap treasures at wholesale prices. Collectors can find bargains but they can also find heartache.
8. If a collector and a dealer want the same movie item at an auction, chances are the dealer will realize the winning bid.
9. Dealers have built-in antennae for helping other dealers at auctions. Know what you're doing if you attempt to cross their airwaves.

10. Dealers rely on other dealers for much of their overall business. Therefore, they like to help one another out whenever possible. This is why there exists something called "dealer's price." Stay away!

11. The best prices should go to collectors, not to other dealers (see above).

12. The best market for a collector is another collector.

13. Most collectors like to haggle over prices. Pay only what you think an item is worth.

14. Some collectors have knowledge, some have greed, some are foolish. Many have a combination of all three. Stick with knowledge.

15. Some collectors will pay outlandish prices for inferior movie memorabilia that they think is scarce or rare (see No. 6).

16. True collectors never stop looking for new pieces of movie memorabilia to add to their collections. These collectors aren't in it for the money but for the enjoyment that collecting brings them.

17. Build up a collection slowly. Be methodical. Stick to a goal.

18. Anything good will remain good. Remember that condition and content are important criteria when purchasing movie memorabilia. Aim for the best material you can find.

19. Don't throw away yesterday's collectible. It could be tomorrow's "hottest" discovery.

20. Read and study everything you can find in print and in talking to other collectors about your specialized area of interest.

21. Buy collectibles whenever possible at church bazaar sales, flea markets, garage, tag, and yard sales. There are hidden treasures galore to be discovered. Stay away from estate sales unless you enjoy losing money. Family members will bid against you for items of inferior quality. Do you really want to pay $20 for a plastic Donald Duck Pez dispenser (without any candy)?

22. Marketing research shows that over 90% of today's young adults who watch videos at home don't know who Buster Keaton was. Study everything available about the movie star's memorabilia you want to own.

23. Price ranges don't necessarily coincide with the movie item sold.

24. Movie memorabilia varies widely in price in different regions of the country. Los Angeles collectors tend to pay more

than do New York collectors. West Coast collectors are heavy buyers in Disneyana. Midwest prices are lower than prices in the South and New York. Collectors in San Francisco usually aren't as knowledgeable as collectors who live in Los Angeles or New York. Photographs and stills can be cheaper in Maine and New York than in Texas or Los Angeles. Toy memorabilia is expensive everywhere but especially in New York, New Hampshire, Connecticut, Massachusetts, and sometimes in Ohio. Movie magazines are overpriced in Atlanta. Sheet music (the really good stuff) is overpriced almost everywhere. Animation art is very, very expensive and tends to be confined to auctions in New York and Los Angeles. Posters and lobby cards can be fairly expensive in San Francisco as can be Big Little and Big Big Books. Pennsylvania, Maryland, and Virginia are good buys for movie ephemera and books. Signatures of Greta Garbo and Humphrey Bogart are prohibitively expensive throughout the United States.

25.   The golden age of movie memorabilia is roughly somewhere between 1910 and 1950, subject to change upon the vagaries of the movie memorabilia marketplace.

Add one for the road: *Everything set down in print is not always right. Hopefully, everything is right in this book.*

KEY TO MOTION PICTURE STUDIOS

The following list is a reference guide to help readers identify the abbreviations used for motion picture studios in the price guide.

AA—	Allied Artists Pictures Corporation
COL—	Columbia Pictures Industries, Inc.
FN—	First National Pictures (later combined with Warner Brothers)
FOX—	Fox Film Corporation (later Twentieth Century-Fox Film Corporation)
MGM—	Metro-Goldwyn-Mayer, Inc.
MON—	Monogram Pictures Corporation
PAR—	Paramount Pictures Corporation
PRC—	Producers Releasing Corporation
RKO—	RKO Radio Pictures, Inc.
REP—	Republic Pictures Corporation
20th—	Twentieth Century-Fox Film Corporation
UA—	United Artists Corporation
UNIV—	Universal Pictures, Inc.
WB—	Warner Brothers, Inc. (Warner Bros.)

Motion picture studio names for Essanay, Hal Roach, Kalem, Lippert, and Pathe are spelled out.

TAKE 2

MOVIE
MEMORABILIA

ANIMATION ART

INTRODUCTION

Nowhere in the field of movie memorabilia is collecting more exciting and expensive than in the area of animation art. The market has literally exploded. Prices for color and black and white animation art have set new auction records. In November of 1988 at Christie's East New York gallery, two Disney animated cels sold in the same day for $110,000 and $148,500. Then in May 1989 another cel from the same Disney cartoon, *Orphan's Benefit*, sold for a whopping $286,000, setting an all-time record for animation art and bringing the total of cels or drawings sold by Christie's East that broke records to six.

There is a fervor among collectors of animation art. There is also a lot of money changing hands between collectors and auction houses, dealers, and other collectors for the best examples of animated art. Years ago, collecting cels and drawings occurred privately among a select group of collectors who bought the art for pleasure and profit. But all that has changed. After an exhibition of Disney animation art at the Whitney Museum of Art in 1981, animation art became a respected art form. The public caught on and quickly became a strong influence in a market that is now extraordinarily competitive and expensive.

Within three years of the Whitney exhibition, Christie's began devoting two sales a year to animation art. Prices doubled and tripled. The heyday when animation art could be brought for a song had ended.

The most popular category of animation art was produced by the Walt Disney Studios (Bambi, Dumbo, Donald Duck, Mickey Mouse, Pinocchio, Snow White), followed by Warner Brothers (Bugs "What's Up Doc?" Bunny, Daffy Duck), Walter Lantz (Woody Woodpecker), Metro-Goldwyn-Mayer (Tom and Jerry), Depatie-Frelang (the pink panther), and Hanna Barbera.

Besides *The Orphan's Benefit* previously mentioned, record

sales of animation art have included a 1932 Walt Disney sketch from *Trader Mickey* which depicts Mickey Mouse held over a boiling kettle, which sold for $12,100, some $10,000 over its estimate; a colored multi-cel set-up from Disney's *Lady and the Tramp*, realizing $44,000 more than double its estimate; and Disney's *Jungle Book* which sold for $23,100, a whopping $10,000 over its estimate (Sotheby's, December 1988).

It is obvious that high-priced animation art is here to stay. This is a shame in one respect because middle- and low-range collectors are being pushed out of the market by the greediness of wealthy collectors whose wallets contain a multitude of one thousand dollar bills.

The following list of animation art is arranged alphabetically by studio beginning with Depatie-Frelang and ending with Walt Disney Studios, of which there is the majority of material. After the studio name comes the title of the cartoon or feature, year released or produced, type of animation art, animation character or characters, notation on matting or frames, size of the piece, seller, date sold, price, and price range/estimate.

A LIST OF PRODUCTION TERMS
FOR ANIMATION ART

Courvoisier Background—a gallery in San Francisco that markets licensed Walt Disney celluloids.
Full Celluloid—a full celluloid sheet, trimmed or untrimmed.
Hand-Prepared Background—the image is highlighted by a specially prepared background.
Key Background—celluloid and master backgrounds correlate to each other.
Master Background—a Walt Disney-prepared background.
Multi-Cel Set-Up—two celluloids together, one of which is a full celluloid.
Partial Celluloid—celluloid sheet trimmed down to image size represented.

 A production cel was used in the actual make-up of a cel; a limited edition cel was made expressly for sale as a form of art; and a serigraph cel is a screen-printed cel with images that are not hand-painted but with front cel outlines and background colors that have been screened on a clear base media. Rice paper was used in very early animation art and is considered to be very rare.

ANIMATION ART LISTINGS

DEPATIE-FRELANG

Pink Panther, circa 1960s/1970s, three celluloids from unknown productions, gouache on celluloid, grease pencil and xerox character outlines, 10 1/2 " × 12 1/2 ", Camden House, May 1989, $75.   *$150–$250*

FLEISCHER STUDIOS

Gulliver's Travels, 1940, prince and princess on a bridge holding hands, gouache on full celluloid applied to watercolor master overlay and background, 11 1/4 " × 15 1/4 ", Christie's East, June 1988, $15,400.   *$7000–$9000*

WINSOR McCAY

Gertie the Dinosaur, 1914, four pen and ink on rice paper animation drawings of Gertie, 7 1/8 " × 9 1/4 " and similar, Christie's East, June 1988, $3520.   *$4000–$6000*

METRO-GOLDWYN-MAYER

Don Schaffer, dancing wood nymphs and snapdragons in a forest, gouache on multi-cel set-up applied to a master watercolor panning background, 10 " × 83 ", Christie's East, June 1988, $2200.   *$2000–$4000*

Don Schaffer, haunted house and a forest clearing: two backgrounds, master watercolor backgrounds, 9 1/2 " × 30 1/2 " and smaller, Christie's East, June 1988, $2090.   *$2000–$3000*

Life With Tom, 1953, 12 background drawings, red, black, and blue pencil, 11 detailed and finished, and one sketchy layout drawing from Tom and Jerry cartoon, five with detailed figures of Tom, 9 " × 12 " × 18 ", Collectors' Showcase, December 1988, $441.   *$200–$300*

Production Unknown, circa 1940s, Tom and Jerry, gouache on celluloid with watercolor master background, framed, 9 " × 12 ", Camden House, May 1989, $1600.   *$1500–$2500*

Tom and Jerry Cartoon, circa 1950s, production unknown, gouache on celluloid, matted, 6½" × 9½", Camden House, May 1989, $150.   *$100–$150*

Touche Pussy Cat, 1954, 12 storyboard sheets, pencil, 12 animation sheets of three or four scenes in sequence with captions, drawn by Joe Barbera, co-director of the famous cartoon series, 10½" × 12½", Collectors' Showcase, December 1988, $441.

$200–$300

What Price Fleadom, 1948, model sheet of dog and fleas from Tex Avery cartoon, 9½" × 15", Collectors' Showcase, September 1988, $79.   *$20–$30*

PARAMOUNT CARTOON STUDIO

Popeye, 1959, original model sheet of Bluto in full pose and a head shot, also Popeye and Olive, Collectors' Showcase, September 1988, $57.   *$15–$25*

UNITED ARTISTS STUDIOS

Yellow Submarine, 1968, four original celluloids of scenes showing Jeremy and a policeman; a dancing "diamond" couple; John with a cut-out Ringo, Lord Mayor, and other figures (one with a "collectors" treasure seal); and Ringo with a cut-out and a blue Meanie; 12½" × 16½", Phillips, December 1988, $700.

$800–$1000

UPA STUDIOS

Mr. Magoo, circa 1960s, production unknown, gouache on celluloid, studio mat/frame, 7½" × 10½", Camden House, May 1989, $175.   *$150–$200*

WALTER LANTZ STUDIO

Woody Woodpecker, 1940s, full-color cel of a running Woody, 2½" × 2½", Collectors' Showcase, September 1988, $205.

$100–$200

WARNER BROTHERS STUDIOS

Baseball Bugs, 1946, 143 pencil storyboard drawings of Bugs playing baseball in New York, 4½" × 6" and similar, Christie's East, June 1988, $4400.   *$800–$1200*

Production and Date Unknown, three animation cels, Speedy Gonzalez, Elmer Fudd and Bugs Bunny, and Bugs Bunny and Daffy Duck, gouache on celluloid, 8″ × 10″ each, Camden House, May 1989, $225.   *$250–$300*

Production and Date Unknown, three animation drawings, Bugs Bunny, Yosemite Sam, and Daffy Duck, one of each, 8″ × 10″, Camden House, May 1989, $175.   *$75–$100*

Production and Date Unknown, four cut cels with oil master production background, Roadrunner and Wile E. Coyote, 9″ × 43″, framed, Camden House, May 1989, $1500.

$1500–$2500

Production Unknown, circa 1960s, Bugs Bunny, gouache on celluloid with hand-inked background, matted, Camden House, May 1989, $575.   *$600–$800*

Leon Schlesinger, The Major Lied Til Dawn, 1938, elephant in boxing ring, gouache on full celluloid applied to a watercolor master background, also two celluloids of elephants from same production, 9″ × 12″, Christie's East, June 1988, $2090.

$2000–$3000

WALT DISNEY STUDIOS

Alice in Wonderland, 1951, The Playing Cards, gouache on celluloid, matted, 9½″ × 12½″, Camden House, May 1989, $450.   *$450–$600*

Alice in Wonderland, 1951, Alice holding the unbirthday cake, gouache on full celluloid applied to a photographic reproduction of a master background, 9″ × 14″, Christie's East, June 1988, $2420.   *$1200–$1500*

Alice in Wonderland, 1951, unframed gouache on full celluloid of a live flower, 10″ × 7¼″, Christie's East, June 1988, $495.

$200–$400

Alice in Wonderland, 1951, unframed gouache on multi-cel set-up of Alice surrounded by bread and butterflies, 11″ × 13″, Christie's East, June 1989, $3300.   *$1800–$2200*

Alice in Wonderland, 1951, gouache on full celluloid applied to a master watercolor background of the Mad Hatter and the March Hare having tea, 10¾″ × 14¾″, Christie's East, June 1988, $13,200.   *$7000–$9000*

Aristocrats, The, 1970, framed gouache on celluloid with lithographed background of Marie and Berlioz, 8″ × 10″, Camden House, May 1989, $525.   *$450–$650*

Aristocrats, The, 1970, gouache on celluloid of Toulouse and Chinese Cat, Camden House, May 1989, $350.   *$250–$400*

Art of Skiing, The, 1941, unframed gouache on laminated celluloid applied to a Courvoisier watercolor and airbrush background of Goofy stuck in the snow, 9½″ × 10″, Christie's East, June 1988, $935.   *$700–$900*

Art of Skiing, The, 1941, gouache on laminated celluloid applied to a Courvoisier watercolor and airbrush background of Goofy with tangled skis, 9¾″ × 10″, Christie's East, June 1988, $1100.   *$700–$900*

Autograph Hound, The, 1939, colored pencil on paper of Greta Garbo embracing Clark Gable, 10″ × 12″, Christie's East, June 1988, $495.   *$700–$900*

Bambi, 1942, pencil storyboard drawing of Bambi, Thumper, and Flower, unframed, 10″ × 12″, Christie's East, June 1988, $308.   *$400–$600*

Bambi, 1942, Maurice Noble watercolor on board of the Burning Forest, 5″ × 6″, Christie's East, June 1988, $770.
          $800–$1200

Bambi, 1942, gouache on multi-cel set-up applied to a watercolor master background of Bambi and his mother in a flower patch, 8″ × 10¾″, Christie's East, June 1988, $19,800.
          $4000–$6000

Bambi, 1942, gouache on full celluloid applied to a key watercolor and airbrush background of Flower discovering his girlfriend in the daisies, 8½″ × 13½″, Christie's East, June 1988, $19,800.   *$12,000–$14,000*

Bambi, 1942, gouache on multi-cel set-up applied to a watercolor master background of Bambi discovering a butterfly on his tail while surrounded by Thumper and rabbits, 8″ × 10¾″, Christie's East, June 1988, $15,400.   *$5000–$7000*

Bambi, 1942, gouache on laminated celluloid applied to a Courvoisier watercolor background of Bambi, Thumper, and two rabbits, 6½ × 8¼", Christie's East, June 1988, $26,400.

$1800–$2200

Beach Picnic, The, 1939, a later studio print model sheet of Donald Duck, ants, and rubber horse, two poses, 11" × 14", Collectors' Showcase, September 1988, $50. $10–$15

Black Cauldron, The, 1985, four model sheets (photoprint) of Huntsmen, Gwythaints, King Eidilleg, and Orwen, 11" × 14", Collectors' Showcase, September 1988, $45. $20–$30

Brave Little Tailor, 1938, colored pencil on paper, framed, of the king seated at his throne, 10" × 12", Christie's East, June 1988, $308. $300–$500

Chef Donald, 1941, gouache on multi-cel set-up applied to a master background of Donald demonstrating how to crack an egg, 7½" × 9½", Christie's East, June 1988, $1210.

$1200–$1600

Cinderella, 1950, gouache on celluloid with photo background of Gus the Mouse, matted, 8" × 11", Camden House, May 1989, $600. $600–$800

Cinderella, 1950, unframed gouache on full celluloid of Cinderella bowing in her gown, 8" × 7½", Christie's East, June 1988, $1430. $300–$500

Cinderella, 1950, gouache on full celluloid applied to a key master background of the Evil Stepmother welcoming the Duke, 19½" × 12½", Christie's East, June 1988, $1760.

$1500–$1800

Cinderella, 1950, gouache on full celluloid applied to a photographic reproduction background of Cinderella dancing with the Prince, 0¼" × 7¼", Christie's East, June 1988, $1320.

$1400–$1600

Clock Cleaners, 1937, two animation drawings, colored pencil on paper and unframed, of Goofy angels flying in a circle, 10" × 12", Christie's East, June 1988, $440. $300–$400

Country Cousin, 1936, two animation drawings from the Academy Award-winning cartoon, graphite and colored pencil on paper depicting Abner and Monty, 10″ × 12″, Camden House, May 1989, $800.   *$900–$1200*

Der Fuehrer's Face, circa 1943, Donald Duck, airbrush spotlight and shadow background in mat, a full-color cel of an angry Donald Duck in full pose talking on a telephone, 7½″ × 9″, Collectors' Showcase, November 1988, $1996.   *$1000–$2000*

NOTE: This is just one of the very limited number of cels created by Walt Disney for sale and publicity purposes, and it is stamped "original WDP" with a label of authenticity as prepared by Courvoisier Galleries. During the last 13 months (June 1988 through June 1989), there have been a few of these cels up for auction and selling through dealers.

Dognapper, The, 1934, animation drawing, graphite on paper of Mickey Mouse and Donald Duck on a motorcycle, 10″ × 12″, Camden House, May 1989, $800.   *$900–$1200*

Donald Duck, circa 1940, gouache on full celluloid applied to a hand-prepared wood veneer background of Donald Duck posing as J. Worthington Foulfellow in front of a picture of J. Worthington Foulfellow, 12½″ × 16½″, Christie's East, June 1988, $2200.   *$4000–$6000*

Donald Duck, undated, gouache on full celluloid, Donald playing baseball, 9″ × 8″, Christie's East, June 1988, $1760.
$800–$1200

Donald Gets Drafted, 1942, unframed gouache on laminated celluloid applied to a hand-prepared background of Donald Duck at attention with a gun, 8¼″ × 7½″, Christie's East, June 1988, $825.   *$400–$600*

Donald's Duck Trouble, 1946, full cellulloid applied to a key master watercolor background of Donald and his double, Christie's East, June 1988, $4400.   *$1600–$1800*

Donald's Golf Game, gouache on partial celluloid applied to a Courvoisier airbrush background of Donald's nephew swinging a club, 6¼″ × 6″, Christie's East, June 1988, $550.

$200–$400

Donald's Nephew, circa 1970s, gouache on celluloid with gouache production background on board, an educational short, matted, 8″ × 10″, Camden House, May 1989, $100.

$200–$300

Dumbo, 1941, graphite and colored pencil on paper animation drawing of Timothy Mouse, 10″ × 12″, Camden House, May 1989, $125. $200–$300

Dumbo, 1941, gouache on laminated celluloid applied to a Courvoisier watercolor and airbrush background of a mother and baby hippo entering their train compartment, 9½″ × 11½″, Christie's East, June 1988, $825. $800–$1200

Dumbo, 1941, gouache on laminated celluloid applied to a Courvoisier airbrush background of Dumbo in makeup with Timothy, 4¼″ × 6½″, Christie's East, June 1988, $935.

$700–$1000

Dumbo, 1941, gouache on laminated celluloid applied to Courvoisier airbrush background of a smiling Dumbo being led by Timothy Mouse, 7¼″ × 10″, Christie's East, June 1988, $2200. $1000–$2000

Dumbo, 1941, gouache on laminated celluloid applied to a Courvoisier airbrush background of Baby Dumbo protected by his mother, 8″ × 10½″, Christie's East, June 1988, $1980.

$2000–$3000

Dumbo, 1941, gouache on laminated celluloid applied to a Courvoisier airbrush background of elephants riding a bicycle on the high wire, 8½″ × 11″, Christie's East, June 1988, $1045.

$1000–$1500

Fantasia, 1940, gouache on laminated celluloid applied to a Courvoisier airbrush background of an elephant staring at a goldfish in a bubble, 7″ × 8½″, Christie's East, June 1988, $1760. $1800–$2200

Fantasia, 1940, pastel on black paper of the Thistle Boys from "Nutcracker Suite," 10″ × 12″, Christie's East, June 1988, $880.   *$1000–$1500*

Fantasia, 1940, gouache on partial celluloid applied to a Courvoisier watercolor and airbrush background of dancing mushrooms in two rows, 7¼″ × 8¼″, Christie's East, June 1988, $12,100.   *$6000–$8000*

Fantasia, 1940, gouache on full celluloid applied to a Courvoisier airbrush background of the Family Pegasus landing in the water, 9″ × 13¾″, Christie's East, June 1988, $28,600.
                                    $10,000–$12,000

★

NOTE: *One of the most beautiful of the airbrushed celluloids from Fantasia.*

★

Fantasia, 1940, green, yellow, and black animation drawing from "The Sorcerer's Apprentice" sequence picturing a sheepish-looking Mickey Mouse removing the Wizard's magical hat as he returns it to his rightful owner, 6½″ × 5½″, Collectors' Showcase, December 1988, $1287.   *$400–$600*

Fantasia, 1940, gouache on full celluloid applied to a Courvoisier airbrush background of Baby Pegasus, 7″ × 9″, Christie's East, June 1988, $4180.   *$700–$1000*

Fantasia, 1940, colored pencil concept drawing of a fawn playing a pipe to a Baby Pegasus, 7½″ × 10″, Christie's East, June 1988, $990.   *$1000–$2000*

Fantasia, 1940, colored pencil on paper, framed, hippo and alligator dancing, 10″ × 12″, Christie's East, June 1988, $880.
                                    $200–$400

Fantasia, 1940, gouache on laminated celluloid applied to a Courvoisier airbrush background of an elephant balancing a goldfish in a bubble on its trunk, 7¾″ × 9¼″, Christie's East, June 1988, $1760.   *$1800–$2200*

Fantasia, 1940, pencil on paper of the Sorcerer with raised arms, 10″ × 12″, Christie's East, June 1988, $770.   *$600–$800*

Fantasia, 1940, gouache on full celluloid applied to a Courvoisier watercolor and airbrush background of a mother unicorn and her three babies, Christie's East, June 1988, $12,100.
                                                                $6000–$8000

Father Noah's Ark, 1933, gouache on multi-cel set-up applied to a key master background of animals leaving the Ark, 9½″ × 11½″, Christie's East, June 1988, $7700.   *$6000–$9000*

Ferdinand the Bull, 1938, gouache on partial celluloid applied to a specially prepared airbrush background of Young Ferdinand with his mother, 6″ × 7″, Christie's East, June 1988, $1210.
                                                                $800–$1200

Ferdinand the Bull, 1938, gouache on partial celluloid applied to a hand-prepared background of a group of matadors and a horse, 8¼″ × 10½″, Christie's East, June 1988, $880.
                                                                $800–$1200

Ferdinand the Bull, 1938, gouache on partial celluloid applied to a hand-prepared background of a matador smoking a cigarette, 7″ × 8½″, Christie's East, June 1988, $330.   *$400–$600*

Ferdinand the Bull, 1938, gouache on partial celluloid applied to a hand-prepared background of Ferdinand and a bee, 9″ × 9½″, Christie's East, June 1988, $1650.   *$1000–$1500*

Flying Mouse, The, circa 1930s, gouache on celluloid publication cel for the D.C. Heath Book Series, of flying mice, framed, 5″ × 9½″, Camden House, May 1989, $375.   *$500–$700*

Goofy and Daisy Duck, circa 1970s, gouache on celluloid with production background on board, 8″ × 12″, Camden House, May 1989, $250.   *$300–$500*

Photo courtesy of Camden House, Los Angeles, CA

D.C. Heath Book Series, 1939, framed gouache on celluloid publication cel of Mickey Mouse and Nephew, 7″ × 8½″, Camden House, May 1989, $1500.   *$1800–$2800*

Hockey Champ, The, 1938, gouache on partial celluloid applied to a hand-prepared airbrush background of Donald Duck and his nephews on the ice, 8¼″ × 9¾″, Christie's East, June 1988, $2090.   *$1000–$1500*

How to Have an Accident in the Home, 1956, full-color cel and background painting, cartoon color and tempera of Donald Duck hung up on a clothesline, 11″ × 25″, Collectors' Showcase, January 1989, $2662.   *$2000–$4000*

Ichabod and Mr. Toad, 1949, full-color animation cel, a full pose of Mr. Toad's loyal friend Rat, very scarce, 2½″ × 5½″, Collectors' Showcase, October 1988, $665.   *$500–$700*

Jungle Book, 1967, Bill Justice (artist), framed gouache on cel-luloid with hand-inked background of Shere Khan, 11″ × 15″, Camden House, May 1989, $900.   *$800–$1000*

Jungle Book, 1967, gouache on full celluloid applied to a mas-ter background of Baloo the bear with coconut headdress, 11¾″ × 15½″, Christie's East, June 1988, $1760.

$1500–$2000

Jungle Book, 1967, gouache on full celloloid applied to a key master background of King Louie on his throne, 10¼″ × 13¼″, Christie's East, June 1988, $3300.   *$4000–$6000*

Lady and the Tramp, 1955, gouache on multi-cel set-up applied to a photographic reproduction background of Lady and the Tramp outside of Tony's Restaurant, 10″ × 13½″, Christie's East, June 1988, $2860.   *$1800–$2200*

Lady and the Tramp, 1955, gouache on multi-cel set-up applied to a master pan background of Tramp fighting two dogs to save Lady, 11″ × 32″, Christie's East, June 1988, $7150.

$10,000–$12,000

Lady and the Tramp, 1955, gouache on full celluloid of Lady and Tramp seated at a table, 7½″ × 8″, Christie's East, June 1988, $2200.   *$1500–$2000*

Little Hiawatha, 1937, gouache on celluloid with Courvoisier airbrushed background of Little Hiawatha and grasshopper, Courvoisier mat/frame, signed Walt Disney, 5½″ × 6½″, Cam-den House, May 1989, $1800.   *$1500–$2000*

Mad Doctor, The, 1933, gouache on full celluloid applied to a master watercolor background of Mickey Mouse peering into a hole on top of skeleton stairs, 9½″ × 11¼″, $63,800.

$7000–$9000

NOTE: *Sold to a private Canadian collector, this black and white cel set a world record for animation art in June of 1988. It had the distinction of being the first black and white cel to come up at auc-tion. To see it in person can steal your breath away.*

Make Mine Music, 1946, gouache on full celluloid of one of the Mudville Nine at bat, 8½″ × 6¾″, Christie's East, June 1988, $880.   *$700–$1000*

Mickey Mouse, gouache on full celluloid applied to hand-prepared cartoon background, 8 1/2 " × 11 1/2 ", Christie's East, June 1988, $2640.   *$1200–$1600*

Mickey's Nightmare, 1932, four animation pencil drawings for four levels of animation in same scene of a black/white cartoon of (1) Mickey Mouse, (2) Mickey and Minnie's children riding on Mickey's back, and (3 & 4) one child on each, 3 " × 3 ", 4 " × 5 1/2 ", 1 1/2 " × 2 ", Collectors' Showcase, November 1988, $465.
                                                    $200–$400

Mickey's Polo Team, 1936, three animation drawings, all pencil on paper, of Mickey Mouse, Frank Buck, Charlie Chaplin, and the Big Bad Wolf, 10 " × 12 ", Christie's East, June 1988, $1320.   *$1600–$1800*

Moose Hunters, 1937, colored pencil on paper of Mickey Mouse, Donald Duck, and Pluto paddling a canoe, 10 " × 12 ", Christie's East, June 1988, $2860.   *$800–$1200*

Mother Goose Goes Hollywood, 1938, original studio photostat model sheet of Charles Laughton as Captain Bligh from Silly Symphony with movie star caricatures, 10 " × 12 1/4 ", Collectors' Showcase, October 1988, $33.   *$40–$60*

Mother Goose Goes Hollywood, 1938, gouache on full celluloid applied to a hand-prepared airbrush background of Charles Laughton, Spencer Tracy, and Freddie Bartholomew as three men in a boat, 6 3/4 " × 7 ", Christie's East, June 1988, $1320.
                                                    $800–$1200

Mother Goose Goes Hollywood, 1938, two animation drawings, colored pencil on paper, of Laurel and Hardy, 10 " × 12 ", Christie's East, June 1988, $605.   *$300–$500*

Mother Goose Goes Hollywood, 1938, colored pencil on paper of Edward G. Robinson and Gloria Swanson on a seesaw, 10 " × 12 ", Christie's East, June 1988, $440.   *$200–$400*

Mother Goose Goes Hollywood, 1938, two animation drawings, both colored pencil on paper, of the Marx Brothers, 10″ × 12″, Christie's East, June 1988, $660. $300–$500

Nifty Nineties, The, 1941, colored pencil on paper of Mickey and Minnie Mouse out for a spin, 10″ × 12″, Christie's East, June 1988, $1430. $800–$1200

Photo courtesy of Camden House, Los Angeles, CA

101 Dalmations, 1961, gouache on celluloid with lithographed background of Pongo, 9″ × 11″, Camden House, May 1989, $1000. $850–$1000

101 Dalmations, 1961, framed gouache on celluloid of Cruella de Ville, 8″ × 10″, Camden House, May 1989, $1100.
                    $1000–$2000

Photo courtesy of Christie's East Animation Art Department

Orphan's Benefit, 1934, black and white gouache, full cel applied to a watercolor background, 10" × 12½" Christie's East, May 1989, $286,000.   *$40,000–$50,000*

Out of Scale, 1951, full-color, dye-transfer print of Donald Duck, inscribed mat and label, made in limited quantity, 8" × 10", 15" × 16", Collectors' Showcase, November 1988, $130.
                                                    $100–$150

Peter Pan, 1953, colored pencil on paper of Captain Hook with a hot water bottle, 12½" × 15½", Christie's East, June 1988, $660.   *$800–$1000*

Pinocchio, 1940, colored pencil on paper of the Blue Fairy, 10" × 12", Christie's East, June 1988, $528.   *$300–$500*

Pinocchio, 1940, partial celluloid applied to a Courvoisier air-brush background of a drowsy Figaro lying under the covers, 5″ diameter, Christie's East, June 1988, $990.   *$1000–$1500*

Pinocchio, 1940, gouache on partial celluloid applied to a Cour-voisier airbrush background of Figaro with a bobber and hook wrapped around his tail, 5¾″ × 6½″, Christie's East, June 1988, $1650.   *$1000–$2000*

Pinocchio, 1940, partial celluloid applied to a Courvoisier air-brush background of Geppetto in his nightshirt, 6¾″ × 7½″, Christie's East, June 1988, $2200.   *$3000–$5000*

Pinocchio, 1940, gouache on multi-cel set-up applied to a Cour-voisier airbrush background of Jiminy Cricket riding a seahorse underwater, 9″ × 11½″, Christie's East, June 1988, $10,450.
     $4000–$6000

Pinocchio, 1940, gouache on partial celluloid applied to a Cour-voisier airbrush background of Jiminy Cricket with rags and bag, 5¼″ × 6½″, Christie's East, June 1988, $935.   *$800–$1200*

Pinocchio, 1940, gouache on partial celluloid applied to a wa-tercolor master background of Lampwick dangling Jiminy Cricket, 9″ × 11″, Christie's East, June 1988, $12,100.
     $3000–$5000

Pinocchio, 1940, gouache on partial celluloid applied to a master watercolor background of Pinocchio with his donkey tail tied to a rock searching for Monstro among the fish, 12″ × 17″, Chris-tie's East, June 1988, $39,600.   *$12,000–$15,000*

Pinocchio, 1940, gouache on partial celluloid applied to a Cour-voisier airbrush background of Cleo jumping up to kiss Pinocchio while Figaro dangles from the fish bowl, 9¾″ × 12″, Christie's East, June 1988, $10,450.   *$6000–$8000*

Pluto's Heartthrob, 1950, gouache on celluloid applied to a key master background, Pluto and Dinah among pink hearts and a puppy Cupid, 9¼″ × 11½″, Christie's East, June 1988, $2090.   *$1800–$2200*

Production Unknown, circa 1960s, framed gouache on cellu-loid with lithographed background of Ludwig Von Duck, 7½″ × 9½″, Camden House, May 1989, $250.   *$400–$600*

Purloined Pup, The, 1946, green and black pencil animation drawing of Pluto and puppy, 5" × 11½", Collectors' Showcase, November 1988, $280.   *$100–$200*

Rescuers, The, 1977, multi-cel set-up gouache on celluloid with "WDP" insignia and label, of Bernard, Biance, and Rufus, 9½" × 13", Camden House, May 1989, $250.   *$300–$500*

Saludos Amigos, 1943, gouache on partial celluloid applied to a hand-prepared watercolor background of Donald Duck and Joe Carioca dancing, 9" × 11¾", Christie's East, June 1988, $2090.   *$2000–$2500*

Sleeping Beauty, 1959, gouache on multi-cel set-up applied to a lithographic background of Briar Rose dancing in the woods with the owl, squirrel, and rabbits, 8½" × 11", Christie's East, June 1988, $1540.   *$1500–$2000*

Sleeping Beauty, 1959, gouache and watercolor master background of the winding staircase in Malificent's castle, 12" × 40", Christie's East, June 1988, $5500.   *$5000–$7000*

Sleeping Beauty, 1959, gouache on two pan celluloids, applied to a key master background of the two kings nodding off, 10" × 22½", Christie's East, June 1988, $12,100.

        $12,000–$16,000

Sleeping Beauty, 1959, gouache on full celluloid applied to a photographic reproduction background of Prince Philip on horseback, 10" × 8", Christie's East, June 1988, $1100.

        $400–$600

Sleeping Beauty, 1959, two animation drawings, graphite on paper of Prince Philip and Aurora, 12½" × 15½" each, Camden House, May 1989, $300.   *$200–$400*

Sleeping Beauty, 1959, graphite and colored pencil on paper, animation drawing of Prince Philip, 12½" × 15", Camden House, May 1989, $100.   *$200–$300*

Snow White and the Seven Dwarfs,* 1937, pencil on paper of Bashful showing various poses on a character model sheet, 12¹/₂″ × 15¹/₄″, Christie's East, June 1988, $2420.

$1000–$1500

Snow White and the Seven Dwarfs, 1937, two matted concept drawings of Dopey from the sequence at the lodge meeting, 4¹/₂″ × 5¹/₂″, Camden House, May 1989, $500.

$800–$1000

Snow White and the Seven Dwarfs, 1937, gouache on full celluloid applied to a hand-prepared background of Doc, 6³/₄″ × 4¹/₂″, Christie's East, June 1988, $1045. $1000–$1500

Snow White and the Seven Dwarfs, 1937, gouache on full celluloid applied to a hand-prepared airbrush background of a dreaming Dopey, 11″ × 11¹/₂″, Christie's East, June 1988, $4620. $2000–$3000

Snow White and the Seven Dwarfs, 1937, gouache on partial celluloid applied to a hand-prepared wood veneer background of Dopey, 7¹/₂″ × 7¹/₂″, Christie's East, June 1988, $1430.

$1000–$1500

Snow White and the Seven Dwarfs, 1937, gouache on multi-cel set-up applied to a watercolor master background of the evil Queen seated in the peacock throne, 9″ × 11³/₄″, Christie's East, June 1988, $52,800. $15,000–$20,000

Snow White and the Seven Dwarfs, 1937, gouache on full celluloid applied to a hand-prepared background of Grumpy, 7″ × 5″, Christie's East, June 1988, $1210. $1000–$1500

Snow White and the Seven Dwarfs, 1937, gouache on partial celluloid applied to a hand-prepared background of forest animals playing with a ball of yarn, Christie's East, June 1988, $605. $400–$600

Snow White and the Seven Dwarfs, 1937, gouache on full celluloid applied to a hand-prepared background of Happy, 6³/₄″ × 4¹/₂″, Christie's East, June 1988, $2420. $1000–$1500

**Snow White and the Seven Dwarfs* was the first full-length feature produced by Walt Disney.

Snow White and the Seven Dwarfs, 1937, graphite and colored pencil on paper of the old Witch peering into Snow White's window, 10″ × 12″, Camden House, May 1989, $600.

$650–$850

Snow White and the Seven Dwarfs, 1937, colored pencil on paper of the Seven Dwarfs building Snow White's bed, 12½″ × 15½″, Christie's East, June 1988, $3300.   *$2500–$3500*

NOTE: *This drawing was cut from the final version of the film and was to be a part of the "bed building" sequence.*

Snow White and the Seven Dwarfs, 1937, gouache on multi-cel set-up applied to a hand-prepared wood veneer background of the Seven Dwarfs looking down, 5½″ × 7½″, Christie's East, June 1988, $3520.   *$1800–$2000*

Snow White and the Seven Dwarfs, 1937, graphite and colored pencil on paper animation drawing of the Queen, 12½″ × 15½″, Camden House, May 1989, $750.   *$500–$700*

Snow White and the Seven Dwarfs, 1937, gouache on partial celluloid applied to a hand-prepared background of the squawking raven perched upon the skull, 9½″ × 11″, Christie's East, June 1988, $2200.   *$2000–$3000*

Snow White and the Seven Dwarfs, 1937, gouache on full celluloid applied to a hand-prepared wood veneer background of six dwarfs leaving the mine, 6¾″ × 11½″, Christie's East, June 1988, $3300.   *$1500–$2500*

Snow White and the Seven Dwarfs, 1937, gouache on multi-cel set-up applied to a hand-prepared airbrush background of Snow White surrounded by her forest friends, 7½″ × 7″, Christie's East, June 1988, $5500.   *$1500–$2000*

Snow White and the Seven Dwarfs, 1937, graphite and colored pencil on paper animation drawing of Snow White, 12½″ × 15½″, Camden House, May 1989, $600.   *$600–$850*

Snow White and the Seven Dwarfs, 1937, gouache on multi-cel set-up applied to a hand-prepared airbrush background of Snow White at the well surrounded by doves, 8½″ × 10½″, Christie's East, June 1988, $5500.   *$2000–$3000*

Snow White and the Seven Dwarfs, 1937, red and black pencil animation drawing of a lively expressive pose, of a surprised Dopey, 3¼″ × 5″, Collectors' Showcase, March 1989, $400.
$300–$400

Society Dog Show, 1939, full-color animation cel, full and un-trimmed, of Pluto carrying his girlfriend, Fifi, in his teeth as he slides down ramp on roller skates, rescuing Fifi from burning building, Collectors' Showcase, September 1988, $481.
$300–$500

Song of the South, 1946, gouache on partial celluloid applied to a hand-prepared background of a thinking Brer Rabbit, 7½″ × 9″, Christie's East, June 1988, $3080.
$3000–$5000

Song of the South, 1946, gouache on full celluloid of Brer Fox holding Brer Rabbit by his ears, 7″ × 11″, Christie's East, June 1988, $4180.
$2000–$2500

Steeple Chase, The, 1933, graphite on paper animation drawing of Minnie Mouse, 10″ × 12″, Camden House, May 1989, $150.
$250–$400

Sword in the Stone, The, 1963, pair of animation cels of the Wolf, one cel pictures the Wolf in shades of dark brown with a black and white eye and a red mouth with a pink tongue, and the other cel pictures his eyes and mouth closed and only a white fang shows, 12½″ × 15″, Hake's, February 1989, $226.
$100–$200

Symphony Hour, 1942, gouache on multi-cel set-up applied to a master watercolor background of Black Pete crying, 8½″ × 11″, Christie's East, June 1988, $2420.
$2500–$3000

Touchdown Mickey, 1932, graphite on paper animation drawing of Mickey Mouse and Minnie Mouse, 10″ × 12″, Camden House, May 1989, $900.
$1200–$1600

Ugly Duckling, The, 1938, gouache on partial celluloid applied to a Courvoisier airbrush background of the mother swan and five ducklings, 8¾″ × 11½″, Christie's East, June 1988, $1430.
$1000–$1500

Ugly Duckling, The, 1938, gouache on multi-cel set-up applied to a hand-prepared background of mother with five ducklings, 8¼″ × 10¾″, Christie's East, June 1988, $2200.

$1500–$2500

Winnie the Pooh and the Blustery Day, gouache on a multi-cel set-up applied to a key master background of Pooh floating along in his chair while the Owl flies overhead, 11¾″ × 15½″, Christie's East, June 1988, $2420.

$1800–$2000

Winnie the Pooh, circa 1970s, educational short, gouache on celluloid with watercolor master background on board, 10″ × 12″, Camden House, May 1989, $300.

$350–$500

Winnie the Pooh, circa 1970s, educational short, gouache on celluloid with watercolor background on board of Winnie the Pooh, Roo, Tigger, and the Owl, 8½″ × 11½″, matted, Camden House, May 1989, $450.

$300–$500

Wynken, Blynken, and Nod, 1935, gouache on multi-cel set-up applied to a hand-prepared background of Wynken, Blynken, and Nod on the boat with starfish, 9½″ × 11½″, Christie's East, June 1988, $4180.

$2000–$4000

AUTOGRAPHS

INTRODUCTION

This is a story of a young man who owned a delivery receipt signed by the actress and singer, Lena Horne. The young man was very proud to own this autograph and showed it to his family and friends whenever the proper occasion arose. He had received the autograph when he was a college student working part-time as a delivery boy for a fancy housewares store on the Upper East Side of New York.

Eventually, the delivery receipt collected a few wrinkles, a coffee stain, and a prominent vertical fold down its middle. When the mystique of owning it wore off, the young man decided to bring the autograph to a dealer before it fell apart. The autograph dealer took one look at the delivery receipt and offered the young man a dollar. Disappointed, our young hero turned and walked out the front door. The delivery receipt went into a bureau drawer and was soon forgotten.

Now, what this young man didn't know was that, despite Lena Horne's name and talent, her signature on a wrinkled, coffee-stained delivery receipt wasn't a very desirable item on the autograph market. For with any type of movie memorabilia, be it autographs or souvenir programs, condition, content, and celebrity name are everything.

Had the delivery receipt been signed by James Dean, Clark Gable, or Marilyn Monroe, it would probably have been scooped up in a second—warts and all. Or had it been a typed letter signed, an autograph note signed, or even better, an autograph letter signed,* the dealer would have offered much more.

As with the autographs of presidents, statesmen, prominent

---

*A letter that is signed and written by person described.

authors, and musicians, there is a hierarchy among autographed material of movie celebrities. A signed and dirty delivery receipt just doesn't have the panache of a handwritten or typed letter (the former entirely written by a celebrity and signed with an authentic signature, the latter usually typed by a secretary and then signed by the celebrity), or even a driver's license application filled out and signed with a handsome signature (examples of signed license applications are included in the following price list).

Remembering that condition, content, and celebrity name are the most important criteria for a collector to know, assembling a collection can be very profitable. In addition to Dean, Gable, and Monroe, other movie celebrities whose signatures, whether on applications, contracts, documents, letters, or scripts, are desirable to collect are Fred Astaire (especially if Ginger Rogers' signature is also present), John Barrymore, Humphrey Bogart, Louise Brooks, Charlie Chaplin (rarely answered letters), Bette Davis, Marlene Dietrich, Errol Flynn, Greta Garbo, Judy Garland, Cary Grant, Jean Harlow, Katharine Hepburn (particularly on photographs), Boris Karloff, Laurel and Hardy, Vivien Leigh (more valuable when signed with Laurence Olivier), Harold Lloyd, Jayne Mansfield (at one time, the poor man's Marilyn Monroe), the Marx Brothers (Groucho's signature being the most highly prized), the Three Stooges, Spencer Tracy, Rudolph Valentino, and John Wayne.

Unfortunately, not every celebrity's authograph can be among the favored few; some less desirable examples include Lauren Bacall (unless her signature accompanies Humphrey Bogart's), Gary Cooper, Olivia de Havilland, and her sister, Joan Fontaine, Ava Gardner (a shame), Greer Garson, Gene Kelly, Kathryn Grayson, Rita Hayworth, Myrna Loy, Walter Pidgeon, Debbie Reynolds, Mickey Rooney, Jane Russell, Barbara Stanwyck, James Stewart, Irving Thalberg (regrettably), and Lana Turner. Of course, both lists would include other celebrity names, but I think the reader will get the idea.

There was a period within the last few years when collecting the autographs of movie stars was frowned upon by serious philologists (philology being the study and collecting of autographs of famous people). But that has changed. According to noted autograph expert, Charles Hamilton, a letter written and signed by Greta Garbo is worth more than a letter by Abraham Lincoln (and his signature has always been very expensive).

Outstanding autographs of movie celebrities that were sold during June 1988 and June 1989 include a document signed by Greta Garbo, a mere 1 1/2 pages, and a carbon copy of an amendment to her contract for the 1939 MGM movie *Ninotchka*, selling for $3500 (February 1989 at Herman Darvick); Clark Gable's personal leather-bound script from *Gone With the Wind*, 1939, MGM, including 17 black and white movie stills which sold at Sotheby's in December 1988 for $70,000 ($77,000 with the 10% buyer's premium); two letters written by Marilyn Monroe and sold to Rabbi Robert Goldburg (who officiated at Monroe's marriage to playwright Arthur Miller) for $2200 and $1540, at New York's Swann Gallery in October 1988; and a sepia photograph signed by the zany Three Stooges (picturing Moe Howard and Curly Joe DeRita dressed in formal clothes, and Larry Fine dressed in a striped bathrobe), selling for $2500 at Herman Darvick in June 1989 (a photograph that realized almost $1000 over its price range).

The coup of the year, however, belongs to Helen and George Sanders (authors of *The Price Guide to Autographs*, Wallace Homestead, 1988), with their discovery of several old boxes of correspondence at an auction in the mountains of North Carolina. The correspondence was from an estate of a Broadway producer, director, and publicity agent, and there were many pieces of autograph material signed with the pseudonyms Harriet Brown and Hammond Brown, and the initials "H," "HB," and "GG." Written in pencil on yellow lined paper, these autographs were of Greta Garbo. In her lifelong quest to live her life anonymously, "to be left alone," she had resorted to camouflage to protect her identity. The Sanders discovered a rich treasure of correspondence autographed by the most elusive of movie stars. Almost every serious collector of movie star autographs hopes for at least one piece of signed material by Greta Garbo. The Sanders, however, now have well over $100,000 worth of such material. Not bad for a Saturday afternoon.

Autographs of movie stars offer one of the best investment opportunities for collectors of movie memorabilia. In the following list, there are many autographed letters, applications, documents, photographs, etc., that sold during the 13-month period between June 1988 and June 1989 in the United States and England. There are autographs worth thousands and autographs worth a few dollars.

However, there is no autograph material written by Ronald Reagan during his presidency or as Governor of California, by Shirley Temple as a United States Representative to the United Nations (Temple material from her political career does not have much attraction to collectors), and by Grace Kelly as the Princess of Monaco.

It is important to note that autographed material of Ronald Reagan from his Warner Brothers years in the 1940s was often signed by his mother. And it has been rumored that some photographs of Joan Crawford were signed by volunteers invited to her Brentwood house for war bond rallies during the war years.

AUTOGRAPHS LISTING

Autographs are listed alphabetically. Following each description is the name of the auction house, autograph or collectibles dealer where the autograph was sold, the month it was sold, the price paid for the autograph, and the estimated price range of the autograph. Almost all of the material is one-of-a-kind and a few autographs do not have price ranges. Complete addresses and telephone numbers for all auction houses and dealers are listed at the end of the book.

Abbott and Costello, one page, evening dinner menu from the restaurant Zimmerman's, undated, inscribed on verso by Lou Costello and Bud Abbott, approximately 8″ × 10″, Herman Darvick, June 1989, $300.　　　　　　　　　　$200–$250

Abbott and Costello, card titled "signature" with Bud Abbott and Lou Costello having signed side by side, 6″ × 1½″, fine, Herman Darvick, April 1989, $200.　　　　　　　　　$200–$250

Abbott and Costello, candid signed photo framed in black and white and picturing the comedians entering a crowded room, Kenneth W. Rendell Gallery, December 1988, $1500.

Academy Award Programs (1952–1982), contains autographs of Bette Davis, Olivia de Havilland, Ava Gardner, Sidney Poitier, Barbara Stanwyck, Loretta Young, among others. Camden House, May 1989, $1900. (From the collection of the publicist, Dore Freeman.) *$1000–$1500*

Actors, title page of the book *Movie Lot to Beachhead*, published 1945, signed on blank areas of page by Leo B. Gorcey (one of the original Dead End Kids), Robert Armstrong (of King Kong fame), Bill Frawley (Fred Mertz of "I Love Lucy"), Jimmy Dorsey, Charles Coburn, Ruby Keeler, George Murphy, and others, signed on blank verso by Jack Carson, "Gabby" Hayes, Edgar Kennedy, Lt. Buddy Rogers/USNR/1945 (husband of Mary Pickford), Harry von Zell (neighbor of Burns and Allen on their popular television show), and others, 6½″ × 9½″, Herman Darvick, December 1988, $250. *$250–$300*

Actresses, photographs/printed portraits signed by Academy Award winners: Claudette Colbert, Faye Dunaway, Joan Fontaine, Janet Gaynor, Helen Hayes, Diane Keaton, Luise Rainer, Maggie Smith, Mary Steenburgen, and Loretta Young, mostly 8″ × 10″, Herman Darvick, September 1988, $85. *$100–$120*

Akroyd, Dan, matted color photo with signature, 8″ × 10″, Autographics, May 1989, $22.50. *$20–$30*

Anderson, Judith, seven photographs, two signed, including portrait shots, stage shots, and a rare shot of the actress with a young Humphrey Bogart, 11″ × 14″, Phillips, December 1988, $50. *$200–$300*

Arbuckle, Fatty, bank check, partly printed Roscoe C. Arbuckle, one page, New York, July 24, 1916, The Greenwich Bank, 1531 Broadway, oblong 3″ × 5″, Herman Darvick, June 1989, $400. *$450–$500*

Ashby, Hal, script from *Harold and Maude*, 1972, signed on title page by Ashby, Ruth Gordon, Bud Cort, and author Colin Higgins, Camden House, May 1989, $700. *$250–$400*

Astaire, Fred, signed in black ink on *American Film* magazine cover, 1981, Cordelia and Tom Platt, June 1989, $95. *$75–$100*

Astaire, Fred and Rogers, Ginger, black and white photograph of Fred and Ginger dancing and looking into each other's eyes, boldly signed Fred Astaire and Ginger Rogers, double matted and framed under glass, approximately 8″ × 10″, about 12″ × 14″ overall, Herman Darvick, April 1989, $275.

$300–$350

Astaire, Fred, black and white photograph of Astaire dancing with Rogers, boldly signed by Astaire, approximately 8″ × 10″, Jerry Granat/Herman Darvick, November 1988, $75.   *$60–$95*

Astaire, Fred, one-page typewritten letter on RKO stationery, 2/21/35, signed in black ink, letter mounted beneath a framed photograph, 10″ × 8″, of Astaire, both glazed together, 25″ × 12″, Phillips, December 1988, $250.   *$250–$350*

Autry, Gene, double-matted, signed black and white photo, 8″ × 10″, Autographics, May 1989, $25.   *$20–$40*

Bacall, Lauren, original still from movie *Key Largo* (1948), double-matted and signed, 8″ × 10″, Autographics, May 1989, $22.50.   *$20–$35*

Ball, Lucille, photograph, circa 1944, 8″ × 10″, very fine, Collectors' Showcase, January 1989, $233.   *$100–$150*

NOTE: *Since her death last year, Lucille Ball memorabilia has become highly sought after by collectors.*

Bara, Theda, sentiment signed on her personal monogrammed stationery, with original envelope addressed by Bara and postmarked Beverly Hills, September 21, 1936, 3″ × 5″, two items, Herman Darvick, December 1988, $140.   *$140–$160*

NOTE: *Theda Bara was the first of the silent screen vamps. Her career lasted from 1914 through 1919 where she was under contract to the old Fox Studio. She made a brief comeback in the mid-twenties.*

★

Barrymore, John, black and white bust photograph inscribed by Barrymore, approximately 8″ × 10″, Herman Darvick, June 1989, $200. $250–$300

Barrymore, Lionel, actor's copy of script for *David Copperfield* (1935), 169 pages (one-side printing), and bound with metal fasteners, signed on cover by director George Cukor, David O. Selznick, producers, and stars including Barrymore, W.C. Fields, Basil Rathbone, Freddie Bartholomew, and Maureen O'Sullivan, among others, approximately 8″ × 10″, Herman Darvick, December 1988, $2500. $1800–$2000

Bartholomew, Freddie, signature on piece of paper, "With best wishes," Jerry Granat/Herman Darvick, November 1988, $25.
$25–$35

Beatles, souvenir program for their movie *A Hard Day's Night* (1964), autographed by all four Beatles and their manager, Brian Epstein, program printed for the film's opening on July 10, 1964 at the Liverpool Odeon, Sotheby's, June 1988, $3575.

Belushi, John and Akroyd, John, scene photograph from the movie *Blues Brothers* (1980), both actors are wearing dark glasses and hats, two full signatures, mint, Collectors' Showcase, November 1988, $448. $85–$125

NOTE: *It is rare to find the signatures of both these actors on the same photograph.*

Bogart, Humphrey, correspondence detailing a chess game between Bogart and a friend, Irving Korner, during shooting of the movie *Casablanca,* which began filming May 25, 1942; chess game correspondence began through the mail on January 5, 1942 and includes about 17 pieces that were mailed between Bogart, on location in California, and Korner, in Brooklyn; complete correspondence of Bogart highlighting his chess moves as played in the movie, Jerry Granat/Herman Darvick, September 1988, $1350.

Bogart, Humphrey, black and white photograph of the actor informally dressed (the word "Sluggy" embroidered on his shirt), perhaps taken on his beloved boat, the Santana; signature in bold handwriting along the lower portion of the photograph, 7″ × 9½″, scarce item, Herman Darvick, April 1989, $1200.
$700–$800

NOTE: *Bogart formed his own production company with Robert Lord and Mark Hellinger as his partners in the late 1940s, naming it Santana Productions in honor of his boat,* Santana. *The films were released primarily through Columbia Pictures and included* Knock On Any Door *(1949),* In A Lonely Place *and* Tokyo Joe *(1950), and* Sirocco *(1951).*

Bogart, Humphrey, driver's license application dated December 12, 1950 from the Department of Motor Vehicles, State of California; Bogart has answered questions on the form and signed his name on the lower right side of the application, 8″ × 5″; framed with a color photograph of Bogie, 15″ × 19″, Christie's East, June 1989, $2420.
$800–$1000

Boone, Pat, "Rock—Jesus is your Rock and He'll never let you down. God bless you, pal—Pat," booklet "A New Song," 192 pages, 1981, sent by Boone to Rock Hudson shortly before the actor died of AIDS, very good condition, 5½″ × 8″, Collectors' Showcase, February 1989, $68.
$75–$100

Bow, Clara, the "It" girl of the late 1920s, signed black and white photograph of Clara holding her baby, Oregon State Autograph Co., January 1989, $400.
$350–$450

Boyd, William, black and white signed photograph, Boyd dressed as Hopalong Cassidy, reaching for his guns and smiling, three-quarter length, approximately 8″ × 10″, Herman Darvick, April 1989, $275.
$200–$250

Brando, Marlon, letter, typed, on Paris hotel stationery, dated 1977, unframed, P.M. Antiques & Collectibles, June 1988, $35.
$30–$50

Brando, Marlon, signed black and white original still of the actor in *On the Waterfront* (1954), COL, for which Brando received his first Academy Award, 8″ × 10″, Oregon State Autograph Co., January 1989, $250.
$200–$300

Brooks, Louise, very rare photograph by Eugene Robert Richee, inscribed and signed by Brooks in bold black ink on a light background featuring a head and shoulders view of this silent film actress, matted and framed, 11″ × 14″, William Linehan Autographs, May 1989, $1600. *$1500–$1800*

NOTE: *Richee was an important photographer at PAR where Brooks was under contract in the late 1920s. As with the later PAR contract star, Francis Farmer, Brooks was her own worst enemy. In turning her back on Hollywood, she sabotaged her own career. Signed Brooks' photographs rarely turn up in the collectible marketplace.*

Burns, George, letter signed, one page, on the actor's personal stationery, dated June 26, 1969, to songwriter Harry Ruby, approximately 8″ × 10″, Herman Darvick, April 1989, $325.
$140–$160

Burns, George and Allen, Gracie, signatures on autograph album page, circa 1940, with "woo woo" Hugh Herbert, inscribed signature on verso, 5½″ × 4¼″, Jerry Granat/Herman Darvick, November 1988, $100. *$90–$100*

Cagney, James, black and white movie still from *Yankee Doodle Dandy*, signed boldly by Jim Cagney, approximately 8″ × 10″, Herman Darvick, April 1989, $85. *$100–$120*

Cagney, James, sepia reprint showing scene from *Angels With Dirty Faces*, WB (1938), signed boldly, Jim Cagney, 14″ × 11″, Herman Darvick, December 1988, $140. *$120–$140*

Cagney, James, portrait, a reprint from an early 1930s gangster film, signed circa 1980s, in a shaky hand, mint, Collectors' Showcase, November 1988, $82. *$65–$95*

Cantor, Eddie, SAG application, 1938, 4″ × 1¼″, fine, Collectors' Showcase, January 1989, $50. *$60–$90*

Caron, Leslie, signed contract, 1975, mint, Collectors' Showcase, January 1989, $48. *$35–$40*

Chaplin, Charles, oblong black and white still from early silent film *Easy Street* (1917), Chaplin is dressed as a policeman, signed on lower blank margin by Chaplin in his later years, approximately 8" × 10", Herman Darvick, December 1988, $250.

$300–$350

Chaplin, Charles, SAG form, circa 1930s, full signature, fine +, 4" × 1/2", Collectors' Showcase, January 1989, $196.

$100–$150

★

NOTE: *Chaplin signed many of his stills and photographs with a simple "hello," followed by his name.*

★

Chevalier, Maurice, clip signature, Jerry Granat/Herman Darvick, February 1989, $35. $25–$35

Clive, Colin, black and white photograph, inscribed, of Clive close-up, rare photograph, approximately 8" × 10", Herman Darvick, June 1989, $225. $200–$250

★

NOTE: *Colin played Baron Frankenstein in the 1931 movie. He died in 1937 at the age of 39.*

★

Cooper Gary, inscribed black and white vintage bust photograph (circa late 1930s), approximately 8" × 10", Herman Darvick, June 1989, $200. $250–$300

Cooper, Gary, sepia bust photograph in profile, inscribed, photo has been repaired on verso with tape, approximately 8" × 10", Herman Darvick, April 1989, $300. $120–$140

Crabbe, Buster, reprint still, full signature, with the actor dressed as Flash Gordon, fine, approximately 8" × 10", Collectors' Showcase, March 1989, $88. $25–$40

Crawford, Joan, black and white glossy photograph, signed and inscribed, Crawford is pictured with John Wayne in a scene from the 1942 MGM movie *Reunion in France*, approximately 8″ × 10″, Cordelia and Tom Platt, June 1989, $30.

$25–$50

NOTE: *This is a rough estimate for Crawford photograph signatures/inscriptions as the actress was a great promoter of self-publicity and a large amount of her autographed material is in the collectible marketplace. More ambitious inscriptions bring higher estimates, particularly if the material is from Crawford's early film career—a career that spanned the years 1925–1972.*

Crawford, Joan, signed letter, 1964, with full signature on her personal letterhead, Brian Kathenes, January 1989, $65.

$60 $75

Crosby, Bing, signed letter, 1½ separate pages, dated November 7, 1950, to songwriter Harry Ruby, Crosby discusses the problems incurred with a record he had made with his teenage son, the record was a success and Crosby wants to keep most of the royalties for himself, a very interesting letter, approximately 8″ × 10″, Herman Darvick, April 1989, $275. $250 $300

Cruise, Tom, color bust photograph, signed, approximately 8″ × 10″, Jerry Granat/Herman Darvick, November 1988, $45.

$40–$55

Darin, Bobby, black and white nearly half length photograph of this actor/singer ("Mack the Knife"), 3″ × 5″, Herman Darvick, April 1989, $250. $160–$180

NOTE: *Darin was nominated for an Academy Award as best supporting actor in 1963 for the film* Captain Newman, M.D. *He died of heart failure at 37 in 1973. Signatures of Bobby Darin are scarce.*

Davis, Bette, signed autograph letter, two pages, Beverly Hills, 1936, in which Davis calls Hollywood a cesspool of humanity, with postmarked envelope addressed by Davis, approximately 6″ × 8″, Herman Darvick, December 1988, $250.

$100–$150

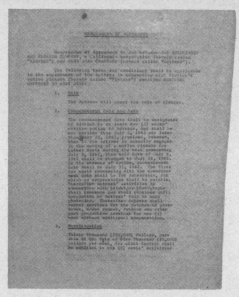

Davis, Bette and *Crawford, Joan,* signed contracts for the 1962 movie *Whatever Happened to Baby Jane?* (WB), Davis contract is five separate pages, dated May 9, 1962, signed and initialed in three places by B.D. and the movie's director, Robert Aldrich (R.A.), Crawford's contract is also dated May 9, 1962, and initialed on one page by the actress and R.A., both contracts are approximately 8″ × 10″, Herman Darvick, February 1989, $1900.   *$600–$700*

NOTE: *Crawford's salary was $30,000 for six weeks of work plus 15% of the net profits, whereas Davis' contract called for a salary twice that amount for six "consecutive" weeks of work, but with only 10% of the net profits. Her contract also gave her approval of a makeup man, hairdresser, and personal wardrobe woman, and Davis could nix the choice of Pearl Bailey in a supporting role, which she did. Davis received her tenth Academy Award nomination for Baby Jane, Crawford wasn't nominated. Who was the smarter business woman?*

★

Dean, James, yearbook "The Take-Off," Fairmont High School, Fairmont, Indiana, class of 1948, Dean has signed his name in pencil opposite his picture on the basketball team, Dean, who wore glasses, was known as Jim or Jimmy, Herman Darvick, June 1988, $1600.   *$1000–$1200*

DeMille, Cecil B., original and confidential script of the 1934 movie *The Crusades,* 194 separate pages, with printed paper wrappers dated "Second/January 29, 1935," inscribed, 8½" × 14", Herman Darvick, September 1988, $200.   *$200–$250*

DeMille, Cecil B., white calfskin binder containing group of fan letters, primarily thank you notes, including a telegram from Winston Churchill, binder is inscribed "Cecil B. DeMille" and embossed with Ten Commandment tablets, Christie's East, October 1988, $2200.   *$300–$400*

DeMille, Cecil B., check from DeMille's production company, dated 1946, for $5926.06 covering production costs for his movie *The Unconquered* (1947) starring Gary Cooper, very fine, 8½" × 3", Collectors' Showcase, January 1989, $121. *$40–$50*

Dietrich, Marlene, black and white photograph, signed, approximately 8" × 10", Willow Valley Collectibles, February 1989, $30.   *$30 $60*

DeHavilland, Olivia, black and white bust photograph, signed, 3" × 5", Jerry Granat/Herman Darvick, February 1989, $20.
                    $20–$40

Disney, Walter, typed letter dated July 29, 1966, signed, framed with a photo of a smiling Disney, Kenneth W. Rendell Gallery, November 1988, $1500.   *$800–$1200*

Donat, Robert, signature on sheet of paper, 3″ × 5″, Jerry Grant/Herman Darvick, November 1988, $45.   *$20–$50*

NOTE: *Donat won the Academy Award for best actor in 1939 for* Goodbye Mr. Chips, *MGM.*

Fairbanks, Douglas, half-length, sepia-printed photograph, ornate border, picturing Fairbanks dressed in a suit and using his left hand to twirl his moustache, signed, lower border (1923), Herman Darvick, April 1989, $110.   *$180–$200*

Fairbanks, Douglas, sepia bust photograph, wearing bandana and earrings, sans shirt, in a scene from his silent film *The Thief of Bagdad* (1924), approximately 8″ × 10″, Herman Darvick, February 1989, $250.   *$200–$250*

NOTE: *Fairbanks made* The Thief of Bagdad *at the peak of his career and athletic powers. It was his most successful silent film both financially and critically.*

Farmer, Frances, vintage sepia photograph and signature, copyrighted PAR, 1936, Herman Darvick, June 1989, $300.

$200–$250

NOTE: *Vintage signatures of Frances Farmer are extremely hard to find.*

Fields, W.C., photograph and separate bold signature, framed together, of Fields in *My Little Chickadee,* 1940, Kenneth W. Rendell Gallery, December 1988, $1500.   *$1200–$1500*

Photo courtesy of William Doyle Galleries

Fields, W.C., inscribed photograph, dated October 11, 1928, to Arthur Samuels "Poppy," William Doyle Galleries, June 1989, $1700. *$400–$500*

NOTE: *This is a respectable looking photograph of Fields, a man who was enormously unattractive, unpleasant in nature, who not only hated children and dogs, but who was also anti-Santa Claus. Ironically, Fields died on Christmas Day in 1946.*

Flynn, Errol, linen-backed photo with separate signature, circa 1935, 11″ × 14″, Camden House, May 1989, $375.

$150–$250

Flynn, Errol, full-length signed portrait, circa 1944, fine +, approximately 6″ × 8″, Collectors' Showcase, November 1988, $339. *$125–$150*

Flynn, Errol, signed letter Errol, two separate pages, from Hotel Comodoro in Havana, Cuba, and dated March 30, 1959, sent to Earl Conrad, the co-author of Flynn's autobiography, *My Wicked, Wicked Ways,* with an unsigned black and white photograph of Flynn and an autographed signed letter of the actor's wife, Beverly Aadland, also written to Conrad and dated May 14, 1959, and signed "Woodsie & Errol," it includes the original mailing envelope, both letters approximately 8″ × 10″, Herman Darvick, March 1989, $1200.   *$500–$600*

NOTE: *Before 1959 was over,* My Wicked, Wicked Ways *had been published and Flynn was dead at the age of 50.*

Fonda, Jane, signed card with original envelope, announcing her as an Academy Award winner for best actress in the 1978 film *Coming Home,* and a signed color photograph of Fonda holding her Oscar, separate frames, 11″ × 14″, Camden House, May 1989, $225.   *$200–$400*

Gable, Clark, signed and inscribed MGM studio portrait, circa 1940, framed, Camden House, May 1989, $450.   *$250–$400*

Gable, Clark, signed check (Security First National Bank of Los Angeles), in ink, dated March 13, 1950, Phillips, December 1988, $200.   *$300–$400*

Gable, Clark, contract for the 1957 WB movie *Band of Angels* between WB and Clark Gable, 60 separate pages, dated January 14, 1957, full signature on the concluding page, and one C.G. initial in the contract, 8½″ × 13″, Herman Darvick, February 1989, $550.   *$800–$900*

Gable, Clark, pencil inscription and signature on the August 1936 edition of *Gone With the Wind,* on blank inside front cover, missing dust jacket, Nasca, October 1988, $160.   *$300–$500*

Garbo, Greta, scribbled ink message on piece of paper, 1930, to a young autograph seeker: "Your a naughty boy," child's mother has written in *Garbo* under the message, 3″ × 4″, Christie's East, June 1989, $990.   *$900–$1200*

Garbo, Greta, signed and inscribed in blue ink, a bust portrait from *The Painted Veil,* 1934, MGM, to a friend in the elevator of Tiffany & Co. in New York on May 4, 1970, 8″ × 5″, Christie's East, June 1989, $4180.   *$4000–$5000*

Garland, Judy, personal letter, one page, date unknown, Camden House, May 1989, $700.   *$500–$600*

Garland, Judy, black and white MGM bust photograph, circa late 1940s, boldly inscribed, approximately 8″ × 10″, Herman Darvick, April 1989, $600.   *$250–$300*

Gielgud, John, clip signature, Jerry Granat/Herman Darvick, February 1989, $10.   *$10–$15*

Gish, Lillian, signed letter on stationery from The Hotel and Bungalows at Beverly Hills, June 27, 1925, one page, approximately 6″ × 8″, Jerry Granat/Herman Darvick, February 1989, $45.   *$35–$65*

Goldwyn, Samuel, short letter, signed and dated 1967, Jerry Granat/Herman Darvick, November 1988, $40.   *$40–$50*

NOTE: *Collectors are waking up to the value of Goldwyn's signature since the publication of his biography by A. Scott Berg (1988).*

Gone With the Wind, October 1938, Macmillan & Co., Margaret Mitchell, hardcover, signed on the inside cover and subsequent pages, cast members have signed their real names opposite their character's name, also signed by the producer, David O. Selznick, and the director, Victor Fleming, Christie's East, June 1989, $13,200. $6000–$8000

Grayson, Kathryn, signed autograph, circa 1944, very fine, approximately 8″ × 10″, Collectors' Showcase, January 1989, $61. $75–$95

Griffith, D.W., bank check with full signature, dated May 5, 1944, Hollywood, in the amount of $20, Herman Darvick, December 1988, $200. $200–$250

NOTE: *Griffith was the silent film director of* Birth of a Nation *(1915) and* Intolerance *(1916), among other classic silent films. He is responsible for discovering and nurturing the careers of Mary Pickford and Lillian Gish.*

Griffith, Hugh, scarce signature of the actor who won the best supporting actor Oscar for *Ben Hur* (1959), Jerry Granat/Herman Darvick, November 1988, $50. $40–$60

Hamilton, Margaret, inscribed black and white still from *The Wizard of Oz* (1939) showing Dorothy and the Scarecrow walking down the yellow brick road as Hamilton, playing the Wicked Witch of the West, lurks behind a tree, great inscription with "witchfully . . ." signature, approximately 8″ × 10″, Jerry Granat/Herman Darvick, February 1989, $125.   *$115–$140*

Hardy, Oliver, SAG application with membership number, circa 1930s, signed, 3½″ × 1½″, Collectors' Showcase, January, 1989, $198.   *$100–$150*

Harlow, Jean, original music folio with signed cover from the MGM movie *Reckless* (1935), 9″ × 12″, Oregon State Autograph Co., January 1989, $1950.

NOTE: *Harlow's singing voice was reputedly dubbed for this movie.*

Harlow, Jean, George Hurrell portrait, signed with inscription from Harlow to her agent/discoverer, Arthur Landau, circa 1931, a one-of-a-kind item, very fine +, Collectors' Showcase, December 1988, $3309.   *$750–$1000*

NOTE: *George Hurrell was a portrait photographer at MGM. This portrait was from the estate of Landau's wife.*

Harrison, Rex, check dated 1967 to a limousine service, fine, 6″ × 3″, Collectors' Showcase, January 1989, $38.   *$20–$25*

Hayes, Gabby, bust photograph, signed George "Gabby" Hayes, scarce, approximately 8″ × 10″, Herman Darvick, April 1989, $275.   *$180–$200*

NOTE: *Hayes was a sidekick to both Roy Rogers and Hopalong Cassidy, and the host of a children's television show in the early 1950s.*

Hayworth, Rita, clip signature, blue background, Jerry Granat/Herman Darvick, February 1989, $100.   *$50–$100*

Henie, Sonja, inscribed small sheet, approximately 6″ × 8″, Jerry Granat/Herman Darvick, February 1989, $75.   *$30–$75*

★

NOTE: *Henie was a contract star at 20th (1936–1943), and with her ice skates she was to 20th what Esther Williams in her swimming pool was to MGM. After winning Gold Medals in the 1928, 1932, and 1936 Olympic Games, Henie came to Hollywood to try the movies. By late 1937, and after only two films, she was in the top 10 money-makers. In 1938 she astutely revised her contract and became the highest paid of stars.*

★

Hepburn, Audrey, signed black and white still from *Sabrina* (1954), pictured with co-star William Holden, approximately 8″ × 10″, Jerry Granat/Herman Darvick, February 1989, $50.
$50–$120

Hepburn, Katharine, signed letter on her personal stationery wherein she tells a fan that she doesn't sign photos, dated 1983, fine, 6″ × 8″, Collectors' Showcase, January 1989, $103.
$25–$30

Hepburn, Katharine, black and white glossy photograph, a bust portrait pose, circa late 1940s, scarce, 7″ × 9″, Cordelia & Tom Platt, March 1989, $1000.   *$850–$1100*

★

NOTE: *Signatures of Katharine Hepburn on photographs are rare. When they do turn up, they tend to be very expensive.*

★

Hepburn, Katharine, RKO continuation contract, dated November 29, 1937, one sheet of typed paper (carbon), signed in ink by Hepburn, matted, Phillips, December 1988, $350.
$300–$400

Hitchcock, Alfred J., matted photo with signature, fine, 16″ × 20″, Nasca, October 1988, $100.   *$75–$150*

Hitchcock, Alfred J., signed album page, includes a small self-portrait signed with a black felt-tip pen, matted with a photograph with Hitchcock's printed signature, both framed and glazed together, 11″ × 14″, Phillips, December 1988, $350.
$250–$350

Holliday, Judy, printed document, signed, one page, dated February 27, 1948 (New York), concerning publicity rights for use of her name, picture or portrait in *Chicago Tribune–New York News Syndicate* publications, approximately 8″ × 10″, Herman Darvick, April 1989, $100. *$180–$200*

Houston, John, signed still portrait from *The Unforgiven* (1960), a Houston-directed picture starring Burt Lancaster, very good, approximately 8″ × 10″, Collectors' Showcase, November 1988, $121. *$60–$80*

Howard, Leslie, inscribed early vintage black and white bust photograph from *The Scarlet Pimpernel* (1934), approximately 8″ × 10″, Herman Darvick, June 1989, $225. *$200–$250*

NOTE: *Howard played Ashley Wilkes in* Gone With the Wind. *He died in an airplane crash in 1943.*

Jolson, Al, inscribed early vintage black and white bust photograph of a smiling Jolson, a captioned photo "Al Jolson—Warner Bros. and Vitaphone Pictures, 1934," approximately 8″ × 10″, Herman Darvick, June 1989, $250. *$200–$250*

Jones, Buck, card signed in red pencil, full signature, plus photograph with signature below (Jones in western clothes), matted, Autographics, March 1989, $75. *$50–$80*

Karloff, Boris, studio script, 108 pages, from *Black Castle* (1954), including early UNIV stationery with Karloff's name, address, and phone number written by him, and a photograph of the actor in the makeup room, also includes reviews of *Black Castle* (10), and a hairpiece supposedly worn by Karloff, Camden House, May 1989, $350. *$350–$500*

Keaton, Buster, self-portrait drawn on an album page with a fine autograph of the actor matted with a postcard and framed, 11″ × 13″, Phillips, December 1988, $5000.

$5000–$10,000

Kelly, Gene, photograph, 1944, very fine, approximately 8″ × 10″, Collectors' Showcase, January 1989, $60. *$65–$95*

Kelly, Grace and Holden, William, black and white movie still from *The Bridges of Toko-Ri* (1954), a sexy bust pose of the stars kissing, signed "Best Wishes" by both, approximately 8″ × 10″, Herman Darvick, April 1989, $300.   *$160–$180*

★

NOTE: *Kelly would leave Hollywood in 1956 to marry the Prince of Monaco. Ironically, both Kelly and Holden met accidental deaths; Holden in 1981 and Kelly in 1982, exactly 28 years after each won an Oscar. Holden won for* Stalag 17 *in 1953, and Kelly won for* The Country Girl *in 1954.*

★

Lasky, Jesse L., signed letter, one page, dated May 31, 1951, Culver City, California, on MGM stationery, approximately 8″ × 10″, Jerry Granat/Herman Darvick, September 1988, $75.   *$65–$75*

★

NOTE: *By 1951, Lasky was an independent producer but his roots in the film industry went back to 1913 when, along with partners Samuel Golfish (later Goldwyn) and Cecil B. DeMille, he formed the Jesse L. Lasky Feature Play Company (their first feature was* The Squaw Man *filmed in 1914). In 1916, the company combined with Adolph Zukor's Famous Players Film Company and became Famous Players-Lasky. Jesse was made first vice-president of all production and served in that capacity through June 1932, when the studio, which had since become Paramount Publix Corporation, went into receivership and Lasky was forced out, losing a personal fortune of over $10 million. He later formed Jesse L. Lasky Productions and released his films through Fox Film Company, and then formed a partnership with Mary Pickford (Pickford-Lasky Productions, Inc.). Lasky died in 1958.*

★

Laurel and Hardy, typed letter with signature Stan Laurel, and a large signature in pencil of Oliver Hardy, matted with a movie still (approximately 6″ × 8″), 11″ × 14″ overall, Herman Darvick, April 1989, $180.   *$200–$250*

Laurel, Stan, signed letter, one full page, dated December 3, 1958, Santa Monica, California, with original envelope, approximately 8″ × 10″, Jerry Granat/Herman Darvick, September 1988, $300.   *$300–$350*

Leigh, Janet, signed letter on MGM stationery (1950), discussing Leigh's relationship with co-star Elizabeth Taylor on the *Little Women* remake, fine, Collectors' Showcase, January 1989, $89.
$40–$50

Leigh, Vivien, full signature on sheet of pink paper, 5″ × 3″, Herman Darvick, December 1988, $200. $100–$120

Lloyd, Harold, signed check, Rolin Film Co., Los Angeles, June 19, 1915, to Lloyd for $50, verso endorsement by H.C. Lloyd, Herman Darvick, December 1988, $225. $180–$200

NOTE: *Lloyd was only 21 years old when he received this check and just beginning his film career portraying the character of Lonesome Luke.*

Loren, Sophia, oblong black and white still from *Two Women* (1961), signed, approximately 8″ × 10″, Jerry Granat/Herman Darvick, September 1988, $50. $20–$70

Lorre, Peter, sepia bust photograph inscribed with Vintage signature, approximately 8″ × 10″, Herman Darvick, April 1989, $275. $180–$200

Loy, Myrna, signed note, one page, on her personal memo paper, brief message and signature, 3″ × 5″, Jerry Granat/Herman Darvick, February 1989, $35. $25–$40

Lugosi, Bela, signature on paper sheet, 3″ × 5″, Herman Darvick, June 1989, $140. $200–$250

MacDonald, Jeanette, original hand-colored lobby photo, inscription and signature, approximately 8″ × 10″, Autographics, March 1989, $250. $225–$275

Magnani, Anna, lined card with signature in red ink, dated April 1968, with color photographs (approximately 6″ × 8″), matted together and framed under glass, 13″ × 16″ overall, Herman Darvick, April 1989, $250. $300–$350

NOTE: *Magnani won the best actress Oscar for her performance in the 1955 movie* The Rose Tattoo. *Her signature is considered rare among collectors.*

Marx, Chico, autograph album page, inscription, circa 1940, 5 1/2" × 4 1/2", Jerry Granat/Herman Darvick, November 1988, $120.   *$100–$125*

Marx, Groucho, letter signed Groucho, dated January 7, 1952, 1 1/4 separate pages of personal stationery, approximately 6" × 8", Herman Darvick, February 1989, $425.   *$200–$250*

Marx, Groucho, contract of 17 pages, dated November 30, 1950, for role in *They Sell Sailors Elephants,* signed Groucho Marx and Julian Marx (Groucho's given name), and a representative of RKO, Christie's East, June 1989, $880.   *$800–$1200*

NOTE: They Sell Sailors Elephants *was a screen adaptation of a book that was retitled* A Girl in Every Port, *and produced in 1952.*

Marx, Groucho, SAG application with membership number, signed, Collectors' Showcase, January 1989, $220.   *$75–$95*

Marx, Harpo, SAG application, pencil signature, 4" × 2", Collectors' Showcase, January 1989, $182.   *$75–$95*

Marx, Zeppo, autographed album page with "best wishes" inscription, 5 1/2" × 4 1/2", Jerry Granat/Herman Darvick, November 1988, $75.   *$75–$95*

NOTE: *Zeppo only appeared in the first five Marx Brothers comedies at PAR (1929–1933), and then retired.*

McCarey, Leo, autograph album sheet of paper, signed and inscribed, 4" × 6", Herman Darvick, June 1989, $80.
$100–$200

NOTE: *McCarey was the director of* The Awful Truth *(1937) and* Going My Way *(1944). He won the Oscar for both pictures.*

McDaniel, Hattie, Screen Actors Guild application with signature and membership number, fine, 4″ × 2″, Collectors' Showcase, January 1989, $275. $50–$75

NOTE: McDaniel's signature is rare. Memorabilia of this actress is known as a "crossover" collectible in that collectors of black memorabilia want her signature, as do collectors of movie memorabilia.

McQueen, Steven, black and white bust photograph, inscribed boldly, and with a handwritten and signed statement from the house detective at the Beverly Wilshire Hotel in Beverly Hills explaining how he came into possession of the photograph (approximately 8″ × 10″), Herman Darvick, September 1988, $225. $100–$120

NOTE: Authentic signed material of Steve McQueen is hard to find.

Menu, PAR Continental Cafe (the studio commissary), signed by 15 stars on March 16, 1949, four pages, approximately 11″ × 14″, including Charles Bickford, Claudette Colbert, Bing Crosby, Marlene Dietrich, Paul Henreid, Alan Ladd, Burt Lancaster, and Barbara Stanwyck, also included is a circa 1940 menu from Mike Lyman's Grill in Hollywood with Eddie Cantor's and Billy De Wolfe's signatures on the cover, approximately 11″ × 14″, Nasca, October 1988, $80. $200–$300

Menu, Jack Benny, Jack Dempsey, Errol Flynn, and Ramon Novarro, among others, signed the cover of the New York Central Railroad's famed Twentieth Century Limited menu, four pages, dated September 10, 1938, Mickey Rooney signed an inside page, approximately 8″ × 10″, Herman Darvick, June 1989, $250. $200–$250

Menu, another four-page menu from the Twentieth Century Limited, signed on the cover by Gracie Allen, George Burns, Harpo Marx (in pencil), George Jessell (in pencil), Pat O'Brien, Edward G. Robinson (in pencil), and Norma Shearer; inside pages have signatures of Joan Crawford, Jim Cagney, Gary Cooper (1938), and, in pencil, Annabella (Mrs. Tyrone Power), Power himself, Harold Lloyd (with a small eyeglass drawing), and Spencer Tracy; Dolores Del Rio has signed in purple pencil, approximately 8″ × 10″, Herman Darvick, June 1989, $200.

$500–$600

NOTE: *There is a small photo affixed inside of both Twentieth Century Limited menus of the daughter of Frank Romano, who was the hairstylist on the train. Romano collected signatures of stars for his daughter.*

Middleton, Charles, signature on sheet of paper, 3″ × 5″, Jerry Granat, Herman Darvick, November 1988, $195.   *$175–$215*

NOTE: *Middleton played Ming the Merciless in the "Flash Gordon" serials. His signature is hard to come by.*

Mineo, Sal, a signed document, one page, dated 1956, New York, wherein the 17-year-old actor gives permission to the *Chicago Tribune–NY News Syndicate* use of his name, picture or portrait in publications for editorial or promotional reasons, approximately 8″ × 10″, Herman Darvick, June 1989, $180.

$100–$120

NOTE: *Mineo was nominated in 1955 for* Rebel Without a Cause *and in 1960 for* Exodus, *both times as best supporting actor. He died violently in 1976 in Hollywood, California.*

Minnelli, Liza, oblong, black and white movie still, boldly signed with full signature from *The Sterile Cuckoo* (1969), approximately 8″ × 10″, Jerry Granat/Herman Darvick, November 1988, $95. $85–$120

NOTE: *Minnelli usually signs "Liza" on most autographed material; her full name is uncommon.*

Mix, Tom, newspaper slip, signed in blank area along with Mix and his horse pictured on an original sepia postcard, 3″ × 2″, Herman Darvick, June 1989, $80. $100–$120

Monroe, Marilyn, cashier's voucher from Stouffers restaurant, New York City, 1955, pencil autograph and sentiment on verso, with light soiling, 4″ × 5½″, Nasca, October 1988, $725.

$500–?

Monroe, Marilyn, photographer's contract, dated 1949, signed, together with a machine color print of Marilyn dressed in a half-opened robe, Christie's South Kensington, December 1988, $4750. $2000–$3000

Monroe, Marilyn, portrait by Cecil Beaton, signed "love and kisses," undated, Neals, November 1988, $5545. $2000–$4000

NOTE: *Marilyn autographed this portrait to a man named Jack. It is not entirely inconceivable that the "Jack" was President Kennedy.*

Monroe, Marilyn, personal note card signed Marilyn Monroe Miller inside, while Mrs. Arthur Miller is engraved on front, Monroe's signature is almost 4″ long, very rare, 4″ × 6″, Herman Darvick, June 1989, $3000. $3000–$3500

NOTE: *This note was written to a friend who had expressed sympathy over Marilyn losing her baby at New York Doctor's Hospital on August 1, 1957.*

Monroe, Marilyn, signed check, dated February 16, 1960, signed in full and drawn on "Marilyn Monroe Productions, Inc.," to Beverly Hills Hotel for $1286.23, MM stamp between her first and last name, very fine, Collectors' Showcase, January 1989, $4400.   *$2000–$4000*

Moore, Clayton (The Lone Ranger), black and white photograph of Moore as The Lone Ranger on his horse Silver, and Jay Silverheels as Tonto on his horse Scout, signed by both actors, Silverheels in a shaky hand, approximately 8″ × 10″, Herman Darvick, April 1989, $350.   *$200–$250*

NOTE: *It is rare to find an autograph of Jay Silverheels.*

Morgan, Frank, autograph album page, circa 1940, with signature of the actor who played the Wizard of Oz, 5½″ × 4½″, Jerry Granat/Herman Darvick, November 1988, $85.   *$75–$85*

Murphy, Audie, three-quarter length inscribed sepia photograph with Murphy in uniform with full World War II medals, together with a one-page agreement, dated 1971, between the actor and one W.C. Knox & Associates for using Murphy's name in an advertising product, photograph and agreement are both approximately 8″ × 10″, Herman Darvick, April 1989, $200.
                                              $200–$250

Olivier, Sir Laurence, black and white movie still of Olivier as Zeus in the film *Clash of the Titans,* full signature (not the more common L. Olivier signature), approximately 8″ × 10″, Jerry Granat/Herman Darvick, November 1988, $95.   *$90–$125*

NOTE: *Olivier usually signs L. Olivier and seldom the full signature: Laurence Olivier or Sir Laurence Olivier. Since the actor's death in 1989, it is very likely his autographs will continue to increase in value.*

Peck, Gregory, black and white photograph, circa 1945, "with regards," approximately 8″ × 10″, Collectors' Showcase, January 1989, $147.   *$75–$95*

Pickford, Mary, letter signed Mary on personal engraved stationery, one full page, with original envelope addressed by the actress, approximately 6" × 8", Jerry Granat/Herman Darvick, February, 1989, $75. *$65–$90*

Pickford, Mary, first edition of her book *The Demi-Widow* (1935), with inscription to friend and actress Betty Bronson (*Peter Pan*, 1925), worn dust jacket, good, Collectors' Showcase, October 1988, $83. *$60–$75*

Pidgeon, Walter, black and white photograph with "greetings," circa 1943, approximately 8" × 10", Collectors' Showcase, January 1989, $60. *$75–$95*

Powell, William and Tracy, Spencer, vintage sepia full-length photograph of Powell, Myrna Loy, Jean Harlow, and Spencer Tracy, arm-in-arm, vintage signature of Powell and Tracy (who has also written an inscription), oblong, approximately 8" × 10", Herman Darvick, June 1989, $250. *$300–$350*

Power, Tyrone, check dated November 20, 1942 from David O. Selznick, signed by him, for $472, Culver City, California, with Power's signature endorsed on verso, Jerry Granat/Herman Darvick, September 1988, $250. *$225–$270*

Raft, George and Cagney, James, black and white oblong photograph, signed by both actors who are dressed in prison uniforms, approximately 8" × 10", Herman Darvick, April 1989, $140. *$200–$250*

Reagan, Ronald, black and white still from the 1939 film *Secret Service of the Air*, picturing Reagan wearing a leather jacket and looking scared, vintage 1939 signature of the then 28-year-old actor, approximately 8" × 10", Herman Darvick, April 1989, $250. *$300–$350*

Reagan, Ronald, two letters written to Doris Lilly, author of *How to Marry a Millionaire*, and gossip columnist for *The New York Post* (late 1950s–1960s), dated late 1940s, Sotheby's, October 1988, $4400.

NOTE: *Reagan and Ms. Lilly were probably an item between Reagan's divorce from Jane Wyman and his marriage to Nancy Davis in the early 1950s. These letters were sold to Malcolm Forbes, publisher of Forbes magazine.*

Reeve, Christopher, original 20-page program for first *Superman* movie, color photographs and a centerfold of a flying Superman which Reeve has signed with a bold 6″ signature, approximately 8″ × 10″, Jerry Granat/Herman Darvick, February 1989, $45.

$45–$55

Reeves, George, black and white photograph of Reeves as Superman (television), framed under glass in a silver metal frame, the actor has signed his full name in dark pencil and signature and photo are double matted, 11¼″ × 14¼″ overall, Herman Darvick, February 1989, $400. $350–$400

NOTE: *Reeves was best known for his portrayal of Superman on television but he was also a fine character actor in movies as well. He died under mysterious circumstances with a bullet to the back of his head. Officially ruled a suicide, there are some people who think he might have been murdered.*

Ritter, Tex, photograph of the western star, September 1945, Dell's Book Outlet, February and June 1989, $75. $60–$90

Roach, Hal, autographed sheet postmarked Beverly Hills, May 27, 1975, with a 10¢ U.S. stamp attached honoring the silent film director, D.W. Griffith, approximately 8″ × 10″, Jerry Granat/Herman Darvick, September 1988, $75. $65–$80

NOTE: *Roach was best known as the director of the "Our Gang" comedies. His career began in silent films, circa 1915.*

Rogers, Ginger, black and white photograph, circa 1945, with inscription and signature, very fine, approximately 8″ × 10″, Collectors' Showcase, January 1989, $88. $95–$125

Rogers, Ginger, one full-page autographed letter dated March 23, 1973, refusing a role in *The Day of the Locust* (1975), approximately 6″ × 8″, Herman Darvick, June 1989, $200.

$140–$160

Rogers, Roy and Evans, Dale, two full-color photographs. Rogers has signed his name in full and added Trigger (the name of his horse), Evans has signed "God Bless You" and her name, Nasca, October 1988, $10. $35–$70

Rooney, Mickey, signed black and white photograph, circa 1944, very fine, approximately 8″ × 10″, Collectors' Showcase, January 1989, $61. $50–$75

Rooney, Mickey, black and white photograph depicting the Andy Hardy family, circa 1939, signed by Rooney and co-stars Fay Holden, Cecilia Parker, and Lewis Stone, good, 11″ × 14″, Collectors' Showcase, October 1989, $192. $75–$100

NOTE: *The Andy Hardy movies at MGM ran from 1937 through 1946. The first Hardy movie starred Lionel Barrymore as Judge Hardy in* A Family Affair *(1937); Lewis Stone took over as the Judge in* You're Only Young Once *(1938). There were 15 movies in the series, 16 if one counts Mickey Rooney's return to his hometown of Carvel in the 1958 movie* Andy Hardy Comes Home.

Saint, Eva Marie, signed black and white still from *A Hatful of Rain* (1957), scarce, approximately 8″ × 10″, Jerry Granat/Herman Darvick, September 1988, $75. $35–$45

Scolfield, Paul, black and white photograph, inscribed and signed in lower blank margin, approximately 6″ × 8″, Jerry Granat/Herman Darvick, September 1988, $35. $35–$45

Scott, George C., signed one-page letter, dated January 11, 1973, to cowboy star Don Barry, approximately 8″ × 10″, Jerry Granat/Herman Darvick, November 1988, $30. $25–$40

Scott, Randolph, signed photograph with inscription in black ink, framed and double-matted, 11″ × 14″, Phillips, December 1988, $100. $100–$200

Selznick, David O., signed full-page letter on Selznick's personal stationery to Daniel T. O'Shea, president of RKO, in which the producer of *Gone With the Wind* (1939) suggests a movie featuring Tarzan and King Kong; included are two letters about Tarzan stories and copyright law, and a signed booklet entitled: "The Legal Protection of Fictional Characters," as well as a carbon of O'Shea's response (he was favorable to the idea), five items, Selznick's letter, approximately 8″ × 10″, Herman Darvick, September 1988, $300.   *$200–$250*

Shearer, Norma, vintage black and white photograph, inscribed and signed, approximately 8″ × 10″, Jerry Granat/Herman Darvick, February 1989, $50.   *$40–$60*

Sinatra, Frank and Capra, Frank, typed agreement, carbon, dated December 27, 1957 for Frank Capra Productions and concerning the 1959 movie *A Hole in the Head*, which starred Sinatra, Ernie Kovacs, and Maureen O'Hara, original full signatures of both Sinatra and Capra, very fine +, 8½″ × 10″, Collectors' Showcase, November 1988, $242.   *$150–$200*

Southern, Ann, signed black and white photograph, circa 1945, very fine, approximately 8″ × 10″, Collectors' Showcase, January 1989, $61.   *$75–$95*

Spanky (George McFarland), autographed letter, one full page, oblong, from the seven-year-old child actor of "Our Gang" comedies, undated, but circa 1935, framed under glass, letter is approximately 6″ × 8″, with frame, 21″ × 22″, Herman Darvick, April 1989, $550.   *$400–$450*

NOTE: *Given Spanky's age, this letter is considered rare.*

Stanwyck, Barbara (and others), two volumes of an original script and treatment for *Union Pacific* (1939), signed by Stanwyck, her co-stars Joel McCrea and Robert Preston, and the director/producer Cecil B. DeMille, Camden House, May 1989, $800.   *$800–$1000*

Steiger, Rod, autographed letter signed of two separate full pages, dated December 4, 1965, in which Steiger writes to his agent that he has decided to sign with the William Morris Agency, approximately 8″ × 10″, Herman Darvick, June 1989, $150.
$100–$120

Stewart, James, signed script for the movie *Bandolero,* dated September 6, 1967, Stewart and several cast members, among them Donald Barry, Harry Carey, Will Geer, Dean Martin, and Raquel Welch, have signed their real names below their film names, 153 pages, 8½″ × 11″, Collectors' Showcase, November 1988, $1278.
$250–$350

Stooges, The Three, black and white printed photograph, signed Larry (Larry Fine), Moe (Moe Howard), and Curly Joe (Curly Joe DeRita), each dressed in Roman togas, approximately 8″ × 10″, Herman Darvick, April 1989, $200.
$180–$200

Stooges, The Three, address of the Three Stooges Fan Club on a printed card (for information, send 50¢, etc.). Larry Fine has signed 3 Stooges/Larry, Moe Howard has signed Moe, and Joe DeRita has signed Curly Joe, 3″ × 5″, Herman Darvick, February 1989, $200.
$120–$140

Stooges, The Three, standard black and white photograph, signed by Moe Howard for all Three Stooges, fine, 5" × 4", Collectors' Showcase, January 1989, $242. *$125–$150*

NOTE: This photograph was signed by Moe shortly before his death.

Tate, Sharon, black and white photograph, a serious pose of the actress who has signed and inscribed the photo with a black felt-tip pen on dark portion of photo, approximately 8" × 10", Herman Darvick, September 1988, $375. *$100–$120*

NOTE: Tate was 26 years old when she and three friends were murdered in August 1969 at her Hollywood Hills home by Charles Manson and members of his nomadic tribe of misfits. Tate was married to director Roman Polanski at the time. Her signatures tend to be in scarce supply.

Temple, Shirley, inscribed and signed sepia bust photograph of Temple as a teenager, approximately 8" × 10", Herman Darvick, April 1989, $80. *$100–$120*

Temple, Shirley, autograph album page, circa 1940, inscribed and signed, 5½" × 4½", Jerry Granat/Herman Darvick, November 1988, $75. *$65–$90*

Thalberg, Irving, signed check drawn upon Louis B. Mayer Studios (later MGM), dated 1923, fine, 8½" × 3", Collectors' Showcase, January 1989, $137. *$50–$75*

NOTE: Irving B. Thalberg (the boy wonder of Hollywood), was second vice-president and supervisor of production at MGM from 1924 through 1936. He was married to MGM star Norma Shearer on September 29, 1927, and died on September 14, 1936 at the age of 37. It is this writer's opinion that Thalberg inscriptions and/or signatures are undervalued.

Todd, Thelma and Grable, Betty, pencil signature on photograph of Todd talking on the phone in bed, vertical fold, matted, together with a signature of Betty Grable on a photograph of the star's famous World War II pin-up pose, matted, two items, fine, 11″ × 14″ each overall, Herman Darvick, April 1989, $140.

$100–$120

NOTE: *Thelma Todd was a blonde comedienne who made her debut in silent films in 1926. She initially worked for PAR and FN studios, before signing a contract with the Hal Roach/MGM Studios in 1929. She remained with Roach through 1935. Todd appeared with the Marx Brothers in two of their early PAR comedies,* Monkey Business *(1931) and* Horse Feathers *(1932). She died under "mysterious" circumstances in December 1935, supposedly of carbon monoxide poisoning in the garage of her home off the old Roosevelt Highway (now Pacific Coast Highway) on the California Palisades/Malibu border. In 1989 Todd was the subject of a biography called* Hot Toddy *wherein the author offered evidence that Todd was murdered and gave her own version of the actress' last hours.*

Tracy, Spencer, vintage black and white photograph, almost half-length, with vintage inscription, *Libeled Lady* (1936), stamped on verso, approximately 8″ × 10″, Herman Darvick, June 1989, $190.

$200–$250

Turner, Lana, black and white photograph, signed and inscribed, circa 1945, approximately 8″ × 10″, Collectors' Showcase, January 1989, $124.

$95–$125

Valentino, Rudolph, signed black and white photograph, picturing Valentino in courtier's clothing, gilt framed, very romantic photo, Kenneth W. Rendell Gallery, November 1988, $2750.

Valentino, Rudolph, boldly signed R. Valentino check drawn on The National City Bank of New York for $14, dated December 18, 1922, with vintage bust photograph showing Valentino wearing a bow tie and signed with a rubber stamp, approximately 8″ × 10″, Herman Darvick, February 1989, $1500.

$1200–$1400

NOTE: *Valentino autographs are considered extremely rare and very, very desirable with collectors, about on par with signatures of Marilyn Monroe and Greta Garbo.*

Vallee, Rudy, three original Preston Struges' scripts, including *Unfaithfully Yours* (1948), annotated and signed by Vallee; *The Palm Beach Story* (1942), without cover; and *The Beautiful Blonde From Bashful Bend* (1948), also signed by Vallee; Phillips, December 1988, $400.

$300–$500

★

NOTE: The Beautiful Blonde From Bashful Bend, *released in 1949, was Grable's first unprofitable picture for 20th. After having been in the movies for a decade, she began her career with 20th in* Down Argentine Way *(1940).*

Welles, Orson, boldly signed movie still from *Black Magic* (1949), oblong, approximately 8″ × 10″, Herman Darvick, April 1989, $180. *$160–$180*

West, Mae, a signed pink personal check, drawn to PAR for publicity photos, dated February 27, 1939, with a framed photograph of the actress, 11″ × 14″, Camden House, May 1989, $100. *$150–$250*

Winger, Debra, black and white photograph with matted signature, 8″ × 10″, Autographics, March 1989, $22.50.

$15–$25

Withers, Jane, small self-drawing of Withers, inscribed with sentiment, Jerry Granat/Herman Darvick, November 1988, $20.

$20–$30

Wizard of Oz, The, three signatures of cast members—Bert Lahr (Cowardly Lion), a signature cut from a document; Billie Burke (Good Witch), a signed black and white photograph cut from a book; and Margaret Hamilton (Wicked Witch of the West), signed and with a sketch of a witch's hat and broom; Burke photograph is 2½″ × 3½″, Hamilton card, 3″ × 5″, three items in all, Herman Darvick, June 1989, $140. *$150–$200*

Wizard of Oz, The, signed black and white stills (two), one of Jack Haley (Tin Man), and the other of Ray Bolger (Scarecrow), both approximately 8″ × 10″, Camden House, May 1989, $350. *$200–$300*

Wray, Fay, book (*Photoplay* edition) of *King Kong* (1933), signed by Wray in the mid-1980s, 249 pages, dated 1932, 5½″ × 8½″, Collectors' Showcase, March 1989, $883. *$350–$500*

Wray, Fay, signed reissue pressbook for *King Kong*, dated 1942, 13 pages, includes *Kong* comic strip, 8½″ × 24″, Collectors' Showcase, December 1988, $357. *$200–$250*

BOOKS

INTRODUCTION

I have a friend who is very pessimistic. When I told him that I was writing a price guide on movie memorabilia, he exclaimed in typical fashion: "Just what the world needs, another price guide!"

My friend had a point. There are a lot of price guides around these days. Just the number of price guides published by House of Collectibles alone is staggering. Yet none of the price guides I've seen give very much coverage to movie memorabilia. Oh, there have been a few books devoted to the subject, but they covered the major areas of collecting such as animation cels, costumes, Disneyana, posters, and sheet music and left out many other collecting categories. And general price guides covering a vast amount of different collectibles usually only gave a cursory look at movie memorabilia.

Of all the price guides that include coverage on movie memorabilia, the chapter on books tended to concentrate only on children's books such as Big Little books, Big Big books, Better Little books, and paper doll activity books, and a large section on Walt Disney titles. There was seldom any mention made of general film titles and movie star biographies or autobiographies.

This price guide is different. There are movie star biographies and autobiographies, film genre titles, coloring books, movie-star fiction, screenplays, dance and cowboy books, film books whose subjects worked behind the camera, *Photoplay-* and *Photo-Drama*-type movie edition books, and even a measurement book of handwritten costume sizes for stars who worked at MGM. Of course, there are listings for Better Little Books (BTLP), Big Little Books (BLB), Big Big Books (BBB), Big Tell-a-Tale and D.C. Heath books, Little Golden Books, and books and boxed sets (kits) on paper dolls.

* * *

Some of the specialized books included in the listing are movie tie-in editions which supposedly began around 1913 when the serial *The Adventures of Kathlyn* was first novelized. In 1914, the *Perils of Pauline* followed suit with a bound hardcover edition that included almost two dozen stills from the popular serial. The following year the first really important movie tie-in appeared as *The Clansmen* by Thomas Dixon. Later re-titled *The Birth of a Nation*, it became the first silent film epic (and possibly the best), as directed by D.W. Griffith, the great pioneering film director.

Big Little Books made their debut in 1933 and were published by the Whitman Publishing Co. in a $3\frac{1}{4}'' \times 4\frac{1}{4}''$ format that included pictures and text. The first BLB was *The Adventures of Dick Tracy*. More than 200 titles followed based on comic strip and Disney cartoon characters, westerns, movies, literature, and radio. Favorite heroes included Tom Mix, Buck Jones, Gene Autry, and Buck Rogers. The first movie-oriented BLB featured Jackie Cooper. Others that followed were about Laurel and Hardy, Our Gang, Will Rogers, Shirley Temple, and Jane Withers. Movie books featured black and white stills instead of drawings.

Whitman's biggest competitor was the Saalfield Publishing Co. of Akron, Ohio, which began publishing books in 1909, and BLBs in 1934. These were called Little Big Books (LBB). Other companies jumped on the bandwagon and began producing similar books.

Popular illustrators of these children's books included Alex Raymond, Henry Vallely, Al Capp, Allen Dean, Alfred Andriola, and Will Gould. Books with their illustrations sell at a premium.

Books and kits of paper dolls are preferred by most collectors to be in uncut condition. Some of the listings have cut dolls and clothes but prices are usually lower for them. Cut sets are usually about half of what an uncut set would cost.

Many paper doll books have been reprinted, which is okay,

but if the dolls have been redrawn, then the price drops considerably. Celebrity paper dolls are the most popular and expensive and most desired by collectors. Look for unstained sets. Paper dolls are an excellent barometer of the different fashion styles over the years.

On a final note, novice collectors should stay away from buying books at auction. They tend to be overpriced and can usually be bought for much less at a used book dealer. Ignorance and "auction fever" often sabotage the good intentions of a novice collector. They assume that bidding against another person, who is often a dealer and who seems to know his books, will result in winning a bid on a book worth its value. But that isn't always the case. Novice collectors who have the last bid will often overbid for a book that is worth much less. Their rationale is that if the other person bid so high the book must be very valuable. Most times it's not and is probably much cheaper at the bookstore down the street. Novice collectors should stay away from book auctions until they learn the ropes and acquire knowledge of book values. This is advice, not preaching.

BOOKS LISTING

GENERAL

Adventures of Mickey Mouse, The, 1931, David McKay, 1st edition, dust jacket, very good, Paper Collectables & Memorabilia Show, November 1988, $95.   *$80-$105*

Adventures of Mickey Mouse, The, 1932, David McKay, 2nd edition, dust jacket, good (loose pages), Wex Rex Collectibles, May 1989, $70.   *$60-$105*

Adventures of Pinocchio, The, 1955, Carlo Collodia, illustrated, very good, Blue Bird Books, June 1989, $6.   *$8-$15*

All My Yesterdays, 1973, Signet Classic Book, re: Edward G. Robinson, softcover, Limelight, August 1988, $3.   *$3-$5*

Around the World in 80 Days Almanac, 1956, full-color illustrations, Wizard of Os Antiques, February 1989, $8.   *$7-$12*

Art of W.C. Fields, 1967, Crown, William K. Everson, dust jacket, out of print, very good, Limelight, August 1988, $10.
          $9-$15

Bashful Billionaire, 1967, Lyle Stuart, Albert B. Gerber, re: Howard Hughes, dust jacket, fine, Paper Collectables & Memorabilia Show, October 1988, $4.   *$4–$9*

Behind the Scenes of Otto Preminger, 1974, William Morrow, by Willi Frischauer, 1st edition, illustrated, dust jacket, fine, Paper Collectables & Memorabilia Show, November 1988, $6.
                    $6–$10

Bells of St. Mary's, The, 1946, movie edition, photos, dust jacket, fine, Collectors' Showcase, February 1989, $27.   *$14–$20*

Ben-Hur Punchout Book, 1959, Golden Press, six sheets of cardboard punchouts, including two chariots plus soldiers, horses, etc., very fine, 7 1/2" × 13", Hake's, April 1989, $69.
                    $25–$50

Bing Crosby: The Hollow Man, 1981, St. Martin's Press, dust jacket, 2nd printing, Limelight, August 1988, $14.
                    $12–$20

Biography of Marlon Brando, 1973, Offen, Ron Offen, dust jacket, out of print, good, Limelight, August 1988, $20.
                    $15–$22

Blue Dahlia, The, 1976, Elm Tree Books, Raymond Chandler w/memoir by John Houseman, screenplay w/black and white lobby card type photos, dated March 15, 1945, dust jacket, out of print, fine, Paper Collectables & Memorabilia Show, February 1989, $35.   *$30–$40*

Bogart, 1965, Fawcett Gold Medal Book, Richard Gehman, illustrated, softcover, fine, Twentieth Century Nostalgia, October 1088, $5.   *$5–$10*

Bogey and Me: A Love Story, 1962, St. Martin's Press, Verna Thompson, 1st edition, out of print, dust jacket, Limelight, August 1988, $12.95.   *$10–$15*

Bogey's Baby, 1976, St. Martin's Press, Howard Greenberger, out of print, fine, Limelight, August 1988, $15.   *$10–$16*

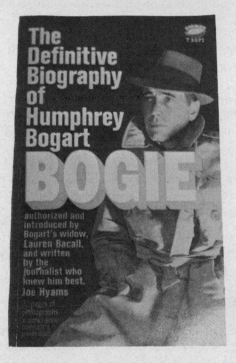

Bogie (definitive biography of Humphrey Bogart), 1966, New American Library, Joe Hyams, softcover, 1st printing, fine, Larry Edmunds Bookshop, August 1988, $6.95.   *$6–$9*

Broadway Melody of 1929, 1929, Grosset & Dunlap, Jack Laight (novelization), Edmund Goulding (scenario), dust jacket, fine, Limelight, August 1988, $20.   *$15–$25*

Bus Stop, 1956, Bantam, William Inge (1955 copyright), #1518, illustrated, softcover, fine, Nussbaum, June 1989, $20.

$15–$20

NOTE: Marilyn Monroe gave the best performance of her career as Cherie in Bus Stop. *Her picture is on the cover of this paperback book, and co-star Don Murray, who played the cowboy named Bo, is pictured on the back cover.*

Cellarful of Noise, A (The Beatles), 1964, Doubleday, Brian Epstein, this is Pyramid Books R-1200 1965 edition, illustrated, softcover, near mint, Twentieth Century Nostalgia, October 1988, $10.   *$10–$25*

Center Door Fancy, 1972, Delacorte Press, Joan Blondell, dust jacket, very good, Limelight, August 1988, $2.   *$2–$9*

Chaplin, 1974, Little, Brown, Roger Manvell, dust jacket, very fine, Mid-Manhattan Library, May 1989, $2.   *$6–$15*

NOTE: This is the first listing for the weekly Mid-Manhattan Book Sale which is held in New York on Wednesdays starting at 11:00 A.M. This is a special sale of books that the library sells as a benefit for their various branch libraries. There are usually many books on film biography, criticism, and genre studies included in the sales. It is an excellent way to buy books at very reasonable prices. For the price range, however, I am using prices charged by dealers since this is a better gauge of prices as most collectors will find them.

Charlie Chaplin Up in the Air, 1917, Donohue & Co., J. Keeley (by arrangement with Essanay), 12 coloring pages of black and white comic strip cartoons of Chaplin, color strips on the inside covers, heavy pages, good, 10″ × 17″, Hake's, February 1989, $71.   *$75–$100*

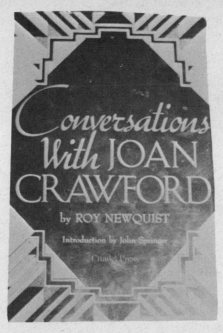

Conversations With Joan Crawford, 1980, Citadel Press, Roy Newquist, 1st edition, dust jacket, near mint, Larry Edmunds Bookstore, August 1988, $10.   *$10–$15*

Cowardly Lion of Oz, Reilly & Lee, 12 colorplates, 1st edition, good, Collectors' Showcase, March 1989, $50.   *$55–$75*

Daily Express Film Book, 1935, five pages on production of Disney's *Silly Symphonies*, illustrated, very good, Collectors' Showcase, March 1989, $101.   *$100–$150*

NOTE: Greta Garbo is pictured on the cover.

Diamonds Are Forever, 1956, Macmillan (first Jove edition, April 1980), Ian Fleming, softcover, very good, Paper Collectables & Memorabilia Show, September 1988, $2.   *$2–$7*

Photo courtesy of Hake's Americana, York, PA

Disneyana, 1974, Hawthorne Books, Cecil Munsey, dust jacket, near mint, 9″ × 11″, Hake's, February 1989, $150.

$75–$200

NOTE: *This is the first biography of Walt Disney and the classic Disney reference.*

Disney Films, The, 1973, Crown, Leonard Maltin, illustrated, one color, dust jacket, fine, 8½″ × 11″, Hake's, February 1989, $32.

$15–$50

NOTE: *All the Disney films, from* Snow White *through* The Happiest Millionaire, *are arranged in chronological order. There is also an appendix that lists the names and dates of all Disney shorts.*

★

Donald Duck Dots, 1954, Whitman, dot pictures of Disney characters to complete, fine, 8″ × 11″, Hake's, November 1988, $14.   *$10–$25*

NOTE: This book is low in price because a few of the dot pictures have been colored.

Doug and Mary: Biography of Douglas Fairbanks and Mary Pickford, 1977, Dutton, Douglas Carey, 1st printing, dust jacket, Limelight, August 1988, $10.   *$7–$14*

Douglas Fairbanks: The Fourth Musketeer, 1953, Henry Holt, Ralph Hancock, and Letita Fairbanks, 1st edition, out of print, dust jacket, Limelight, August 1988, $15.   *$12–$20*

NOTE: I haven't been able to ascertain if Letita Fairbanks was the daughter of Beth Sully, Fairbanks' first wife, if and when she remarried, or if Letita is the name of Douglas Fairbanks, Jr.'s second wife (his first wife was Joan Crawford). Perhaps a reader might know the answer.

Dracula, 1931, Grosset & Dunlap, movie edition with Bela Lugosi pictured on back of dust jacket, fine, 5½″ × 8″, Collectors' Showcase, January 1989, $126.   *$100–$150*

Dream Palaces (Hollywood at Home), 1981, Charles Lockwood, 1st edition, dust jacket, out of print, fine, Paper Collectables & Memorabilia Show, May 1989, $9.   *$9–$15*

Elvis Presley Story, The, 1960, Hillman Books, James Gregory, (introduction by Dick Clark), illustrated, Hake's, February 1989, $29.   *$25–$50*

NOTE: This book includes photographs of four Presley movies made prior to his induction in the army. They are Love Me Tender *(1956),* Loving You *(1957),* Jailhouse Rock *(1957), and* King Creole *(1958). The front page has an Elvis fact sheet.*

Elvis: The Final Years, 1980, St. Martin's Press, Jerry Hopkins, dust jacket, near mint, Limelight, August 1988, $6.95.

$6–$15

Errol and Me, 1960, Signet, Nora Eddington Flynn Haymes (as told to Cy Rice), softcover, 1st printing, very good, Limelight, August 1988, $10.

$10–$15

Fabulous Fanny, The, 1953, Alfred Knopf, Norman Katkov, re: Fanny Brice, dust jacket, Limelight, August 1988, $12.

$10–$16

Fabulous Tom Mix, The, 1957, Prentice-Hall, Olive Stokes Mix and Eric Heath, illustrated, dust jacket, fine, Hake's, February 1989, $59.

$15–$25

Fantasia, 1940, Simon & Schuster, Deems Taylor, tipped-in art plates from Disney film, very good, 10″ × 13″, Collectors' Showcase, January 1989, $253.

$250–$400

NOTE: Reputedly, the best book ever produced for a film. This is a classic Disney title which should be in the library of every collector of Disneyana. Frequently turns up at auctions and in dealer shops. Another copy sold in March 1989 through Collectors' Showcase for $298.

Ferdinand the Bull, 1938, #903 linen book, fine, The Mouse Man Ink, September 1988, $35.

$30–$40

Film Pictorial Annual, 1939, very fine, Collectors' Showcase, March 1989, $121.

$150–$200

Film Review Annual, 1951–1952, English-published title, illustrated w/film scenes, 160 pages, fine, 7½″ × 10″, Hake's, February 1989, $24.

$25–$50

Film Revue Annual, 1950, same as above, $23.

$25–$50

Films of Greta Garbo, The, Citadel Press, Parker Tyler, dust jacket, very good, Mark Twain Library Book Fair, September 1988, $5.   *$10–$18*

NOTE: *The book fair is held every Labor Day weekend in Redding, Connecticut. Very low prices on books including film titles. Since the fair's books are marked down, I have listed a dealer price range for this title.*

Films of Jean Harlow, The, 1965, Citadel Press, Conway & Ricci, illustrated, dust jacket, very fine, 8.5″ × 11″, Paper Collectables & Memorabilia Show, May 1989, $12.   *$10–$25*

Flesh and Fantasy, 1978, Penny Stallings, Howard Mandelbaum, St. Martin's Press, softcover, very good, Twentieth Century Nostalgia, October 1988, $10.   *$10–$20*

For Whom the Bell Tolls, 1944, Jonathan Cape, London, and Thacker & Co., Ltd., Bombay, 1st Indian edition, illustrated w/ photos from the 1943 film starring Gary Cooper and Ingrid Bergman, very fine, Waiting for Godot Books, October 1988, $85.

$75–$90

NOTE: *The book was published in Bombay with an English text.*

Frankenstein, 1932, The Readers Library Publishing Co., Mary Shelley, movie edition, Boris Karloff pictured on dust jacket as the monster, scarce, very good, Pepper & Stern, April 1989, $250.   *$200–$275*

Fred Astaire and Ginger Rogers Book, The, 1977, Vintage Books, Arlene Croce, softcover, 1st edition, good, True Value Books, January 1989, $22.   *$15–$25*

NOTE: *At top right corner of each page there is an action-flip dance photo so readers can quickly flip the pages to see Astaire and Rogers dance.*

★

Fred Astaire Dance Book, The, 1955, w/two 45 rpm records, mint, 7″ × 9″, Collectors' Showcase, September 1988, and Collectors' Showcase, November 1988, $29 and $31.   *$25–$50*

Gable, 1975, Signet (film series), Chester Williams, softcover, 1st printing, out of print, Limelight, August 1988, $5.

$5–$10

Garbo, 1962, Dell, John Bainbridge, illustrated, 1st printing, very good, Limelight, August 1988, $4.   *$4–$10*

Garden of Allah, The, 1970, Crown, Sheilah Graham, 2nd printing, illustrated, dust jacket, very good, Collectors' Bookstore, August 1988, $15.   *$12–$22*

Gene Autry and the Golden Ladder Gang, 1950, Whitman, W.H. Hutchinson, black and white illustrations, dust jacket, very good, Hake's, November 1988, $14.   *$15–$25*

George Raft (biography), 1974, McGraw-Hill, Lewis Yablonsky, dust jacket, very good, Limelight, August 1988, $7.98.

$5–$10

★

NOTE: Raft made his film debut in Queen of the Night Clubs *with Texas Guinan at WB in 1929. He was under contract to PAR from 1932 through 1939, and then signed with WB. Raft was a very popular actor in the 1930s and 1940s, but his stubbornness and pride sabotaged what could have been a far better career. He was notorious for turning down this and that role because, he thought, it would make him look bad. Such roles often went to other stars who became famous because of them. Raft is best remembered for* Scarface (1932), *which he made for UA, and* They Drive by Night, *which he made in 1940 for WB.*

★

Ginger Rogers and the Riddle of the Scarlet Cloak, 1942, Whitman, Lela E. Rogers, illustrated, dust jacket, out of print, street vendor, NYC, October 1988, $15.   *$9–$17*

Photo courtesy of Hake's Americana, York, PA

Gone With the Wind, 1936, Macmillan, Margaret Mitchell, 1st edition, True Value Books, January 1989, $100.   *$75–$100*

Photo courtesy of Hake's Americana, York, PA

Gone With the Wind Movie Book, 1940, Macmillan, Margaret Mitchell, motion picture edition w/six pages of full-color film scenes and portraits of Clark Gable and Vivien Leigh, fine, 7" × 9½", Hake,'s February 1989, $25.   *$25–$50*

Good Night, Sweet Prince, 1945, The Blakiston Co., Gene Fowler, good, Limelight, August 1988, $4.98.   *$4.98–$8*

★

NOTE: *The definitive biography of John Barrymore.*

★

Great Movie Stars, The, 1970, Hill & Wang, David Shipman, revised edition, dust jacket, good, Limelight, August 1988, $20.   *$10–$20*

Green Murder Case, The, 1928, Grosset & Dunlap, S.S. Van Dine, movie edition, illustrated, fine, Auston Books, June 1989, $5.   *$5–$10*

Hemingway and Film, 1980, Frederick Ungar Publishers, Gene D. Phillips, illustrated, 1st edition, dust jacket, Waiting for Godot Books, October 1988, $25.   *$20–$25*

Hero Behind the Mask, The, 1986, St. Martin's Press, Keith McKay, re: Robert De Niro, 1st edition, dust jacket, Limelight, August 1988, $8.   *$8–$10*

High Barbaree, 1945, Grosset & Dunlap, Charles Nordhoff and James Norman Hall, very good, Limelight, August 1988, $12.50.   *$10–$20*

His Eye Is on the Sparrow, 1951, Doubleday, Ethel Waters with Charles Samuels, book club, dust jacket, Limelight, August 1988, $10.   *$8–$12*

Hollywood Cage, The, 1969, Hart Publishing Co., Charles Hamblett, original copyright title: *Who Killed Marilyn Monroe?* (1966), illustrated, dust jacket, fine, Mid Manhattan Library, November 1988, $4.   *$8–$15*

Hollywood Detectives, 1972, Citadel Press, William K. Everson, 1st edition, dust jacket, fine, Pepper & Stern, April 1989, $65.   *$65–$75*

★

NOTE: *Excellent book on fictional detectives in movies.*

★

Hollywood Speaks: An Oral History, 1974, G.P. Putnam, Mike Steen, dust jacket, very good, Mid-Manhattan Library, November 1988, $3. $5–$9

Hollywood Stories, no copyright, Frederick Fell, Corinne Griffith, illustrated, 1st edition, dust jacket, out of print, fine, Limelight, August 1988, $8. $7–$10

NOTE: *Corinne Griffith was a silent film actress known for her beauty. One of her best remembered roles was in* The Divine Lady, *which was released in 1929 by WB. The movie portrayed Griffith as Emma Hamilton and her liaison with Lord Nelson. The director, Frank Lloyd, won an Academy Award.*

Hollywood in 3-D, 1987, 3-D Zone, Vol. 1, No. 7, comic book movie with picture of Jayne Mansfield on both front and back covers, with 3-D glasses, Limelight, August 1988, $3. $3–$6

Hud, Popular Library, Larry McMurty, picture of Paul Newman and Patricia Neal on cover, 1st printing, softcover, Twentieth Century Nostalgia, October 1988, $3. $3–$5

NOTE: *Book was published by Harper & Row in 1961; this edition must be later, as film was not released until 1963. No Popular Library copyright in book.*

Humphrey Bogart, 1975, Little, Brown, Nathaniel Benchley, 1st edition, dust jacket, out of print, very good, Limelight, August 1988, $20. $15–$25

I.E. An Autobiography, 1965, G. Putnam, Mickey Rooney, dust jacket, out of print, Limelight, August 1988, $12.50. $10–$15

I Hate Actors, 1944, Crown, Ben Hecht, dust jacket, very good, Liberty State Park Collectible's Expo, June 1989, $18.

$15–$30

NOTE: *Ben Hecht was a novelist, critic, and very, very expensive (and successful) screenwriter. His fee was reputed to be $1000 a day. Very colorful dust jacket.*

Image of Kate, The, 1962, Dell Publishers, Mary Astor, softcover, out of print, Limelight, August 1988, $1. $1–$4

Isle of Lost Ships, The, 1929, British *Photoplay* edition for FN, dust jacket, fine, 4″ × 6¼″, Collectors' Showcase, March 1989, $25. $30–$40

It Takes More Than Talent, 1953, Alfred A. Knopf, Mervyn LeRoy, director, as told to Alyce Canfield, Louis B. Mayer introduction, out of print, very good, Mid-Manhattan Library, October 1988, $2. $5–$12

James Bond "007" Film Scene Book, undated (circa 1965), Eon Productions and Gildrose Productions Ltd., illustrated w/color and black and white film scenes, very fine, 8 1/4″ × 11 1/4″, Hake's, April 1989, $92.   *$25–$50*

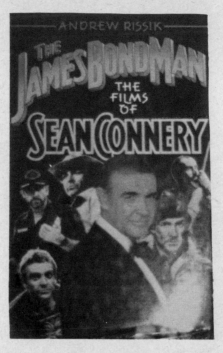

James Bond Man, The (The Films of Sean Connery), 1983, Elm Tree Books, Andrew Rissik, dust jacket, near mint, Limelight, August 1988, $22.   *$18–$30*

James Bond Trivia Quiz Book, The, 1984, Arbor House, Philip Gurin, softcover, 1st edition, fine, Oceanside Books, November 1988, $12.50.   *$10–$15*

James Dean—American Icon, 1984, Dalton, 9″ × 12″, True Value Books, January 1989, $15.   *$15–$20*

James Dean Revisited, 1978, D. Stock, illustrated, Cover to Cover, February 1989, $17.   *$12–$20*

Jazz Baby, 1982, St. Martin's Press, David Houston, re: Joan Crawford, 1st edition, 1st printing, dust jacket, fine, Limelight, August 1988, $13.50.   *$10–$15*

Photo courtesy of Hake's Americana, York, PA

John Wayne Coloring Book, 1951, Saalfield, #2354-15, 32 coloring pages of Wayne in various roles, very good, Hake's, November 1988, $51.   *$50–$75*

King Kong, 1932, Grosset & Dunlap, Edgar Wallace and Merian C. Cooper, novelization by Delos W. Lovelace, *Photoplay* edition, illustrated, 1st edition, dust jacket, fine, Pepper & Stern, April 1989, $1500.

NOTE: *The dust jacket pictures King Kong via a full-color painting in three different scenes from the RKO film. This* Photoplay *edition is extremely rare.*

King of Kings, The, 1927, Grosset & Dunlap, Henry MacMahon and Jeanie MacPherson, *Photoplay* edition, illustrated, fine, Limelight, August 1988, $25.   *$20–$30*

King of Kings, The, 1927, Jeanie MacPherson, illustrated w/photographic reproductions by William Mortenson, with verse on every other page, edition of 50 (#47), red Moroccan binding, 17″ × 13″, Christie's East, October 1988, $3300.

$1200–$1500

NOTE: *This book came from the estate of Cecil B. DeMille.*

King of the Jungle, undated, Jacobson-Hodgkinson, William E. Wing (without Edgar Rice Burroughs copyright), movie book based on the Elmo *Tarzan* Lincoln silent film of 1918, illustrated w/bluetone and black and white film scenes and characters, softcover, very good, 5¼″ × 8″, Hake's, February 1989, $72.

$50–$75

Laugh and Live, 1917, Britton Publishers, Douglas Fairbanks, illutrated, out of print, Limelight, August 1988, $10.

$10–$15

Laughter Is a Wonderful Thing, 1956, A.S. Barnes, Joe E. Brown, 1st edition, dust jacket, very good, Pepper & Stern Books, April 1989, $45.   *$30–$50*

Legends: Joan Crawford, 1986, Little, Brown, John Kobal, illustrated, softcover, 1st edition, near mint, Paper Collectables & Memorabilia Show, September 1988, $5.   *$10–$20*

Les Miserables, 1935, Lynn Book, movie edition of Victor Hugo novel, illustrated, Collectors' Showcase, September 1988, $30.

$15–$30

Life and Curious Death of Marilyn Monroe, The, 1974, Pinnacle House, Robin F. Flatzer, 3rd printing, dust jacket, out of print, Limelight Bookstore, August 1988, $50. *$35–$60*

Life Goes to the Movies, 1975, Time-Life Books, illustrated, black and white and color photos from 1930s to present, dust jacket, fine, 11″ × 13¼″, Hake's, June 1989, $13. *$10–$25*

Lolita: A Screenplay, 1974, McGraw-Hill, Vladimir Nabokov, 1st edition, dust jacket, fine, "Atlantique City" Collectibles Market, March 1989, $45. *$35–$55*

Lon Chaney The Mocking Bird Movie Book, 1925, illustrated, softcover, good, 5½″ × 8″, Hake's, February 1989, $62.
$25–$50

Lonely Life, The, 1982, G. Putnam's, Bette Davis, 3rd printing, dust jacket, Limelight, August 1988, $20. *$15–$25*

Lulu in Hollywood, 1982, Alfred A. Knopf, Louise Brooks, 2nd printing, dust jacket, Pomander Bookshop, February 1989, $12. *$9–$15*

Madonna, Adams High School Yearbook, Rochester, Michigan, class of 1976, black and white photo of Madonna Ciccone (page 118), group scene (page 29), and Thespian Society photo (page 100), unsigned, very good, 9″ × 12½″, Herman Darvick, February 1989, $200. *$200–$250*

Man Who Came to Dinner, The, 1942, Pocket Book, George S. Kaufman/Moss Hart, movie edition, illustrated, Bette Davis, Monty Wooley on front cover, 1st printing, Limelight, August 1988, $5. *$5–$10*

Marilyn, 1973, Grosset & Dunlap, Norman Mailer, 1st printing, illustrated, 10¾″ × 9¼″, very good, Paper Collectables & Memorabilia Show, May 1989, $14. *$12–$20*

Marilyn Monroe Story Biography, 1953, Greenberg Publishers, Joe Franklyn and Laurie Palmer, illustrated, Hake's, November 1988, $101. *$25–$50*

Memo From David Selznick, 1972, Viking, Rudy Behlmer, dust jacket, Mark Twain Library Book Fair, September 1988, $2. *$7–$12.50*

Merely Colossal, 1953, Simon & Schuster, George Price, 1st printing, dust jacket, very good, Paper Collectables & Memorabilia Show, November 1988, $7. *$5–$10*

MGM Cinerama: How the West Was Won, 1963, Random House, illustrated, Wizard of Os Antiques, February 1989, $8. *$8–$10*

MGM Measurement Book of the Stars, compiled by Hanna Lindfors, the chief fitter to Gilbert Adrian (MGM costume designer), contains handwritten measurements for Greta Garbo, Joan Crawford, Janet Gaynor (Mrs. Adrian), Jean Harlow, Mary Pickford, Carole Lombard, and Norma Shearer, among others, Christie's East, June 1989, $3520. *$1200–$1500*

Mickey and Minne Mouse Coloring Book, 1933, Saalfield, #979, 28 pages, black and white illustrations, fine, 10½" × 15", Hake's, April 1989, $75. *$75–$100*

Mickey Mouse Alphabet Book From A to Z, 1936, Whitman, 32 pages, black and white, red illustrations, scarce, fine, 7" × 10", Hakes, February 1989, $202. *$100–$200*

Mickey Mouse Book, 1930, Bibo & Lang, limited edition, 16 pages, black and white illustrations (Disney art), good, 9" × 12", Collectors' Showcase, February 1989, $508. *$300–$400*

★

NOTE: *This is the first published Disney book. In 1931, David McKay of Philadelphia reputedly published the first Disney story book.*

★

Photo courtesy of Hake's Americana, York, PA

Mickey Mouse Illustrated Movie Stories, 1931, David McKay, black and white illustrations of cartoon films, scarce, 6″ × 8½″, Hake's, February 1989, $575. $200–$400

Mickey Rooney Paint Book, 1940, Merrill, illustrated, fine, 10¼″ × 15″, Hake's, June 1989, $23. $25–$50

Monty, 1977, Arbor House, Robert LaGuardia, 3rd printing, dust jacket, Limelight, August 1988, $13. $9–$15

Motion Picture News Blue Book, 1930, illustrated, 6″ × 9″, Collectors' Showcase, November 1988, $56. $40–$50

Movie Gags Book, 1935, Whitman, #1145, very fine, 4½″ × 5¼″, Hake's, June 1989, $62. $50–$70

Movie Lot to Beachhead, 1945, Doubleday, editor of *Look* magazine, illustrated, 1st edition, rare photos, very good, Mark Twain Library Book Fair, September 1988, $4.   *$9–$15*

Movies, The, 1957, Simon & Schuster, Richard Griffith and Arthur Mayer, 60-year history of Hollywood, illustrated, dust jacket, one color, very good, 9″ × 12″, Paper Collectables & Memorabilia Show, January 1989, $7.50.   *$7.50–$15*

★

NOTE: *This definitive book on the movies would ordinarily sell at a higher price range but, as the above example is a library copy, it is priced lower than a non-library copy. These latter copies usually sell for up to $35 in fine condition with the dust jacket.*

★

Movies, Mr. Griffith, and Me, The, 1969, Prentice-Hall, Lillian Gish, dust jacket, fine, Pepper & Stern, April 1989, $45.
$40–$50

★

NOTE: *Lillian Gish began her film career with D.W. Griffith in* The Unseen Enemy *(1912). Her sister, Dorothy, was also featured. Gish stayed with Griffith through 1924 and then signed a contract with MGM for six movies at $800,000.*

★

Mr. Cantowine, 1953, Little, Brown, Lionel Barrymore, out of print, dust jacket, Limelight, August 1988, $7.50.   *$7–$15*

Mrs. Miniver, 1942, Grosset & Dunlap, James Strugher, photo of Greer Garson and Walter Pidgeon on book cover, Limelight, August 1988, $12.50.   *$10–$20*

New Adventures of Tarzan, The, 1935, Pleasure Books (Blue Ribbon Press series), Edgar Rice Burroughs (1935 copyright), Stephen Sleisinger (1935 picture copyright), pop-up, black and white illustrations, full-color pop-up scenes, 20 pages, very fine, 8″ × 9¼″, Hake's, February 1989, $266.   *$100–$200*

New Hollywood, The (American Movies in the '70s), 1975, Thomas Y. Crowell, Axel Madsen, 1st printing, dust jacket, fine, Mid-Manhattan Library, November 1988, $2.   *$7–$12*

Nibbles and Me, 1946, Duell, Sloan & Pearce, Elizabeth Taylor, illustrated, 1st edition, dust jacket, 5″ × 7″, Waiting for Godot Books, June 1988, $45. $22.50–$50

NOTE: *Elizabeth Taylor "wrote" this book at the age of 13. The subject concerns her pet chipmunk.*

Our Gang Crayon Book, 1937, Roebuck (Hal Roach copyright), illustrated, 16 pages, coloring book (crayoned pictures), 8″ × 11″, Hake's, November 1988, $40. $50–$75

Picture of Dorian Gray, The, 1945, movie edition, illustrated, very good, 8½″ × 11″, Collectors' Showcase, March 1989, $27. $15–$25

Picture Show Annual, 1926, Rudolph Valentino on the cover, illustrated, very good, Collectors' Showcase, March 1989, $111. $125–$150

NOTE: *This and all of the following* Picture Show Annuals *are British publications and illustrated with photographs of movie stars on the front covers, and star and film photographs inside.*

★

Picture Show Annual, 1931, illustrated, fine, Collectors' Showcase, March 1989, $56. $75–$100

Picture Show Annual, 1939, illustrated, fine, Collectors' Showcase, March 1989, $101. $150–$200

Picture Show Annual, 1940, illustrated, fine, Collectors' Showcase, March 1989, $83. $150–$175

Picture Show Annual, 1941, illustrated, fine, Collectors' Showcase, March 1989, $79. $75–$100

Picture Show Annual, 1950, illustrated, fine, Collectors' Showcase, March 1989, $45. $60–$75

Picture Show Annual, 1951, illustrated, very good, Collectors' Showcase, March 1989, $23. $50–$75

Picture Show Annual, 1952, illustrated, fine, Collectors' Showcase, March 1989, $36.   *$60–$75*

Picture Show Annual, 1955, illustrated, fine, Collectors' Showcase, March 1989, $39.   *$50–$70*

Picture Show Who's Won on the Screen, 1956, fine, 8″ × 10½″, Collectors' Showcase, March 1989, $170.   *$75–$100*

NOTE: *This is another British publication that features short biographies and small photographs of British and American stars.*

Poor Little Rich Girl (Shirley Temple Movie Book), 1936, Saalfield, illustrated w/photos from 20th, softcover, very good, 9½″ × 10″, Collectors' Showcase, October 1988, $73.

$25–$75

Roy Rogers and The Ghost of Mystery Rancho, 1950, Whitman, Walker A. Tompkins, illustrated, dust jacket, very good, Paper Collectables & Memorabilia Show, March 1989, $17.50.

$10–$20

Roy Rogers and The Gopher Creek Gunman, 1945, Whitman, #2309, Don Middleton, illustrated, good, 5½″ × 8″, Paper Collectables & Memorabilia Show, May 1989, $8.   *$7–$11*

Roy Rogers and The Outlaws of Sundown Valley, 1950, Whitman, #2347, Snowden Miller, illustrated, very good, 5½″ × 8″, Paper Collectables & Memorabilia Show, March 1989, $10.

$10–$15

Ruth Gordon: An Open Book, 1980, Doubleday, Ruth Gordon (biography), dust jacket, out of print, Limelight, August 1988, $10.   *$8–$12*

Sean Connery, 1985, Stein & Day, Michael Feeney Callan, 1st edition, softcover, very good, Twentieth Century Nostalgia, October 1988, $3.50.   *$3.50–$5*

Scarecrow and the Tin Woodman of Oz, The, 1939, Rand McNally, #297, illustrated story book, very good, 5½″ × 7″, Hake's, June 1989, $20.   *$25–$50*

Schnozzola, 1951, Viking, Gene Fowler (Jimmy Durante biography), 1st edition, dust jacket, out of print, Larry Edmunds Bookstore, August 1988, $22.50.   *$15–$27.50*

Screen World, 1961, 1963-1969 (eight volumes), Greenberg, Daniel Blum and John Willis, illustrated, all one color, dust jacket, very good, 6 1/2″ × 9 1/2″, Collectors' Showcase, November 1988, $88.   *$100–$150*

Screen World, 1976, Crown, John Willis, volume 27, softcover, illustrated, dust jacket, fine, street dealer, NYC, May 1989, $2.
$15–$25

NOTE: Screen World *volumes began publishing with the 1949 volume. Originally softcover, the volumes changed to hardcover in the 1950s. Daniel Blum was the original author, and John Willis followed with later editions.*

Secret Word Is Groucho, The, 1976, Putnam, Groucho Marx and Hector Ace, dust jacket, very good, Limelight, August 1988, $20.   *$15–$23*

Shirley Temple Crayon Book, 1935, Saalfield, #1711, diecut pages and cover, illustrated, crayoned pages, good, 13″ × 13″, Hake's, April 1989, $26.   *$25–$50*

Shirley Temple Edition of Captain January and The Little Colonel, 1959, Random House, illustrated, dust jacket, near mint, 6 1/2″ × 7 1/2″, Paper Chase Antiques, January 1989, $25.

$20–$30

Shirley Temple in Stowaway, 1935, movie edition, 8″ × 10″, very good, Artis Books, June 1989, $22.   *$20–$30*

Sign of the Cross, 1932, *Photoplay* edition, illustrated, dust jacket, very good, Collectors' Showcase, March 1989, $58.

$40–$50

Singing Fool, The, 1939, *Photoplay* movie edition, very good, Collectors' Showcase, November 1988, $22.   *$25–$45*

Slide Area, The (Scenes of Hollywood Life), 1968, Dial Press, Gavin Lambert, 1st printing, dust jacket, fine, Mid-Manhattan Library, November 1988, $1.   *$10–$25*

NOTE: *Excellent book on Hollywood. Often quoted in books and articles by writers on the movies.*

Slightly Scarlet, 1930 (Paramount Famous-Lasky Corp.), World Wide, Percy Heath, PAR movie adaptation, very good, The Attic, September 1988, $1.   *$1–$5*

Snow White, A Story Book, 1950, Tower Press (England), illustrated, Hake's, February 1989, $63.   *$15–$25*

Snow White and the Seven Dwarfs, 1938, Linen Book, #925, illustrated, fine, The Mouse Man Ink, June 1988, $45.
$40–$50

Snow White and the Seven Dwarfs, 1937, Grosset & Dunlap, illustrated, very good, The Mouse Man Ink, June 1988, $40.
$30–$45

Snow White and the Seven Dwarfs Stamp Book, 1957, Simon & Schuster, 48 large full-color stamps mounted on blocks, very fine, 8½″ × 11″, Hake's, February 1989, $18.
$25–$50

So Help Me (The Daring Life Story of George Jessel), 1946, Tower Books, George Jessel, 1st edition, out of print, good, Limelight, August 1988, $5.
$5–$10

Some of These Days, 1957, Hammond Co. (English edition), Sophie Tucker (autobiography), dust jacket, very good, Limelight, August 1988, $10.
$10–$15

Some Time in the Sun, 1976, Charles Scribner & Sons, Tom Dardis, out of print, dust jacket, Pomander Bookshop, February 1989, $8.50.
$8–$13

Sonja Henie "Queen of the Ice" Coloring Book, 1939, Merrill Book, #3476, 44 coloring pages, 10¼″ × 15″, Hake's, June 1989, $18.
$25–$50

Son of Groucho, 1972, David McKay, Arthur Marx, dust jacket, very good, Limelight, August 1988, $12.50.
$10–$22

Special Kind of Magic, A, 1968, Rand McNally, Roy Newquist, 2nd printing, dust jacket, out of print, Limelight Bookstore, August 1988, $7.50.
$7.50–$9

Stage Door Canteen, 1943, New Avon Library, movie edition, black and white illustrations, softcover, very good, Limelight Bookstore, August 1988, $12.50.   *$10–$15*

Star Maker, 1959, Duell, Sloan & Pearce, Homer Croy (re: D.W. Griffith), 1st edition, dust jacket, very good, Pomander Bookshop, February 1989, $7.50.   *$7.50–$15*

Story of Bing Crosby, 1946, World Publishing, Ted Crosby, (foreword by Bob Hope), 1st edition, dust jacket, out of print, good, Limelight Bookstore, August 1988, $10.   *$8–$12*

Strange Death of Marilyn Monroe, The, 1964, Capell, very good, Hughes Papers, January 1989, $8.   *$8–$15*

Sunshine and Shadow, 1955, Doubleday, Mary Pickford (re: Mary Pickford), 1st edition, dust jacket, very good, Limelight, August 1988, $15. *$7–$18*

Tallulah, My Autobiography, 1952, Harper & Bros., Tallulah Bankhead, 1st edition, illustrated, dust jacket, Family Publications, February 1989, $10. *$8–$12*

Talmadge Girls, The, 1978, Viking, Anita Loos, dust jacket, out of print, very good, Limelight, August 1988, $12.50.

$10–$18

They Got Me Covered, 1941, Bob Hope (introduction by Bing Crosby), 1st edition, illustrated, good, J. Goldsmith Antiques, August 1988, $12. *$7–$13*

NOTE: *The paperback edition of this title is fairly common; the hardcover edition is much less common as fewer copies were printed. A hardcover first edition would sell for over $50.*

Thief of Bagdad Coloring Book, The, 1940, Sabu photo on cover, fine, Collectors' Showcase, March 1989, $120. *$50–$75*

Thief of Bagdad Story Book, The, 1940, Saalfield, 36 pages, illustrated, very good, 8″ × 12″, Collectors' Showcase, September 1988, $33. *$15–$25*

Three Comrades, 1978, Southern Illinois University Press, F. Scott Fitzgerald (based on an Erich Maria Remarque novel), 1st edition, dust jacket, scarce, "Atlantique City" Collectibles Market, March 1989, $60. *$50–$65*

Photo courtesy of Hake's Americana, York, PA

Three Stooges, The Punchout Book, 1962, Golden Press, punch-out figures and props in circus scene, near mint, Hake's, February 1989, $98.   *$75–$100*

Thunderball, 1984, Berkley Books, Ian Fleming, 5th printing, fine, Paper Collectables & Memorabilia Show, September 1988, $2.   *$2–$7*

Tom Sawyer Movie Book, 1931, Whitman, 20 pages, full-color film scene on every other page, very fine, 6½″ × 9″, Hake's, November 1988, $18.   *$25–$50*

Too Much, Too Soon, 1957, Henry Holt, Diana Barrymore and Gerold Frank, out of print, dust jacket, fine, Limelight, August 1988, $15.   *$10–$30*

Ugly Duckling, The, 1939, Whitman (Walt Disney), illustrated, full-color covers, scarce, very good, Hake's, June 1989, $136.   *$50–$75*

Unforgettable Hollywood, 1983, Dallinger, 8 1/2″ × 11″, True Value Books, January 1989, $12. $10–$15

Valentino, 1967, Trident, Irving Schulman, 1st edition, dust jacket, very good, Limelight, August 1988, $7.50. $6–$7.50

Venus in Hollywood, 1970, Lyle Stuart, Michael Bruno, out of print, dust jacket, Limelight, August 1988, $9.50. $8–$12

Walt Disney's Bambi Picture Book, 1942, Walt Disney Productions, #930, very good, scarce, 9 1/2″ × 13″, Hake's, November 1988, $26. $25–$50

Walt Disney's Cinderella Golden Open-Door Book, 1965, with five little color "story books" inside, very fine, Collectors' Showcase, March 1989, $22. $30–$40

Walt Disney's Donald Duck and His Cat Troubles, 1948, Whitman, #845, black and white, red illustrations, full-color cover, fine, 5 1/2″ × 5 1/4″, Hake's, June 1989, $37. $50–$75

Walt Disney's Magnificent Mr. Toad, 1949, 32 pages, illustrated, very good, Collectors' Showcase, March 1989, $82. $20–$30

Walt Disney's Mary Poppins Golden Look-Inside Book, 1964, illustrated, five little "books" inside, very fine, Collectors' Showcase, March 1989, $24. $30–$40

Walt Disney's People & Places, 1959 (re: documentary films), 2nd printing, fine, Collectors' Showcase, March 1989, $22.
$20–$30

Walt Disney's Pinocchio, 1949, Little Nipper Series Y-385, w/ two 7″ RCA Victor records, narrated by C. Edwards, good, Paper Collectables & Memorabilia Show, April 1989, $15.
$15–$25

Walt Disney's Pinocchio Paint Book, 1939, Whitman, illustrated, fine, scarce, 11″ × 15″, Hake's, February 1989, $80.
$50–$75

Walt Disney Presents 40 Big Pages of Mickey Mouse, 1936, Whitman, 40 pages of pictures/games to crayon, some used, scarce, 10″ × 12 1/2″, Hake's, February 1989, $98. $75–$100

Way I See It, The, 1959, Prentice-Hall, Eddie Cantor, 1st edition, dust jacket, Limelight, August 1988, $12.95.   *$10–$15*

Westmore of Hollywood, The, 1976, J.P. Lippincott, Frank Westmore and Muriel Davidson, 1st edition, illustrated, dust jacket, fine, Mid-Manhattan Library, November 1988, $3.
$6–$10

Whatever Happened to Hollywood, 1975, Funk & Wagnalls, Jesse Lasky, Jr., dust jacket, fine, Pomander Bookshop, February 1989, $6.   *$5–$8*

What Price Hollywood?, 1932, 1959 RKO copyright, Frederick Ungar, Gene Fowler and Roland Brown screenplay, softcover, illustrated with film scenes, fine, Pageant Book & Print Shop, October 1988, $4.50.   *$4.50–$8*

NOTE: *This movie starred Constance Bennett in what was universally thought to be her best performance. The story was about a waitress who rises to fame and fortune in Hollywood, an early version of* A Star Is Born.

★

What's New Pussycat?, 1965, Dell, Marvin H. Albert, illustrated, original screenplay, very good, Abby Book Shop, October 1988, $1.   *$1–$3*

Where's the Rest of Me?, 1965, Dell, Ronald Reagan and Richard C. Hubler, 2nd printing (August 1981), softcover, out of print, Limelight, August 1988, $2.95.   *$2.95–$7*

Who's Who in the Film World, 1914 (West Coast Edition, re: early silent film stars), Camden House, May 1989, $100.
$25–$50

Will Rogers: His Life Story, 1941, Bobbs Merrill, Betty Rogers, good, Limelight, August 1988, $10.   *$8–$12*

Wind at My Back, The (The Life and Times of Pat O'Brien), 1964, Doubleday, Pat O'Brien, illustrated, dust jacket, out of print, August 1988, $9.   *$8–$12*

Wizard of Oz, The, 1944, Saalfield, L. Frank Baum, animated by Julian Wehr, illustrated (removable), partially spiral-bound, 20 pages, 1st edition, fine, 8″ × 10″, "Atlantique City" Collectibles Market, March 1989, $140. *$110–$150*

Wizard of Oz Story Book, The, circa 1939, English publication, illustrated (eight color, seven black and white plates), Phillips, December 1988, $1500. *$250–$350*

Wizard of Oz Waddle Book, 1934, Blue Ribbon Books, illustrated with cardboard Waddle figures (missing), walking Waddle figures on cover, art by W.W. Denslow, fine, 7¼″ × 9¼″, Hake's, February 1989, $78. *$100–$200*

Yellow Submarine (The Beatles), 1968, Signet, illustrated w/ scenes from animated Beatles film, 1st edition, fine, 4¼″ × 7″, Hake's, February 1989, $17. *$15–$25*

SIGNED BOOKS

Bijou Dream, 1982, Crown, Jack Warner, Jr., #27 of 100 copies authorized for distribution by Signed Editions, Ltd., 1st edition, dust jacket, near mint, Mid-Manhattan Library, October 1988, $4. *$15–$20*

Bogey's Baby, 1976, St. Martin's Press, Howard Greenberger, signed by the author, 1st edition, dust jacket, Mario Carrandi, Jr., March 1989, $18.50. *$15–$22*

Chinatown, 1983, Neville, Robert Townes (screenwriter), one of 350 copies numbered and signed by Townes, this copy is #345, 1st edition, illustrated, near mint, "Atlantique City" Collectibles Market, March 1989, $75. *$75–$90*

Don't Say Yes Until I Finish Talking, biography of Darryl F. Zanuck, 1971, Doubleday, Mel Gussow, presentation copy with author's signature tipped in, 1st edition, dust jacket, Mario Carrandi, Jr., March 1989, $15. *$15–$25*

Famous Film Folk, 1925, Charles Fox, autographed by author, illustrated, fine, Collectors' Showcase, November 1988, $72.
$30–$35

Films of Ingrid Bergman, 1970, Citadel, author autographed, illustrated, fine, Collectors' Showcase, November 1988, $72.
$30–$35

Gone With the Wind, 1938 edition, Macmillan, signed by 23 members of the cast, crew, and production department of the MGM movie including Clark Gable, Vivien Leigh, Olivia de Havilland, Leslie Howard, Hattie McDaniel, Butterly McQueen, Evelyn Keys, Monty Westmore (makeup artist), and Lyle Wheeler (art director), among others. Fred Crane, who played one of the Tarleton twins, consigned this book for auction and signed as well, as did George Besselo, who played his twin brother in the movie (Besselo changed his name to George Reeves and played Superman on television in the 1950s). Camden House, May 1989, $20,000.   *$25,000–$30,000*

Knock On Any Door, 1947, Appleton, Willard Motley, inscribed by Humphrey Bogart, who starred in the movie of the same name in 1949, dust jacket, Pepper & Stern, April 1989, $975.
                                               $900–$1000

My Life East and West, 1929, autobiography of silent western star William S. Hart, and signed by the actor, illustrated black and white photos and color artwork by Charles Russell, noted western artist, Camden House, May 1989, $200.   *$100–$200*

There Really Was a Hollywood, 1985, Jove, Janet Leigh, signed by the actress, 4th printing, illustrated, mint, Collectors' Bookstore, August 1988, $5.   *$5–$10*

Untold Story of Errol Flynn, The, 1980, Charles Hingham, autographed by the author, 1st edition, dust jacket, out of print, Limelight, August 1988, $5.   *$15–$25*

BETTER LITTLE BOOKS

Charlie Chan Solves a New Mystery, 1940, art by Alfred Andriola, very good, Collectors' Showcase, December 1988, $22.
                                                 $20–$30

Donald Duck Says Such Luck, 1941, illustrated, very good, Collectors' Showcase, March 1989, $26.   *$20–$30*

Donald Duck Up in the Air, 1945, illustrated by Carl Barks, very good, Collectors' Showcase, March 1989, $30.   *$20–$30*

Flash Gordon and the Tyrant of Mongo, Whitman, #1484, illustrated, very good, Hake's, February 1989, $36.   *$50–$75*

Inspector Charlie Chan: Villainy on the High Seas, 1942, illustrated, fine, Collectors' Showcase, January 1989, $46.

$30–$40

Jackie Cooper in Gangster's Boy, 1939, illustrated, fine, Collectors' Showcase, January 1989, $25.

$20–$30

Mickey Mouse and the Dude Ranch Bandit, 1943, very good, J. Goldsmith, August 1988, $45.

$30–$40

Mickey Mouse and the Magic Lamp, 1942, illustrated, very good, Collectors' Showcase, March 1989, $35.

$30–$35

Mickey Mouse in the Treasure Hunt, 1941, illustrated, very good, J. Goldsmith Antiques, August 1988, $45.

$30–$40

Tim McCoy and the Sandy Gulch Stampede, 1939, illustrated, fine, Collectors' Showcase, December 1988, $29.

$25–$35

Walt Disney's Bambi, 1942, illustrated, very good, Collectors' Showcase, January 1989, $22.

$20–$30

BIG BIG BOOKS

Story of Mickey Mouse, The, 1933, Whitman, Gottfredson art reprints, 32 pages, good, Collectors' Showcase, March 1989, $60.

$75–$125

Story of Mickey Mouse and the Smugglers, The, 1935, Whitman, rare, good, The Mouse Man Ink, September 1988, $45.

$40–$60

Tom Mix and the Scourge of Paradise Valley, 1937, Whitman, #4068, Vallely art, good, 7¼″ × 9½″, Hake's, November 1988, $52.

$50–$80

BIG LITTLE BOOKS

Buccaneer, The, 1938, Whitman, #1470, illustrated with film scenes of the PAR film starring Frederic March, very fine, Hake's, February 1989, $21.

$25–$50

Buck Rogers Big Little Books (set of 12), Whitman, including the rare *Buck Rogers in the City of Floating Globes* (a Cocomalt giveaway, not numbered); *On the Moons of Saturn* (#1143); *The Depth Men of Jupiter* (#1169); *The Planetoid Plot* (#1197); and *War With Planet Venus* (#1437), illustrated, Christie's East, December 1988, $715.

$500–$700

David Copperfield, 1934, Whitman, #1148, story and film scenes from MGM movie starring W.C. Fields and Freddie Bartholomew, very fine, 5″ × 5¼″, Hake's, February 1989, $100.

$25–$50

Photo courtesy of Hake's Americana, York, PA

Felix the Cat All Pictures Comic, 1945, Whitman, #1465, illustrated in cartoon picture panels, good, Hake's, June 1989, $41.

$25–$50

Jackie Cooper in Peck's Bad Boy, 1934, Saalfield, #1084, illustrated with film scenes from movie, fine, 5″ × 5¼″, Hake's, February 1989, $21.

$25–$50

Law of the Wild, The, 1930s, Saalfield, softcover, based on *Rin-Tin-Tin and Rex* movie, illustrated, good, Collectors' Showcase, December 1988, $9.   *$15–$25*

NOTE: *Difficult to pin down the exact date of this book and year the movie was released and by what studio. Rin-Tin-Tin was introduced to moviegoers in 1923 in a film called* Where the North Begins, *released by WB. The dog was under contract to the studio and appeared in a total of 19 movies. His salary was $1000 weekly, and some of his contract benefits included a small orchestra for mood music during his scenes, a diamond-studded collar, and a Chateaubriand steak with all the trimmings at mealtimes. It was the profits made from Rin-Tin-Tin movies that kept WB afloat during the silent era, and also prevented many theaters across the country from closing due to lack of business.*

Lost Patrol, The, 1934, Whitman, #753, illustrated with film scenes from movie starring Boris Karloff, fine, 5″ × 5¼″, Hake's, February 1989, $60.   *$25–$50*

Mickey Mouse, 1933, Whitman (unnumbered), first Disney Big Little Book, illustrated, scarce, good, Hake's, April 1989, $218.
                                                                           $50–$100

Mickey Mouse and Bobo the Elephant Book, 1935, Whitman, #1160, very good, Hake's, June 1989, $62.   *$25–$50*

Mickey Mouse in the Foreign Legion, 1940, Whitman, #1428, illustrated, fine, Hake's, February 1989, $72.   *$25–$50*

Mickey Mouse Runs His Own Newspaper, 1937, Whitman, illustrated, Gottfredson art and text, fine, Collectors' Showcase, September 1988, $39 and March 1989, $22.   *$30–$50*

Mickey Mouse and the Sacred Jewel, 1936, Whitman, #1187, fine, Collectors' Showcase, March 1989, $31.   *$30–$40*

Mickey Mouse Sails for Treasure Island, premium Big Little Book, scarce, fine, Hake's, June 1989, $51.   *$50–$75*

New Adventures of Tarzan, 1935, Whitman, #1180, text and photos from film starring Herman Brix (later Bruce Bennett), very good, Collectors' Showcase, March 1989, $27.   *$30–$40*

Plainsman, The, 1936, Whitman, #1123, Gary Cooper–Jean Arthur movie, illustrated, very good, Collectors' Showcase, January 1989, $22.　　　　　*$20–$25*

Popeye in Quest of His Poopdeck Pappy, 1937, Whitman, #1450, art by L.C. Segar, very good, Collectors' Showcase, January 1989, $27.　　　　　*$30–$35*

Power Smoke Range, 1935, Whitman, #1176, illustrated, very good, Collectors' Showcase, December 1988, $11.　　　*$20–$30*

Secret Agent X-9, 1936, Whitman, #1144, art by Charles Flanders, fine, Collectors' Showcase, January 1989, $27.　　*$20–$30*

Silver Streak, The, 1935, Whitman, #1155, movie story with illustrations, very good, Collectors' Showcase, January 1989, $13.　　　　　*$10–$25*

Tom Mix and the Hoard of Montezuma, 1937, Whitman, #1462, full-color and black and white illustrations, fine, Hake's, June 1989, $36.　　　　　*$25–$50*

Treasure Island, 1934, Whitman, #1141, illustrated with film scenes from MGM picture starring Jackie Cooper, very fine, 5″ × 5¼″, Hake's, February 1989, $14.　　　　*$25–$50*

Walt Disney's Silly Symphony Stories, 1936, Whitman, #1111, illustrated, good, Collectors' Showcase, March 1989, $35.

$20–$30

BIG TELL-A-TALE BOOKS

Winnie-the-Pooh, 1965, Whitman, #2443, poems by A.A. Milne, Walt Disney Productions, text copyright 1927 (E.P. Dutton), authorized edition, illustrated, very good, Paper Collectables & Memorabilia Show, February 1989, $5.　　　　　*$5–$10*

D.C. HEATH

Bambi, 1942, good, The Mouse Man Ink, September 1988, $12.　　　　　*$10–$15*

Donald Duck and His Friends, 1939, fine, The Mouse Man Ink, September 1988, $35.　　　　　*$25–$38*

Mickey Never Fails, 1938, School Readers series, illustrated, very fine, 6″ × 8½″, Hake's, February 1989, $42. $25–$50

Walt Disney's Pinocchio, School Readers series, illustrated, very good, scarce, 6″ × 8½″, Hake's, June 1989, $32. $25–$50

NOTE: *School Readers series were fairly well used by school-age children and it's usually difficult to find better-than-average copies.*

★

Water Babies Circus and Other Stories, 1940, near mint, The Mouse Man Ink, September 1988, $35. $25–$40

LITTLE GOLDEN BOOKS

Cinderella Friends, 1950, 1st edition, very good, Hake's, February 1989, $10. $15–$20

Walt Disney's Pinocchio, 1948, Simon & Schuster (earliest Little Golden Book edition), very fine, Hake's, November 1988, $25.
          $15–$25

PAPER DOLLS

Assorted Paper Dolls, 1930s, cut figures and clothes of Deanna Durbin, Alice Faye, Sonja Henie, and Shirley Temple, plus a group of teenagers with "Paper Doll Family and Their House"; babies with clothes/furniture; fine, Skinner, November 1988, $110. $150–$200

Assorted Paper Dolls, 1930s/1940s, *Gone With the Wind* cut set; Sonja Henie, two cut sets; cut set of Deanna Durbin with two figures; partially cut sets with two figures of Greer Garson; Skinner, November 1988, $130. $100–$150

"Blondie" Paper Dolls and Clothing, 1943, Whitman, #975, stiff paper dolls of Blondie, Dagwood, infant Cookie, dog Daisy, and son Alexander, Dagwood is 9½″, cut assortment of clothes and accessories, fine, Hake's, June 1989, $20. $15–$25

Carol Lynley Doll Book, Whitman, #2089, 11″ tall standup doll, eight pages of uncut clothing, 28 costumes/accessories, near mint, 7¼″ × 13″, Hake's, November 1988, $50. $50–$75

Claudette Colbert's Cut-Out Clothing, 1943, Saalfield, #2451, 11 cut clothing pieces, three paper dolls (missing), very fine, Hake's, February 1989, $14. $25–$50

Deanna Durbin's Cut Doll Clothing, 1941, Merrill Book, #4804, two missing dolls, 10 clothing pieces, very fine, Hake's, February 1989, $5. $25–$50

Elizabeth Taylor, 1957, cut-out dolls, 16 pages, very fine, 10 1/2″ × 12″, Collectors' Showcase, March 1989, $27.

$50–$65

Gene Autry Melody Ranch Cut-out Doll Book, 1950, Whitman, #990-10, full-color cover with 9″ tall punchout Gene Autry, ranch characters punchout figures, six pages of clothing, near mint, Hake's, November 1988, $99. $100–$200

Greer Garson Dolls and Clothing, 1944, Merrill Book, three 10″ punched-out doll figures, 16 cut clothing pieces, good, Hake's, November 1988, $33. $25–$50

Hayley Mills, 1964, Whitman, #1960, mint, Alan Levine, June 1988, $25. $20–$30

Jane Withers Paper Doll and Clothing, 1940, Whitman #99, full-color punchout paper doll, eight complete one-piece outfits, good, Hake's, February 1989, $35. $25–$50

Mary Poppins, 1964, Whitman, four paper dolls, mint, Alan Levine, June 1988, $20. $18–$25

Natalie Wood Cut-Out Dolls, 1958, very fine, 10 1/2″ × 12″, Collectors' Showcase, September 1988, $61. $35–$50

Oklahoma Cut-Out Dolls, 1956, paper doll folder with "statuette dolls" and clothing changes for stars of movie, Gordon Macrae and Shirley Jones, very fine, 10″ × 12″, Collectors' Showcase, September 1988, $72. $40–$50

Our Gang, multi-colored cut-outs, with clothes and pets, very good, Richard Opfer, February 1989, $65. $50–$75

Shirley Temple Masquerade Costumes for Paper Doll, 1940, Saalfield, paper clothing with 12″ paper dolls (missing), Hake's, February 1989, $30. $50–$75

Photo courtesy of Hake's Americana, York, PA   Photo courtesy of Hake's Americana, York, PA

Shirley Temple Paper Doll, 1936, Saalfield, 34″ heavy paper doll from "life-size paper doll book," full-color w/one dress, Hake's, February 1989, $75.   *$75–$100*

Tuesday Weld Boxed Paper Doll Kit, 1960, Saalfield, #5112, two 9″ unpunched standup dolls, large uncut sheet of 58 costume pieces, illustrated, original box, near mint, 9″ × 14½″ × 1″, Hake's, June 1989, $46.   *$50–$75*

COSTUMES

INTRODUCTION

In December of 1984, Sotheby's auctioned off a pair of sequined Ruby Red Slippers worn by Judy Garland in *The Wizard of Oz* for $15,500. This auction helped to change the status of movie costumes forever. To suspect that in June of 1988, less than four years later, another pair of slippers would hit the auction block for a staggering $150,000 ($165,000 with the 10% buyer's premium) boggles the brain.

Movie costumes have been increasingly "hot" since the MGM and Max Berman auctions on the West Coast in the early 1970s. These two auctions helped to ignite the flame that has been burning collectors with costume fever ever since.

The Ruby Red Slippers that sold at Christie's set a world record for costume memorabilia, but with prices and collector interest accelerating every day, that record will undoubtedly be eclipsed during the 1989–1990 auction season or through a collectibles dealer. Even the most simple movie costumes are bringing high prices, and a few "not quite costumes" too, such as the initialed handkerchief belonging to Marilyn Monroe that was found in her purse the night she died. It sold for $2145 in October of 1988, and the handbag it was found in went for $1126.

Going back to four years ago at the Sotheby's auction and the Ruby Red Slippers, a simple pantsuit worn by Lana Turner in the MGM film *The Bad and the Beautiful* (1952) sold for $225, mere chicken-feed compared with prices for costumes realized in 1988 and early 1989. In December of 1988, for instance, a two-piece gold lurex pantsuit supposedly worn by Marilyn Monroe in her "Joe DiMaggio days" sold for $7450, and just seven months earlier, at Christie's South Kensington Auction Gallery in London, a simple, albeit skinny, black dress worn by Monroe in

Some Like It Hot brought auction goers to their feet when the final bid realized a whopping $36,600.

That dress was bought for the Museum of the Moving Image in London (and we all know that Marilyn Monroe sure knew how to move). Watching her play the ukelele and sing "Running Wild" on a train in that slinky dress, while Tony Curtis and Jack Lemmon dressed in drag played backup, was enough to recruit legions of new Monroe fans. Hmmmmm! Wonder if those drag outfits are going on the block!

In the following costume listings, readers will find descriptions of fiberglass lace-up boots which the rock singer Elton John wore in the 1975 movie *Tommy* selling for $20,570; a blouse worn by M.M. in *Let's Make Love* fetching $4650; a pair of black patent leather tap shoes which Fred Astaire danced in during the "Continental" number in the classic 1934 RKO musical *The Gay Divorcee*; and the two gingham dresses Judy Garland wore in *The Wizard of Oz*, one for the color sequences of the movie ($18,000) and one for the black and white sequences ($9000).

Costumes are listed alphabetically by type, i.e., dress, gown, hat, suit, and so on, the actor or actress who wore the costume, the film in which they wore it, the movie releasing studio and date, a general description of the costume, place, and date it sold, and the price and price range.

Often there will be a notation as to a "label," and this means that the costume was either signed or inscribed with the actor or actress' name who had worn it and/or a studio production number. I have also included the words "photograph or still included." This is a photo or still that accompanied a costume and pictures the actor or actress wearing it.

Other notations where applicable involve costume condition, such as very good, mint, and fine.

Price and price ranges cover the period from June 1988 through June 1989.

COSTUMES LISTING

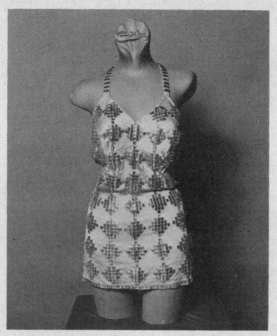

Photo courtesy of Camden House, Los Angeles, CA

Bathing Suit, worn by Esther Williams in *Bathing Beauty,* MGM, 1944, designed by Irene Sharaff, beige satin heavily adorned with crystal stones in a geometric pattern and w/matching stones on the shoulder straps, included with April 17, 1944 issue of *Life* magazine, picturing the actress on the cover in this bathing suit, Camden House, May 1989, $1100.   *$500–$700*

Blouse, worn by Marilyn Monroe in *Let's Make Love,* 20th, 1960, pink silk, Christie's South Kensington Auction Gallery, December 1988, $4750.

Bodice, worn by Joan Crawford in *The Women,* MGM, 1939, designed by Adrian, completely covered with fishscale gold celluloid sequins, Camden House, May 1989, $950.   *$300–$500*

Boots, worn by Ava Gardner in *Show Boat*, MGM, 1951, designed by Walter Plunkett, in button-up black kidskin lined with gray leather, studio initials and Ms. Gardner's name are inscribed in boots, Camden House, May 1989, $150.   *$200–$250*

Boots, worn by Elton John, the rock singer, in *Tommy*, COL, 1975, pair of Doc Marten's fiberglass lace-up boots, Sotheby's (London), September 1988, $20,570.

NOTE: *These boots were auctioned as part of a four-day sale of rock star possessions and memorabilia that was the largest accumulation of such material to hit the international auction houses in the last seven years.*

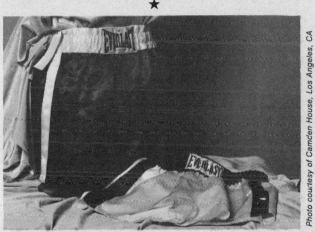

Photo courtesy of Camden House, Los Angeles, CA

Boxing Trunks, worn by Robert De Niro in *Raging Bull*, 1980, two pairs of trunks, one of white satin with black trim, and one of black satin with white trim, Camden House, May 1989, $750.   *$900–$1100*

NOTE: *One pair of the trunks were worn by De Niro in the early part of the film when he was thin, and the other pair were worn in the later parts of the movie when he was heavy. De Niro won the best actor Oscar for his performance as the prize fighter, Jake La Motta.*

Costume, worn by John Candy in *Spaceballs*, MGM, 1987, consisting of a custom-made, beige, textured fabric jumpsuit with a red and white patch over the left pocket with the actor's character name "Barf," a beige undershirt, black and white tennis shoes, two fur feet and paws, a fur tail, black leather gloves, and an elaborate styrofoam mold of the actor's head with an original eye patch and ears attached, Camden House, May 1989, $600.

$700–$800

Costume, worn by Richard Gere in *No Mercy*, Tri-Star, 1986, gray cotton pants and undershirt, blue print shirt and sweat jacket with hood, blue parka vest, belt, scarf, knit cap, socks, brown leather boots and brown leather jacket, Camden House, May 1989, $300.

$150–$200

Costume, worn by Mel Gibson in *Tequilla Sunrise*, 1988, pair of blue jeans, pale green silk shirt with a maroon jacket, actor's initials "M.G.#1" handwritten in waistband, photograph included, Collectors' Showcase, March 1989, $605.

$200–$300

Costume, worn by Maureen O'Sullivan in *Tarzan's Secret Treasure*, MGM, 1941, suede leather costume laces up both right and left sides with self-lacing, label, two photographs included, Camden House, May 1989, $1500.

$1200–$1500

Costume, worn by Tyrone Power in *The Mark of Zorro*, 20th, 1940, designed by Travis Banton, two-piece, gray-blue wool suit adorned with silk velvet and gold bullion, the jacket has a gray velvet collar, label, Camden House, May 1989, $2250.

$1500–$3000

Costume, worn by Gus Rethwisch (the character "Buzzsaw," in *The Running Man*, Tri-Star, 1987), black nylon slacks with two silver stripes down the legs, a black cotton tank top, black cotton fishnet shirt, a pair of black leather gloves, custom-made black leather motorcycle boots with straps, leather belt with name "Buzzsaw" tooled into the leather, black/silver panels dropping to the legs, and a silver helmet with clear visor, photograph included, Camden House, May 1989, $400.

$300–$400

Costume, worn by Arnold Schwarzenegger in *The Running Man*, Tri-Star, 1987, World Gym sweat shirt, brown pants, striped suspenders and black rubber boots, with a second costume of white tank top and boxer shorts, label, photo included, Collectors' Showcase, March 1989, $550.   *$200–$300*

Costume, worn by Bruce Willis in *Sunset*, Tri-Star, 1988, a white cotton dress shirt, brown suede hatband with silver buckle, two pairs of custom-made white leather gloves with black stitching, one pair of custom-made gloves of black leather with white stitching, a tooled black leather belt with sterling silver buckle set with four silver conchos, an elaborate pair of cowboy boots of black leather with tulips running up the leg in white leather, initial label, photographs included, Camden House, May 1989, $400.   *$300–$400*

NOTE: *Willis played the cowboy actor Tom Mix.*

Dance Leotard, worn by Leslie Caron in *Lili*, MGM, 1953, designed by Mary Ann Nyberg, multi-colored shades of pink chiffon dotted with opaque sequins, also a pair of satin ballet slippers, label, Camden House, May 1989, $325.   *$300–$400*

Dance Leotard, worn by Judy Garland in *Till the Clouds Roll By*, MGM, 1946, designed by Helen Rose and Irene, beige satin with attached undergarment trimmed with silk, label, photograph included, Camden House, May 1989, $600.   *$600–$800*

Dress, worn by Billie Burke in *The Ghost Comes Home*, MGM, 1940, 1940s day dress of blue and white checked gingham with 3/4-length sleeves, gathered and pleated ornamentation at the front and back of the bodice, label, Camden House, May 1989, $100.   *$150–$250*

Dress, worn by Doris Day in *Jumbo*, MGM, 1962, two-piece pale pink cotton eyelet dress with vested bodice under attached skirt, pink tulle hat with flowers, Collectors' Showcase, December 1988, $518.   *$400–$600*

Dress, worn by Judy Garland in *The Wizard of Oz*, MGM, 1939, blue and white gingham "test" pinafore fastened at the rear with hooks and snaps, shoulder straps attached to the body of the dress with four white buttons, name tag inside the back panel of the dress reads "Judy Garland, 4228," 24" length, Phillips, December 1988, $18,000.   *$20,000–$25,000*

NOTE: *This dress is supposedly one of four or five made for Ms. Garland during the production tests for the movie. This particular dress was rejected by the producers because it was too short, i.e., "revealing." The actual dress that was used was longer and fell below the knees.*

Dress, worn by Judy Garland in *The Wizard of Oz*, MGM, 1939, designed by Adrian, yellow ocher and black checked cotton gingham jumper, ornamented with white buttons at the front, also a white blouse trimmed with a blue bow tie with polka dots, photographs included, Camden House, May 1989, $9000.   *$6000–$8000*

NOTE: *This dress was worn by Garland in the black and white (sepia) portion of* The Wizard of Oz. *It is not known if this was a test dress or the actual dress worn by Ms. Garland in the Kansas sequence of the movie when the actress sings "Somewhere Over the Rainbow." The blouse was worn by Garland in the first few weeks of filming but was later abandoned and it does not appear in the movie.*

Dress, worn by Geraldine Page in *Sweet Bird of Youth*, MGM, 1961, designed by Orry Kelly, black silk chiffon over nude silk, trimmed at the collar, cuff, and waist with black velvet, velvet bow at the waist, label, two photographs included, Camden House, May 1989, $200.   *$300–$400*

Dress, worn by Vivien Leigh in *Gone With the Wind*, MGM, 1939, two-piece cotton day dress with blue-gray bolero jacket, matching full skirt, both trimmed in black cord, label, two stills included, Alexander Gallery, December 1988, $15,000.

NOTE: *Vivien Leigh wore this dress in the scene where Scarlett O'Hara drives her carriage into "Shanty Town" and is rescued from attackers by "Big Sam."*

Gloves, worn by Joan Crawford in *Mannequin*, MGM, 1938, designed by Adrian, black velvet and suede, embroidered with silver sequins and beads, Christie's East, June 1989, $1210.
$700–$900

Gown, worn by Ann Blyth in *The Great Caruso*, MGM, 1951, designed by Helen Rose, yellow silk period gown, complete silk undergarment, labels, photograph included, Camden House, May 1989, $400. $200–$300

Gown, worn by Susan Hayward in *With a Song in My Heart*, 20th, 1952, designed by Charles LeMaire, halter dance gown of turquoise silk brocade, floral motif with silver threads, bodice and neck ribbon ornamentation with silver beads, sequins, and glass stars, full-length skirt with organ pleats, label, Camden House, May 1989, $525. $350–$450

Gown, worn by Virginia Mayo in *The Iron Mistress*, WB, 1952, pale green linen, studio label, photograph included, Camden House, May 1989, $200. $200–$250

Gown, worn by Ann Southern in *Nancy Goes to Rio*, MGM, 1949, designed by Helen Rose, custom evening gown of rust lace, net, and chiffon, photograph included, Camden House, May 1989, $250. $200–$300

Gown, worn by Joanne Woodward in *From the Terrace*, 20th, 1960, designed by William Travilla, gold satin brocade dressing gown trimmed at the collar and cuffs with mink, studio label, photograph included, Camden House, May 1989, $325.
$150–$250

Gown, worn by Mae West in *Every Day's a Holiday*, PAR, 1938, 1900s-style black velvet, leg-o-mutton sleeves, scoop neck, overall sequined plume motifs, black velvet hat crowned with tufted feathers, three movie stills included, Alexander Gallery, December 1988, $25,000.

NOTE: A bottle of perfume is also included with the gown. The designer, Schiaparelli, was inspired to create the perfume expressly for Ms. West. It is called "Shocking," a name the designer used after he received the actress' measurements. The perfume bottle is in the shape of an hourglass.

Gown, worn by Loretta Young in *Key to the City*, MGM, 1950, designed by Irene, peach crepe-backed satin, bodice of ecru lace covering satin, front-waist satin bow, label, Camden House, May 1989, $375.   *$200–$300*

Handbag, used by Marilyn Monroe, alligator hide, brown, with strap and M.M.'s initials engraved on top, 1950s, 10″ × 7½″, Collectors' Showcase, October 1988, $1126.   *$1000–?*

Handkerchief, used by Marilyn Monroe, light blue with pink roses embroidered on side, M.M.'s initials embroidered in blue, 1950s, 13″ × 13″, very fine, Collectors' Showcase, October 1988, $2145.   *$750–?*

NOTE: Both the purse and the handkerchief were found in Monroe's bedroom the night she died. The handkerchief was inside the handbag.

Hat, worn by Judy Garland in *Ziegfeld Girl*, MGM, 1941, designed by Adrian, candy-kiss hat with hundreds of fishscale silver sequins over a straw foundation, ornamented with Austrian crystal rhinestones and beads in a floral motif at the front of the cone, photograph included, Camden House, May 1989, $925.
$1100–$1300

Hat, worn by Margaret Hamilton in *The Wizard of Oz*, MGM, 1939, black wool and silk scarf on wire meshing, Sotheby's, December 1988, $33,000.   *$30,000–$50,000*

Hat, worn by Vivien Leigh in *Gone With the Wind*, MGM, 1939, wide-rim straw scalloped at back with wide pink silk ribbon across front, label, Alexander Gallery, December 1988, $15,000.

Headpiece, worn by Norma Shearer in *Marie Antoinette*, MGM, 1938, designed by Adrian, elaborate metal birdcage with tiny pieces of Austrian crystal, inside the cage is an animatron of a bird covered with feathers which moves its head from side to side and opens and closes its beak when the cage apparatus is turned on, photograph included, Camden House, May 1989, $3000.   *$4000–$5000*

Ice Skating Outfit, worn by Joan Crawford in *Ice Follies of 1939*, MGM, 1939, designed by Adrian, black silk velvet heavily embellished with Austrian lead crystal beads, with matching gloves, photograph included, Camden House, May 1989, $1250.
                                                       $1800–$2000

Jacket, worn by Ray Bolger in *The Harvey Girls*, MGM, 1945, designed by Helen Rose, blue wool with plaid stitching in light gold thread, trimmed with three black mother-of-pearl buttons, waistcoat of orange wool trimmed with many white buttons down the front, labels, still included, Camden House, May 1989, $200.   *$100–$200*

Jacket, worn by Judy Garland at her second engagement at the Palace Theater in NY, 1956, in the "Get Happy" number, black tuxedo-type jet-beaded jacket, codemarks, fine, Collectors' Showcase, October 1988, $3025.   *$3000–$5000*

Jacket, worn by Elvis Presley in *Double Trouble*, MGM, 1967, designed by Donfeld, custom-made red cotton jacket with black leather snap closures at the front, lobby card included, Camden House, May 1989, $5000.   *$3750–$4000*

Jacket, worn by Stewart Granger in *Young Bess*, MGM, 1953, Elizabethan silk-lined leather with leather design work around neck, puffed shoulders, label, photo included, Collectors' Showcase, January 1989, $572.   *$350–$450*

Mandarin Top, worn by Luise Rainer in *The Good Earth*, MGM, 1937, designed by Dolly Tree, with burgundy silk burlap, satin frogs at the neck and down the right side, beige silk faille and blue silk trim runs down the closure and at the cuff, label, photograph included, Camden House, May 1989, $250.

$200–$300

Matador Jacket, worn by Rudolph Valentino in *Blood and Sand*, PAR, 1922, weighing seven pounds, the jacket is wine-colored satin, heavily encrusted with silver and blue cut-glass gems set in rosettes of silver sequins and stitched with wire thread, label, two photographs included, fine, Collectors' Showcase, March 1989, $5000.

$5000–$10,000

NOTE: *Valentino wore this jacket in the movie's deathbed scene. The costume was altered for goring by the bull.*

Opera Gloves, worn by Joseph Cotten in *Gaslight*, MGM, 1944, embroidered gloves with silver threads and small stones, left glove soiled as it was used by the actor throughout the movie, Camden House, May 1989, $1600.

$1100–$1500

Pajama Outfit, worn by Heather O'Rourke in *Poltergeist III*, MGM, 1987, one-piece red flannel with white trim on collar, cuffs, and feet, trimmed with seven white buttons down the front, photograph included, Camden House, May 1989, $200.

$100–$150

Pantsuit, worn by Marilyn Monroe, two-piece gold lurex, Christie's South Kensington Auction Gallery, December 1988, $4750.

NOTE: *The pantsuit was supposedly given to Marilyn by Jean O'Doul, personal manager of Joe DiMaggio when he was married to Monroe.*

Robe, worn by Tallulah Bankhead in *A Royal Scandal*, 20th, 1945, designed by Rene Hubert, early 18th-century-style open robe of black velvet with ears-of-corn beadwork embroidery, rhinestones on the collar and panniered skirt, draped cuffs on a full petticoat trimmed with ivory silk net ruffles, label, photograph included, Camden House, May 1989, $900.   *$600–$650*

Running Suit, worn by Arnold Schwarzenegger in *The Running Man*, Tri-Star, 1987, one-piece suit of yellow, gray, and red lycra, padded shoulders, arms quilted with black stitching, the left leg decorated with large red letters spelling "Running Man," a pair of pumpkin-colored ankle boots, navy blue boiler suit, and warm-up suit, photograph included, Camden House, May 1989, $800.   *$500–$700*

Sailor's Cap, worn by Jayne Mansfield, autographed, good, P.M. Antiques & Collectibles, June 1988, $165.   *$150–$200*

Shirt, worn by James Cagney in *Yankee Doodle Dandy*, WB, 1942, designed by Milo Anderson, orchid and white silk satin with orchid bows at the sleeves, label, Camden House, May 1989, $4500.   *$2000–$2500*

Shoes, worn by Fred Astaire in *The Gay Divorcee*, RKO, 1934, black patent leather tap shoes (signed by the actor on the insole), and a pair of black patent leather dance shoes worn by Ginger Rogers, Astaire's dance partner in the same movie, Camden House, May 1989, $9000.   *$2000–$4000*

NOTE: *Astaire's tap shoes were used in the "Continental" number, which ran for 18 continuous minutes in the film. Rogers' dance shoes can be seen in the "I'll Be Hard to Handle" number.*

Shoes, worn by Ray Bolger (Scarecrow in *The Wizard of Oz*), of brown suede with leather soles, photograph included, Phillips, December 1988, $200.   *$400–$600*

Shoes, worn by Katharine Hepburn in *The Desk Set*, 20th, 1957, pair of dark brown leather high-heeled shoes with toe ornamentation, size 7B, handwritten name and production number under arch, fine, Collectors' Showcase, October 1988, $137.

$75–$100

Shoes, worn by Gene Kelly and Frank Sinatra in *Take Me Out to the Ball Game*, MGM, 1949, designed by Valles, two matching pairs of custom-made shoes, orchid leather and beige suede, orchid leather trims the toes, heels, and lace area of the shoes, Camden House, May 1989, $1650.   *$1300–$1500*

Shoes, worn by Ginger Rogers, circa 1940s, pair of black leather Mary Jane shoes, name handwritten on shoes with production #P2777, fine, Collectors' Showcase, October 1988, $176.

$50–$75

NOTE: *These shoes were probably worn by Rogers in the 1942 PAR movie* The Major and the Minor.

Shoes, worn by Norma Shearer in *Romeo and Juliet*, MGM, 1936, designed by Adrian, custom-made silver slipper satin with heavily embellished crystal beads, sequins, silver thread, and large moonstone, in a floral motif, Camden House, May 1989, $500.   *$800–$1000*

Skirt, worn by Linda Darnell in *Forever Amber*, 20th, 1947, designed by Rene Hubert and Charles LeMaire, period garment of brown and green wool skirt with matching brown wool bodice, white collar and cuffs, bodice laces up the front, label, six photographs included, Camden House, May 1989, $300.

$400–$500

Slippers, worn by Judy Garland in *The Wizard of Oz*, MGM, 1939, pair of Ruby Slippers designed by Gilbert Adrian, red silk faille uppers and heels overlaid with hand-sequined georgette, flat jeweled toe bows, painted red soles with red-orange felt, label, Christie's East, June 1988, $165,000.   *$15,000–$20,000*

NOTE: *These slippers were won as a second prize by Roberta Jeffries Bauman in 1940 in a nationwide contest for high school students in which they submitted their choices for the 10 best movies of 1939. Ms. Bauman's slippers were the second or third pair (out of seven or eight pairs) made for Judy Garland, and a label marked "double" in the slippers constitutes a duplicate for this costume item.*

Smock, worn by Edward Everett Horton in *The Lost Horizon*, COL, 1937, 32″ long, intricate jade green Chinese pattern silk, label, very good, Collectors' Showcase, January 1989, $292.
$350–$400

Stockings, worn by Joan Crawford in *Torch Song*, MGM, 1953, designed by Helen Rose, fishnet- and rhinestone-embellished stockings, Camden House, May 1989, $350.   *$150–$250*

Suit, worn by Clark Gable in *Gone With the Wind*, MGM, 1939, designed by Walter Plunkett, three-piece gray wool suit, label, photograph included, Alexander Gallery, December 1988, $12,500.

Suit, worn by Greer Garson in *The Valley of Decision*, MGM, 1945, designed by Irene, two-piece, period green wool suit with bodice trimmed with inset green taffeta at the bust and sleeve, and ornamentation of black lace, plus gold satin undergarment, label, Camden House, May 1989, $450.   *$300–$400*

Tuxedo, worn by James Cagney in *Ragtime*, 1981, three-piece ensemble of matching black tailcoat and trousers with black satin trim, white vest, label, Camden House, May 1989, $400.
$500–$700

Undergarment, worn by Judy Garland in *Presenting Lily Mars*, MGM, 1943, designed by Howard Shoup, beige silk with multiple layers of ecru silk inset lace, ornamented with satin ribbon on cupped sleeves, waist, and above the lace on garment bottom, label, Camden House, May 1989, $850.   *$600–$800*

Photo courtesy of Christie's East, New York

Uniform, worn by Elvis Presley in *G.I. Blues*, PAR, 1960, designed by Edith Head, two-piece khaki Army uniform consisting of a long-sleeved shirt with military patches and pins, belted pants, and a dark green wool hat, still included, Christie's East, June 1988, $1100.   *$1000–$1500*

Vest, worn by Clark Gable in *Gone With the Wind*, MGM, 1939, designed by Walter Plunkett, taupe vest with four pockets, six dark brown buttons on the front, fully lined with gray silk, label, Camden House, May 1989, $3800.   *$1500–$2000*

Vest, worn by James Cagney in *Yankee Doodle Dandy,* WB, 1942, striped woolen vest, fine, Collectors' Showcase, October 1988, $330.   *$125–$200*

NOTE: *Cagney won the Academy Award for best actor for this film.*

DESIGNER SKETCHES

Edith Head, designer, seven 17″ × 14″ costume sketches for Joan Crawford's personal wardrobe, Camden House, May 1989, $850.   *$700–$900*

Edith Head, designer, 14″ × 17″ costume sketch for Eva Gabor for *A New Kind of Love,* 1963, watercolor, signed in full, fine, Collectors' Showcase, September 1988, $184.   *$100–$150*

Edith Head, designer, 14″ × 17″ costume sketch for Rita Hayworth, circa 1950s, signed in full, very fine, Collectors' Showcase, October 1988, $402.   *$200–$400*

Edith Head, designer, 14½″ × 19¼″ lightly colored costume sketch for Mary Tyler Moore in *What's So Bad About Feeling Good?,* 1968, with fabric sample, signed in full, fine, Collectors' Showcase, February 1989, $243.   *$200–$300*

Edith Head, designer, 14½″ × 19¼″ original watercolor costume sketch for Dany Robin in *Topaz,* 1969, fine, Collectors' Showcase, September 1988, $176.   *$150–$200*

Walter Plunkett, designer, 16″ × 21″ costume design in pen and ink with wash on board for Vivien Leigh in *Gone With the Wind,* MGM, 1939, of a full-skirted black mourning gown with heart-shaped bonnet and full-length veil for scene #87 in film, signed in full with studio stamp, still included, Christie's East, June 1989, $8250.   *$3000–$4000*

Walter Plunkett, designer, costume design in pen and ink with wash heightened with gold on board, of Vivien Leigh in *Gone With the Wind,* MGM, 1939, of a deep green velvet gown made from the portières of Tara, trimmed with cord and tassels and matching bonnet for scene #388 in film, signed in full, studio stamp, Christie's East, June 1989, $9990.   *$3000–$4000*

Walter Plunkett, designer, costume design in pen and ink with wash on board, for Vivien Leigh in *Gone With the Wind*, MGM, 1939, of an off-the-shoulder neckline trimmed in ribbon-edged ruffles, green-sprigged muslin party dress with green velvet sash, slippers and leghorn straw hat, for scene #31 (Scarlett's bedroom through the barbeque at Twelve Oaks), signed in full, photo and still included, Christie's East, June 1989, $8250.   *$3000–$4000*

Rett Turner, designer, three 17″ × 11″ costume sketches for Lucille Ball's personal wardrobe, signed lower right, Camden House, May 1989, $1700.   *$250–$350*

DISNEYANA

INTRODUCTION

In an old episode of the 1970s "Colombo" television show starring Peter Falk, a wine connoisseur is sitting with his secretary
at an auction of rare wines. A particularly rare bottle comes up
on the block. As the bidding commences, the secretary asks: "Do
we really need this bottle of wine?" (they have just spent over
$18,000 on other bottles).

"Nobody needs a $5,000 bottle of wine," her boss says, and
adds after a slight pause, "It's just that I don't want anyone else
to have it."

I thought of this remark at an auction of Disneyana collectibles
recently. A rare celluloid Mickey and Pluto toy depicting Mickey
Mouse on the back of a three-wheeled Pluto was up for bid. The
toy was Japanese, tinplate, and had a keywind mechanism in the
front wheel. Only 5½" long, this toy escalated to $6600 by the end
of the bidding, almost 500% over its estimate.

Two bidders were frantic to own the toy at whatever cost.
Their attitude was "why let the other guy have it if I can get it."
Such shenanigans are common at auctions today. And Disneyana
collectibles are no exception, maybe even more so, since all serious collectors of movie memorabilia would like to own a piece
of Walt Disney and so much Disneyana spills over into practi-
cally every other collecting category. The golden age of Disneyana, the 1930s, is particularly desirable. The desire to own a slice
of Mickey Mouse, Donald Duck, the Three Little Pigs or any of
the other comic characters is crazy because there is so much more
demand than supply of Disney collectibles from this era.

This was the age when Mickey Mouse looked like the happy
rodent that he was: pie-eyed, with a huge pot belly, stringy tail,

cigarette thin arms and legs, big round shoes, black ears in the shape of large balloons, and glove-like hands. Born in 1928 in the cartoon short "Steamboat Willie," Mickey was joined by the Three Little Pigs in 1933 and Donald Duck on June 9, 1934 (a Gemini), who debuted in "The Wise Little Hen."

From circa 1934–37, Donald Duck had a long yellow bill and neck, a short, squat, flat body, and, naturally, he waddled. His outrageous nature was capped by having one eye closed in a wink. As might be expected, Donald Duck quickly became Walt Disney's most famous character after Mickey Mouse. The Three Little Pigs weren't any slouches either.

Pinocchio came along in 1940, just outside the golden age of Disneyana collectibles, but a tremendous amount of merchandise featuring Pinocchio was produced in quick order.

Disneyana collectibles were usually marked "Walt Disney Productions," and in late 1939 the initials "WDP" were also seen on collectibles. Later merchandise was marked "Walt Disney Enterprises"—these are three means to identifying Disneyana from a particular era.

Most Disney merchandise was produced from 1940 to 1987 and is still being produced. While prices for collectibles from the early 1940s are increasing by leaps and bounds, the really expensive collectibles are from the golden age of Disneyana. Almost every collector hopes to acquire a Mickey Mouse or Donald Duck that has not been previously seen in the market. Unfortunately, great examples of Disneyana seldom appear at auction or through dealers.

To reiterate about identification and dates for Disney collectibles, it is important to remember that all items that were produced after September 1938 were marked either "Walt Disney Productions" or "WDP." Since there are thousands upon thousands of Disney collectibles produced after 1938, it is important to look around for the best possible examples. Having the original box adds considerably to the toy's value.

Other Disney collectibles that intrigue collectors are Snow White and the Seven Dwarfs, Cinderella, the Three Caballeros, Dumbo, Peter Pan, Lady and the Tramp, and Sleeping Beauty. Davy Crockett, who made his debut in the 1950s, is also very collectible. The 1950s are very hot with collectors of Disneyana right now and items are becoming increasingly expensive.

In this chapter there are no books or sheet music listed (see individual chapters for Disney additions). I also haven't included any Mickey Mouse Club collectibles since they are identified with television. Except for a Chein Disneyland roller coaster, there is also an absence of Disneyland collectibles. These are theme park items that would be better suited to another type of price guide.

DISNEYANA LISTING

BIG BAD WOLF

Figure, Sieberling Products, standing rubber figure with brown and painted details, original box, 10″ high, Christie's East, March 1989, $715.   *$100–$150*

Photo courtesy of Hake's Americana, York, PA   Photo courtesy of Hake's Americana, York, PA

Pocket Watch, 1934, Ingersoll, colorful dial with the Wolf's black and white eye animated to count the seconds, background in red with Pigs in full-color illustration, Hake's, June 1989, $971.
$400–$700

Photo courtesy of Hake's Americana, York, PA

"Who's Afraid of the Big Bad Wolf?" alarm clock, Ingersoll, dial depicts the Three Little Pigs in color and a large figure of the Wolf in the center whose diecut litho arms and hands point at the time as his head nods up and down to tick off the seconds, scarce, Hake's, February 1989, $390. $200–$400

CLARABELLE

Clarabelle, valentine, 1939, full-color card with movable head, 3″ × 5″, Hake's, February 1989, $32. $25–$50

DAVY CROCKETT

Davy Crockett, gun, Marx, circa 1955, brown with silver-accented, plastic flintlock-style gun, 10¼″ long, Hake's, February 1989, $46. $25–$50

DONALD DUCK

Ashtray, double Donald Duck, circa 1935, Japan, twin long-billed Donald Ducks perched on tray, high-gloss glaze finish, 3 1/2" high, Christie's East, December 1988, $528.

$350–$450

Bisque, 1930s, long-billed Donald Duck holding a sword in hand, a scabbard at his waist, 3" tall, Hake's, February 1989, $76.

$25–$50

Bank, late 1940s, white ceramic bank depicting Donald Duck with a raised hand, coin slot at the back of his head, full-color, 4" × 4" × 6", Hake's, February 1989, $76. $50–$75

Bank, Composition, circa 1960s, painted, slot on Donald's back, rubber stopper (missing on this bank), gold original tag inscribed "Donald Composition Bank," 3 1/2" × 4" × 6", Hake's, February 1989, $30. $25–$50

Photo courtesy of Hake's Americana, York, PA

Soda Bottle, 1960s, Donald Duck Cola soda bottle with large head of Donald Duck on each side, smaller head at the top, inscribed "Donald Duck/Not To Be Refilled/Trademark Copyright/Walt Disney Productions," one pint 8 fl. oz., 10" tall, Hake's, February 1989, $44. $25–$50

Cardboard Carrier, early 1950s, green/purple cardboard carrier for six bottles of Donald Duck Lime Cola, also a pair of 8″-tall Donald Duck Cola clear glass bottles with Donald pictured on each side, 5″ × 7″ × 7″ (carrier), Hake's, November 1988, $58.   *$50–$75*

Convertible, Linemar, small blue convertible roadrunner with a pop-in celluloid Donald Duck driver, front-wheel friction drive, 3″ long, Christie's East, March 1989, $110.   *$80–$100*

Chocolate Mold, tinplate, 5″ high, Knight's, October 1988, $30.   *$25–$40*

Cloth Doll, Knickerbocker, long-billed doll with music box and swivel neck dressed in band leader uniform, "bearskin" hat, jacket, brass buttons, 16″ high, Christie's East, March 1989, $1760.   *$2000–$2500*

Cloth Doll, Knickerbocker, long-billed doll of Donald Duck dressed in sailor's suit, bow tie, and cap, original Knickerbocker tag, 13″ high, Christie's East, March 1989, $440.   *$500–$800*

Cloth Doll, Krueger, long-billed doll, velveteen Donald Duck in sailor cap, open mouth, Silly Symphony tag, 16″ high, Christie's East, December 1988, $825.   *$300–$400*

Cookie Jar, white, J. Goldsmith Antiques, August 1988, $72.50. $50–$90

Figure, celluloid, movable feet and arms, Walt Disney copyright, 3¾" tall, Hake's, February 1989, $220. $50–$75

Greeting Card, 1942, Hallmark, diecut Easter card, inked initials, 4" × 6", Hake's, February 1989, $33. $25–$50

Acrobat Gym Toy, Linemar, Donald Duck performing on a high bar, gym toy pennant, original box, Christie's East, March 1989, $352. $100–$150

Acrobat Gym Toy, Donald Duck performing on a keywind wire bar, original box, 9" high, Christie's East, March 1989, $286.
$150–$200

Jack-in-a-Box, celluloid cardboard box with squeaker and jointed arms on Donald Duck, 4½" high, Christie's East, March 1989, $715. $800–$1200

Jack-in-a-Box, Spear, composition Donald Duck, wooden box covered with Duck design, spring-up push-button, Christie's East, December 1988, $154. $80–$100

Kart, Marx, Japan, Donald Duck driving a wheel friction-powered cart, lever-action handle bars, 6″ long, Christie's East, March 1989, $242.   *$100–$150*

Keywind Climbing Fireman, Linemar, tinplate, Donald Duck in fireman's gear climbing a ladder, 13¾″, Christie's East, December 1988, $440.   *$200–$300*

Keywind Crazy Car, lithographed with various Disney characters, spinning head Donald Duck at the wheel, 5¼″ long, Christie's East, December 1988, $154.   *$100–$150*

Keywind "Straight Shooter" Walker, Mavco, hard plastic toy, original box, with hard plastic Pluto nodder, 7″ long, Christie's East, March 1989, $154.   *$100–$150*

Keywind Walker, Creation Toys, French composition Donald Duck with painted features, original box, 7″ high, and a Donald Duck composition walker, Wilson, 4½″ high, Christie's East, December 1988, $352.   *$200–$300*

Label, 1942, Walt Disney Productions, grapefruit juice can label with Donald Duck and other Disney characters on a bright green background, John Wade, February 1989, $15.   *$12–$20*

Pez Dispenser, Walt Disney Enterprises, undated, Hong Kong, white head of Donald Duck opens to dispense candy, yellow bill, blue base, Brookside Place, September 1988, $1.   *$1–$4*

Pluto, Donald Duck and, Cart, Japanese, tinplate, three wheels, Donald Duck drawn by a dashing Pluto, 9″ long, Christie's East, March 1989, $2420.   *$1200–$1500*

Pocket Watch, circa 1939, Donald Duck on the dial, Mickey Mouse on the back, and a Bayard alarm clock; Donald Duck's arms point to hours and minutes, head nods away the seconds, Christie's East, December 1988, $1045.   *$250–$300*

Rocket Toy, Donald Duck steering a friction-wheeled drive missile, original box, 7″ long, Christie's East, March 1989, $418.   *$200–$300*

Six Pack, Walt Disney Productions, full bottles with caps in cardboard carton of Donald Duck Lime Cola, picture of Donald Duck on carton, Manhattan Antiques and Collectibles Show, Triple Pier 90, November 1988, $45.   *$35–$50*

Tile With Thermometer, circa 1940s, Kemper-Thomas, ceramic tile with Donald Duck depicted as a policeman operating a "Stop/ Go" traffic sign, silver cardboard thermometer with glass tube on side, hanging loop, 6″ × 6¼″, Hake's, November 1988, $41.
                                                                $25–$50

Toothbrush Holder, circa 1935, Japan, bisque, twin long-billed Donald Ducks, 4″ high, Christie's East, December 1988, $352.
                                                              $200–$300

Toy, circa 1950s, Fisher-Price, #544, tall wood pull toy depicting Donald Duck moving his arms up and down as toy rolls with a clicking sound, paper labels, 4″ × 11″ × 9″, Hake's, February 1989, $100.   *$75–$100*

Toy, Linemar, lithographed tinplate Donald Duck toy waddles forward and quacks by pulling Huey back who is with Donald, original box, 5″ high, Christie's East, December 1988, $715.
                                                              $200–$300

Train Set, Mauday, Japanese, two lithographed cars, tunnel, track, original box, with a Donald Duck convertible, Linemar, original box, Mickey Mouse puzzle game, Donald Duck puzzle game, and three Donald Duck charms, Christie's East, December 1988, $550.   *$200–$250*

Truck, Linemar, gasoline truck with articulated cab and friction-powered mechanism, lithographed tanker with Donald Duck and Mickey Mouse, original box, 12″ long, Christie's East, March 1989, $935.   *$500–$700*

Wind-up Toy, Marx, tin, Donald Duck duet, painted, Knight's, October 1988, $300.   *$200–$300*

Wristwatch, Bradley, 1960s running wristwatch of Donald Duck image of figural arms and hands telling the time, original strap, Hake's, February 1989, $90.   *$50–$75*

DOPEY OF SEVEN DWARFS

Fabric Figure, 6½″ high, full dwarf costume, Calico Cat Antiques, December 1988, $150.   *$125–$160*

Original Theater Display Composition, 1938, 18″ automation with speaker in Dopey's stomach, movable mouth, Wex Rex Records & Collectibles, May 1989, $375.   *$300–$400*

DUMBO

Ceramic Pitcher, 1947, Leeds China, spout on Dumbo's mouth, pink pastel color on Dumbo's cheek and ears, large handle, two-quart pitcher, stamped "Disney/Dumbo," Hake's, February 1989, $55.   *$25–$100*

Stuffed Animal, 1947, original box, Carol Zittel at Manhattan Triple Pier Expo, November 1988, $85.   *$75–$100*

FERDINAND THE BULL

Tin Wind-up Toy, Marx, 6″ high, Knight's, October 1988, $80.   *$75–$100*

FIGARO

Wind-up Toy, Marx, lithographed, toy moves a few inches when wound, then Figaro's tail turns, making him roll over before repeating the movement, $1\,^3/_4″ \times 4\,^1/_2″ \times 2\,^1/_2″$, Hake's, February 1989, $160.   *$100–$200*

GEPPETTO

Composition Wooden Figurine, circa 1940, original paint, 5″ high, Kane's Antiques & Collectibles, June 1989, $50.

$40–$55

NOTE: *Geppetto is Pinocchio's father.*

GOOFY

Pelham Puppet, a smiling Goofy dressed in shirt, vest, yellow shoes, and a hat, 37″ high, Christie's East, September 1988, $715.   *$900–$1200*

MICKEY MOUSE

Airport, Keywind, Marx, Disneyville graphics and Mickey Mouse as pilot, $8\,^1/_2″$ diameter, original box, Christie's East, March 1989, $550.   *$400–$600*

Blackboard, School, Richmond School Furniture Co., pictures of Mickey Mouse and Minnie Mouse with letters of the alphabet and numbers featured in upper portion of blackboard, wood crafted, "Atlantique City" Collectibles Market, March 1989, $200.   *$175-$225*

Bottle Cap Set, circa early 1930s, six colored metal bottle caps, full-color images of Goofy and Horsecollar, Clarabelle and Minnie Mouse, and Mickey Mouse and Pluto on tops of bottle caps for different flavors (lemon, orange, lime), 1⅛" diameter each cap, Hake's, November 1988, $397.   *$200-$400*

Bowl, enamel child's bowl, 8" diameter, Knight's, October 1988, $40.   *$30-$50*

Bubble Gum Cards, Mickey Mouse bubble gum #23, #24, #26, and #29, Hake's, February 1989, $42.   *$25-$50*

Bubble Gum Wrapper, 1030s, Gum, Inc., illustrated wax wrapper, 5" × 7", Collectors' Showcase, October 1988, $66.
                                                                           $15-$30

Button, early 1930s, image of Mickey Mouse in black and white on blue fabric set in brass rim with mint gold luster, scarce, ⅞", Hake's, April 1989, $69.   *$75-$100*

Button, early 1930s, image of Mickey Mouse in white fabric with dark red background, Hake's, April 1989, $23.   *$25-$50*

Car, Fire Department, 1940s, Sun Rubber Co., rubber wheels, Mickey Mouse is driving and Donald Duck is in the back holding onto his fire helmet, 2½" × 6½" × 4" tall, Hake's, February 1989, $95.   *$25-$75*

Cello Charm, 1930s, Japanese, depicting Mickey Mouse with guitar with one bent leg, scarce, Hake's, February 1989, $36.
                                                                           $25-$50

Christmas Lights, Mazda, The British Thompson-Houston Co., Ltd., England, circa 1936, 12 plastic lights of Disney characters, boxed, Skinner, November 1988, $150.   *$150-$250*

Christmas Lights, Nima, plastic shade lights with decals of Disney characters, original box, includes unboxed set, Christie's East, December 1988, $176.   *$100–$150*

Circus, four-piece circus train with tent and accessories, Caropreso Gallery, December 1988, $2900.   *$2000–$2500*

NOTE: *The high price paid for this circus train was due to the presence of the circus tent, which is exceedingly rare to find in excellent condition, as was the case with this set. Although the original box was missing, the tent being present overshadowed this loss.*

Costume, top, shorts, four finger gloves, bonnet, printed gauze mask, and four Mickey Mouse-printed doll clothes pieces, Christie's East, December 1988, $88.   *$200–$300*

Doll, early 1930s, Deans Rag Book Co.; England, black velour doll with yellow felt hands and yellow velour feet, the doll's large plastic google eyes are missing, rare, 16″ tall, Hake's, February 1989, $640.   *$400–$700*

Doll, Cloth, probably Dean's Rag Book Co., England, 1932-35, velveteen Mickey Mouse over wire armature, velveteen shorts, hands and shoes have leather soles, shoe button eyes, felt ears, 7½″, Skinner, November 1988, $250.   *$200–$300*

Advertising Figure, circa 1935, French composition semi-round Mickey Mouse tied into a shadowbox frame, 38″ high, 44″ × 30″ framed, Christie's East, September 1988, $2420.   *$1500–$2000*

NOTE: *This is an example of an early Mickey Mouse figure with yellow gloved hands on hips, sharp nose, large moon ears, pie-cut eyes, and swirling "rat's" tail. A highly desirable figure with collectors.*

★

Figure, late-celluloid construction showing Mickey Mouse standing and waving with a swivelled head, Christie's East, March 1989, $176. *$200–$300*

Films, circa late 1930s–early 1940s, four 8mm cartoon films, three of Mickey Mouse and one of Donald Duck, original boxes with Mickey Mouse pictured on the covers, 50' each film, Camden House, May 1989, $100. *$100–$150*

Photo courtesy of Hake's Americana, York, PA

Greeting Card, 1942, Hallmark, get well card of Mickey Mouse as a surgeon getting his equipment from a mail-order tool chest, illustration inside of Mickey by a hospital door with a sign reading: "We cure everything but bacon," Hake's, February 1989, $25. *$15–$25*

Hurdy-Gurdy, circa 1931, Distler, Mickey with sharp nose and rat grin pushing a band organ which, when wound, makes Mickey turn the crank and Minnie dance to a tune (her arms missing), organ lithographed with various mousecapades, 6" long, Christie's East, March 1989, $7150.   *$5000–$7000*

Kart, Marx, Japanese, Mickey Mouse driving a four-wheel, friction-powered Disney kart with lever-action handlebars, 6" long, Christie's East, March 1989, $242.   *$100–$150*

Keywind Carousel, Japanese, celluloid Mickey Mouse standing on one foot atop a red ball, holding an umbrella with dangling stars, 8", Christie's East, March 1989, $825.   *$1000–$1200*

Mickey Mouse Magazine, June/August 1935, volume one, first issue, third series, color illustrations, 44 pages, 10¼" × 13¼", Collectors' Showcase, October 1988, $206.   *$100–$200*

Mickey Mouse Magazine, March 1935, volume two, number five, second series, Collectors' Showcase, February 1989, $62.
        $30–$50

Mickey Mouse Magazine, March 1936, volume one, number six, third series, 36 pages, Collectors' Showcase, December 1988, $120.   *$40–$60*

Mickey Mouse Magazine, October 1937, volume two, number 13, third series, color illustrations, 36 pages, Collectors' Showcase, September 1988, $110.   *$75–$125*

Mickey Mouse Magazine, January 1938, volume three, number four, color comics, stories, 36 pages, 8½" × 11½", Collectors' Showcase, February 1989, $75.   *$40–$60*

Mickey Mouse Magazine, September 1938, volume three, number 12, color illustrations, 42 pages, Collectors' Showcase, September 1988, $66.   *$50–$80*

Mickey Mouse Magazine, October 1939, volume five, number one, comics, stories, etc., 8¼" × 10½", Collectors' Showcase, February 1989, $79.   *$100–$125*

Marionette, composition head, sharp nose, pie-cut eyes, fur-covered stick body and pull-string control, 7¼″ high, Christie's East, March 1989, $308.   *$400–$600*

Marionette, circa 1933, Tony Sarg, early black and white papier-mâché head with rat nose, painted pie-cut eyes, felt ears, open mouth smile, and on Mickey's cloth body, a shirt, shorts, gloves, and boots, Christie's East, December 1988, $3080.   *$700–$900*

NOTE: *Tony Sarg wrote and illustrated children's books, designed textiles, and worked on early animated cartoons. He was born in Guatemala in 1881 and schooled in Europe. He also designed toys, as well as the huge balloons for many of the Macy's Thanksgiving Day parades. He died in 1942.*

Mask, early 1930s, Warnova/under license from Walt Disney, linen face mask, black and white pie-cut eyes, 9″ × 10½″, Hake's, November 1988, $52.   *$75–$100*

Melody Player, original box, "Atlantique City" Collectibles Market, March 1989, $275.

Newspaper, weekly, November 14, 1936, English Mickey Mouse weekly, volume one, number 41, 12 pages, full-color, black and white illustrations, 11″ × 15″, Hake's, April 1989, $21.
                                             $25–$50

Paint Box, circa 1960s, lithographed tin box of Mickey Mouse and Donald Duck on the moon painting a rocket with Earth in the background, 4½″ × 5″ × 1½″, Hake's, November 1988, $12.   *$15–$25*

Pencil Sharpener, celluloid figure, black, white, and red, scarce, 2½″, Hake's, April 1989, $199.   *$75–$100*

NOTE: *Pencil sharpeners often have the metal sharpening mechanism missing. This can affect the price. However, this example of a Mickey Mouse pencil sharpener was desirable enough to a collector without the sharpening mechanism.*

Pocket Watch, Ingersoll, leather and metal fob, Mickey Mouse second dial with running Mickeys, boxed, Phillips, December 1988, $750.   *$750–$1250*

Puzzle, circa 1950s, Parker Brothers, four complete 16" × 18" comic picture puzzles of 12 comic book or newspaper panels with balloon captions, 7" × 18" × 1¼" box, Hake's, November 1988, $69.   *$75–$100*

Recipe Book Cards, Weber Baking Co., colored recipe cards to be pasted in "Recipe Scrapbook," 3¼" × 5", Hake's, February 1989, $41.   *$25–$50*

Rocker, circa 1935, Mengel Co., painted wooden sides depicting an early Mickey Mouse lying in a pool of water, 35", Christie's East, September 1988, $462.   *$400–$500*

Rollercoaster, 1950s, Chein, two cars, tin, Wex Rex Records & Collectibles, May 1989, $250   *$225–$275*

Roly-Poly, Chad Valley, lithographed cardboard figure of Mickey Mouse balancing on two rotating discs, also a lithographed cardboard and wood Mickey Mouse swing toy, 7½" and 11" high, Christie's East, March 1989, $220.   *$150–$220*

Rubber Ball, circa 1930s, Seiberling, baseball design with stitching and image of Mickey Mouse on one side, 2¼" diameter, Hake's, February 1989, $150.   *$75–$100*

Slippers, fleece-lined sheepskin Mickey Mouse children's slippers with Mickey decals on front, printed Mickey and Minnie Mouse figures on each side of the pair, size 11, Christie's East, December 1988, $77.   *$150–$200*

Soldier Set, 1934, eight full-color cardboard Mickey Mouse targets and wood/metal, toy, pop-gun Daisy rifle with five corks, original colored box, 18" × 8¼" × 1", Collectors' Showcase, October 1988, $465.   *$200–$300*

Talking Telephone, 1974, Hasbro, plastic, Wex Rex Records & Collectibles, May 1989, $10.   *$8–$15*

Train Set, circus, early 1930s, one circus car missing, mint and boxed at "Atlantique City" Collectibles Market, March 1989, $6000.   *$5500–$6500*

Train Set, Walt Disney meteor train set, tin wind-up, painted, Knight's, October 1988, $435.   *$100–$500*

Trapeze Toy, keywind tinplate frame with celluloid Mickey Mouse, 12″ high, Christie's East, March 1989, $242.
                                                            $100–$150

Photo courtesy of Hake's Americana, York, PA

Watch, 1930s, Ingersoll, Hake's, February 1989, $465.

$200–$700

NOTE: *This is one of the first 1930s Mickey Mouse watches with a small second wheel picturing little Mickeys between the legs of a larger Mickey Mouse.*

Wristwatch, Ingersoll, two metal Mickey Mouse figures depicted on each side and a running Mickey Mouse in a circular second counter, original leather strap, Phillips, December 1988, $750.

$750–$1000

Wristwatch, circa 1939, Ingersoll Mickey Mouse dial shows Mickey and two figural Mickeys on links on metal band, which is from an earlier Mickey #1 watch, Christie's East, December 1988, $605.   *$300–$400*

Wristwatch, circa late 1940s, Ingersoll rectangular with Mickey Mouse in black and white, red, and yellow on a silver dial, red numbers, yellow gloved hands, original red plastic strap, Hake's, February 1989, $151.   *$100–$200*

MICKEY MOUSE AND MINNIE MOUSE

Dolls, pair of dolls with early features, Minnie Mouse wears a skirt and cap, Mickey Mouse's name is embroidered on his chest, both dolls wear gloves and boots, 15″ high each doll, Christie's East, September 1988, $495.   *$500–$600*

NOTE: *See Introduction for details of the early features found on Mickey Mouse and Minnie Mouse.*

Marionettes, wooden bodies and composition heads, Mickey Mouse with pie-cut eyes, rat-teeth grin, plush hands, velvet pants; Minnie Mouse with painted closed eyes, closed mouth smile, dressed in skirt and shoes; each 9″ high, Christie's East, December 1988, $1760.   *$700–$900*

Playing Cards, 1932, boxed set, Minnie Mouse is pictured on one set, Mickey Mouse on the other set, Hake's, April 1989, $82.
$75–$100

Bisque, wearing blue dress and green hat, playing a mandolin, Hake's, November 1988, $46.   *$50–$75*

Doll, Steiff, with pie-cut eyes, sharp nose, open-mouth smile, velvet body, and high-heel shoes, 9″ high, Christie's East, March 1989, $1760.   *$1000–$1200*

Wind-up Toy, tin, 6″ high, Knight's, October 1988, $385.
$300–$400

101 DALMATIONS

Photo courtesy of Hake's Americana, York, PA

Pencil Case, 1960, dark blue box with full-color label, 5 " × 10 " × 2 " deep, Hake's, February 1989, $15.   *$10–$15*

OSWALD THE RABBIT

China Planter, 1958 (Walter Lantz copyright), Napco Ceramic, Japan, molded figure of Oswald dressed in blue baseball umpire uniform with orange chest protector, 4½ " figure, 3 " × 3½ " planter, Hake's, February 1989, $120.   *$100–$200*

Doll, first Walt Disney-designed doll, "Atlantique City" Collectibles Market, March 1989, $5000.

NOTE: *Bought by New York dealer Mel Birnkrant from dealer Richard Wright.*

★

Keywind Walker, velvet face, pie-cut eyes, and floppy ears on Oswald, who is dressed in orange and black, label reading "Oswald the Lucky Rabbit copyr'td Universal Pictures Corp. an Irwin," 13″ high, Christie's East, March 1989, $5500.

$6000–$8000

NOTE: *Walt Disney designed Oswald the Rabbit in the mid-1920s. The first Oswald film was called* Troller Troubles, *which Disney made at his studios and rented through UNIV. This film was later destroyed by Disney. The Oswald copyright was retained by UNIV, Disney gave up all claims to the rabbit over contract problems, and he moved on to discover Mickey Mouse. The likeness of Oswald was used on promotional items such as candy and badges.*

PINOCCHIO

Carousel, diecast Pinocchio, shaped carousel seats of Disney characters Mickey Mouse, Donald Duck, Bambi, Dumbo, and Joe Carioca, 12″ high, Christie's East, March 1989, $550.

$700–$900

Doll, Knickerbocker, composition jointed doll with slightly crazed eyes, painted, Knight's, October 1988, $250.

$200–$300

Doll, wood and composition, 1930s, 11″ high, Wex Rex Records & Collectibles, March 1989, $375.　　　　*$300–$400*

Figure, Ideal, composition and wood jointed figure, 10¼″ high, Hake's, February, $250.　　　　*$75–$200*

Figure, 1940, Crown Manufacturing Co., large composition and jointed Pinocchio, red and white clothes, Kay Kamen paper label, 34″ high, Christie's East, December 1988, $770.

$400–$600

Film Trailer, 1960s, reissue trailer for 1939 Walt Disney movie with other trailers on reel, 35mm, technicolor, 10″ wide, Collectors' Showcase, October 1988, $75.   *$60–$90*

Game, 1939, Merry Puppet Game, no instructions, boxed, 9″ × 19½″ × 1¾″, Hake's, February 1989, $60.   *$25–$50*

Marionette, composition and wood marionette dressed in shirt, vest, and pants, movable plastic eyes, ½″ rubber nose extends to over 1″, strings and cardboard hand control, scarce, Hake's, February 1989, $500.   *$100–$400*

Puppet, Crown Toy and Novelty, red fabric body, white hands, "W. Disney Ent." mark, scarce, 9″ tall, Hake's, February 1989, $85.   *$100–$200*

PLUTO

Badge, mid-1960s, thin molded plastic badge of Pluto in a colorful flasher picture balancing on a ball in a doorway as a young strong man stands alongside a circus tent, image moves when pin is turned, 2½″ × 3″, Hake's, February 1989, $21.

$15–$25

Electric Clock, circa 1955, hard orange plastic figural clock, bone-shaped hands, tongue and eye movement, original box, 9″ high, Christie's East, December 1988, $132.   *$150–$200*

Figure, 1930s, Sieberling, hard rubber figure, 1″ × 3½″ × 2″, Hake's, November 1988, $75.   *$100–$200*

Kart, Marx, Japanese, Pluto driving a Disney four-wheel friction-powered kart, lever-action handlebars, 6″ long, Christie's East, March 1989, $220.   *$100–$150*

Keywind Acrobat "Gym Toy," Linemar, celluloid Pluto performing on a high bar with gym toy pennant, original box, 13″ high, Christie's East, March 1989, $462.   *$200–$250*

Keywind "Rollover" Toy, Linemar, plush-covered Pluto, runs forward, rolls over, begs with raised feet, original box, 6½" long, Christie's East, March 1989, $242.   *$150–$200*

Keywind Walking Toy, Linemar, plush-covered Pluto, wags tail, moves head, walks forward, original box, 8" long, Christie's East, March 1989, $242.   *$200–$300*

Pop-up Critter, 1930s, Fisher-Price, jointed wood figure of Pluto assuming various positions when string attached to pair of metal rings is pulled, 2½" × 9½" × 7" tall, Hake's, February 1989, $54.   *$25–$45*

NOTE: *Fisher-Price toys made during the years 1931-1963 are very collectible, particularly if the toys are in fine to mint condition.*

PROFESSOR VON DRAKE

Keywind Walker, Linemar, Von Drake dressed in lithographed coat, vest, tie, original box, 5½" high, Christie's East, December 1988, $660.   *$200–$300*

SEVEN DWARFS (SNOW WHITE)

Pencil Case, Walt Disney Enterprises, picturing Dopey, Bashful, and Sneezy, Wex Rex Records & Collectibles, May 1989, $30.
        $25–$35

Christmas Ornaments, composition figures, painted facial features, sparkle-glitter candy storage bodies, set of eight, Christie's East, December 1988, $110.   *$150–$250*

Composition Seven Dwarfs With Names, Knickerbocker, dressed in velveteen jackets, pants, and hats, jointed arms, 8½" high (average), Christie's East, December 1988, $1045.   *$700–$900*

SNOW WHITE AND THE SEVEN DWARFS

Bisque Set, Japanese, Dwarfs holding musical instruments, Snow White 6½" tall, dwarfs 4½" tall, Hake's, February 1989, $805.   *$400–$1000*

Puzzle, 1940s, colored puzzle with Snow White, the Dwarfs, and forest animals in forest clearing with cottage in background, boxed, 14″ × 22″, Hake's, February 1989, $92.   *$25–$50*

Safety Blocks, circa 1939, Halsam, 16 large wooden blocks, Donald Duck appears on a few blocks, 7″ × 7″ × 2″ deep box, Hake's, February 1989, $65.   *$50–$75*

Toy, Knickerbocker (Walt Disney Productions), original tag, Knight's, October 1988, $2000.   *$1200–$1600*

THE THREE CABALLEROS

Film Slides, 1950, Hollywood Film Enterprises, set of 10 full-color 35mm slides, folded sheet pictures the Three Caballeros on one side, 10 printed story captions coinciding with 10 slides on the other side, rare, 2″ × 2″ each slide, Hake's, February 1989, $50.   *$50–$75*

THREE LITTLE PIGS

Film Slides, 1950, Hollywood Film Enterprises, same as above but folded sheet pictures the Three Little Pigs, Hake's, February 1989, $65.   *$50–$75*

Hanky, early 1930s, white and red hanky with black detailing, 8½″ × 8½″, Hake's, February 1989, $40.   *$25–$50*

Plate, 1938, Patriot China, Wex Rex Records & Collectibles, May 1989, $60.   *$45–$60*

Puzzle, 1940s, Jaymar, depicts Pigs dancing down a pathway while the Wolf lurks behind a tree with his carpetbag, 8″ × 10″ × 2″ deep box, Hake's, February 1989, $14.   *$15–$25*

Hooked Rug, Skinner, July 1988, $396.   *$300–$350*

NOTE: This rug came from the estate of Paul Revere and Helen Douglas Ladd. Skinner's auctioned the rug at an on-site sale at the Ladd's "Windmill Cottage" in East Greenwich, Rhode Island. The Ladds collected antiques and collectibles for over 65 years.

★

Photo courtesy of Hake's Americana, York, PA   *Photo courtesy of Hake's Americana, York, PA*

Sand Pail, depicts the Three Little Pigs at the seashore with the Wolf lurking behind some wooden pilings, Disney Enterprises/ Ohio Art copyrights, 3″ tall, Hake's, June 1989, $100.

$75–$100

Toothbrush Holder, early 1930s, bisque toothbrush holder depicting the Three Little Pigs, 1¼″ × 4″ × 4″, Hake's, June 1989, $69.   *$75–$100*

Tray, circa 1933, beer-parlor tray made to celebrate Prohibition repeal, color lithograph on metal, Phillips, December 1988, $750.   *$500–$1000*

UNCLE SCROOGE

Uncle Scrooge, bank, glazed ceramic, Uncle Scrooge in brown bed with pink blanket and green paper money decoration, rubber stopper, "Dan Brechner" sticker, 4″ × 5½″ × 4″ tall, 4″ × 6″ × 5″ box, Hake's, February 1989, $115.   *$100–$200*

WALT DISNEY

Photo courtesy of Camden House, Los Angeles, CA

Animation Model, 1940, walking broom from *Fantasia*, wood and straw, wire-framed arms, Camden House, May 1989, $8250.   *$6000–$8000*

NOTE: *This three-dimensional animation model of the Walking Brooms was brought to life in the film by Mickey Mouse as the Sorcerer's Apprentice. The brooms could be moved into a variety of positions to allow the animator to study movement in sequence. This broom is a magnificent artifact from the glory days of Disney animation.*

Bisque Comic Characters, various makers, including characters Mickey Mouse, Minnie Mouse, Donald Duck, Ferdinand the Bull, Pluto, Seven Dwarfs, among others, 2½″ to 4″ tall, Skinner, November 1988, $1000.   *$100–$150*

Comic Character Toys, six wooden and jointed toys of Mickey Mouse, Popeye, Olive Oyl, Wimpy, and two of Minnie Mouse, early Disney Co. style, 3¹⁄₂″ × 5″ each, Skinner, November 1988, $425. $100–$150

Doll House Play Set, 1950s, Marx, deep-brown cardboard box holds a large two-story lithographed disassembled tin doll house, walls covered with Disney character wallpaper, floors carpeted, five separate rooms and garage with roof patio, house furniture, equipment, 12″ × 26″ × 3¹⁄₂″, Hake's, February 1989, $240. $100–$200

Flivver, friction-drive yellow convertible with long-necked Donald Duck driver, lithographed with Mickey Mouse, Thumper, Dopey, and other Disney characters, Christie's East, March 1989, $352. $250–$350

Keywind #6 Race Cars, Occupied Japan, tinplate, celluloid Mickey Mouse in one race car and celluloid Donald Duck in another race car, 3", Christie's East, March 1989, $528.

$300–$400

Keywind Television Car, Marx, lithographed with various Disney characters on yellow car, roof inset with "television screen" with Mickey Mouse and Donald Duck, original box, 7" long, Christie's East, March 1989, $528. $300–$400

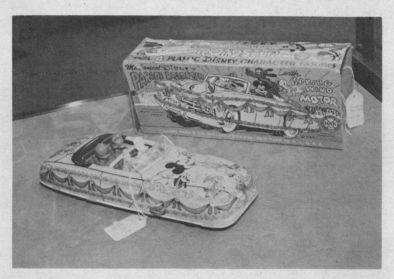

Parade Roadster, Marx, keywind, tinplate convertible, lithographed with variety of Disney characters, tan color, Donald Duck driving with three passengers, original box, 11" long, Christie's East, March 1989, $385. $250–$300

Playing Cards, 1946, Russell Manufacturing Co., miniature playing cards in matchbook-size boxes featuring Disney characters, instructions in each box, illustrated, Annex Arts and Antiques Outdoor Flea Market, October 1988, $60. $50–$100

NOTE: *There are six volumes to a set; however, individual volumes are often sold to collectors.*

★

Playing Cards, same as previous listing, except one volume (#5) of Three Little Pigs sold separately, Twentieth Century Nostalgia, October 1988, $10.   *$8–$10*

Premiums, late 1940s/early 1950s, Disney comic books offer from Wheaties, featuring Donald Duck, Mickey Mouse, and the Three Little Pigs, Paper Collectables & Memorabilia Show, February 1989, each $12.   *$10–$15*

Photo courtesy of Hake's Americana, York, PA

Roller Coaster, circa 1950s, Chein, Disneyland roller coaster with Disney characters pictured on sides of toy in amusement park settings, including scene of Alice being pulled in a cart by Pluto while the White Rabbit gives chase, built-in key, Hake's, February 1989, $435.   *$200–$400*

NOTE: This book does not include Disneyland memorabilia except for the above piece, which is very attractive and in fine condition.

★

Rug, character area rug picturing Mickey Mouse, Minnie Mouse, Bambi, Chip 'n' Dale, Donald Duck and his nephews, Goofy, Lady, Thumper, and Tramp, 68″ × 100″, Christie's East, March 1989, $440.   *$500–$700*

Rugs, Three, woolen, one picturing Donald and Daisy Duck, another Huey, Dewey, and Louie, and the third, Uncle Scrooge, Knight's, October 1988, $200.   *$150–$250*

Talkie-Jecktor Record and Paper Films, 1930s, 7″ record to be used with Movie-Jecktor features "Mickey Mouse Presents Silly Symphony in The Sand Man," paper films are wooden spools for titles, covered color boxes with Disney characters pictured, Hake's, February 1989, $30.   *$75–$100*

Top, 1930s, Fritz Bueschel, full-color rotating tin top picturing Mickey and Minnie Mouse, Donald Duck, Horace, and Nephew, 6½″ × 7″ diameter, Collectors' Showcase, October 1988, $135.   *$100–$200*

Train, parade, Durham, plastic, battery operated, original box, Wex Rex Records and Collectibles, May 1989, $65.   *$50–$75*

Viewmaster Reels, late 1960s, three GAF Viewmaster reels of *Mary Poppins* (1964), color story book, envelope, Hake's, November 1988, $10.   *$10–$15*

Wristwatches, one with portrait of Snow White and one with portrait of Alice in Wonderland, leather straps, Phillip's, December 1988, $250.   *$250–$350*

WALT DISNEY STUDIOS

Photo courtesy of Hake's Americana, York, PA

Christmas Card, 1936, single-sheet stiff card depicting Mickey Mouse, Minnie Mouse, and Donald Duck stuffing a large envelope inscribed "Season's Greetings, Walt Disney" into a mailbox, envelope, 7″ × 9″, Hake's, February 1989, $265.   *$200–$400*

Christmas Card, 1937, paper card with blank inside and color scene on cover of Mickey and Minnie Mouse, Pluto, and Donald Duck wearing mufflers and playing in the snow, inscribed "—And Greetings From Us Too," 4″ × 5″, Hake's, February 1989, $528.   *$200–$400*

Christmas Card, 1938, original full-color card with Snow White, Mickey Mouse, Donald Duck, 8 pages, 6″ × 7½″, Collectors' Showcase, October 1988, $123.   *$150–$200*

Christmas Card, 1940, *Fantasia*-theme color scene with Frost Fairy ice skating and word "Greetings" inside, card opens again to depict Frost Fairy with words "From Walt Disney," then fully opened, card depicts caricature of a conductor (Stokowski) assisted by Donald Duck conducting chorus of Disney characters singing "God Rest You Merry Gentlemen," from *Fantasia*, and also Goofy, Pinocchio, Snow White, Minnie Mouse, Pluto, and the Reluctant Dragon, 5½" × 22", rare, Hake's, February 1989, $213.   *$200–$400*

Duckster Award, undated, uninscribed, metal statuette with wood base, 9½" tall, Camden House, May 1989, $1800.

$1800–$2000

NOTE: *These statuettes were given to distinguished employees at Walt Disney Studios.*

MAGAZINES

INTRODUCTION

Magazines are collected for various reasons including star covers, star material, movie tearsheet ads (see next chapter), illustrators of star covers and ads, authors and biographers, and film reviews.

Prices of magazines are affected by the quantity that is available of a certain issue and also by how desperately a collector might want an issue. Star covers usually bring the higher prices, but depending on demand and supply, dealer prices tend to be flexible for many movie magazines, especially for copies that were published in the 1940s and 1950s. Most star covers from the 1930s are scarce, and therefore more expensive and difficult to find in fine or better condition.

Star covers on *Life* magazine are very popular among collectors, especially if they are dated from the late 1930s to early 1940s. Most of these issues have black and white covers, and there were many movie star photographs on covers during this period. Most of the issues from the 1950s through the early 1970s were published with colored photographs, and covers picturing Marilyn Monroe, Elizabeth Taylor, and John Wayne are highly sought after. *Time* and *Newsweek* covers of the same personalities are also desirable to collectors; James Dean and the Marx Brothers are other draws.

If magazine contents include photo stories of movie stars, directors, writers, or include information on life in Hollywood, then such issues are sometimes more collectible than if there was a movie star on the cover or a photograph of an airplane, fox terrier or fashion model.

Playboy is a major crossover collectible that appeals mainly to two types of collectors—those who like "girlie" magazines (*Cab-*

aret, *Fling*, *Modern Man*, *Penthouse*), and those who like movie stars. Sometimes the two categories intermingle. The premier issue of *Playboy*, in December 1953, featured Marilyn Monroe on the cover and in a nude centerfold. In very fine to mint condition that issue sells for almost $2000. Other popular covers and photo stories feature Ursula Andress, Jane Fonda, Gina Lollobrigida, Jayne Mansfield, and Stella Stevens.

The most desirable of movie magazines, however, are those devoted exclusively to movie stars and the film industry. Most were published from the 1920s through the 1960s. Issues from the 1930s are more expensive and desirable to collectors. Female star covers outrank male star covers, and Disney cartoon characters fall somewhere in between. Most of these magazines are found in good to fine condition.

Movie magazine titles include *Hollywood*, *Modern Movies*, *Movie Classic*, *Motion Picture*, *Movieland*, *Photoplay*, *Screen Album*, *Screenland*, *Screen Guide*, *Silver Screen*, and *True Confessions*.

Magazines can be found primarily through dealers and at collectible shows. Sometimes they turn up at auction but are usually grouped together in a bundle as one lot. Single issues are usually signed or accompanied by other types of movie memorabilia that are part of a collection.

MAGAZINES LISTING

American Classic Screen, March/April 1978, volume two, number four, Jean Harlow on cover, A & S Books, February 1989, $10.   *$8–$12*

American Photographer, Marilyn Monroe, July 1984, text/photographs of Monroe inside in "The Last Sitting: Marilyn Monroe Masquerade for Richard Avedon," Paper Collectables & Memorabilia Show, March 1989, $5. $5–$9

NOTE: *Monroe is dressed as Lillian Russell atop a bicycle on cover of magazine.*

Cabaret, Marlene Dietrich, May 1955, volume one, number one, article on Las Vegas with Dietrich picture inside, also Cafe Singers article re: Betty Hutton, Dorothy Dandridge, Lena Horne, Sophie Tucker, among others, back cover pictures the actress Abby Lane, excellent, John Van Doren, March 1989, $15.
$10–$15

Cabaret, June Allyson, January 1956, article called "Those Fabulous Copa Girls," Northeast Collectibles Extravaganza, December 1988, $5. $5–$10

NOTE: *June Allyson was a former Copa showgirl.*

Classic, Viola Dana, February 1923, Schoyer's Books, March 1989, $12.50. $10–$20

Cue, Jayne Mansfield, October 1, 1955, article inside on Mansfield with a black and white photo of the actress on a massage table, Hake's, November 1988, $16. $15–$25

Eros, Marilyn Monroe, Autumn 1962, 96 pages, famous Marilyn Monroe issue with many "last" photographs taken of the actress, 10″ × 12½″, Collectors' Showcase, October 1988, $95.
$50–$75

Photos courtesy of Hake's Americana, York, PA

Everyday Science and Mechanics, February 1934, full-color cover
illustration of scene from 1934 movie *The Invisible Man*, plus
inside article with black and white film scenes and illustrations,
64 pages, 8½″ × 11″, Hake's, February 1989, $35. $25–$50

★

NOTE: *Brilliant magazine cover showing how the bandages are
stripped off by the Invisible Man. Inside the issue is an article with
illustrations showing how various scenes of the movie were achieved
by trick photography and props.*

★

Family Circle, May 19, 1946, early photograph of Marilyn Monroe inside, her name is not mentioned on the cover, 8½" × 11", Collectors' Showcase, February 1989, $176.   *$100–$150*

Famous Monsters of Filmland, 1958, second issue, Wood art, plus material on Lon Chaney, Boris Karloff, Bela Lugosi, Collectors' Showcase, December 1988, $74.   *$50–$100*

Films in Review, April 1967, reviewed inside are "The Films of Ronald Reagan" from *Love Is in the Air* (1937, WB), to *The Killers* (1964, UNIV), text/film scenes, also an article on Cecil B. DeMille and another on opera singers on the screen, A & S Books, July 1988, $10.   *$8–$15*

Fling, Jayne Mansfield, June 1965, black and white photo article inside on movie star sex queens, Nussbaum, January 1989, $8.
          $8–$15

Hollywood, Clara Bow, June 1929, feature articles on "Our Gang" first talking picture, Gloria Swanson's aborted film *Queen Kelly*, 28 pages, Collectors' Showcase, December 1988, $139.
          $25–$40

Hollywood, Jean Harlow, March 1937, Collectors' Showcase, November 1988, $57.   *$25–$35*

Hollywood, Ginger Rogers, May 1937, Collectors' Showcase, September 1988, $13.   *$25–$30*

Hollywood, Merle Oberon and Laurence Olivier (*Wuthering Heights*), May 1939, Collectors' Showcase, September 1988, $8.
          $30–$35

Hollywood, Gene Tierney, September 1942, inside Hedy Lamaar, Linda Darnell, Keye Luke, among others, John Van Doren, December 1988, $22.   *$20–$25*

Horoscope Screen Album, June 1931, #2, 50 stars covered with one-page portraits and biographies, 64 pages, Collectors' Showcase, November 1988, $28.   *$30–$35*

Liberty, Donald Duck, Mickey Mouse, Dumbo, and Pluto, March 1942, Collectors' Showcase, January 1989, $18.
          $10–$15

Liberty, Abbott and Costello, May 1942, article on the comedy team inside, Collectors' Showcase, January 1989, $18.

$10–$15

Life, November/December 1936, first six issues of *Life* magazine formerly in the collection of Cecil B. DeMille, his name and subscription on the spine of the bound issues, bookplate, Collectors' Showcase, January 1989, $330. $150–$200

Life, September 26, 1938, Papermania, January 1989, $12.

$10–$20

NOTE: *The cover of this issue is a crazy-quilt background photograph of the Crazy Horse at the Greenbrier Valley Fair in West Virginia. An artist has drawn comic-strip heroes of the period on the cover and they include Captain and the Katzenjammer Kids, Wimpy, Little Benny facing Big Andy Gump, Mickey and Minnie Mouse, and Mr. Jiggs.*

★

Life, Tallulah Bankhead, March 6, 1939, on the inside front cover is a full-page movie ad for *The Little Princess*, with Shirley Temple, Hughes Papers, March 1989, $6. $6–$12

Life, Rosalind Russell, September 4, 1939, text and photos inside of MGM's *The Women*, Papermania, January 1989, $8.
$5–$12

Life, Betty Grable, December 1939, People's Magazine Service, June 1989, $12. $10–$20

Life, Fred Astaire and son, August 25, 1941, article inside on Astaire, Tama Fair, September 1988, $6. $6–$15

NOTE: *This issue would have sold for a higher price had there not been pencil scribbles all over the cover.*

Life, Ginger Rogers, March 2, 1942, text and photographs of Rogers' ascent to stardom and arrival in Hollywood, her hometown, and her southern Rogue River Valley ranch, Papermania, January 1989, $10. $8–$15

Life, Roy Rogers and Trigger, July 12, 1943, five-page article and photos of Roy and his family, Hake's, November 1988, $16. $12–$25

Life, Margaret Sullivan, January 24, 1944, Papermania, January 1989, $8. $8–$12

Life, Spencer Tracy, December 3, 1945, June 1989, Annex Antique & Collectible Flea Market, $7. $5–$12

Life, Paulette Goddard, December 17, 1945, the actress in costume for her role in the movie *Kitty*, Triple Pier Expo, November 1988, $12. $10–$20

Life, Bing Crosby/Joan Caulfield, October 7, 1946, Triple Pier Expo, November 1988, $10. $10–$12

Life, Gloria Grahame, October 21, 1946, inside are photos of the actress and MGM boss, Louis B. Mayer, also a movie ad for RKO's "The Best Years of Our Lives," Papermania, January 1989, $8. $6–$10

Life, Jane Greer, June 2, 1947, Annex Antiques & Collectibles Flea Market, October 1988, $7.   *$6–$10*

Life, Elizabeth Taylor, July 14, 1947, Papermania, January 1989, $15.   *$12–$20*

Life, Viveca Lindfors, February 14, 1949, Northeast Collectibles Extravaganza, December 1988, $5.   *$5–$8*

Life, Marilyn Monroe, April 7, 1952, DeVolder Antiques, March 1989, $10.   *$10–$27*

Life, Greta Garbo, January 10, 1955, first of three parts on Greta Garbo, her arrival from Sweden in Hollywood, and her movie career at MGM in Hollywood, Paper Collectables & Memorabilia Show, February 1989, $8.   *$8–$30*

★

NOTE: *Cover photo by Steichen. The remaining two installments appeared in the winter of 1955.*

★

Life, Jayne Mansfield, April 23, 1956, A & S Books, June 1989, $16.   *$10–$20*

NOTE: *As mentioned elsewhere in this book, Jayne Mansfield memorabilia has become a very "hot" collectible. This author is mad about her.*

Life, Adlai Stevenson and Mrs. Roosevelt, August 27, 1956, color, Papermania, January 1989, $12.   *$8–$18*

NOTE: *Not a star cover but the inside contents warrant inclusion here. Both Marilyn Monroe and Elvis Presley are included in the issue. Monroe is featured in text and black and white photos in the movie* Bus Stop, *and Elvis Presley is featured in a nine-page article with black and white photos and text concerning his impact on his fans. There is also a great black, white, and green ad for baseball memorabilia fans of Yogi Berra for Kraft Italian Dressing. This is a very desirable collector's issue and should be left intact.*

Life, Elizabeth Taylor, October 15, 1956, color, A & S Books, February 1989, $20.   *$8–$22*

Life, Shirley Temple and daughter, February 3, 1958, color, Hughes Papers, February 1989, $6.   *$6–$10*

Life, Marilyn Monroe and Yves Montand, August 1960, Paper Collectables & Memorabilia Show, March 1989, $15.   *$12–$20*

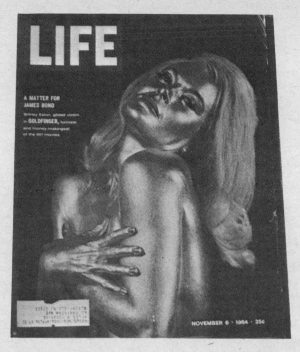

Life, Shirley Eaton, November 6, 1964, color, text and color, black and white photos of James Bond "007" movie *Goldfinger*, Happier Days, June 1988, $15.   *$9–$16*

NOTE: This is a crossover collectible as fans of James Bond will want it as well as magazine memorabilia collectors. Shirley Eaton played Jill Masterson who met her fate by being painted in gold by Oddjob, Goldfinger's henchman in the 1964 movie.

Life, John Wayne, May 7, 1965, color, the actor in western costume is back in action after a bout with cancer, Paper Collectables & Memorabilia Show, December 1988, $20.   *$10–$25*

Life, Sean Connery, January 7, 1966, color, picture of the actor in role of James Bond in 1965 UA movie *Thunderball*, three pages with six black and white scenes inside, brief text and captions plus review of the movie, Hake's, April 1989, $35. $25–$40

NOTE: Another crossover collectible that was purchased through a mail-order auction by an over-zealous collector who didn't mind shelling out $35. Hake's price range for this particular issue is excessive and I have lowered it by $10.

Life, Paul Newman, November 15, 1968, color, Paper Collectables & Memorabilia Show, February 1989, $8. $8–$10

Life, Mae West, April 18, 1969, color, Family Publications, February 1989, $3. $3–$8

NOTE: Ms. West came out of a 26-year retirement to play the role of talent agent Letitia Van Allen opposite 1960s sex siren Racquel Welch in Myra Breckinridge, 20th, 1970. The movie was based on the Gore Vidal bestseller.

Life, John Wayne, January 28, 1972, color, Papermania, January 1989, $7. $5–$10

Life, Marilyn Monroe, September 8, 1972, color, article inside, Hughes Papers, January 1989, $8. $8–$15

Literary Digest, Charlie Chaplin, November 1935, article inside, cover pictures the actor in *Modern Times* released in 1936, Collectors' Showcase, January 1989, $12. $20–$25

Look, Charlie Chaplin, September 1940, article inside, Collectors' Showcase, January 1989, $29. $15–$20

Look, John Wayne, October 6, 1942, color, Wayne pictured in movie *Flying Tigers* (REP) on cover, inside are 13 scenes from the black and white film and a film review, Hake's, April 1989, $30. $25–$50

Look, James Dean, 1956, article on Dean inside, Collectors' Showcase, March 1989, $22. $15–$20

Look, Mickey Mouse, April 6, 1971, Disney story inside, Hughes Papers, January 1989, $3.   *$3–$10*

Mechanix Illustrated, 1954, article on *The Creature From the Black Lagoon*, Collectors' Showcase, March 1989, $55.
                                                         $10–$15

Modern Man, Jayne Mansfield, January 1958, article on Mansfield inside, Northeast Collectibles Extravaganza, December 1988, $5.   *$5–$15*

Modern Man, Jayne Mansfield, March 1961, article inside which discusses Mansfield's penchant for publicity and family life, very provocative color cover, Northeast Collectibles Extravaganza, December 1988, $5.   *$5–$15*

Modern Mechanics, Mickey Mouse and Donald Duck, 1937, lengthy technical Disney article inside, Collectors' Showcase, November 1988, $49.   *$10–$15*

Modern Screen, Marlene Dietrich, May 1931, plus inside an article on Rudolph Valentino by Eleanor Glyn, Collectors' Showcase, December 1988, $19.   *$40–$45*

Modern Screen, Claudette Colbert, December 1935, Christy cover, inside material on Luise Rainer, Miriam Hopkins, Fredric March, others, John Van Doren, December 1988, $45.
                                                         $35–$45

Modern Screen, Jeanette MacDonald, October 1936, article inside on Katharine Hepburn, Collectors' Showcase, November 1988, $19.   *$35–$40*

Modern Screen, Bing Crosby, September 1948, Papermania, January 1989, $20.   *$15–$26*

Modern Screen, Elizabeth Taylor, June 1950, material inside on Ingrid Bergman, Joan Crawford, Jane Powell, Ronald Reagan, others, Northeast Collectibles Extravaganza, December 1988, $15.   *$15–$25*

Modern Screen Pin-Ups, Marilyn Monroe, 1955, first issue, Collectors' Showcase, March 1989, $102.   *$35–$60*

Motion Picture, Ruth Roland, June 1916, Schoyer's Books, March 1989, $13.50.   *$12–$18*

Motion Picture, Loretta Young, April 1938, Schoyer's Books, March 1989, $15. $15–$30

Motion Picture, Clark Gable, February 1943, Paper Collectables & Memorabilia Show, April 1989, $30. $25–$35

Motion Picture, Deanna Durbin, December 1945, Northeast Collectibles Extravaganza, December 1988, $20. $15–$25

Motion Picture Classic, Alice Joyce, November 1916, Schoyer's Books, March 1989, $15. $15–$20

Motion Picture Classic, J. Warren Kerrigan, October 1917, Kerrigan pictured in cowboy clothes, Schoyer's Books, March 1989, $20. $20–$30

NOTE: J. Warren Kerrigan is best known for his role in the 1923 PAR movie The Covered Wagon.

Motion Picture Magazine, Wallace Reid, February 1917, Schoyer's Books, March 1989, $15. $12–$25

Motion Picture Magazine, Anita Stewart, May 1917, Schoyer's Books, March 1989, $15. $12–$20

Motion Picture Magazine, Douglas Fairbanks, 1918, Collectors' Showcase, March 1989, $46. $30–$40

Motion Picture Magazine, William S. Hart, 1918, Collectors' Showcase, March 1989, $50. $30–$40

Motion Picture Magazine, Anna Q. Nilsson, August 1924, cover by Alberto Vargas, Schoyer's Books, March 1989, $25.

$20–$35

NOTE: Covers by noted artists such as Vargas are more expensive than covers by artists of lesser stature. Anna Q. Nilsson was a major silent film actress. She was also one of the guests playing bridge with Gloria Swanson in a scene from Sunset Boulevard, *PAR, 1950; the other bridge guests were silent film actors Buster Keaton and H.B. Warner.*

Motion Picture Story Magazine, Thomas Alva Edison, January 1914, this was the "Edison Number," Schoyer's Books, March 1989, $20.   *$20–?*

Movie Classic, Joan Blondell, April 1932, Clara Bow interview inside, her first since marrying the cowboy actor, Rex Bell, in December of 1931, Collectors' Showcase, December 1988, $17.
                                                                    $25–$35

★

NOTE: *Clara Bow was known as the "It" girl of silent films, and actually starred in a movie called* It *in 1927. She was a happy-go-lucky flapper who liked a good time and a good man. In the days before the production code went into effect, she was known to be quite mischievous both on and off the set. Bow retired from films in 1933 at the age of 26, her last film being* Hoopla *for FOX films.*

★

Movie Classic, Mae West, August 1933, Collectors' Showcase, September 1988, $31.   *$20–$25*

Movieland, Marilyn Monroe, January 1953, Collectors' Showcase, February 1989, $44.   *$15–$20*

Movie Mirror, Norma Shearer, March 1939, cover soiled, fair, Schoyer's Books, March 1989, $6.   *$15–$25*

★

NOTE: *Price range is much higher than price paid because of the poor condition of the magazine.*

★

Movie-Radio Guide, Rita Hayworth, December 1942, story inside "Queen of the Camps," Collectors' Showcase, January 1989, $49.   *$20–$35*

Movie Spotlight, October 1955, story inside by actress Terry Moore called "The Real James Dean," Illustrator Collector's News, March 1989, $14.   *$10–$20*

Movie Stars Parade, September 1953, features articles and photos on Rock Hudson, Virginia Mayo, Debbie Reynolds, Esther Williams, Illustrator's Collector's News, March 1989, $10.
                                                                    $10–$15

New Movie, Marion Davies, February 1931, Collectors' Showcase, December 1988, $33.   *$35–$40*

Newsweek, April 18, 1955, Disney color cover and four-page story inside, Collectors' Showcase, November 1988, $40.
                                                    $10–$20

New York Mirror Magazine, Marilyn Monroe, June 23, 1957, magazine within the famous tabloid newspaper, 16 pages, 11″ × 14″, Collectors' Showcase, November 1988, $94.   *$30–$50*

Photo, Marilyn Monroe, July 1953, and *Tab*, May 1954, several photos of Monroe including "Monroe vs. Harlow," each 8″ × 5″, Poster Mail Auction Co., February 1989, $30.   *$30–$45*

Photoplay, Gloria Swanson, September 1928, stories inside include one on Chaplin's movie *City Lights*, Clara Bow and Jack Gilbert, airbrush cover, RNL Books, June 1989, $18.   *$15–$25*

Photoplay, Greta Garbo, August 1930, Collectors' Showcase, September 1988, $34.   *$20–$25*

Photoplay, Janet Gaynor, August 1934, cover by Christy, Papermania, January 1989, $35.   *$30–$45*

Photoplay, Myrna Loy, September 1937, Northeast Collectibles Extravaganza, December 1988, $30.   *$25–$35*

Photoplay, Lana Turner, October 1946, Northeast Collectibles Extravaganza, December 1988, $21.   *$20–$30*

Photoplay, Ava Gardner, February 1952, yard sale, Beverly Hills, CA, July 1988, $9.   *$9–$15*

Photoplay, January 1957, material inside on Joan Collins, Judy Garland, Elvis Presley, Illustrator's Collector's News, March 1989, $5.   *$5–$10*

Picturegoer, Alice Faye, August 15, 1934, Paper Collectables & Memorabilia Show, February 1989, $20.   *$12–$20*

NOTE: Picturegoer *is a national film and entertainment weekly pub-lished in England every Thursday.*

Picturegoer, Lola Albright, May 5, 1956, Roger's Comics, Oc-tober 1988, $3.   *$3–$7*

Picture Play, Greta Garbo, December 1935, Collectors' Show-case, September 1988, $41.   *$35–$40*

Playboy, February 1955, playmate is Jayne Mansfield, Northeast Collectibles Extravaganza, December 1988, $80.   *$75–$110*

NOTE: Playboy *condition is judged very seriously, and the majority of issues in this listing are in fine or better condition, but not mint. Mint copies sell for much more money; for example, a mint copy of the Monroe issue mentioned above would sell for close to $2000 (see Introduction).*

Playboy, September 1955, pictorial on Marilyn Monroe called "Pink Elephants and Purple Hair," Northeast Collectibles Ex-travaganza, December 1988, $45.   *$40–$60*

Playboy, April 1956, pictorial of Diana Dors ("DD in 3D"), Northeast Collectibles Extravaganza, December 1988, $20.
                                                          $15–$25

Playboy, Jayne Mansfield, February 1957, also a pictorial inside on the actress, Nussbaum, September 1988, $18.   *$15–$25*

Playboy, January 1960, pictorial of the actress Stella Stevens, Northeast Collectibles Extravaganza, December 1988, $28.
                                                          $15–$40

Playboy, January 1964, pictorial of Marilyn Monroe in this 10th anniversary issue, also a reprint of the famous nude pose of Mon-roe that appeared in the first issue, Hake's, June 1989, $41.
                                                          $25–$50

Playboy, November 1965, pictorial essay on James Bond's girls, Northeast Collectibles Extravaganza, December 1988, $15.
                                                          $6–$15

Playboy, March 1966, first installment of Ian Fleming's novelette *Octopussy*, the James Bond adventure, and a pictorial on Italian actress Rossana Podesta and English actress Shirley Anne Field ("This Sporting Life"), Rogers Comics, December 1988, $2.

$8–$12

Playboy, March 1966, second and final installment of *Octopussy*, plus Part VIII of "History of Sex in Cinema," re: Jean Harlow, Marlene Dietrich, Greta Garbo, Hedy Lamarr, and Mae West, Rogers Comics, December 1988, $2. *$8–$12*

NOTE: Both this and the above issue were in less than fine condition. Hence, lower prices.

Playboy, June 1966, Triple Pier Expo, November 1988, $15.

$8–$15

NOTE: This issue is a treasure chest of Humphrey Bogart reference material. Three pieces appear on the actor: "The Bogart Boom: The Man and the Myth," by Kenneth Tynan; "The Career and the Cult," by Bosley Crowther; and a Bogart quiz.

Playboy, July 1979, movie pictorial on the girls of *Moonraker*, 1979, UA, James Bond movie, Nussbaum, November 1988, $6.

$5–$10

Quick, Lucille Ball, November 1950, Collectors' Showcase, March 1989, $7. *$15–$20*

Rexall Magazine, Clark Gable, April 1933, the actor revealed through his handwriting, Family Publications, May 1989, $8.

$8–$10

Salute Magazine, Marilyn Monroe, August 1946, one of Monroe's first modeling jobs to appear in print, included also is a September 1953 issue of *Tab* magazine with Monroe on the cover, Camden House, May 1989, $100. *$100–$125*

Screen Album, Myrna Loy, 1937, portrait of movie stars on each page and biographies, 50 pages, Collectors' Showcase, November 1988, $20. *$30–$40*

Screen Book, Norma Shearer, December 1931, Collectors' Showcase, December 1988, $33.   *$40–$45*

Screen Book, Jean Harlow, October 1932, Collectors' Showcase, December 1988, $102.   *$40–$50*

Screen Book, Mae West, May 1935, Collectors' Showcase, March 1989, $18.   *$25–$35*

Screenplay, Jean Harlow, April 1936, Paper Collectables & Memorabilia Show, September 1988, $20.   *$20–$30*

Screen Stars Album, Norma Shearer, 1933–34, each page devoted to a different star with photos and a biography, 50 pages, 8½″ × 11″, Collectors' Showcase, November 1988, $35.

$30–$50

Silver Screen, Claudette Colbert, February 1932, Collectors' Showcase, December 1988, $23.   *$25–$30*

Silver Screen, Mae West, February 1935, Collectors' Showcase, September 1988, $30.   *$30–$40*

Silver Screen, Shirley Temple, December 1935, cover by the artist Marland Stone, Hake's, April 1989, $23.   *$25–$50*

Silver Screen, Irene Dunne, November 1936, cover by the artist Marland Stone, Northeast Collectibles Extravaganza, December 1988, $28.   *$25–$35*

Silver Screen, Ann Sheridan, January 1943, Northeast Collectibles Extravaganza, December 1988, $25.   *$25–$35*

Stage Magazine, Alice Frost, Helen Hayes, Katharine Hepburn, Lily Pons, November 1940, three-page pictorial inside of Walt Disney's *Fantasia*, Alan Levine, June 1988, $22.50.   *$20–$25*

Tell Magazine, Jane Russell, 1950s, inside are pin-up photo features and a six-page article of Russell in *The Outlaw*, plus a photo feature on Sophia Loren, 5¼″ × 7½″, Hake's, June 1989, $16.   *$15–$25*

Theater Arts, Citizen Kane, 1941, inside are articles on Frank Capra, Alfred Hitchcock, and the Disney movie *Fantasia,* Collectors' Showcase, November 1988, $74. $20–$25

NOTE: *Another example of an issue that should be left intact for its collectible value.*

This Was Hollywood, Clark Gable and Jean Harlow (*Red Dust*), 1955, volume one, number one, annual by Sidney Skolsky, the columnist, depicts Gable and Harlow in a scene from MGM's *Red Dust* (1932), and inside pictures of Greta Garbo, Shirley Temple, Robert Taylor, and Rudolph Valentino, Roger's Comics, October 1988, $4. $10–$20

NOTE: *A crease on the bottom right-hand corner of the cover affected the value of this magazine. Most collectors do not like creases or folds on the covers of movie magazines. This is also very true of* Playboy *magazines.*

Time, Marx Brothers, August 15, 1932, cover features the comedians in *Horse Feathers,* PAR, Collectors' Showcase, February 1989, $66. $140–$150

NOTE: *This issue is highly sought after by collectors. It missed its price range considerably because the copy had been bound, and, when removed, a hole was left in the issue.*

Time, John Wayne, March 3, 1952, story inside on Groucho Marx by the author, Leo Rosten, and a news item on Marilyn Monroe, Nussbaum, January 1989, $8. $5–$10

True Confessions, Greta Garbo, 1930, inside is a full-page photo of Joan Crawford plus an article on new sex codes in Hollywood, Collectors' Showcase, December 1988, $48. $25–$40

True Confessions, Greta Garbo, February 1935, Collectors' Showcase, December 1988, $45. $25–$35

True Story, Jean Harlow, April 1932, Collectors' Showcase, December 1988, $71.   *$40–$45*

True Story, Gary Cooper and Claudette Colbert, May 1938, Collectors' Showcase, December 1988, $20.   *$25–$30*

Western "Movie Thrills" Magazine, Johnny Mack Brown, November 1950 (Ideal Publishing Corp.), bi-monthly, photos and features of western stars including John Wayne, Red Barry, Roy Rogers, Rex Allen, and a tribute to Will Rogers by Gene Autry, 96 pages, 8½″ × 11″, Hake's, February 1989, $72.   *$25–$50*

Western Stars Magazine, Tim Holt, April/June 1950, volume one, number 5, inside are hundreds of photos, portraits, film scenes of western stars including Roy Rogers and Dale Evans, Hopalong Cassidy, Lash LaRue, John Wayne, plus film reviews of western movies, 98 pages, 8½″ × 10½″, Hake's, February 1989, $60.
$25–$50

Westerner Magazine, Tom Mix, July/August 1972, bi-monthly, features articles about oldtime cowboy stars and western history including Art Acord, Buck Jones, Tex Jordan, Ken Maynard, Jack Hoxie, William S. Hart, Bob Steel, and Hoot Gibson, 68 pages, 8½″ × 11″, Hake's, June 1989, $17.   *$15–$25*

Western Stars, Spring 1950, number five, *Dell* magazine, 98 pages, spine bad condition, fair, Collectors' Showcase, November 1988, $9.   *$10–$20*

Whisper, Frank Sinatra and Ava Gardner, October 1956, inside is a two-page article on Jayne Mansfield, 68 pages, Hake's, June 1989, $12.   *$15–$25*

MAGAZINE
TEARSHEET
MOVIE ADS

INTRODUCTION

Some movie memorabilia collectibles are worth more broken apart than they are kept intact. For example, an autograph book containing many celebrity signatures might be more valuable if taken apart and sold separately than as a whole.

The same is true for magazine tearsheet movie ads that appeared in *Life*, *Esquire*, *Newsweek*, *Playboy*, *Time*, *Home Magazine*, *Saturday Evening Post*, *Good Housekeeping*, and *Collier's*, among other publications. Sometimes these individual tearsheet movie ads are more valuable than the magazine itself, particularly if there is damage to the front or back covers or interior pages. Soiled, creased, taped, or torn covers of uninteresting copies that yield one or two excellent movie ads inside should definitely be removed.

I wouldn't suggest tearing apart valuable magazines that feature important movie articles or have a photograph on the cover of a movie star who is particularly hard to find on a magazine. *Life* magazine had many celebrity faces on their covers and some were of very important stars. If a collector owns *Life* issues of stars such as Betty Grable, Bette Davis, Paulette Goddard, Marilyn Monroe, Elizabeth Taylor, Claudette Colbert, John Wayne, or Fred Astaire, I would advise them to leave the issue intact. If there is a movie ad of special interest that the collector might want to rip out, he or she should stifle the urge until a second copy is found, preferably in an inferior condition.

Magazine tearsheet movie ads hold the same criteria for desirability as do posters, autographs, books, photographs, press-books, souvenir programs or any other type of movie memorabilia where a star's picture is apt to be included. The better movie tearsheets are those that feature stars like Orson Welles, Errol Flynn, Ronald Reagan, Cary Grant, Gary Cooper, Ingrid Bergman, Marilyn Monroe, James Cagney, Humphrey Bogart, and any of the Disney animated features or a movie ad that is particularly beautiful to look at or has unusual or outstanding graphics. Color tearsheets are more expensive than black and white, or black, red, and white tearsheets, and if an illustrator's name should appear in the ad, then that too would increase the value.

Actual photographs of movie stars pictured in the ad are more desirable than a simple illustration, an example being the 1945 20th movie *Billy Rose's Diamond Horseshoe*, where there is only an illustrated likeness of Betty Grable that looks so vague that it could also be Carole Landis or Hazel Brooks. Movie stars who are prominently featured are also higher in price than stars whose faces are in the background.

All the major studios placed movie ads in *Life* magazine, where, in the opinion of this author, the best movie tearsheet ads appeared.

Standard tearsheet movie ads are $5\frac{3}{4}$ " $\times$ 14", 8" $\times$ 11", and the most common size, 11" (or $10\frac{1}{2}$ ") $\times$ 14". Both *Life* and the *Saturday Evening Post* featured the majority of their movie ads in this latter size.

Tearsheet movie ads should be removed carefully so as not to leave too much torn paper on the extreme left side of the ad. Also, ads that are creased and dirty aren't collectible material. Some of the black lettering in certain movie ads (re: *Letty Lynton*, 1932, MGM), might be faded with specks of white showing through, but this shouldn't be a problem affecting price, especially if the ad is of a major movie or pictures major stars.

Many collectible shows feature magazine tearsheet movie ads in several dealer booths. The ads are usually protected in poly bags with a white backing board or are shrinkwrapped. Aim for the poly bags. You can always remove the ad at a later date and insert another ad. Collectible shows include Paper Collectables & Memorabilia Show, New York; the Manhattan Triple Pier Expo (Thanksgiving weekend, and a weekend in the winter); Papermania in Hartford, Connecticut, an annual show held in

January; "Atlantique City" Collectibles and Antiques Market, held every March; and Northeast Collectibles Extravaganza, a relatively new show, which is held in Boston in December, and also in Massachusetts during the winter.

Prices in this chapter are taken from movie ads that were seen in dealer booths at several of the major collectible shows held in the Northeast. The general price range was from $1 to $15, with the most expensive piece being a 1938 WB ad for *Angels With Dirty Faces* starring James Cagney. The ad was listed as rare and marked $35 at a dealer's table at the Paper Collectables & Memorabilia Show in May 1989. The cheapest ad I have seen was for the movie *Trial*, 1955, MGM, at $1.

There is also a separate category of magazine tearsheet ads for advertising products endorsed by movie stars or featuring movie stars in the ad. Some examples are the Royal Crown Cola ads which featured many female stars of the 1940s and 1950s, Chesterfield and Lucky Strike cigarettes, Western Union, Lane Chests, International Sterling, DeSoto automobiles, Lux Soap, Lustre-Creme Shampoo, Pabst Blue Ribbon beer, Ayds reducing plan candy, Pacquins hand cream, and Royal Gelatin desserts. However, I have not included such ad prices in the following listings because of my unfamiliarity with the category. In a later edition of this price guide I plan to include such ads.

It should also be noted that in this chapter, the listings are arranged chronologically by year, not alphabetically.

MAGAZINE TEARSHEETS LISTING

MOVIE ADS 5¾" × 14"

Dream Girl, 1948, PAR, Betty Hutton, MacDonald Carey, Patrick Knowles, black, red, and white, $3.

Miracle Can Happen, A, UA, Paulette Goddard, James Stewart, Henry Fonda, Dorothy Lamour, Fred MacMurray, Harry James, black, red, and white, $2.

★

NOTE: This movie was released as On Our Merry Way.

★

Command Decision, 1949, MGM, Clark Gable, Walter Pidgeon, Van Johnson, Brian Donlevy, Charles Bickford, black and white, $2.

Tammy and the Bachelor, 1957, UNIV-International, Debbie Reynolds, Leslie Nielsen, Walter Brennan, Fay Wray, black and white, $1.

Where the Hot Wind Blows, 1960, MGM, Gina Lollobrigida, Marcello Mastroianni, Yves Montand, black, red, and white, $3.

MOVIE ADS 8″ × 11″

Letty Lynton, 1932, MGM, Joan Crawford, Robert Montgomery, Nils Asther, May Robson, black and white, $4.

MOVIE ADS 11" × 14"

Maytime, 1937, MGM, Jeanette MacDonald, Nelson Eddy, black and white, $7.

Top of the Town, 1937, UNIV, Gertrude Nielsen, George Murphy, Doris Nolan, Hugh Herbert, Ella Logan, black and white, $5.

Dodge City, 1939, WB, Errol Flynn, Olivia de Havilland, Ann Sheridan, black, red, and white, $15.

The Philadelphia Story, 1940, MGM, Cary Grant, Katharine Hepburn, James Stewart, Ruth Hussey, black, red, and white, $6.

Desperate Journey, 1942, WB, Errol Flynn, Ronald Reagan, Nancy Coleman, Raymond Massey, black and white, $18.

Pride of the Yankees, The, 1942, RKO, Gary Cooper, Teresa Wright, Babe Ruth, Walter Brennan, black, red, and white, $12.

Ten Gentlemen From West Point, 20th, George Montgomery, Maureen O'Hara, John Sutton, Laird Cregar, black, red, and white, $3.

NOTE: *The red in this magazine tearsheet is almost a pinkish hue.*

To Be or Not To Be, 1942, UA, Carole Lombard, Jack Benny, Robert Stack, Lionel Atwill, black and white, $8.

NOTE: *This was Carole Lombard's last picture before her tragic death in a plane crash.*

Jack London, 1943, UA, Michael O'Shea, Susan Hayward, Virginia Mayo, black and white (Jack London title is in red), $2.

Stage Door Canteen, 1943, UA, all-star cast including Tallulah Bankhead, Katherine Cornell, Helen Hayes, George Jessel, Gypsy Rose Lee, Alfred Lunt, Paul Muni, primarily black, red, and white with some faint gray, green, and yellow tones, $4.

What a Woman!, 1943, COL, Rosalind Russell, Brian Aherne, Willard Parker, black and white, $2.

NOTE: *Willard Parker was advertised as "What a 'Find'! . . . Sensation of the Year!" Anybody know his whereabouts?*

Hail the Conquering Hero, 1944, PAR, Eddie Bracken, Ella Raines, Franklin Pangborn, black, red, and white, $5.

Wilson, 1944, 20th, Alexander Knox, Charles Coburn, Geraldine Fitzgerald, Thomas Mitchell, Vincent Price, black, red, and white, $7.

NOTE: *This movie was a monumental flop. The magazine tearsheet, however, is very pictorial.*

Incendiary Blonde, 1945, PAR, Betty Hutton, Arturo de Cordova, Charles Ruggles, Barry Fitzgerald, color, $10.

Spanish Main, The, 1945, RKO, Paul Henreid, Maureen O'Hara, Walter Slezak, Binnie Barnes, black and white, $2.

Week-End at the Waldorf, 1945, MGM, Ginger Rogers, Lana Turner, Walter Pidgeon, Van Johnson, Robert Benchley, black and white, $6.

NOTE: *This was a remake of* Grand Hotel *moved to New York. Lana Turner played the Joan Crawford role, Ginger Rogers was a movie star instead of a ballerina, and Walter Pidgeon played a war correspondent.*

Breakfast in Hollywood, 1946, UA, Tom Breneman, Bonita Granville, Zasu Pitts, Hedda Hopper, black and white, $2.

Bride Wore Boots, The, 1946, PAR, Barbara Stanwyck, Robert Cummings, Diana Lynn, black, red, and white, $4.

Masquerade in Mexico, 1946, PAR, Dorothy Lamour, Arturo de Cordova, Patrick Knowles, Ann Dvorak, black, red, and white, $5.

Monsieur Beaucaire, 1946, PAR, Bob Hope, Joan Caulfield, Patrick Knowles, black, red, and white, double-page ad, $8

Notorious, 1946, RKO, Cary Grant, Ingrid Bergman, Claude Rains, directed by Alfred Hitchcock, black and white, $10.

NOTE: *Great magazine tearsheet showing the faces of Grant and Bergman in a huge black key.*

Our Hearts Were Growing Up, 1946, PAR, Gail Russell, Diana Lynn, Brian Donlevy, Billy De Wolfe, black, red, and white, $5.

NOTE: *Sequel to the movie* Our Hearts Were Young and Gay.

Intrigue, 1947, UA, George Raft, June Havoc, Helena Carter, black, red, and white, $8.

NOTE: *Great graphics but mundane star line-up for this "B" film noir of not any great distinction.*

Emperor Waltz, The, 1948, PAR, Bing Crosby, Joan Fontaine, Roland Culver, Lucile Watson, color, $6.

Enchantment, 1948, RKO (Samuel Goldwyn), David Niven, Teresa Wright, Evelyn Keyes, Farley Granger, color, $12.

NOTE: *Very sensual magazine tearsheet movie ad for its time. Beautiful color and design.*

★

Good Sam, 1948, RKO, Gary Cooper, Ann Sheridan, Joan Lorring, black and white, $4.

Joan of Arc, 1948, RKO, Ingrid Bergman, Jose Ferrer, color, $7.

Key Largo, 1948, WB, Humphrey Bogart, Edward G. Robinson, Laureen Bacall, Lionel Barrymore, Claire Trevor, black and white, $8.

Lady From Shanghai, The, 1948, COL, Rita Hayworth, Orson Welles, Everett Sloane, Glenn Anders, black and white, $10.

NOTE: Hayworth with blond-hair coiffure looking very sensual leaning on her hands in a negligee-type gown in Orson Welles' shadow.

Melody Time, 1948, RKO (Walt Disney), Roy Rogers, Dennis Day, Frances Langford, Freddy Martin, color, $10.

Rachel and the Stranger, 1948, RKO, Loretta Young, William Holden, Robert Mitchum, black and white, $2.

State of the Union, 1948, MGM, Spencer Tracy, Katharine Hepburn, Van Johnson, Angela Lansbury, Lewis Stone, black, red, and white, $7.

Battleground, 1949, MGM, Van Johnson, John Hodiak, Ricardo Montalban, George Murphy, black, red, and white, $3.

John Loves Mary, 1949, WB, Ronald Reagan, Jack Carson, Edward Arnold, Patricia Neal, black and white, $15.

Knock on Any Door, 1949, COL, Humphrey Bogart, John Derek, black and white, $14.

Man on the Eiffel Tower, The, 1949, RKO, Charles Laughton, Franchot Tone, Burgess Meredith, Robert Hutton, and the City of Paris, color, $12.

NOTE: *One of the best colored magazine tearsheet movie ads from* Life *magazine. Spectacular design and graphics.*

Woman's Secret, A, 1949, RKO, Maureen O'Hara, Melvyn Douglas, Gloria Grahame, Bill Williams, black and white, $2.

Cinderella, 1950, RKO (Walt Disney), animated film, color, $10.

His Kind of Woman, 1951, RKO, Robert Mitchum, Jane Russell, Vincent Price, color, double-page ad, $12.

NOTE: *The movie was a hodgepodge of melodramatic cliches and there was probably more screen chemistry on the set than in the movie between Mitchum and Russell, but the magazine tearsheet movie ad as advertised in* Life *magazine is a winner. Wonderful color and strong likenesses of the two stars.*

Beau James, 1957, PAR, Bob Hope, Vera Miles, Paul Douglas, black and white, $3.

Funny Face, 1957, PAR, Audrey Hepburn, Fred Astaire, Kay Thompson, black, red, and white, $5.

Gunfight at the O.K. Corral, 1957, PAR, Burt Lancaster, Kirk Douglas, Rhonda Fleming, black, red, and white, $6.

Sayonara, 1957, WB, Marlon Brando, James Garner, Red Buttons, Miyoshi Umeki, Patricia Owens, black and white, $3.

MISCELLANEOUS COLLECTIBLES

INTRODUCTION

This is the chapter for all categories of movie memorabilia that do not fit within a specific collector's category. Although several collecting areas such as buttons, games, playing cards, and minor pieces of film ephemera could be classified as separate collecting areas, they have been combined here into one miscellaneous chapter because there is simply not enough items within each category to warrant a full chapter.

This chapter includes everything from artworks to wristwatches. In between there is a myriad of movie memorabilia including badges, a Gene Autry bicycle, cigarette cards and cigarette cases, Dixie Ice Cream lids, gum cards (and gum wrappers), movie props, a payroll sheet for Marilyn Monroe, lunch boxes, motorcycles, pianos, a ship's wheel used in a Cecil B. DeMille epic, a bull whip, studio publications, and even a "witch remover." Read the chapter to learn about that one.

Individual categories are described with some brief but pertinent notes about that particular collectible. The chapter is in alphabetical order with multiple listings in a particular category also in alphabetical order. I have tried to list collectibles under the most accurate heading; for example, exhibit cards, exhibitors' manuals, and a fan petition sheet for the cowboy William S. Hart are listed under film ephemera.

That readers might take offense at seeing one of their favorite collectible categories clumped together into one long miscellaneous chapter probably won't endear them to the author. However, there is just so much room in a price guide, and the amount of material that can be fit into any one collectible area really determines whether it rates a separate chapter.

Hopefully, all this makes sense. If I, the author, have failed to compile this chapter to any of my readers' tastes, please do not lose any sleep over it. That I am still alive and sane after writing this chapter is a miracle.

MISCELLANEOUS COLLECTIBLES LISTING

ACADEMY AWARDS

For many years, the gold-plated Oscar statuette was traded privately and sold on the black market before Malcolm Willits of Collectors' Bookstore in Hollywood began to include Oscars in his mail-order auctions. In March 1988, he was commissioned to sell the best picture Oscar for *An American in Paris*, MGM, 1951, and it realized a bid of $15,760. A goldmine was born, much to the consternation of Academy members who frown upon the practice of selling Oscars (winners must sign an agreement that they won't sell the Oscar to anyone but the Academy). Ironically, Oscars have been found at garage and tag sales, and even in pawn shops, selling for around $30 to $50 apiece.

With the *An American in Paris* and *How Green Was My Valley* (see below) Oscars bringing high prices the future looks bright. Willits' personal goal is to acquire the Oscar given to Walt Disney for *Snow White and the Seven Dwarfs*. It is seven tiny Oscars climbing a staircase to a regular-sized Oscar. Willits thinks it would bring about $100,000.

Oscar, 1941, *How Green Was My Valley*, 20th, awarded to Thomas Little for best set decoration, also includes an 18″ × 17″ scrapbook with Little's name embossed in gold, 11 signed letters from Fox president, Darryl F. Zanuck, souvenir program, movie invitations, tickets, studio letters, and other materials, Oscar, very fine, scrapbook, fine, Collectors' Showcase, December 1988, $17,715.   *$10,000–$12,000*

NOTE: *Thomas Little was nominated a total of 21 times for best set decoration; out of those 21 nominations, he won six Oscars.*

★

Program, 1951, 23rd annual ceremony, includes two gold tickets, Collectors' Showcase, September 1988, $110. *$50–$60*

Program, 1963, 35th annual ceremony, Collectors' Showcase, September 1988, $39. *$30–$40*

Program, 1964, 36th annual ceremony, Collectors' Showcase, September 1988, $29. *$20–$30*

Program, 1967, 39th annual ceremony, Collectors' Showcase, September 1988, $26. *$15–$25*

Programs, 1973, 1975, 1976, 1979, 1981 (5), 24 pages each, annual award ceremonies, each program gold stamped with an Oscar figure on the cover, Collectors' Showcase, December 1988, $75. *$80–$100*

NOTE: *These programs were given to members of the audience.*

ART

Caricature Collage, Eleanor Powell, three-dimensional, by famed Hollywood artist Krapilik, Camden House, May 1989, $250. *$1000–$1500*

Caricature Collage, Clark Gable, three-dimensional, original work by Krapilik, 5″ × 7″, framed, Camden House, May 1989, $500. *$1500–$2000*

Caricature Prints (6), from *Motion Picture Herald*, Krapilik, caricatures of Katharine Hepburn, Mickey Rooney, and Spencer Tracy, others, embossing, heavy stock, 9″ × 12″, Camden House, May 1989, $150. *$100–$150*

Charcoal on Board, Joan Crawford, 1937, used as cover for *Photoplay*, February 1937, framed, 13″ × 16″, Guernsey's, April 1989, $3500.　　　　　　　　　　　　　　　　　*$3000–$5000*

Charcoal Sketch, Marilyn Monroe, Joe Sabataro, artist, 1962, original art for poster printed for Marilyn Monroe Fan Club, framed, 21″ × 18″, Camden House, May 1989, $100.

　　　　　　　　　　　　　　　　　　　　　　$200–$300

Charcoal Sketch, King Kong, depicted atop Empire State Building, Fay Wray in hand, artist, date unknown, Camden House, May 1989, $150.　　　　　　　　　　　　　*$150–$200*

Charcoal, Watercolor, and Gouache, production and set design for film *Marie Antoinette*, MGM, 1938, signed by artist Jack Martin Smith, framed, 15½″ × 21″, Camden House, May 1989, $800.　　　　　　　　　　　　　　　　　*$1000–$1500*

Illustration, hand-painted, Milton Caniff (artist), signed and inscribed, framed, 12″ × 19″, Camden House, May 1989, $3800.　　　　　　　　　　　　　　　　　*$2000–$3000*

NOTE: *This was an illustration of "The Dragon Lady," a character in Caniff's cartoon strip "Terry and the Pirates." Caniff presented the illustration to Joan Crawford for a birthday gift in 1964. Crawford served as the inspiration for the illustration.*

Lithograph, red and white canvas of Marilyn Monroe, Doolittle (artist), framed, 36″ × 54″, Camden House, May 1989, $475.

　　　　　　　　　　　　　　　　　　　$1000–$1200

Painting, Shirley Temple, circa 1935, oil on canvas of Shirley dressed in pink dress under a blue sky, Dillon (artist), signed, 20″ × 16″, Jim Collins, January 1989, $3200.　　*$2500–$3500*

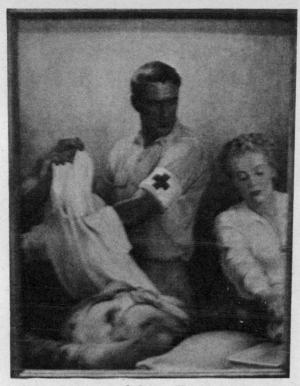

Painting, Gary Cooper and Signe Hasso, oil on canvas, circa 1944, John Falter (artist), framed, 35″ × 26″, Christie's East, October 1988, $7150.   *$1000–$1500*

NOTE: *This painting was from the estate of Cecil B. DeMille, as are the following two paintings. This painting depicts the actors in a scene from* The Story of Dr. Wassel, *1944, PAR, which was based on a true story.*

Painting, "Samson Tearing Down the Temple," *Samson and Delilah*, 1949, PAR, oil on canvas of Victor Mature as Samson,
Norman Rockwell (artist), signed, framed, 5′ × 9″ × 3″, Christie's East, October 1988, $82,500.   *$70,000–$90,000*

Painting, "Wool," circa 1950, Hedy Lamarr and Victor Mature
as Delilah and Samson, signed upper left, framed, 24″ × 20″,
Christie's East, October 1988, $1870.   *$800–$1200*

Painting, "Shot Red Marilyn," circa 1964, Andy Warhol (artist),
40″ square, Christie's, May 1989, $4.07 million.

NOTE: *This was a record paid for an Andy Warhol painting.*

Painting, Charlie Chaplin, self-portrait, 1921, 24″ × 17″, Christie's East, June 1989, $26,400.

NOTE: *Chaplin painted this self-portrait on the set of* The Kid, *1921, FN, and gave the painting to Jackie Coogan, who played the kid in the movie.*

Pin-up, print, color, of Jayne Mansfield, "Blonde Bomber," in a red and white one-piece bathing suit, plus a colored record album cover, 16″ × 12″, Poster Mail Auction Co., February 1989, $35.   *$25–$40*

NOTE: *This print was probably pulled from a calendar. It is best to keep calendars intact as it increases their value.*

Portrait, Veronica Lake, circa 1946, Soubie (artist), 24″ × 32″, Guernsey's, April 1989, $2000   *$500–$700*

Print, promotional prints for re-release of *Gone With the Wind*, of Clark Gable, Vivien Leigh, Olivia de Havilland, and Leslie Howard, Camden House, May 1989, $1100.   *$100–$150*

Print, "Flash Gordon," limited edition print, #1027 of 1500 full-color prints from the 1930s serials, signed by Buster Crabbe, 1977, Alex Raymond (artist), Collectors' Showcase, October 1988, $312.   *$250–$300*

Production Design, set backdrop for nightclub dream sequence in Alfred Hitchcock's *Spellbound*, 1945, RKO, cloth (muslin) backdrop, Salvador Dali (artist), 18′ × 37′, Camden House, May 1989, $10,000.   *$20,000–$40,000*

NOTE: *It is disputable if this piece was wholly created by Salvador Dali. The backdrop was used in the famous nightmarish dream sequence of the movie where Gregory Peck encounters Ingrid Bergman in his dream.*

★

Standee, original, hand-colored photos and artwork on masonite for *Casablanca*, 1942, WB, picturing Humphrey Bogart, Ingrid Bergman, and Sydney Greenstreet, Sotheby's, December 1988, $22,000.   *$5000–$7000*

NOTE: *The "standee" was used to promote the 1942 premiere of the film.*

Watercolor and Crayon, caricature of Joan Crawford, Milton Caniff (artist), inscribed, framed, 36″ × 24″, Camden House, May 1989, $1700.   *$1500–$2000*

Watercolor and Gouache, production and set design for *Cat On a Hot Tin Roof*, 1958, MGM, Gene Johnson (artist), signed, matted, 6″ × 17″, Camden House, May 1989, $250.   *$100–$200*

Watercolor and Gouache, production and set design for *Marie Antoinette*, 1938, MGM, Duane Alt (artist), matted, 9″ × 12″, Camden House, May 1989, $725.   *$600–$800*

NOTE: *Both of these artworks come with an MGM auction certificate of authenticity.*

AUCTION CATALOGS

MGM Auction, 1970, complete set of five catalogs, sealed in original shipping cartons, Camden House, May 1989, $700.
                                                    $200–$400

NOTE: *This is the auction that started it all with movie memorabilia becoming the "hot" collectible it has become today.*

Swann Galleries (New York), 1978, collection of L. Frank Baum, author of *The Wizard of Oz*, and related Oziana, illustrated, 140 pages, with price sheet, supreme reference material, Pepper & Stern, April 1989, $45.   *$40–$45*

AWARDS

Golden Globe, presented to Cecil B. DeMille by The Hollywood Foreign Correspondent's Association, 9″ high, Christie's East, October 1988, $1760. $400–$600

Plaque, to Cecil B. DeMille as top producer and director of 1956 for *The Ten Commandments,* 12″ × 8″ overall, Christie's East, October 1988, $770. $300–$400

BADGES

Badges listed in this guide are in very fine to mint condition. Badges should retain their luster and also be free of dents and scratches.

Buck Jones Club, circa 1930s, black and red on brass club member's badge, Collectors' Showcase, February 1989, $40.
$25–$50

NOTE: *Recent reproductions of the Buck Jones Club badge have been spotted.*

Gene Autry Fan Club, official club member's badge, circa 1940s, black and white and orange cello, scarce, 1 1/4″, Hake's, February 1989, $52. $50–$75

Keystone Kops, 12 items including six seven-point, star-shaped badges, three matching hat badges, and three "State Police" badges, mounted, framed under glass, Camden House, May 1989, $5000. $4000–$4500

NOTE: *These badges were accompanied by an original notarized statement from the Logan Costume Co., where they were purchased, attesting to their authenticity. Also included were newspaper pictures showing the badges worn by Keystone Kops.*

Special Police "007" Badge Pin, circa late 1960s, silvered metal, unauthorized "007" number diecut into pin, 1 3/4″ × 2″, Hake's, February 1989, $14. $15–$25

Tom Mix "Wrangler," brass inset with red, blue, and gold-foil checkerboard design, 1938, Hake's, February 1989, $85.

$75-$100

BANKS

Value of banks is determined by condition and rarity. Cast-iron, tin, and metal banks outclass tin advertising banks and banks made of plastic, glass or ceramic. There are mechanical and still banks. Mechanical banks have a mechanism that moves coins into a slot. They are more desirable and expensive than still banks.

Harold Lloyd, tin mechanical bank, lithographed, possibly German, Sotheby's, June 1988, $11,000. $4000-$5000

NOTE: *The Harold Lloyd bank is from the collection of the aluminum and metals millionaire, Al Davidson, who started collecting mechanical banks in the mid-1960s.*

Stan Laurel, circa 1962, hard vinyl plastic coin bank, caricature of the actor seated on a chest, coin slot is in the back of his head, 3″ × 3″ × 10″ tall, Hake's, November 1988, $18. $25-$50

BICYCLE

Gene Autry, circa 1950, Monark, Gene Autry holster and cap pistol saddle, glass "gems" inset at fenders and on the chain guard, gun-shaped horn, horseshoe-framed reflector plus other cowboy features, 36″ high, Christie's East, September 1988, $1870. $2000-$3000

BUTTONS

Academy Award "Official" Buttons, press committee pins and host committee badges, dating from 1952, Camden House, May 1989, $100. $25-$50

All Quiet on the Western Front, 1930, black and white, 1¼″, Hake's, April 1989, $48. $50-$75

007/Always on Target, 1980s, Bond logo in purple, dark blue background, design of a telescopic gunsight, 2¼″, Hake's, April 1989, $21. $10-$15

Freddie Bartholomew, 1930s, button #17 from a movie set, black and white fleshtone, lithographed, Hake's, February 1989, $16.
$10-$15

Wallace Beery, 1930s, from movie star set, black and white with orange lettering, 1", Hake's, November 1988, $14. $15-$25

Billy Jack for President, black and white lithograph for 1971 film, 2¼", Hake's, February 1989, $18. $10-$15

Humphrey Bogart, circa 1951, "Humphrey Bogart Starring in *The African Queen*," rim reads "Mr. Plateau Invites You to the Plateau Party," black and white with brown and black type, scarce, 2½", Hake's, November 1988, $40. $25-$50

Boy Meets Girl, 1938, illustration of man and woman for movie of same name starring James Cagney and Pat O'Brien, dark blue on dark pink, ⅞", Hake's, February 1989, $11. $10-$15

John Mack Brown, 1935, black and white, red rim button advertising the actor's UNIV film *Rustlers of Red Dog*, 1¼", Hake's, February 1989, $46.　　　　　$50–$75

Buck Rogers in the 25th Century, circa 1935, club member's button, 1", Hake's, February 1989, $65.　　　　　$75–$100

Close Encounters of the Third Kind, 1977, white and dark blue flasher button, 2½", Hake's, February 1989, $12.　　　　　$10–$15

Sean Connery Is James Bond 007, black and white and red with 1982 copyright, 1½", Hake's, February 1989, $16.　　　　　$10–$15

Grace Cunard/Francis Ford in The Purple Mask, 1916, serial, purple on white, ⅞", Hake's, February 1989, $15.　　　　　$15–$25

James Dean, circa 1955, photo cello button, with black and white photo on yellow background, 3½", Hake's, April 1989, $41.
　　　　　$50–$75

For Your Eyes Only/James Bond 007, 1981 copyright, English, plastic rim, 2¾", Hake's, February 1989, $23.　　　　　$10–$15

Photo courtesy of Hake's Americana, York, PA

Greta Garbo, 1930s, lithographed button, black and white and fleshtone button from movie set, #3, scarce, Hake's, February 1989, $38.　　　　　$25–$50

Judy Garland/MGM's Wizard of Oz, blue on white illustration with orange rim, blue lettering, 1¼″, Hake's, April 1989, $199.
$100–$200

NOTE: *This button was issued as part of a movie contest. It is numbered "293" at the top.*

I Saw E.T., 1982, UNIV copyright, purple on dark blue, 2¼″, Hake's, June 1989, $4.
$5–$10

Leo the Metro-Goldwyn-Mayer Lion on World Tour—The Greatest Star on the Screen, 1930s, black and white with lion's head tinted in dark yellow, ⅞″, Hake's, November 1988, $23.
$15–$25

Harold Lloyd, blue and white lithographed button from a set from the 1930s, ¾″, Hake's, April 1989, $25.
$15–$25

Loew's Our Gang Club, 1930s, black, gray, and red movie contest button picturing the five gang members plus a dog lined up behind a fence, 1¼″, Hake's, February 1989, $67.
$25–$50

Ken Maynard Club/First National Pictures, 1930s, black and white, ⅞″, Hake's, February 1989, $26.
$15–$25

May the Force Be With You, 1977, white on blue button from Star Wars, 20th, 3″, Hake's, April 1989, $10.
$10–$15

Tim McCoy's Vigilantes, 1930s, lithographed, ⅞″, Hake's, February 1989, $26.
$25–$50

Photo courtesy of Hake's Americana, York, PA

Metro-Goldwyn Pictures, black and white and red button showing speeding locomotive, pre–1924 (before Louis B. Mayer joined the company), 1″, Hake's, February 1989, $24.
$15–$25

Tom Mix Circus, 1930s, circus souvenir button, black and white on black background, 1 3/4 ", Hake's, February 1989, $68.

$50-$75

Photo courtesy of Hake's Americana, York, PA

Tom Mix for Vice President, 1930s, 1 1/4 ", Hake's, November 1988, $101. $75-$100

Paramount Pictures, 1930s, multi-colored corporation logo, 7/8 ", Hake's, November 1988, $15. $15-$25

M. Rooney/J. Garland Babes in Arms, yellow button from a Philadelphia movie theater, 1939, 1 1/4 ", Hake's, November 1988, $53. $75-$100

Sabu Club/Sabu in The Thief of Bagdad, black and white, 7/8 ", Hake's, April 1989, $21. $25-$30

Photo courtesy of Hake's Americana, York, PA

Shadow of Fu Manchu, The, 1930s, dark green and bright yellow movie button, 1 1/4 ", Hake's, February 1989, $65. $50-$75

Smokey and the Bandit, full-color photo button with title of 1977 film (1980 UNIV copyright), 3″, Hake's, February 1989, $6.
$10–$15

Star Trek, the Motion Picture, 1979, full-color, 2¼″, Hake's, February 1989, $17.
$10–$15

Genuine Shirley Temple, An Ideal Doll, 1930s, brown lettering on white rim with brown and tan photo, button affixed to 1930s dolls, 1¼″, Hake's, February 1989, $51.
$50–$75

Vote Yes for Sunday Movies, 1930s, white and dark blue button used to promote more liberal Sunday activities, ¾″, Hake's, April 1989, $12.
$15–$25

Welcome Dahlings, black and white button, 2¼″, Hake's, April 1989, $6.
$10–$15

NOTE: *This button was given to guests at a black tie party at Abercrombie & Fitch, a New York luxury sporting goods store, to celebrate the publication of Bankhead's book* Tallulah, *published by Holt, Rinehart & Winston. Party was held November 15, 1972. The store has since closed its Manhattan branch.*

Wizard, 1967, lithographed button with blue background from *Oz* set, copyrighted by MGM, ⅞″, Hake's, February 1989, $20.
$15–$25

CALENDARS

James Dean Calendar, The, 1982, Pomegranate Artbooks, Sanford Roth (photographer), Twentieth Century Nostalgia, October 1988, $20.
$15–$25

Photo courtesy of Hake's Americana, York, PA

Jayne Mansfield, 1965, glossy, thin, cardboard wall calendar, with 12 month sheets intact, photos of actress, 9″ × 14″, Hake's, February 1989, $138.   *$85–$100*

Paramount Pictures, 1923–24, stamped leatherette color cover with photos, ads, 25 pages, 11″ × 14″, Collectors' Showcase, October 1988, $88.   *$100–$150*

CAMERA/PROJECTOR

The first single lens camera was patented in 1888 by Louis Aime Augustin Le Prince. In 1889, Thomas Alva Edison and his assistant, William Kennedy Laurie Deicson, at Edison's laboratories in West Orange, New Jersey, developed what eventually became the Kinetoscope, the first motion-picture machine to be used commercially (1891). The Motion Picture Machine was invented in 1893 by Charles Egar Duryea and J. Frank Dureau (both were Americans), and, in 1894, the Frenchmen, Louis Jean Lumiere and Auguste Marie Lumiere, invented the Motion Picture Projector.

Ansco 8" × 10" Camera, Turner Reich 12-21-28, convertible lens constructed of painted wood with metal trim having a tripod, property of George Hurrell, MGM photographer, 40" high, Christie's East, June 1989, $1650.   *$2000–$3000*

★

NOTE: *Included is a letter of authenticity from George Hurrell.*

★

Hollywood Projector, hand-cranked, 35mm, with film and reels, sold by Montgomery Ward, also a "Kodascope Projector," circa 1930s, 16mm, missing lens and other pieces, and a "Keystone Moviegraph," circa 1920s, hand-cranked, Camden House, May 1989, $400.   *$100–$200*

CIGAR/CIGAR BOX

Santa Maria Havana Cigar, unsmoked, original container, Christie's East, October 1988, $440.   *$100–$150*

NOTE: *This cigar was presented to Cecil B. DeMille in 1957 by Winston Churchill.*

Cardboard Cigar Box, 1920s, the sheik of 5¢ cigars re: Rudolph Valentino, 6″ × 7½″ × 4″, Collectors' Showcase, October 1988, $90.   *$50–$75*

CIGARETTE CARDS

Cigarette cards were published by a great many tobacco companies in Britain, the United States, and Germany. British sets were popular in 24-, 40-, 50-, and 100-card sets and were produced on all kinds of subjects, not only movie stars. Cards have an illustration on one side and written information on the other. They are small enough to be stored easily and are quite educational. Literally millions of cigarette cards have been produced and range in price from under $1 to about $100. Tom Mix cigarette cards are usually fairly expensive. Cigarette cards were also given as premiums. If pasted into an album, cards bring lower prices. World War II bought a leveling off of cigarette cards.

German, circa 1930s, 38 cards, majority in color, including Norma Shearer, Ramon Novarro, *The Good Earth* (1937, MGM), very fine, Collectors' Showcase, February 1989, $27.   *$15–$20*

German, 1937 album of 274 full-color cards, depicting Jean Harlow, Marlene Dietrich, Douglas Fairbanks, Shirley Temple, others, fine, Alan Levine, June 1988, $175.   *$150–$180*

German, movie star cards, 1932, album #2 with 275 full-color cards, gold background, mounted, 35 pages, depicting Lon Chaney, Carole Lombard, Joan Crawford, Clara Bow, Buster Keaton, Greta Garbo (3), many others, 12″ × 9″ album, Collectors' Showcase, January 1989, $166.   *$100–$200*

Tom Mix, German, circa 1930s, card #36, Orami Cigarettes of Germany, semi-glossy black and white photo of the actor in western garb, very fine, 1¼″ × 2″, Hake's, February 1989, $19.   *$10–$15*

CIGARETTE CASES

Errol Flynn, 1930s, sterling silver, engraved "Good Luck, Errol, John Barrymore" inside, "EF" engraved on front, 4″ × 3″, Collectors' Showcase, January 1989, $1100.   *$500–$1000*

NOTE: *Flynn and Barrymore were friends and drinking cronies.*

Laura, 1944, 20th, "To Gene Tierney from cast & crew, 'Laura' " engraved on back, small lighter engraved with Tierney's name; Chinese pagoda, half-moon and tree motif, very fine, 2½″ × 3″, Collectors' Showcase, January 1989, $1703.
$500–$700

COOKIE JAR

W.C. Fields, McCoy, Triple Pier Expo, November 1988, $238.
$200–$250

CORKSCREW

W.C. Fields, early 1940s, painted and carved wooden corkscrew for champagne bottles, very fine, Collectors' Showcase, February 1989, $24.   *$40–$50*

CREDIT CARDS

Joan Crawford, nine credit/membership cards including the American Federation of Television and Radio Artists, Eatons, many signatures, Camden House, May 1989, $450.

$300–$400

Joan Crawford, eight credit/membership cards, including American Film Institute, Lord & Taylor, Saks, many signatures, Camden House, May 1989, $600.   *$400–$500*

Joan Crawford, eight credit/membership cards, including Bergdorf-Goodman, Bonwit Teller, Screen Actor's Guild, many signatures, plus "J.C." gold-stamped on small wallet, Camden House, May 1989, $1400.   *$300–$400*

DIXIE ICE CREAM LIDS

Dixie Ice Cream Lids (Dixie Cup Lids) were actually cups of Meadow Gold Ice Cream, 4 fl. oz., with lids that depicted the photographs of movie stars on the underside. The most popular lids among children were cowboy heroes such as Bill "Hopalong Cassidy" Boyd, Gene Autry, Red Barry, and Tom Mix. Buster Crabbe as Flash Gordon was the most highly prized. Stars such as Bette Davis did absolutely nothing for the kids, although to today's adult collectors, her lid is very desirable. Dixie Lids didn't preserve well because of their roundness. They are hard to store. How many round boxes are there? Dixie Cup comes from the container's brand name, Meadow Gold Creamery, but nobody ever called them by that name. They were Dixie Cup Lids to kids and adults in the 1930s through the 1950s, just as they are to collectors today.

Movie Star Dixie Lids, Betty Grable *Pin-Up Girl* (1944, 20th), blue color, also black and white photo of *Footlight Serenade* (1942, 20th), Bob Hope *Road to Utopia* (1945, PAR), blue color, and Van Heflin, brown, no movie indicated, tabs off, good, 2¼″ each, Hake's, June 1989, $15.   *$15–$25*

Elizabeth Taylor, photo, 2¼″, fine, Twentieth Century Nostalgia, August 1988, $7.50.   *$5–$10*

DIXIE ICE CREAM PICTURES

Bill Boyd, undated, full-color photo, yellow margin, black and white scenes on back from 1939 PAR film *Silver on the Sage*, from series by Dixie Ice Cream, 8″ × 10″, fine, Hake's, November 1988, $30.   *$50–$75*

Photo courtesy of Hake's Americana, York, PA

Clark Gable, circa 1935, full-color photo, yellow margin, short biography on reverse, black and white film scenes from MGM's *After Office Hours, Forsaking All Others, Chained*, 9″ × 11″, Hake's, June 1989, $16.   *$15–$25*

Jean Harlow, circa 1935, full-color photo closeup, yellow margin, short biography on reverse, five black and white scenes from *Reckless, The Girl From Missouri, Blonde Bombshell*, all MGM, 9″ × 11″, Hake's, June 1989, $16.   *$15–$25*

Photo courtesy of Hake's Americana, York, PA

Katharine Hepburn, circa 1935, full-color closeup photo, yellow margin, short biography on reverse, five black and white scenes from *The Little Minister, Little Women,* both RKO, 9″ × 11″, Hake's, June 1989, $12.   *$15–$25*

★

NOTE: The above are all in very fine condition.

★

DRESSING ROOM TAG

Clark Gable, MGM, brass medallion of Dressing Room #24, inscribed Clark Gable, MGM lion inscribed on verso, 2″ diameter, Christie's East, June 1989, $2860.   *$1200–$1500*

DOLLS

In the doll hierarchy, China dolls are the most esteemed. China refers to the head and sometimes the hands and feet. Bodies are made of cloth or leather. Next come bisque dolls, which are unglazed, have lifelike faces, set-in glass eyes, and fancy wigs. There are many celebrity dolls produced in bisque. Prices begin in the low hundreds and climb into the thousands. Composition dolls follow bisque dolls and are usually lower in price. These dolls flaked easily. Composition dolls that were American-made during the 1930s are becoming very rare. Next in line are plastic and vinyl dolls, which are fairly inexpensive as dolls go.

Fanny Brice, 12½", Richard Wright Antiques, June 1988, $295.   *$275-$325*

Jackie Coogan, papier-mâché, German, repair to head, 11", Calico Cat Antiques, December 1988, $145.   *$125-$150*

Laurel and Hardy, bisque, hand-painted, Taiwan made, mint, 20/22" tall, Collectors' Showcase, December 1988, $66.
$50-$60

Laurel and Hardy, cloth dolls (2), detailed, produced in 1972 by Larry Marman, includes six smaller figurines of Laurel and Hardy, 13" tall, Camden House, May 1989, $200.   *$100-$200*

Harold Lloyd, cloth doll, 11½" high, with Orphan Annie doll, wooden, jointed, 5" high, Christie's East, May 1989, $132.
$80-$100

Groucho Marx, #32001, Effanbee, 16" high, Wex Rex Records & Collectibles, May 1989, $150.   *$140-$160*

Colleen Moore, 1930s, fairy princess and Effanbee Doll, yellow heart on red background, very fine, ⁹/₁₆ ", Hake's, February 1989, $48.   *$25–$50*

Popeye, limited edition, molded and painted features, dressed in flannel shirt, sailor's cap, and blue pants, holding a can of spinach in left hand, pipe missing, 24 " high, Christie's East, December 1988, $286.   *$500–$700*

Shirley Temple, Ideal, composition, original tagged, blue dotted, organdy dress with pleats, blonde mohair wig, 11¼ " high, Christie's East, March 1989, $462.   *$200–$300*

Shirley Temple, Ideal, composition, green sleep eyes, blonde wig, five-piece body, dressed in pink cotton dress over a red felt coat and hat, 13 ", Christie's East, March 1989, $308.   *$300–$350*

Shirley Temple, circa 1930s, Ideal, composition, original red and green plaid dress, pin, eyes crazed, slight composition damage, 18 ", Skinner, November 1988, $150.   *$300–$400*

Shirley Temple, Ideal, original box, five additional costumes, 13 ", Theriault, October 1988, $1500.   *$1000–$1200*

John Wayne, #2891, Effanbee, dressed in cavalry outfit, 16 ", Wex Rex Records & Collectibles, May 1989, $165.   *$150–$175*

Jane Withers, with trunk and wardrobe, 19 ", Theriault, October 1988, $1300.   *$1000–$1200*

FIGURES

Bugs Bunny, circa 1940s, china, hollow china, colored body, blue eyes, full-dimensional, glazed, molded on base, very fine, 2 " × 4½ " base, Hake's, February 1989, $153.   *$100–$200*

Crab With Fiddle, Alice in Wonderland, Greenwich Auction Room, June 1989, $300.   *$300–$400*

Felix the Cat, circa 1930, velveteen, maroon, arms jointed, movable head, arms, tail, plastic eyes attached to fabric-covered discs, 11″ high, Skinner, November 1988, $425.   *$150–$200*

Our Gang, plaster, group of 10, hand-painted and with cardboard hand-painted "Our Gang" backdrop, fine, Skinner, November 1988, $100.   *$150 $250*

Soldier/Cards, Alice in Wonderland, Greenwich Auction Room, June 1989, $200.   *$250–$300*

FILM EPHEMERA

Brochure, Max Factor, 1936 (new edition), original copyright 1928, Factor studio, Hollywood, Myrna Loy cover picture, stars inside include Joan Crawford, Claudette Colbert, Bette Davis, Jean Harlow, Sylvia Sidney, and Rita Cansino (later Hayworth), contains makeup/beauty tips, also makeup service card picturing Colbert using Factor's face powder, fine, Sherry Dempsey, Annex Arts & Antiques Flea Market, October 1988, $8.   *$10–$20*

Brochure, advertising, Norman Film Manufacturing Co. for *The Lovebug* and *The Crimson Skull*, good, 9 1/2″ × 12″, Richard Opfer, February 1989, $70.   *$50–$75*

Brochure, theater, 1940, *Susan and God*, MGM, Joan Crawford, Fredric March, Rita Hayworth, unfolded, 12″ × 7″, Collectors' Showcase, January 1989, $30.   *$20–$30*

Brochure, theater, 1940, *Waterloo Bridge*, MGM, Vivien Leigh, Robert Taylor, full-color, unfolded, 17″ × 7″, Collectors' Showcase, January 1989, $37.   *$25–$35*

Envelopes, 35th commemorative, Katharine Hepburn, George Arliss, date of birth and picture on left on envelope, Collectors' Bookstore, August 1988, $7.50.   *$7.50–$9*

Exhibit Card, Tom Mix, circa 1925, blue film scene of *The Best Bad Man*, good, 3 1/4″ × 5″, Hake's, February 1989, $12.
$10–$15

Exhibit Card, William S. Hart, 1931, yellow-tone photo of Hart in costume for movie *Two Gun Man*, fine, 3 1/2″ × 5 1/2″, Hake's, November 1988, $8.   *$10–$15*

Exhibitor's Book, RKO, 1935–36, 18 gold and silver pages, portraits of Fred Astaire, Ginger Rogers, Katharine Hepburn, fine, 9″ × 12″, Collectors' Showcase, October 1988, $86.   *$75–$100*

Exhibitor's Manual, 1926–27, Pathe, color ads for *Our Gang*, Chaplin's *Shoulder Arms*, Harold Lloyd, Harry Langdon, Ben Turpin, 324 pages, 9″ × 12″, Collectors' Showcase, December 1988, $112.   *$100–$700*

Exhibitor's Publication, 1922, *The Oakdale Affair* story by Edgar Rice Burroughs for British film, full-page ad, Evelyn Greeley, Reginald Denny, 12 pages, rare, fine, 7 1/2 " × 11 ", Collectors' Showcase, December 1988, $199.   *$50–$100*

Fan Petition Sheet, 1939, reissue of Astor Pictures Corp. film *Tumbleweed*, 1925, William S. Hart's last film, folded, 8 1/2 " × 22 ", Hake's, February 1989, $21.   *$25–$50*

Film Flyer, Green Eyed Monster, framed, good, 12 " × 19 ", Richard Opfer, February 1989, $80.   *$75–$100*

Film Folder Sheet, 1938, COL *Blondie* series, this being the initial film of the series, four-page sheet herald, folded, blue-tone photo of stars Penny Singleton and Arthur Lake, plus a small Chic Young cartoon, fine, 4 " × 5 1/2 ", Hake's, February 1989, $42.   *$25–$50*

Film Sheet, 1936, MGM, *San Francisco*, Clark Gable, Spencer Tracy, Jeanette MacDonald, full-color movie herald, illustrated, fine, 7 " × 12 ", Hake's, November 1988, $37.   *$25–$50*

Film Sheet, 1935, MGM, *Reckless*, Jean Harlow, William Powell, movie herald sheet, folded, full-color scenes, fine, 7 " × 11 1/2 ", Hake's, November 1988, $21.   *$25–$50*

Greeting Card, circa 1939–1940, *Oz* valentine of diecut stiff paper, valentine with full-color picture depicting movie's characters, fine, 4 1/2 " × 7 ", Hake's, February 1989, $67.   *$50–$75*

Menu, 1945, dining car of Santa Fe, full-page color picture of MGM's *The Harvey Girls*, 6 " × 9 ", Collectors' Showcase, March 1989, $102.   *$35–$40*

Newspaper, 4/20/22, *Dayton Daily News*, front-page story entitled: "Arbuckle Is Finished as Movie Star," fine, Willow Valley Collectibles, February 1989, $7.50.   *$5–$10*

NOTE: Fatty Arbuckle had been involved in the death of an actress named Virginia Rappe at a party he tossed for some friends over the 1921 Labor Day weekend at the St. Francis Hotel in San Francisco. Arbuckle was alleged to have had intercourse with Ms. Rappe using a Coke bottle as the instrument of penetration. The actress died a few days later from the "supposed" assault, and Arbuckle was brought to trial. Various women's groups and other right-wing organizations persecuted him in the press; yet, after three separate trials, he was acquitted of all charges. However, the notoriety and bad press effectively ended his career and his films were boycotted. Eventually the actor found work as a director under the name William Goodrich; one of the films he co-directed with King Vidor was the 1927 comedy The Red Mill, *starring Marion Davies. But Arbuckle's heyday as the silent screen's greatest comedian had passed. He died a broken man in 1933.*

Newspaper, 12/18/23, *Dayton Daily News* (Ohio), large full-view photo that ran with story "Jackie Cooper Begins to Doubt Existence of Santa," Willow Valley Collectibles, April 1989, $10.
$8–$12

Newspaper, 6/28/30, *Toledo Blade*, (Ohio), article "Film Stars Are Wed," re: marriage of cowboy star Hoot Gibson to actress Sally Eilers, photo of Ms. Eilers, Willow Valley Collectibles, April 1989, $8.50.   *$7–$10*

Newspaper Insert, 6/20/36, *Motion Picture Herald*, full-page RKO special with photos of Fred Astaire dancing alone and with Ginger Rogers, also Katharine Hepburn, Barbara Stanwyck, others, W.C. Fields photo on back, 38 pages, fine, Collectors' Showcase, October 1988, $90.   *$75–$95*

Newspaper Insert, 1/2/37, *Motion Picture Herald*, 1912–1937 insert, 20 pages, fine, Collectors' Showcase, October 1988, $28.
$50–$60

Notebook, lot of three for Beatles' *Yellow Submarine*, 1969, full-color depictions of rock group as portrayed in animated film, two spiral-bound notebooks, 5″ × 7½″ and 8″ × 10½″, and one three-ring binder, 10½″ × 12″, unopened, near mint, Hake's, November 1988, $324.   *$100–$200*

Payroll Statement, 1/28/54, re: Marilyn Monroe and William Morris Agency, carbon copy check to Monroe for $852.34 for six days work at 20th, suspension mention, framed, mint, 8½″ × 11″, Collectors' Showcase, December 1988, $585.

                                        $100–$150

Photo Card, circa 1920s/early 1930s, Tom Mix, black and white film photo of cowboy star pictured in automobile with Barney Oldfield, famous racing car driver, very good, 3¼″ × 5¼″, Hake's, February 1989, $16.   *$10–$15*

Police Logs, 1938, MGM, original, rare, over 600 pages, Camden House, May 1989, $600.   *$200–$300*

Publicity Mailing, 1958 for *The Young Lions*, Marlon Brando, Dean Martin, Hope Lange, Montgomery Clift, May Britt, star photos, 12 pages, fine, Collectors' Showcase, September 1988, $22.   *$20–$40*

Serial Card, circa 1940s, black and white card for attendance at chapter showings of 15-chapter *The Lone Ranger* film serial, Sears ad on back for free cowboy suit (earned by attending each episode), rare, fine, 3¼″ × 5″, Hake's, November 1988, $64.
                                        $75–$100

GAMES

Games should be complete and in very good or better condition. The cover content is very important in selling to collectors. Size of the game is also an important criterion for pricing games. Beware of taped box lids because tape tends to remove the lithography. Collectors tend to specialize in themes, i.e., Adventure, Disney, Westerns, etc.

Around the World in 80 Days, 1957, David Niven and other stars pictured on box cover, cards, money, dice, croupier cups included with game, Annex Arts & Antiques Flea Market, October 1988, $10.   *$10–$12*

Dr. No, 1961, Victory Games, role-playing game, complete, boxed, very good, Wex Rex Records & Collectibles, May 1989, $25. $20–$28

Enter the Dangerous World of James Bond, 1965, Milton Bradley, very good, Wex Rex Records & Collectibles, May 1989, $35. $30–$40

Photo courtesy of Hake's Americana, York, PA

Gulliver's Travels, 1939, Milton Bradley, "Official Edition adapted from Paramount's Technicolor Production by Max Fleischer" on cover, colorful, 10″ × 19″ × 2″, Hake's, June 1989, $72. $25–$50

James Bond/Secret Agent 007, 1964, Milton Bradley, colorful 16″ × 18½″ playing board, figure pieces, cards, complete, very fine, box 9½″ × 19″ × 1½″, Hake's, February 1989, $41.
                                                              $22–$50

James Bond 007, 1965, Milton Bradley, playing board, plastic tiles with 007 symbols, diecut black suedelike sheet board, plastic chips, mint game, near mint box, 8½″ × 12″ × 2″, Hake's, February 1989, $98. $75–$100

James Bond 007 Thunderball, 1965, Milton Bradley, complete, colorful 16″ × 18½″ playing board, cardboard character sheets in scuba outfits, many unused "Secret 007 Notebook" sheets, full-color illustrated box lid, fine, 9½″ × 19″ × 2″, Hake's, November 1988, $50. $15–$25

Photo courtesy of Hake's Americana, York, PA

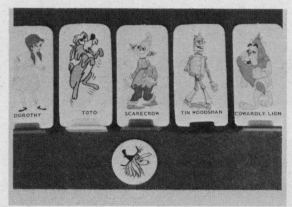

Photo courtesy of Hake's Americana, York, PA

Off to See the Wizard, 1968, Milton Bradley, MGM copyright, colorful board, 16″ × 18½″, game parts include cardboard standup pieces with full-color characters pictured, small cardboard disk depicting witch, complete, fine, Hake's, February 1989, $75. *$50–$75*

Stars Wars Destroy Death Star, 1977, Kenner, boardgame with playing board 16″ × 16″, death star spinner, secondary spinner, tiny spaceship tokens, full-color lid design, boxed, complete, fine, 16½″ × 16½″ × 1″, Hake's, February 1989, $12. *$15–$25*

Travel With Woody Woodpecker, 1956, Cadaco-Ellis, Lantz copyright, scarce, fine, 12½" × 19" × 1½", Hake's, February 1989, $59. $75–$100

Wings, 1928, tie-in of 1927 movie from PAR (won the first Academy Award as best picture), card game with instructions, two decks of cards, Sekino & Gray, November 1988, $28. $25–$35

GLASS

Glasses should be free of scratches and anything else that might remove the printed design. Tip: Keep glasses out of the dishwasher. Repeated washings destroy the design.

Mae West, Arby's collectors' series, from *I'm No Angel*, 1933, PAR, Twentieth Century Nostalgia, October 1988, $10.
                                                        $8–$12

GLASS LANTERN SLIDES

Slides were taken from the graphic elements of 22" × 28" displays in movie theaters from the early silents through the late 1940s. They were the earliest forms of advance advertising for theaters, and tended to be shown both before and after the feature to intrigue the audience for what was to come.

Harbor Lights, 1923, Ideal Films Ltd., Tom Moore, Excelsior Illustrating Co., very good, Constance Nadig, June 1989, $35.
                                                        $25–$35

Pied Piper Malone, 1924, PAR, Thomas Meighan (book by Booth Tarkington), Excelsior Illustrating Co., Constance Nadig, June 1989, $35. $25–$35

The Humming Bird, 1924, PAR, Gloria Swanson movie, also *Prodigal Daughters*, 1923, *Bluebeard's Eighth Wife*, 1923, both PAR, full-color, very fine, 4" × 3", Collectors' Showcase, February 1989, $86. $50–$60

GUM CARDS

Gum cards are produced on every imaginable subject, from animals to World War II. Complete sets in fine condition are what collectors want; individual cards are fine if they can be used to fill in the missing cards to complete a set. Like baseball cards, creased and dirty cards are off-limits to the majority of collectors. They should be stored in individual plastic envelopes for excellent preservation. Some companies that produced celebrity gum cards are Carreras Ltd., Rothmans Ltd., Godfrey Phillips Ltd., Letraset and Watford Biscuits in Great Britain, and Topps and Fleer's in the United States.

James Bond Secret Agent 007, 1965, Philadelphia Chewing Gum Co., lot of six cards depicting scenes from *Dr. No*, 1962, *From Russia With Love*, 1963, and *Goldfinger*, 1964, card numbers 9, 11, 22, 26, 48, and 58, from a set of 66, creased, good, 2½" × 3½", Hake's, February 1989, $12. $10–$15

Photo courtesy of Hake's Americana, York, PA

James Dean Hit Stars, late 1950s, Topps Gum, two cards from 88-card set, with full-color photo on each card, brief biography on back, numbered, fine, 2½" × 3½", Hake's, November 1988, $21. $15–$25

Walt Disney's Zorro, 1950s, complete set of 88 full-color cards, 2½″ × 3½″, Collectors' Showcase, March 1989, $150.

$60–$75

Three Stooges, 1959, Fleer's, color photos of comedians, complete set of 96, very fine, Collectors' Showcase, September 1988, $238.

$100–$200

GUM WRAPPER

A Hard Day's Night, 1964, Topps, waxed paper wrapper gum pack set, sepia film scenes, Beatles pictured on wrapper in black and white, fine, 5″ × 6″, Hake's, November 1988, $18.

$15–$25

JEWELRY

Charm, Brass, 1930s, Shirley Temple, brass rim, cut-out center with picture of Shirley, 5/8″ diameter, Hake's, November 1988, $71.

$75–$100

Charm, Movie, circa 1950s, silver link bracelet depicting stars Gary Cooper with Lauren Bacall, June Allyson, Cary Grant, Susan Hayward, Roy Rogers, very good, 6″ long, Hake's, February 1989, $51.

$50–$75

Hair Clip, 1960s, Mae West, diamond-like white stone with 18 small diamonds and four larger ones, 2″ × 1″, Collectors' Showcase, January 1989, $181.

$150–$200

★

NOTE: *Clip came with a letter of authenticity.*

Money Clip, Cecil B. DeMille, presented to him and engraved on verso, 14K textured gold surmounted by figure of Academy Award, 3/4 oz. gross, Christie's East, October 1988, $1870.

$100–$200

Pocket Mirror, 1920s, Mary Pickford, black and white cello photo mirror, scarce, fine, 2¾″ tall, Hake's, April 1989, $94.

$50–$100

Ring, Tom Mix, look-in, brass, inscribed "Boston" over pictures of Tony and a sixgun, Tom Mix brand on top of ring, small hole on ring side depicts black and white picture of Mix and horse, Tony, with inscription "To My Straight Shooter Pal, Tom Mix," good luster, fine, Hake's, February 1989, $212.   *$100–$200*

Ring, 1945, Marilyn Monroe, gold, adjustable, engraved inside "Norma Jean Baker 1945," Collectors' Showcase, January 1989, $4202.   *$1500–$3000*

★

NOTE: *This ring was previously owned by one of Monroe's intimate friends, a friend who was the first person in her house the night she died. This person is mentioned in many biographies about the actress.*

★

Ring, Elvis Presley, gold, designed and worn by the actor and singer, sheik's head with pear-shaped ruby in turban, diamond eyes, Sotheby's, June 1988, $14,300   *$4000–$6000*

KEYS

Keys to the City, set of 10, given to Joan Crawford by different city and state officials, Camden House, May 1989, $400.

$100–$150

LAMP

Gone With the Wind, red on gold, poppies, original paint, 17″ high, Triple Pier Expo, November 1988, $200.   *$170–$225*

LUNCH BOXES

Lunch boxes have become very collectible within the last two years or so. Boxes should be complete with the thermos. Handles must be in good condition (they are easily damaged), and the metal should be free of rust and dents. Beatles and Disneyana lunch boxes are the most popular now among collectors, and the most expensive. Space and science-fiction boxes are also very collectible.

Roy Rogers and Dale Evans, Double R Bar Ranch logo, very good, Skinner, February 1989, $66.   *$45–$75*

Yellow Submarine, 1968, King-Seeley Thermos Co., lithographed metal box with thermos (6½"), yellow plastic cap, orange box depicting scenes from animated film continuously around box sides, fine, 7" × 8½" × 4", Hake's, February 1989, $215. *$75–$200*

MASKS

Abominable Dr. Phibes, The, 1977, Vincent Price horror film, original foam master mold worn by the actor, Camden House, May 1989, $125. *$300–$500*

Charlie McCarthy and Mortimer Snerd, latex masks seen in Disney's *Fun and Fancy Free*, Greenwich Auction Room, June 1989, $300. *$500–$600*

MONSTER MODEL

Frankenstein's Monster, realistic stand-in model for the actor Boris Karloff in this 1931 UNIV film, one-of-a-kind item (made by the designer Jack Pierce to relieve Karloff of the 48-pound outfit during filming), Christie's South Kensington Auction Gallery, London, December 1988, $29,700. *$25,000–$35,000*

NOTE: *The model was bought by the Museum of Moving Image in London.*

MOTORCYCLES

These are excellent examples of crossover collectibles.

Cyclone, former property of actor Steve McQueen, yellow with white balloon tires, one-of-a-kind, Urban Archeology (Sandy Smith's Modernism Show), November 1988, $75,000.

Excelsior Auto Cycles, former property of actor Steve McQueen, two cycles with white balloon tires, one red, one green, Urban Archeology (Sandy Smith's Modernism Show), November 1988, $30,000.

Harley-Davidson, former property of Arnold Schwarzenegger, owned by Warner LeRoy, proprietor of Maxwell's Plum, a restaurant in New York, William Doyle Galleries, January 1988, $15,000.

MUGS

Photo courtesy of Camden House, Los Angeles, CA

Joan Crawford, circa 1945, Barclay, hand-painted heads of a wide-eyed Joan Crawford with handles shaped like gold Oscars, created as a one-of-a-kind item for the actress after she won the Academy Award for best actress in *Mildred Pierce*, 1945, WB, Camden House, May 1989, $2400.   *$2500–$3000*

MUSICAL

Folk Guitar, Elvis Presley, Gibson, Model J-200, used in *Elvis and Me*, Sotheby's, 1988, $25,000.

Piano, nightclub "Paris Flashback" piano used in *Casablanca*, 1942, WB, for Bogart-Bergman love scene in La Belle Aurore Cafe, Sotheby's, December 1988, $154,000.   *$75,000–$100,000*

NOTE: *This piano was consigned to Sotheby's by a dentist in Beverly Hills and sold to a Japanese buyer. The piano bench was also included. It is not the piano used at Rick's Cafe in* Casablanca. *The price of $154,000 included a 10% buyer's premium.*

PENCIL SHARPENER

Most pencil sharpeners are made in foreign countries such as Japan and Germany. They are composed chiefly of metal or celluloid. Pencil sharpeners with an intact blade bring higher prices than those without a blade (blades were installed with a screw for easy removal).

Hopalong Cassidy, flat black and white and dark blue plastic, image of Hoppy and a sharpener mounted on back, scarce, very fine, Collectors' Showcase, February 1989, $35.   *$25–$35*

PILLOW

Wizard of Oz, The, 1939, merchandising tie-in, pictured are Judy Garland, Jack Haley, Ray Bolger, Bert Lahr, and the Witch, plus two Munchkins and Toto, actor's name printed at bottom of pillow, very fine, Collectors' Showcase, March 1989, $319.   *$200–$300*

PLATES

Cafe De Paris, 20th, canape and dessert plates, circa 1950s, white with restaurant logo, set of six, J. Goldsmith Antiques, August 1988, $57.   *$39–$60*

PLATTER

Cecil B. DeMille, American silver, wreath and floral motif banding, inscribed at center with signatures of Ronald Coleman, Gary Cooper, Bette Davis, Deanna Durbin, Bing Crosby, Betty Grable, Lana Turner, others, 12 1/4", Christie's East, October 1988, $16,500.   *$800–$1200*

PLAYING CARDS

Many collectors collect playing cards by a particular topic. Sets should have 52 cards and a joker. Single cards are also desirable if particularly rare.

Photo courtesy of Hake's Americana, York, PA

Photo courtesy of Hake's Americana, York, PA

Photo courtesy of Hake's Americana, York, PA

Movie Souvenir, 1916, M.J. Moriarty Movie Souvenir Card Co., 52-card original playing deck, joker with Chaplin picture, cards have black and white photo portraits of silent film stars, reverse full-color chariot scene from *Ben Hur*, 1927, MGM, cardboard box, 3″ × 3¾″ × 1″, Hake's, November 1988, $128.

$100–$200

PREMIUMS

The first cereal premium was offered in 1919 by Kellogg's cereal of Funny Jungleland Moving Pictures, which depicted the antics of show animals in flip-flop strips. Many companies gave away premiums to purchasers of their products. Whitman Publishing began producing softbound premiums in 1933, the most common being the Coco Malt giveaways. In 1935 they began production of premiums for Big Little Books, which contained less pages than the regular editions of the books. Other companies included Phillips Dental Magnesia, Amoco Gas, Kool-Aid, Sears, Pan Am Gas, and Macy's. As with any other collectible, price is an important factor as is content, condition, and scarcity of the premium. In the 1950s, Wheaties offered Disney premiums, and Bond Bread ("Hoppy's favorite") did the same.

Coco Malt, circa 1933, Buck Rogers, map of the solar system, 21 1/2″ × 27 1/2″, Christie's East, September 1988, $198.

$300–$400

Gone With the Wind, 1940, toothpaste premium, cookbook, very good, 5 1/2″ × 7 1/2″, Collectors' Showcase, December 1988, $113.

$60–$70

Lux Soap, 1930s, sepia portrait photos, lot of three on printed simulated frames, back of frame includes film title from 1934 movie and star, i.e., Ginger Rogers in *The Gay Divorcee*, very fine, 9″ × 12″, Hake's, April 1989, $21.

$25–$50

Ralston, undated, Tom Mix, cardboard mechanical movie viewer with two-reel film for movie *Rustler's Roundup*, complete, rare, very fine, 1″ × 4″ × 6 1/2″, Hake's, February 1989, $306.

$100–$300

PROPS

Bull Whip, 1921, PAR, braided, full-size elaborate whip, supposedly used by Rudolph Valentino in *The Sheik*, Camden House, May 1989, $1500.

$1000–$2000

★

NOTE: *Consigned by the music librarian at PAR; his grandfather received the bull whip from Valentino.*

★

Forearm, 1984, *Romancing the Stone*, foam rubber with gloved hand (bitten off by an alligator in film), 20″ long, Phillips, December 1988, $110.   *$500–$1000*

Head, 1969, *Skidoo*, Groucho Marx's head used as a prop sculpture, mounted on a large silver screw, fantastic likeness, 3½″ × 5″, Camden House, May 1989, $1000.   *$700–$900*

Pistols, E.M. Reilly & Co., London, pair of composite flintlock pistols with sighted blue octagonal barrels, used by Gary Cooper in *The Unconquered*, 1947, PAR, signed "Roh Andre Kuchenreiter" on strapwork, Christie's East, October 1988, $46,200.
                                                   $2000–$3000

NOTE: *From the estate of Cecil B. DeMille, these pistols are strongly favored to be crossover collectibles. Pistols, as a separate category of collectible, bring some of the highest prices at auction and through dealers.*

Ship Wheel, 1942, *Reap the Wild Wind*, PAR, Cecil B. DeMille estate, oak and pine, typical form, 10 spokes division, from U.S. Cruiser "Marblehead," 66‛ diameter, Christie's East, October 1988, $990.   *$400–$600*

Throne, 1963, *Cleopatra*, 20th, wood, hand-made, hand-painted, antiqued, adorned with snakes of cast metal, torch flames, Sacred Cats, padded velvet seat and cushion, used by Rex Harrison (Julius Caesar) in movie, Camden House, May 1989, $5000.   *$5000–$7000*

Photo courtesy of Christie's East, New York

Witch Remover, 1939, *The Wizard of Oz*, MGM, used by the Cowardly Lion, giant sprayer with large canister-form holding tank with screw top, cylinder chamber pump, plunger rod with wooden handle, gray paint, red bands, marked "Witch Remover," red cylinder, 28″ long, Christie's East, June 1989, $22,000.   *$15,000–$22,000*

NOTE: From scene in film where Dorothy and companions enter the haunted forest.

PUPPETS

Humphrey Bogart, early 1940s, wooden, Bogart likeness, dressed in brown wool trench coat, gray felt hat, painted wood shoes, Louis Hunt, carving, 25″ tall, Camden House, May 1989, $550.   *$500–$600*

Duchess and Baby, *Alice in Wonderland*, sitting on throne chair, Greenwich Auction Room, June 1989, $2500.   *$5000–$6000*

Frog Doorman, *Alice in Wonderland*, with letter prop, Greenwich Auction Room, June 1989, $3000.   *$600–$700*

Jiminy Cricket, 1939 World's Fair, Disney Studios, re: Campbell Soup, hand puppet, Greenwich Auction Room, June 1989, $4250.   *$3000–$4000*

King of Hearts, *Alice in Wonderland*, Greenwich Auction Room, June 1989, $6500.   *$5000–$6000*

Stan Laurel and Oliver Hardy, rubber marionettes, Greenwich Auction Room, June 1989, $20.   *$50–$70*

White Rabbit, *Alice in Wonderland*, with monocle, gloves, Greenwich Auction Room, June 1989, $13,000.
                                              $10,000–$12,000

PUZZLES/POSTCARDS

I've combined these two categories because they are both absent from this price guide. I took a folder of index cards with prices, descriptions, and general literature on these collecting categories up to the country and left the folder on the train when disembarking. I only hope they were found by an interested collector. In the next edition of this book, I promise to have lengthy coverage of both these collecting categories. In the interim, please accept my apologies for their not being included here. (See reference chapter.)

Double Donald Duck ashtray, Japanese, c. 1935, $528 ($350–$450). *Photo courtesy of Christie's East, New York.*

Gilbert Adrian designed "ruby slippers" worn by Judy Garland in *The Wizard of Oz*, 1939, MGM, $165,000 ($15,000–$20,000). *Photo courtesy of Christie's East, New York.*

Note: All prices in parentheses are the estimated price ranges. All other prices are what the item actually sold for.

Cabaret, June Allyson cover, January 1956, $5 ($5–$10).

Andy Hardy's Double Life, 1942, MGM, insert, $60 ($50–$90).

The Invisible Man, 1933, UNIV, classic half-sheet, $11,000 ($9000–?).

Enchantment, 1948, RKO (Samuel Goldwyn), David Niven, Teresa Wright, $12.

Stan Laurel/Oliver Hardy marionettes, $20 ($50–$70).

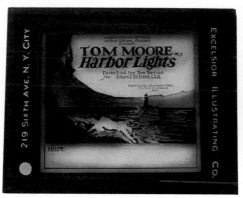

Glass Lantern slide, *Harbor Lights*, 1923, Ideal Films, Ltd., $35 ($20–$35).

When Worlds Collide, 1951, PAR, three-sheet, $600 ($1000–$1500).

To Have and Have Not, 1944, WB, Humphrey Bogart, Lauren Bacall, three-sheet, $1500 ($700–$900).

Jiminy Cricket, hand puppet,
$4250 ($3000–$4000).

Mae West gown in black
velvet from *Every Day's A
Holiday*, 1938, PAR, $25,000.
*Photo courtesy of Alexander
Gallery, New York.*

The Man on the Eiffel Tower,
1949, RKO, Charles Laugh-
ton, Franchot Tone, movie
tearsheet ad, $12.

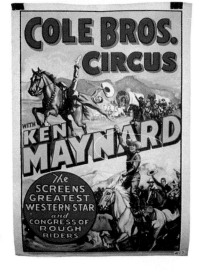

The Blue Dahlia, English book of Raymond Chandler screenplay, $35 ($30–$50).

Ken Maynard, 1940, Cole Brothers circus half-sheet, $125 ($150–$200).

Pathe News Car, Louis Marx, $528 ($400–$600). *Photo courtesy of Christie's East, New York.*

The Seven Year Itch, 1955, 20th, Marilyn Monroe, Tom Ewell, three-sheet, $250 ($400–$500).

"I'm Nobody's Baby," from *Andy Hardy Meets Debutante*, Judy Garland, Mickey Rooney, words and music by Benny Davis, Milton Ager, Lester Santly, c. 1921 Leo Feist, Inc., $20 ($5–$30).

The City That Never Sleeps, 1953, REP, and *The Frightened City*, 1950, COL, two one-sheets, $150 ($250–$350).

Poor Little Rich Girl, 1936, 20th, Shirley Temple movie book, Saalfield, $73 ($25–$75).

RECORDS/RECORD ALBUMS

Dumbo, 1945, Walt Disney Studios, RCA Victor three-record album, jacket, fair, Collectors' Showcase, September 1988, $16.   *$30–$50*

Edith Head, 1970, 42nd Academy Award ceremony, open-end interview with costume designer on 33 1/3 rpm special radio material record, 7", Collectors' Showcase, December 1988, $25.
                                                         $20–$50

Story of Johnny Appleseed, The, circa 1940s, Walt Disney's *Melody Time*, 1948, RCA Victor 78 rpm records, three, #1048, with voices of characters by Dennis Day, scarce, 10" × 11", Hake's, November 1988, $21.   *$25–$50*

Whale Who Wanted to Sing at the Met, The, 1946, Walt Disney, Columbia Masterworks Album, three-record set, 78 rpm, Nelson Eddy, singer, very rare, Collectors' Showcase, September 1988, $167.   *$60–$80*

Woody Woodpecker and His Talent Show, 1949, Walter Lantz, two-record 78 rpm record album, full-color Woody score, recorded by Mel Blanc, 12" × 10 1/4", Collectors' Showcase, December 1988, $37.   *$30–$40*

SOUNDTRACKS

Blackbeard's Ghost, Walt disney, #DQ-1305, narrated by actor Peter Ustinov, 12" LP, Collectors' Showcase, November 1988, $15.   *$20–$25*

Gone With the Wind, MGM, original score recording, Max Steiner, Clark Gable and Vivien Leigh pictured on jacket, official full-range recording, 33 1/3 rpm, Abby Bookshop, October 1988, $3.   *$3 $12*

Gone With the Wind, 1954, RCA Victor, two 45 rpm records of complete film music, cardboard album, 7" × 7 1/4", Hake's, April 1989, $46.   *$25–$50*

Lucky Lady, Arista, #1322, original soundtrack album, high-fidelity, Burt Reynolds and Liza Minelli caricature sketch on jacket, 33⅓ rpm, Abby Bookshop, October 1988, $3.   *$3–$9*

March Along With Mary Poppins, Walt Disney, DQ-1288, UCLA Marching Band, shrinkwrapped album, rare, 12″ LP, Collectors' Showcase, November 1988, $5.   *$15–$25*

Moonspinners, The, Walt Disney, Vista, BV-3323, with Hayley Mills, shrinkwrapped, rare, Collectors' Showcase, November 1988, $22.   *$20–$30*

Old Yeller/The Legend of Lobo, Walt Disney, DQ-1258, shrinkwrapped album, 12″ LP, Collectors' Showcase, November 1988, $12.   *$12–$15*

Quiet Man, The, 1952, Decca Records, DL-4511, REP picture, John Wayne, Maureen O'Hara, Barry Fitzgerald, vocal by Bing Crosby, Victor Young, orchestra, Wayne and O'Hara pictured on jacket in scene from film, 33⅓ rpm LP, Tama Fair, September 1988, $3.   *$3–$8*

STAMPS

D.W. Griffith, complete sheet of 50 U.S. 10¢ stamps, pasted, black paper, very fine, Collectors' Showcase, January 1989, $38.   *$20–$25*

STUDIO PUBLICATIONS

These are studio publications with movie star material, photographs, film synopsis, and general information on film productions, directors, and publicity. They were produced on heavy stock paper and are 11″ × 14″ in size.

Lion's Roar, 1942, March, MGM, Conrad Veidt, second anniversary showing of *Gone With the Wind*, very good, Collectors' Showcase, October 1988, $324.   *$125–$150*

Lion's Roar, 1942, June, MGM, *Tarzan's New York Adventure*, *Her Cardboard Lover* with Norma Shearer (Shearer's last movie), 48 pages, Collectors' Showcase, December 1988, $385.
    $75–$100

Lion's Roar, 1942, September/October, MGM, 80 pages, very good, Collectors' Showcase, October 1988, $388.   *$100–$150*

Lion's Roar, 1943, April, MGM, Laurel and Hardy, *Cabin in the Sky*, with Lena Horne, Varga foldout of a DuBarry Girl, also Lucille Ball, Lana Turner, 135 pages, Collectors' Showcase, February 1989, $297.   *$125–$250*

Lion's Roar, another copy of above, October 1988, $550.
$125–$175

Lion's Roar, 1943, September, MGM, Judy Garland, Lucille Ball, Lassie, Red Skelton, 112 pages, Collectors' Showcase, February 1989, $266.   *$150–$200*

New Dynamo, 1944, October, 20th, with star photos, movie stills, articles on forthcoming films, in two sections, 167 pages, 11″ × 16″, Collectors' Showcase, March 1989, $211.
$100–$150

New Dynamo, 1945, April, 20th, anniversary publication, volume one, number fifteen, 50 pages in color, 212 pages, 9″ × 12″, Collectors' Showcase, December 1988, $399.   *$125–$150*

THERMOMETER

Some Like It Hot, enameled, colored, promotional thermometer in orange, black, and white, depicting Marilyn Monroe down the center, 39″ long, Phillips, December 1988, $1500.
$1500–$2000

TICKETS

Don Juan, 1926, WB, John Barrymore, original envelope (dirty, chipped), for evening performance, Vitaphone film, two tickets (unused and mint), Constance Nadig, June 1989, $10.
$10–$15

TRADE PUBLICATIONS

Trade publications are "runs" or individual issues of profusely illustrated industry trade magazines and newspapers which date from the early 1900s to the present. Some other publications not included in this listing are *Motion Picture News*, *Moving Picture World*, and *Wids*. Trade publications contain ads, film news, day-to-day records of Hollywood history, star photos and portraits, lists of films, movie scenes, theater exteriors, statistics, etc. The July 14, 1987, single issue of *Hollywood Reporter* is particularly desirable among collectors because it is a special issue devoted to James Bond films. In the 13 months that I was researching and writing this price guide, I was not able to find a copy of this particular issue. Collectors and dealers tell me that it sells for around $25–$45.

Boxoffice, 1934, January–December, bound volume, complete year of publication, re: Mae West, Carole Lombard, Katharine Hepburn, Shirley Temple, W.C. Fields, Fred Astaire, and Ginger Rogers, others, 9″ × 12″, Collectors' Showcase, March 1989, $385.   *$250–$350*

Boxoffice, 1944–49, cloth, 500 pages, 9″ × 12″, Collectors' Showcase, December 1988, $122.   *$150–$200*

Boxoffice, 1951–58, eight bound issues of annual second "preview" section, 9½″ × 12¼″, Collectors' Showcase, October 1988, $121.   *$100–$150*

Hollywood Reporter, 1935, July 1–December 1935, complete half-year volume, Collectors' Showcase, October 1988, $172.
$150–$200

Hollywood Reporter, 1939, April 1–30, leather-bound, embossed in gold, 600 pages, Camden House, May 1989, $300.
$500–$600

Reel Journal, The (later *Boxoffice*), 1930, complete year for this weekly publication, 9″ × 12″, Collectors' Showcase, February 1989, $125.   *$200–$300*

Showman's Trade Review, 1942, December 16, full-page portraits of Abbott and Costello, Gary Cooper, Bette Davis, Clark Gable, Judy Garland, Betty Grable, Dorothy Lamour, also Dis-

ney and western movies, 92 pages, 9″ × 12″, Collectors' Showcase, October 1988, $42. *$60–$75*

Variety, 1945, January 3, softcover, anniversary edition, with
Walt Disney's *Three Caballeros*, Abbott and Costello, etc., 178
pages, 11″ × 16″, Hake's, February 1989, $29. *$50–$75*

WATCHES

Photorific Celebrity Watches (three), wide band and chain dials
feature portraits of Marilyn Monroe, Jean Harlow, Rudolph Valentino, worn on belt, pocket or wrist, original boxes, Christie's
East, December 1988, $176. *$80–$120*

Tom Mix, circa 1933, Ingersoll, dial features Mix with lasso in
hand, on his horse, long horn on subsidiary dial, steel "buckle"
links on band with Mix portrait on top link, rare, Christie's East,
December 1988, $1100. *$500–$700*

MOVIE POSTERS
AND LOBBY CARDS

INTRODUCTION

The most actively collected movie memorabilia is movie paper
which includes posters, banners, lobby cards, and window cards.
   Poster sizes include the one-sheet (27″ × 41″), half-sheet
(22″ × 28″), two-sheet (45″ × 59″), three-sheet (41″ × 81″),
six-sheet (81″ × 81″), and twenty-four-sheet (109″ × 236″).
There is also a mini one-sheet bearing identical art to the one-
sheet but 17″ × 24″ in size.
   Other poster sizes include 14″ × 36″, 22″ × 38″, 30″ × 40″,
and 40″ × 60″, each bearing the exact size to its proper name.
There is also a British Quad Poster which is different from the
American poster and 40″ × 30″ in size.
   Some collectors prefer to classify all movie paper as posters;
other collectors differentiate posters from the following movie
paper—banners (24″ × 82½″), inserts (14″ × 36″), lobby
cards (11″ × 14″), and window cards (14″ × 22″). Window
cards were printed in three different sizes including mini, regular, and over-size. The mini-window card carried the same art
as the one-sheet poster but in a reduced size of 8″ × 14″. The
regular window card measured 14″ × 22″, and the over-size
window card was 14″ × 28″, about the same size as a half-sheet.
   Lobby cards were produced in sets of eight (a title card and
seven scene cards), and before the 1950s were printed on heavy
stock. Lobby cards are either color photos measuring the full
11″ × 14″ size of the card, or 8″ × 10″ color stills bordered
by a film's logo and credits; films released by United Artists,

Universal, and Warner Brothers prior to 1981 were bordered 11″ × 14″ sets.

One-sheet and half-sheet posters, inserts, and lobby cards are the most actively sought after of all movie paper. They are easiest to display or store (a collector would need the size of a Versailles to hang a collection of six-sheet or twenty-four-sheet posters), and are exceptionally beautiful in design, particularly posters produced during the 1930s and 1940s.

Title cards are more desirable and usually more expensive than scene cards, unless the scene card pictures a major star in closeup. Cards with the major star(s) in the background, or with supporting players and the major star, or just supporting players, are priced lower and are less desirable to collectors. Scene cards that only display an object such as a falling airplane or a group of extras standing around are the least desirable of all cards.

An exception are science-fiction or horror movie cards that picture monsters, spaceships, or robots. They are quite often in demand and are fairly expensive. A scene card, for example, from the 1954 Warner Brothers movie *Them*, which pictures the giant ants, is a highly sought after image. The same is true of a scene card picturing Robby the Robot in the 1956 Metro-Goldwyn-Mayer film *Forbidden Planet*.

All movie paper, whether posters or lobby cards, really is a question of supply and demand affecting price. Some movie paper is more common than others, some scarce, and some really extremely rare. It's up to the collector as to how much he or she wants to spend. And, of course, the dealer and auction house have to realize a profit as well.

Condition also plays a major role in evaluating movie paper. Posters and lobby cards that are free of any noticeable flaws (and there are few in mint condition) bring the highest prices. But even pinholed, soiled, taped, folded, or creased movie paper, and to some extent, water-damaged paper, can also bring fairly high prices. It is the poster, for example, that has chunks missing or is faded or trimmed that is off-limits to the most serious of collectors. Unless such movie paper is needed to complete a collection of a particular star or genre, it is best to stay away and spend one's money on better quality posters or lobby cards.

In the list that follows, I have used the correct names of all movie paper, i.e., inserts, one-sheets, half-sheets, window cards, title, and scene cards in lieu of using sizes, which I felt might confuse the reader. I have only used size dimensions for foreign posters as they are usually categorized under size and not by the types of movie paper within the general "poster" heading. And speaking of foreign posters, there are some very fine examples listed here. Most are French stone lithographed posters; a few are Belgian. As a rule, Belgian posters are better preserved than those made in France. Also, Belgian posters were produced in the one-sheet size which helped in preserving and storing them.

Linen-backed movie paper is also noted in the list. Linen, cotton, and other materials were used as a preservation method to protect the paper. In and of itself, linen-backed movie paper can never be considered as mint and any listings that mention such paper are either excellent, very good, or in good condition only. (However, linen-backed movie paper will last indefinitely.)

A word now about reissues. When a movie was re-released by a studio, the movie paper went through a metamorphosis. Artwork and advertising changed. Most collectors frown on reissues and prefer the original movie paper. Only important movies such as *Casablanca*, *Gone With the Wind*, and several of Disney's animation films are desirable reissues. Of course, this doesn't imply that reissues of lesser movies won't sell, but if given the choice between an original poster and a reissue, choose wisely. And make sure that the reissue has the letter "R" somewhere in the border of the poster. Otherwise, it is questionable what one will be getting for their money.

As a final note, stay away from movie paper that has been glued to a backing. Time, and especially sunlight, will cause the glue to seep through the surface and completely destroy the movie paper.

MOVIE POSTERS AND LOBBY CARDS LISTING

INTRODUCTION

Movie paper is listed alphabetically by movie title, followed by movie release date, studio, major star(s), category of movie paper, pertinent information about the movie paper if applicable (linen-backed, scarce, rare, etc.), name of auction house or collectible dealer, month movie paper was sold from June 1988 through June 1989, price paid, and then to the extreme right, the price range.

Since the majority of the posters are in color, I have only mentioned black and white movie paper where appropriate, and also if the poster is a re-release or reissue (this notation pertaining to either colored or black and white movie paper).

Several poster descriptions and price ranges are followed by the word *Note*, wherein I have written some historical information about the movie paper sold or the movie stars associated with said movie paper that would be of interest to the reader.

Abbott and Costello Meet the Mummy, 1955, UNIV, title card, matted and framed, Guernsey's, April 1989, $45.   *$100–$150*

Abbott and Costello Meet the Killers, 1955, UNIV, Boris Karloff, 18″ × 14″ Belgian poster, linen-backed, Camden House, May 1989, $50.   *$100–$150*

Across the Pacific, 1942, WB, Humphrey Bogart, insert, Guernsey's, April 1989, $125.   *$400–$500*

Action in the North Atlantic, 1943, WB, Humphrey Bogart, one-sheet, Guernsey's, April 1989, $200.   *$400–$600*

Adventures of Sherlock Holmes, The, 1939, 20th, Basil Rath-bone, Ida Lupino, one-sheet, linen-backed, rare, Camden House, May 1989, $4000.   *$4000–$4500*

Affair in Trinidad, 1952, COL, Rita Hayworth, Glenn Ford, 19″ × 14″ Belgian poster, linen-backed, Camden House, May 1989, $50.   *$100–$150*

Algiers, 1938, UA, Hedy Lamarr, Charles Boyer, half-sheet, Guernsey's, April 1989, $550.   *$500–$600*

Alice in Wonderland, 1933, PAR, Gary Cooper, W.C. Fields, half-sheet, excellent, Guernsey's, April 1989, $700.
          $1500–$2000

NOTE: Charlotte Henry played the title role.

Ali Baba and the Forty Thieves, 1944, UNIV, Jon Hall, Maria Montez, three-sheet, Guernsey's, April 1989, $175.   *$300–$450*

Ali Baba and the Forty Thieves, 1944, UNIV, Jon Hall, Maria Montez, title card and four scene cards, Guernsey's, April 1989, $45.   *$200–$250*

NOTE: Jon Hall, of the loincloth image, was a champion swimmer who did his own water stunts in movies, including a 131′ dive. He was often paired with Dorothy Lamour or Maria Montez. Born on a train in Fresno, California, Hall worked at 20th during the mid-1930s under his real name, Charles Locher.

★

All About Eve, 1950, 20th, Bette Davis, Anne Baxter, one-sheet, Guernsey's, April 1989, $250.   *$150–$200*

All About Eve, 1950, complete set of lobby cards, Guernsey's, April 1989, $450.   *$400–$700*

All of Me, 1933, PAR, Miriam Hopkins, Fredric March, George Raft, half-sheet, mint, Guernsey's, April 1989, $300.

$500–$700

All This and Heaven Too, 1940, WB, Bette Davis, Charles Boyer, 63″ × 47″ French stone lithographed poster, linen-backed, Camden House, May 1989, $400.   *$600–$700*

All Through the Night, 1942, WB, Humphrey Bogart, lobby title card, good, Collectors' Showcase, March 1989, $171.

$95–$125

Ambassador Bill, 1931, Fox (later 20th), Will Rogers, lobby scene card, excellent, Poster Mail Auction Co., February 1989, $15.

$45–$65

American Madness, 1932, COL, Walter Huston, one-sheet, Collectors' Showcase, January 1989, $125.   *$200–$300*

An Ideal Husband, 1948, 20th, Paulette Goddard, Michael Wilding, one-sheet, Guernsey's, April 1989, $50.   *$200–$300*

An Ideal Husband, 1948, complete set of lobby cards (eight), Guernsey's, April 1989, $25.   *$100–$150*

Andy Hardy's Double Life, 1942, MGM, Mickey Rooney, Esther Williams, Lewis Stone, lobby scene card, fine, Paper Collectables and Memorabilia Show, February 1989, $165.   *$15–$40*

NOTE: *A fairly high price for this particular scene card from the Andy Hardy series.*

Andy Hardy's Double Life, 1942, MGM, insert, excellent, Hollywood Poster Exchange, August 1988, $60.   *$50–$90*

Andy Hardy's Private Secretary, 1941, MGM, Mickey Rooney, Lewis Stone, Kathryn Grayson, lobby scene card, very good, Paper Collectables & Memorabilia Show, February 1989, $10.

$10–$25

Angel, 1937, PAR, Marlene Dietrich, 24″ × 33″ French poster, linen-backed, excellent, Phillips, December 1988, $400.

$400–$600

Anna Karenina, 1935, MGM, Greta Garbo, Fredric March, window card, excellent, Guernsey's, April 1989, $500.

$1200–$1500

Annie Get Your Gun, 1950, MGM, Betty Hutton, Howard Keel, half-sheet, Guernsey's, April 1989, $150.   *$150–$250*

NOTE: Judy Garland was originally set to do this movie but bowed out due to illness.

Asphalt Jungle, The, 1950, MGM, Sterling Hayden, Marilyn Monroe, six-sheet, rare, Guernsey's, April 1989, $1300.

$400–$600

NOTE: The sheets have been taped together on the reverse with water-soluble tape.

Auntie Mame, 1958, WB, Rosalind Russell, one-sheet, excellent, Phillips, December 1988, $100.   *$150–$200*

Babe Ruth Story, The, 1948, AA, William Bendix, Claire Trevor, poster for a Chesterfield cigarette advertisement picturing Bendix as Babe Ruth holding a bat and smoking a Chesterfield, Christie's East, September 1988, $440 (includes 10% buyer's premium).   *$300–$350*

Babes in Toyland, 1934, MGM, Stan Laurel, Oliver Hardy, window card, excellent, Guernsey's, April 1989, $5000.

$1500–2000

Baby Take a Bow, 1934, FOX, Shirley Temple, James Dunn, lobby scene card, excellent, Phillips, December 1988, $250.

$250–$350

NOTE: This was Shirley Temple's first major film at FOX.

Bad and the Beautiful, The, 1952, MGM, Kirk Douglas, Lana Turner, one-sheet, excellent, Phillips, December 1988, $100.

$150–$250

Bad For Each Other, 1953, COL, Lizbeth Scott, Charlton Heston, insert, Camden House, May 1989, $50. $50–$75

Bambi, 1942, RKO (Walt Disney Productions), complete set of lobby cards, Camden House, May 1989, $1100.   *$1000–$1500*

Barefoot Contessa, The, 1954, UA, Ava Gardner, Humphrey Bogart, one-sheet, Camden House, May 1989, $70. $50–$75

Bar 20, 1943, UA, William Boyd, three-sheet, framed, fair, Camden House, May 1989, $175. $50–$100

NOTE: Boyd played Hopalong Cassidy in this movie as well as in other movies, and on television. He began his career in silent films as a matinee idol of the late 1920s.

Batman, 1966, 20th, Adam West, 22″ × 18″ French poster, very good, Poster Mail Auction Co., February 1989, $80.

$35–$50

Battle Circus, 1953, MGM, Humphrey Bogart, June Allyson, 31″ × 23″ French poster, good, Poster Mail Auction Co., February 1989, $40. $75–$125

NOTE: Preposterous casting of Bogart and Allyson, which had about as much electricity as pairing Anna Sten with Rin-Tin-Tin.

Beach Blanket Bingo (and eight other *Beach* movies of the 1960s), 1965, American International, Frankie Avalon, Annette Funicello, all inserts, excellent, Phillips, December 1988, $325.

$250–$350

Because You're Mine, 1952, MGM, Mario Lanza, lobby title card and five scene cards, Guernsey's, April 1989, $25. $50–$75

Bedtime for Bonzo, 1951, UNIV, Ronald Reagan, half-sheet, Guernsey's, April 1989, $275. $350–$450

Belle of the Nineties, 1934, PAR, Mae West, window card, excellent, Guernsey's, April 1989, $425. $700–$900

Belle of the Nineties, 1934, window card, very good, Guernsey's, April 1989, $750. $1000–$1500

Bells of Coronado, 1950, REP, Roy Rogers, Dale Evans, three-sheet, good, Poster Mail Auction Co., February 1989, $86.

$100–$150

Bengal Brigade, 1954, UNIV, Rock Hudson, Arlene Dahl, lobby scene card, fine, Roger's Comics, October 1988, $6. $5–$10

Best Foot Forward, 1943, MGM, Lucille Ball, Harry James, half-sheet, Guernsey's, April 1989, $50. $150–$200

NOTE: *During this movie, Ball was under contract to MGM, having suffered for years as a contract star at RKO where she was dubbed the "queen of B-movies." A former Goldwyn girl in the early 1930s, the actress didn't hit her stride until television in the early 1950s in the hit comedy series "I Love Lucy."*

Between Midnight and Dawn, 1950, COL, Mark Stevens, Edmund O'Brien, Gale Storm, lobby title card and six scene cards, Guernsey's, April 1989, $25. $75–$125

Between Two Worlds, 1944, WB, John Garfield, Sydney Greenstreet, insert, Guernsey's, April 1989, $50. $150–$200

Bhowani Junction, 1956, MGM, Ava Gardner, one-sheet, framed, Camden House, May 1989, $225. $100–$150

Big House, The, 1955, COL, Broderick Crawford, 40″ × 60″ heavy stock silkscreen drive-in release poster, Guernsey's, April 1989, $70. *$150–$200*

Birds, The, 1963, UNIV, Rod Taylor, Tippi Hedren, lobby scene card, fine, Collectors' Showcase, November 1988, $63.

$40–$50

Birth of a Nation, 1915, Epoch Producing Co., Lillian Gish, Mae Marsh, Henry B. Walthal, Miriam Cooper, one-sheet, 1927 re-release stone lithograph, restored, linen-backed, very rare, Camden House, May 1989, $4000. *$3500–$4000*

Black Rose, The, 1950, 20th, Tyrone Power, Orson Welles, five lobby scene cards, Guernsey's, April 1989, $25. *$50–$100*

Black Swan, The, 1942, 20th, Tyrone Power, Maureen O'Hara, insert, very good, Guernsey's, April 1989, $375. *$400–$600*

Black, Swan, The, 1942, lobby title card and five scene cards, Guernsey's, April 1989, $300. *$600–$900*

Blind Husbands, 1919, UNIV, Erich Von Stroheim, lobby title card, rare, Guernsey's, April 1989, $3250. *$2000–$3000*

Blondie Hits the Jackpot, 1949, COL, Penny Singleton, Arthur Lake, three-sheet, Hake's, February 1989, $75. *$50–$100*

Blondie's Big Deal, 1949, COL, same cast as above, display card, good, Collectors' Showcase, December 1988, $28. *$40–$50*

Blood and Sand, 1941, 20th, Tyrone Power, Rita Hayworth, Linda Darnell, three-sheet, Guernsey's, April 1989, $225.

$500–$1000

Blood and Sand, 1941, six-sheet (unbacked in four sheets), Guernsey's, April 1989, $600. *$500–$1000*

Blood and Sand, 1941, two lobby scene cards with Power and Hayworth pictured, Guernsey's, April 1989, $175. *$450–$550*

Blue Skies, 1946, PAR, Bing Crosby, Fred Astaire, Joan Caulfield, one-sheet, Guernsey's, April 1989, $275.   *$200–$300*

NOTE: *The character of Holden Caulfield in J.D. Salinger's classic
novel* The Catcher in the Rye *was named after Joan Caulfield, who
was Salinger's favorite actress. The actress was under contract to
PAR during the 1940s.*

Blue Skies, 1946, insert, Guernsey's, April 1989, $125.

$200–$250

Bonnie Scotland, 1935, MGM, Stan Laurel, Oliver Hardy, window card, very good, Guernsey's, April 1989, $500.

$1000–$1200

Boogie Man Will Get You, The, 1942, COL, Boris Karloff, Peter
Lorre, lobby title card, fine, Collectors' Showcase, February
1989, $122.   *$75–$100*

Boom Town, 1940, MGM, Spencer Tracy, Clark Gable, Claudette Colbert, Hedy Lamarr, lobby scene card, very good, Poster
Mail Auction Co., February 1989, $26.   *$40–$60*

Bride Came C.O.D., The, 1941, WB, James Cagney, Bette Davis, insert, Guernsey's, April 1989, $250.   *$250–$300*

Bride of Frankenstein,The, 1935, UNIV, Elsa Lancaster, Boris
Karloff, one-sheet, very good, Guernsey's, April 1989, $3250.

$4000–$6000

NOTE: *Highly sought after by collectors.*

Bright Eyes, 1934, FOX, Shirley Temple, James Dunn, window
card, good, Guernsey's, April 1989, $250.   *$300–$500*

Broadway Bill, 1934, COL, Myrna Loy, Warner Baxter, window card, Guernsey's, April 1989, $425.   *$400–$600*

Broadway Melody, The, 1929, MGM, Bessie Love, Charles King, complete set of lobby cards in mint condition, rare, Guernsey's, April 1989, $2000.   *$4000–$6000*

NOTE: This was the first all-talking, all-singing, all-dancing musical.

Broadway Limited, 1941, UA, Victor McLaglen, Patsy Kelly, lobby title card, very good, Paper Collectables & Memorabilia Show, February 1989, $10.   *$10–$20*

Broken Lullaby, 1932, PAR, Nancy Carroll, Lionel Barrymore, half-sheet, excellent, Guernsey's, April 1989, $450.
     $300–$500

Buck Rogers, a set of eight lobby cards from serial chapters #1 "Tomorrow's World," #2 "Tragedy on Saturn," #3 "The Enemy's Stronghold," #4 The Sky Patrol," #5 "The Phantom Plane," #7 "Primitive Urge," and #12 "War of the Planets"; also included is a title card for *Planet Outlaws*, which was a full-length movie made from the serials, Christie's East, September 1988, $198.
     $300–$400

Photo courtesy of Camden House, Los Angeles, CA

Bull-Dogger, The, 1924, Norman Film Mfg. Co., Bill Pickett, stone lithographed one-sheet, linen-backed, rare, Camden House, May 1989, $800.   *$550–$650*

NOTE: *Before Pickett appeared in silent black westerns, he had been a rodeo star in the early 1900s known for his bull-dogging skills. Two of his early assistants were Tom Mix and Will Rogers before their Hollywood careers. Pickett had certain traits in common with fellow cowboy star William S. Hart in that both men were tall, lean, graceful, silent, and very self-confident.*

Bullets or Ballots, 1936, WB, Humphrey Bogart, Edward G. Robinson, six-sheet French stone lithographed poster, Camden House, May 1989, $650.   *$1250–$1500*

Bus Stop, 1956, 20th, Marilyn Monroe, Don Murray, one-sheet, good, Collectors' Showcase, September 1988, $192.   *$150–$200*

Bus Stop, 1956, one-sheet, Camden House, May 1989, $325.
$100–$150

Butterfield 8, 1960, MGM, Elizabeth Taylor, Laurence Harvey, Eddie Fisher, one-sheet, Guernsey's, April 1989, $45.
$100–$150

NOTE: *Based on a 1935 novel by John O'Hara,* Butterfield 8 *was Elizabeth Taylor's last film on her MGM contract, which had begun in 1943. That year she had a small part in* Lassie Come Home *and was immediately signed by the studio. She won an Academy Award for best actress for her role in* Butterfield 8, *after having failed to win the previous three years.*

Cain and Mabel, 1936, WB, Marion Davies, Clark Gable, 23″ × 29″ Belgian poster, linen-backed, Guernsey's, $225.
$500–$700

Call Northside 777, 1948, 20th, James Stewart, Richard Conte, window card, Guernsey's, $30.   *$75–$125*

Call of the Wild, 1935, UA, Clark Gable, Loretta Young, window card, good, Guernsey's, April 1989, $50.   *$150–$250*

Canary Murder Case, The, 1929, PAR, William Powell, Louise Brooks, lobby scene card, good, Collectors' Showcase, September 1988, $127.   *$75–$100*

NOTE: *This was the first movie based on the popular S.S. Van Dine mysteries, with William Powell playing the debonair detective, Philo Vance. He also appeared in* The Greene Murder Case *(1929),* The Benson Murder Case *(1930), and* The Kennel Murder Case *(1933). Basil Rathbone took over the role briefly in MGM's* The Bishop Murder Case *in 1930, Paul Lukas played Vance in* The Casino Murder Case *(MGM, 1935), and in 1939, PAR made* The Gracie Allen Murder Case *with Gracie Allen and Warren William. James Stephenson also took a stab at playing the detective in* Calling Philo Vance, *which was released in 1940 by WB. The Stephenson remake was a pale imitation of the original William Powell version.*

Cape Fear, 1962, Universal-International, Gregory Peck, Robert Mitchum, one-sheet, very good, Poster Mail Auction Co., February 1989, $20.   *$35–$55*

Captain January, 1936, 20th, Shirley Temple, Guy Kibbee, window card, very good, Guernsey's, April 1989, $250.

$300–$500

Captain January, 1936, lobby scene card picturing Shirley Temple, Guy Kibbee, and Slim Summerville, excellent, Phillips, December 1988, $200.   *$200–$250*

Carefree, 1938, RKO, Fred Astaire, Ginger Rogers, lobby scene card, fine, Collectors' Showcase, February 1989, $150.

$225–$375

NOTE: *Not one of the better Astaire-Rogers musicals.*

Casablanca, 1942, WB, Humphrey Bogart, Ingrid Bergman, one-sheet, linen-backed, fine, Collectors' Showcase, January 1989, $6600.   *$6000–$7500*

Casablanca, 1956, reissue half-sheet picturing famous last scene at airport, very good, Collectors' Showcase, February 1989, $400.   *$250–$500*

Cat's Meow, The, circa 1925, Harry Langdon, one-sheet, Guernsey's, April 1989, $1000.   *$800–$1000*

NOTE: *Langdon was a baby-face comedian whose on-screen antics were like those of a little boy. He made more than two dozen two- and three-reelers for Mack Sennett from 1924 to 1926, and one feature in 1927. As an independent actor, he made films for FN and MGM.*

Cattle Queen of Montana, 1955, RKO, Barbara Stanwyck, Ronald Reagan, lobby scene card, Poster Auction Mail Co., April 1989, $8.   *$5–$20*

Charlie Chan in Egypt, 1935, FOX, Warner Oland, Rita Cansino (pre–Rita Hayworth), Stepin Fetchit, window card, also window cards for *Charlie Chan in Paris*, 1935, FOX, Oland with Mary Brian, and *Charlie Chan at the Circus*, 1936, 20th, with Oland and Keye Luke, Guernsey's, April 1989, $650.

$800–$1000

Charlie Chan in London, 1934, FOX, Warner Oland, Raymond (Ray) Milland, Drue Leyton, window card, good, Collectors' Showcase, November 1988, $179. *$100–$125*

NOTE: *Warner Oland played the scholarly and considerate detective in 17 movies, beginning with* Charlie Chan Carries On *in 1931 and ending with* Charlie Chan at Monte Carlo *in 1937. All 17 movies were made at FOX, and later, 20th. Five other actors also played Charlie Chan in the movies: George Kuwa, Kamiyama Sojin, E.L. Park, Sidney Toler, and Roland Winters.*

★

Charlie McCarthy, Detective, 1939, UNIV, Edgar Bergen, Robert Cummings, one-sheet, Guernsey's, April 1989, $150.
$250–$350

Cheaper by the Dozen, 1950, 20th, Clifton Webb, Jeanne Crain, complete set of eight lobby cards, Guernsey's, April 1989, $25.
$75–$125

Chinatown, 1974, PAR, Jack Nicholson, Faye Dunaway, 22″ × 14″ Belgian poster, excellent, Poster Mail Auction Co., February 1989, $40.
$50–$70

Cinderella, 1950, RKO (Walt Disney animated film), insert, fine, Collectors' Showcase, October 1988, $94.
$50–$75

Circus, The, 1928, UA, Charles Chaplin, lobby scene card, very fine, Collectors' Showcase, December 1988, $409.   *$400–$500*

★

NOTE: Chaplin received a special Oscar for writing, acting, directing, and producing The Circus *at the first Academy Awards ceremony held on May 16, 1929, at the Roosevelt Hotel in Hollywood, California.*

★

City That Never Sleeps, The, 1953, REP, Gig Young, Mala Powers, and *The Frightened City* (also called *The Killer That Stalked New York*), 1950, COL, Evelyn Keyes, Charles Kovin, two one-sheets, Guernsey's, April 1989, $150.   *$250–$350*

City That Never Sleeps, The, 1953, title card and four scene cards, excellent, Guernsey's, April 1989, $35.   *$75–$125*

Clash by Night, 1952, RKO, Barbara Stanwyck, Marilyn Monroe, Robert Ryan, half-sheet, fine, Collectors' Showcase, March 1989, $115.   *$200–$250*

Climax, The, 1944, UNIV, Boris Karloff, half-sheet, Guernsey's, April 1989, $175.   *$250–$350*

College Holiday, 1936, PAR, Jack Benny, George Burns, Gracie Allen, one-sheet, Guernsey's, April 1989, $50.   *$250–$350*

Come on Danger, 1941, RKO, Tim Holt, one-sheet, good, Poster Mail Auction Co., $20.   *$50–$75*

Coney Island, 1943, 20th, Betty Grable, George Montgomery, half-sheet, Guernsey's, April 1989, $275.   *$350–$500*

Coney Island, 1943, one-sheet, Guernsey's, April 1989, $700.   *$300–$500*

Coney Island, 1943, complete set of lobby cards, Guernsey's, April 1989, $225.   *$300–$500*

Confidential Agent, 1945, WB, Charles Boyer, Lauren Bacall, insert, Guernsey's, April 1989, $125.   *$100–$150*

Corn Is Green, The, 1945, WB, Bette Davis, half-sheet, very good, Guernsey's, April 1989, $80.   *$200–$250*

Country Girl, The, 1954, PAR, Grace Kelly, William Holden, Bing Crosby, insert, very good, Collectors' Showcase, March 1989, $45.   *$50–$75*

Courtship of Andy Hardy, The, 1942, MGM, Mickey Rooney, Lewis Stone, Donna Reed, scene card, fine, Paper Collectables & Memorabilia Show, January 1989, $15.   *$15–$35*

Cover Girl, 1944, COL, Rita Hayworth, Gene Kelly, three scene cards, Guernsey's, April 1989, $125.   *$150–$250*

Crash Dive, 1943, 20th, Tyrone Power, Dana Andrews, Anne Baxter, insert, Guernsey's, April 1989, $125.   *$150–$250*

NOTE: *Upon completing this film, Power was inducted into the U.S. Marines for the duration of World War II. His first post–war picture was* The Razor's Edge *in 1946.*

Creature From the Black Lagoon, The, 1954, UNIV, Julia Adams, Richard Carlson, 31″ × 24″ French stone lithographed poster, Camden House, May 1989, $200.   *$250–$350*

Creature Walks Among Us, The, 1956, UNIV, Jeff Morrow, Rex Reason, insert, good, Collectors' Showcase, $101.   *$75–$100*

Cuban Love Song, The, 1931, MGM, Lupe Velez, Lawrence Tibbett, half-sheet, Guernsey's, April 1989, $275.   *$300–$400*

NOTE: *Lupe Velez was more famous for her affair with Gary Cooper in the late 1920s–early 1930s, and her 1933 marriage to Johnny "Tarzan" Weismuller than for her movies. Cooper was asked once by a reporter what was the most enthralling thing that had happened to him in the movies, and he answered: "Lupe Velez!" Velez received some prestige in the* Mexican Spitfire *series at RKO (1939–1943) where she parodied her real-life Mexican personality, which was as volatile as a bowl of jalapeño peppers and a ton of tabasco. Her botched suicide in 1944 made her even more famous.*

Cyclone Fury, 1951, COL, Charles Starrett, Smiley Burnette, one-sheet, Poster Mail Auction Co, February 1989, $15.

$45–$65

Daisy Kenyon, 1947, 20th, Joan Crawford, Henry Fonda, Dana Andrews, one-sheet, Guernsey's, April 1989, $50.   *$150–$200*

Daisy Kenyon, 1947, complete set of lobby cards, Guernsey's, April 1989, $70.   *$150–$250*

Dames, 1934, WB, Dick Powell, Ruby Keeler, Joan Blondell, half-sheet, mint, Guernsey's, April 1989, $700.   *$800–$1200*

Dancers in the Dark, 1932, PAR, Miriam Hopkins, Jack Oakie, half-sheet, excellent, Guernsey's, April 1989, $175.   *$250–$350*

Dancing Lady, 1933, MGM, Joan Crawford, Clark Gable, half-sheet, Guernsey's, April 1989, $2250.   *$2000–$2500*

Dangerous Years, 1948, 20th, Marilyn Monroe, title card and six scene cards with Monroe on the title and two of the scene cards, Guernsey's, April 1989, $400.   *$600–$900*

Dark Corner, The, 1946, 20th, Lucille Ball, Clifton Webb, half-sheet, very good, Poster Mail Auction Co., February 1989, $35.   *$60–$80*

Daughter of Shanghai, 1937, PAR, Larry "Buster" Crabbe, Anna May Wong, scene card, Poster Mail Auction Co., February 1989, $15.   *$40–$60*

Day the Earth Stood Still, The, 1951, 20th, Michael Rennie, Patricia Neal, title card, Guernsey's, April 1989, $600.   *$500–$700*

Photo courtesy of Camden House, Los Angeles, CA

Day the Earth Stood Still, The, 1951, one-sheet of Gort dominating poster, Camden House, May 1989, $850.   *$600–$750*

Day the Earth Stood Still, The, 1951, three-sheet (in two sections), fine, Collectors' Showcase, December 1988, $2086.
                                          $1500–$2500

★

NOTE: *Classic 1950s science-fiction movie. Highly sought after by collectors. Some of the artwork is really phenomenal.*

★

Dead End, 1937, UA, Sylvia Sidney, Joel McCrea, Humphrey Bogart, five scene cards with Bogart pictured on four, Guernsey's, April 1989, $60. $300–$400

Deadline, U.S.A., 1952, 20th, Humphrey Bogart, complete set of lobby cards, very good, Collectors' Showcase, $165.
$100–$125

Dead Man's Trail, 1952, MON, Johnny Mack Brown, Jimmy Ellison, one-sheet, Poster Mail Auction Co., February 1989, $25. $30–$50

Defense Rests, The, 1934, COL, Jean Arthur, Jack Holt, half-sheet, very good, Guernsey's, April 1989, $375. $300–$500

Desiree, 1954, 20th, Marlon Brando, Jean Simmons, insert, very good, Collectors' Showcase, March 1989, $51. $50–$75

Dial M for Murder, 1954, WB, Ray Milland, Grace Kelly, one-sheet, linen-backed, Camden House, May 1989, $325.
$250–$300

Diamond Horseshoe (Billy Rose's), 1945, 20th, Betty Grable, Phil Silvers, one-sheet, Guernsey's, April 1989, $375. $500–$700

Dimples, 1936, 20th, Shirley Temple, Frank Morgan, scene card, excellent, Phillips, December 1988, $150. $200–$250

Dinner at 8, 1933, MGM, John Barrymore, Jean Harlow, Marie Dressler, Wallace Beery, Lee Tracy, half-sheet, Guernsey's, April 1989, $2500. $4000–$6000

★

NOTE: This poster of Jean Harlow dressed in a green negligee and draped around other cast members gives the viewer the impression that Harlow appears with each of these co-stars in the movie. However, she has no scenes with John Barrymore or Lee Tracy.

Dino, 1957, AA, Sal Mineo, Susan Kohner, one-sheet, Poster Mail Auction Co., February 1989, $25. $50–$75

Dirigible, 1931, COL, Fay Wray, Jack Holt, scene card, Collectors' Showcase, September 1988, $46. $65–$85

Disraeli, 1929, WB, George Arliss, scene card, Guernsey's, April 1989, $90.   *$100–$150*

Dive Bomber, 1941, WB, Errol Flynn, Fred MacMurray, one-sheet, linen-backed, Guernsey's, April 1989, $175.   *$400–$500*

Dodge City, 1939, WB, Errol Flynn, Ann Sheridan, 63″ × 47″ French stone lithographed poster, linen-backed, Camden House, May 1989, $275.   *$250–$350*

NOTE: *The art for this poster was drawn by Constantin Balinsky.*

Dog's Life, A, 1918, FN, Charlie Chaplin, a complete set of lobby cards, the title card is spectacular, Guernsey's, April 1989, $1100.   *$2000–$4000*

Dog's Life, A, 1918, three-sheet, linen-backed, Guernsey's, April 1989, $3000.   *$6000–$8000*

Dolly Sisters, The, 1945, 20th, Betty Grable, John Payne, title card and four scene cards, Guernsey's, April 1989, $40.
                                                        $150–$200

Down to Earth, 1946, Rita Hayworth, half-sheet, very good, Guernsey's, April 1989, $100.   *$200–$250*

Dracula, 1931, UNIV, Bela Lugosi, Helen Chandler, insert, framed, extremely rare, excellent, Guernsey's, April 1989, $11,000.   *$15,000–$18,000*

NOTE: *Brilliant graphics by artist Karoly Grosz pictures Lugosi as Count Dracula emerging from a spider web. The crème de la crème of movie paper.*

Dragnet, 1954, WB, Jack Webb, four scene cards, Camden House, May 1989, $50.   *$50–$75*

Dr. Jekyll and Mr. Hyde, 1941, MGM, Spencer Tracy, Ingrid Bergman, Lana Turner, window card, good, Guernsey's, April 1989, $100.   *$250–$300*

Drums Along the Mohawk, 1939, 20th, Claudette Colbert, Henry Fonda, six scene cards, Guernsey's, April 1989, $225.

$400–$600

Drums Along the Mohawk, 1947, one-sheet reissue, Guernsey's, April 1989, $400. $1000–$1200

★

NOTE: *Very high estimate for a reissue one-sheet.*

★

Duel in the Sun, 1946, Selznick, Jennifer Jones, Gregory Peck, Lillian Gish, half-sheet, excellent, Phillips, December 1988, $200. $200–$300

Duke Steps Out, The, 1929, MGM, Joan Crawford, William Haines, 47″ × 63″ French release poster, linen-backed, Guernsey's, April 1989, $2750. $900–$1200

Dumbo, 1941, RKO (Walt Disney Productions), half-sheet, fair, Collectors' Showcase, November 1988, $363. $95–$125

★

NOTE: *This is an example of a poster in fair condition that has extensive damage but brought a relatively high price at a mail-order auction. The price range is well below the bid price, which is excessive given the condition of the poster. Collectors on the West Coast tend to spend more for movie paper and other movie memorabilia than do collectors on the East Coast and in other regions of the country.*

★

Edge of Darkness, 1943, WB, Errol Flynn, Ann Sheridan, half-sheet, unfolded, very good, Guernsey's, April 1980, $100.

$300–$400

Elmo Lincoln, circa 1930s, *Tarzan* black and white photo poster on newsprint paper stock issued by Chicago American Newspaper, poster is 23½″ × 30″, folded 8″ × 12½″, fine, Hake's, February 1989, $46. $50–$75

★

NOTE: *Lincoln was the screen's first Tarzan. This photo is from the 1918 film* Tarzan of the Apes.

★

Emma, 1932, MGM, Marie Dressler, half-sheet, mint, Guernsey's, April 1989, $500.   *$250–$350*

★

NOTE: *The artwork on this poster is by the artist John Held, Jr.*

★

Empire Strikes Back, The, 1980, Mark Hamill, Harrison Ford, one-sheet, fine, Collectors' Showcase, September 1988, $82.

$75–$85

Fantasia, 1940, Walt Disney Productions, Mickey Mouse, 30″ × 40″ British poster, Camden House, May 1989, $1000.

$1000–$1200

Farmer's Daughter, The, 1947, RKO, Loretta Young, Joseph Cotton, scene card, Poster Mail Auction Co., February 1989, $10.   *$10–$20*

★

NOTE: *Loretta Young won the Oscar for best actress for this movie.*

★

Female Jungle, 1956, American Releasing, Jayne Mansfield, John Carradine, scene card, Paper Collectables & Memorabilia Show, February 1989, $10.   *$10–$30*

Fighting Fools, 1949, MON, Leo Gorcey, Huntz Hall, and the Bowery Boys, one-sheet, good, Collectors' Showcase, February 1989, $65.   *$50–$75*

Fighting Kentuckian, The, 1949, REP, John Wayne, Vera Hruba Ralston, half-sheet, very good, Guernsey's, April 1989, $60.

$150–$250

Fire Patrol, The, 1924, Chadwick Pictures, Anna Q. Nilsson, window card, Poster Mail Auction Co., $45.   *$75–$100*

Flame of New Orleans, The, 1941, UNIV, Marlene Dietrich, half-sheet, Guernsey's, April 1989, $125.   *$250–$350*

Flying Down to Rio, 1933, RKO, Dolores Del Rio, Fred Astaire, Ginger Rogers, half-sheet, rare, excellent, Guernsey's, April 1989, $4000.   *$4000–$6000*

Follow the Fleet, 1936, RKO, Fred Astaire, Ginger Rogers, one-sheet, linen-backed, Guernsey's, April 1989, $2900.

$2500–$3000

Photo courtesy of Camden House, Los Angeles, CA

Follow the Fleet, 1936, RKO Fred Astaire, Ginger Rogers, Morgan lithographed one-sheet, linen-backed, Camden House, May 1989, $2950. $2500–$3000

Footlight Serenade, 1942, 20th, Betty Grable, Victor Mature, complete set of lobby cards plus one duplication, Guernsey's, April 1989, $450. $300–$500

Forbidden Planet, 1956, MGM, Walter Pidgeon, Anne Francis, one-sheet, Camden House, May 1989, $850.   *$500–$600*

NOTE: *This is the science-fiction movie with Robby the Robot that has become a cult favorite with science-fiction devotees. One of the best posters from the 1950s, a decade not known for great posters.*

Forever Amber, 1947, 20th, Linda Darnell, Cornel Wilde, complete set of lobby cards, Guernsey's, April 1989, $45.

$150–$250

For Me and My Gal, 1942, MGM, Judy Garland, Gene Kelly, one-sheet, Camden House, May 1989, $675.   *$200–$250*

Fort Dobbs, 1958, WB, Clint Walker, Virginia Mayo, scene cards #4 and #5, fine, Paper Collectables & Memorabilia Show, February 1989, $20.   *$20–$30*

NOTE: *Clint Walker was the handsome star of the television series "Cheyenne" before embarking on a film career at WB.*

Four Feathers, 1939, UA, Ralph Richardson, June Duprez, one-sheet, Guernsey's, April 1989, $700.   *$900–$1200*

Foxes of Harrow, The, 1947, 20th, Rex Harrison, Maureen O'Hara, complete set of lobby cards, Guernsey's, April 1989, $25.   *$150–$200*

Frankenstein, 1951, UNIV, Boris Karloff, Mae Clarke, Colin Clive, scene card picturing Karloff, reissue, linen-backed, fine, Collectors' Showcase, September 1988, $356.   *$100–$200*

French Line, The, 1953, RKO, Jane Russell, Gilbert Roland, insert, very fine, Collectors' Showcase, September 1988, $43.

$50–$75

NOTE: *There is some speculation as to the official release date of this movie. I have listed 1953 because the film opened in St. Louis in the fall of that year but was immediately banned by the archbishop of the Archdiocese of St. Louis. Withdrawn, it didn't reopen until the middle of 1954, undergoing some editing in the interim.* French Line *was one of the worst movies of the 1950s and undoubtedly the most atrocious movie of Jane Russell's career, even worse than* The Outlaw *(1943).*

Friendly Persuasion, 1956, AA, Gary Cooper, Anthony Perkins, half-sheet, Camden House, May 1989, $200.   *$50–$75*

From Russia With Love, 1963, UA, Sean Connery, Lotte Lenya, Daniela Bianchi, 40″ × 60″ British poster for the original release, Guernsey's, April 1989, $100.   *$300–$500*

NOTE: *Sean Connery as the debonair James Bond 007 in the second of the Bond movies.*

Fun in Acapulco, 1963, PAR, Elvis Presley, Ursula Andress, one-sheet, Camden House, May 1989, $175.   *$125–$150*

Funny Face, 1957, PAR, Fred Astaire, Audrey Hepburn, three-sheet, linen-backed, Camden House, May 1989, $150.

$200–$300

Gas House Kids in Hollywood, 1949, PRC, Carl "Alfalfa" Switzer, one-sheet, very good, Poster Mail Auction Co., February 1989, $15.   *$35–$55*

Gaslight, 1944, MGM, Ingrid Bergman, Joseph Cotten, Charles Boyer, one-sheet, framed, Camden House, May 1989, $700.

$600–$800

Gasoline Gus, 1921, PAR, Fatty Arbuckle, Lila Lee, three-sheet, rare, French poster, linen-backed, Guernsey's, April 1989, $950.   *$2000–$3000*

Giant, 1956, WB, Elizabeth Taylor, Rock Hudson, James Dean, half-sheet, very good, Collectors' Showcase, February 1989, $302.   *$150–$200*

Giant, 1956, one-sheet, Camden House, May 1989, $350.
                                                    $150–$200

Girl From Jones Beach, The, 1949, WB, Virginia Mayo, Ronald Reagan, insert, Guernsey's, April 1989, $50.   *$200–$250*

Girl From Missouri, The, 1934, MGM, Jean Harlow, Franchot Tone, window card, Guernsey's, April 1989, $475.   *$150–$250*

Glass Key, The, 1935, PAR, George Raft, Claire Dodd, Edward Arnold, window card, Guernsey's, April 1989, $400.

$400–$600

God's Little Acre, 1958, UA, Aldo Ray, Robert Ryan, title card, Poster Mail Auction Co., February 1989, $5. $5–$15

Go Into Your Dance, 1935, WB, Al Jolson, Ruby Keeler, scene card, Phillips, December 1988, $150. $250–$450

NOTE: *Released in Britain as* Casino de Paris, *it was the only film Al Jolson made with his wife, Ruby Keeler.*

Gold of the Seven Saints, 1961, WB, Clint Walker, Roger Moore, scene card, fine, Paper Collectables & Memorabilia Show, May 1989, $10. $3–$30

Golden Boy, 1939, COL, Barbara Stanwyck, William Holden, half-sheet, framed, Phillips, December 1988, $300. $300–$500

Golden Stallion, The, 1949, REP, Roy Rogers, scene card, Poster Mail Auction Co., February 1989, $25. $25–$35

Gone With the Wind, 1947, MGM, Vivien Leigh, Clark Gable, one-sheet reissue, good, Guernsey's, April 1989, $300.

$600–$800

Gone With the Wind, 1947, title card (with damaged border), reissue, Guernsey's, April 1989, $250. $400–$600

Goodbye Mr. Chips, 1939, MGM, Robert Donat, Greer Garson, one sheet, linen-backed, Camden House, May 1989, $400.

$400–$500

Great Lie, The, 1941, WB, Bette Davis, Mary Astor, scene card, excellent, Phillips, December 1988, $150. $150–$200

NOTE: *Mary Astor won an Academy Award as best supporting actress for her role in this movie.*

Greatest Show on Earth, The, 1952, PAR, Betty Hutton, James Stewart, Dorothy Lamour, seven scene cards, Guernsey's, April 1989, $25.   *$50–$150*

Great Waltz, The, Luise Rainer, title card and four scene cards, Guernsey's, April 1989, $60.   *$200–$300*

Hard Day's Night, A, 1964, UA, the Beatles, insert, Guernsey's, April 1989, $125.   *$100–$200*

Hellcats of the Navy, 1957, COL, Ronald Reagan, Nancy Davis, scene card showing both stars (the only one in the set with both shown), excellent, Phillips, December 1988, $80.   *$100–$150*

Hell's Kitchen, 1939, WB, Ronald Reagan and the Dead End Kids, one-sheet, Camden House, May 1989, $375.   *$250–$300*

Hell's Kitchen, 1939, scene card, linen, excellent, Phillips, December 1988, $100.   *$150–$250*

Help!, 1965, UA, the Beatles, one-sheet, scarce, Guernsey's, April 1989, $80.   *$150–$350*

Help!, 1965, scene card, excellent, Poster Mail Auction Co., February 1989, $30.   *$30–$50*

Hold That Baby, 1949, MON, Leo Gorcey, Huntz Hall, and the Bowery Boys, one-sheet, very good, Poster Mail Auction Co., February 1989, $25.   *$35–$55*

Home in Indiana, 1944, 20th, Jeanne Crain, Walter Brennan, one-sheet, excellent, Poster Mail Auction Co., February 1989, $40.   *$75–$95*

Hong Kong, 1951, PAR, Ronald Reagan, Rhonda Fleming, three-sheet, linen-backed, Guernsey's, April 1989, $250.   *$100–$300*

Horror of Dracula, 1958, UNIV, Peter Cushing, 47″ × 63″, French poster, linen-backed, Guernsey's, April 1989, $650.
$400–$600

Horse Soldiers, The, 1959, UA, John Wayne, William Holden, three-sheet, good, Poster Mail Auction Co., February 1989, $45. $90–$120

How Green Was My Valley, 1941, 20th, Walter Pidgeon, Maureen O'Hara, one-sheet, Camden House, May 1989, $300.
$150–$200

How To Be a Detective, 1952, RKO (Walt Disney Productions), one-sheet, excellent, Guernsey's, April 1989, $350. $400–$600

Hucksters, The, 1947, MGM, Clark Gable, Ave Gardner, Deborah Kerr, one-sheet, Camden House, May 1989, $150.
$150–$200

Iceland, 1942, 20th, John Payne, Sonja Henie, scene card, Poster Mail Auction Co., February 1989, $10. $10–$35

I'll Give a Million, 1938, 20th, Warner Baxter, Peter Lorre, scene card, Poster Mail Auction Co., February 1989, $21. $50–$65

Immortal Sergeant, 1943, 20th, Henry Fonda, Maureen O'Hara, three-sheet, good, Poster Mail Auction Co., February 1989, $45. $100–$150

In a Lonely Place, 1950, COL, Humphrey Bogart, Gloria Grahame, scene card, fine, Paper Collectables & Memorabilia Show, September 1988, $10. $10–$40

In Love and War, 1958, 20th, Robert Wagner, Sheree North, scene card, fine, Roger's Comics, October 1988, $3. $3–$9

In Old Chicago, 1937, 20th, Tyrone Power, Alice Faye, Alice Brady, one-sheet, Guernsey's, April 1989, $2750. $2000–$3000

In Old Monterey, 1939, REP, Gene Autry, one-sheet, Guernsey's, April 1989, $80. $100–$200

Invasion of the Body Snatchers, 1956, AA, Kevin McCarthy, Dana Wynter, scene card, very fine, Collectors' Showcase, February 1989, $66. $40–$50

Invisible Man, The, 1933, UNIV, Claude Rains, Gloria Stuart, half-sheet, excellent, Guernsey's, April 1989, $11,000.

$9000 +

NOTE: *The price paid at Guernsey's for this half-sheet is a record. I have never seen this particular film realize a higher bid at auction or through a dealer.* The Invisible Man *is perhaps one of the most sought after posters in the movie memorabilia market.*

Invisible Ray, The, 1936, UNIV, Boris Karloff, Bela Lugosi, window card, rare, good, Guernsey's, April 1989, $1000.

$2500–$3500

Iron Major, The, 1943, RKO, Pat O'Brien, title card, fine, Paper Collectibles & Memorabilia Show, April 1989, $10. $10–$25

Iron Man, 1931, MGM, Lew Ayres, Jean Harlow, window card, Guernsey's, April 1989, $800. $1200–$1500

It Came From Beneath the Sea, 1955, COL, Faith Domergue, Kenneth Tobey, one-sheet, Camden House, May 1989, $125.

$100–$150

NOTE: *This is the poster with Ray Harryhausen's giant animated octopus attacking San Francisco. Faith Domergue was a protégé of Howard Hughes whom he kept under wraps until a suitable role was found for her. The movies she eventually made were "Bs" and released in the late 1940s and 1950s. She was not particularly gifted as an actress.*

It Happens Every Spring, 1949, 20th, Paul Douglas, Ray Milland, Jean Peters, one-sheet, Collectors' Showcase, February 1989, $64. $75–$100

★

NOTE: *Jean Peters married Howard Hughes on March 29, 1954, and retired from films shortly thereafter.*

★

Ivanhoe, 1952, MGM, Robert Taylor, Elizabeth Taylor, Joan Fontaine, six scene cards, Guernsey's, April 1989, $45.

$50–$75

I Want to Live, 1958, UA, Susan Hayward, Theodore Bikel, title card, Poster Mail Auction Co., February 1989, $11. $10–$35

Jeanne Eagels, 1957, COL, Kim Novak, Jeff Chandler, one-sheet, very good, Poster Mail Auction Co., February 1989, $10.

$35–$55

Jeanne Eagles, 1957, half-sheet, Collectors' Showcase, October 1988, $55. $60–$80

Johnny Allegro, 1949, COL, George Raft, Nina Foch, scene card, Poster Mail Auction Co., February 1989, $8. $5–$15

Julius Caesar, 1953, MGM, Marlon Brando, Louis Calhern, three-sheet, Camden House, May 1989, $175. $225–$275

Killers, The, 1946, UNIV, Burt Lancaster, Ava Gardner, 18″ × 14″ Belgian poster, linen-backed, Camden House, May 1989, $75.

$100–$150

★

NOTE: *This movie was based on a short story by Ernest Hemingway.*

★

King for a Night, 1933, UNIV, Helen Twelvetrees and Chester Morris, one-sheet, excellent, Guernsey's, April 1989, $245.

$250–$350

★

NOTE: *Twelvetrees acted in films during the early 1930s. Her roles often called for her to be "weepy." Memorabilia of Twelvetrees rarely comes on the market.*

★

King Kong, 1952, RKO, re-release, three-sheet, duotone, framed, fair, Camden House, May 1989, $450. $300–$500

King's Row, 1942, WB, Ann Sheridan, Ronald Reagan, Robert Cummings, Betty Field, one-sheet, Guernsey's, April 1989, $300. $700–$900

NOTE: This was the film that made Ronald Reagan a "star." It was also the movie in which Reagan has a scene in which, upon discovering that his legs have been amputated, screams: "Where's the rest of me!?" Legend has it that he rehearsed this line for several weeks before the scene was actually filmed, and years later used the line for the title of his autobiography. Despite its powerful performances and controversial elements of murder, madness, and sadism, King's Row was only moderately successful at the box office. The studio held up its release for a year because they were afraid of the effect it might have on the public in a time of war.

Kismet, 1944, MGM, Marlene Dietrich, Ronald Coleman, one-sheet, Guernsey's, April 1989, $125. $150–$200

Kitty, 1946, PAR, Paulette Goddard, Ray Milland, one-sheet, good, Collectors' Showcase, September 1988, $69. $75–$95

Klondike Annie, 1936, PAR, Mae West, window card, excellent, Guernsey's, April 1989, $375. $600–$700

NOTE: Had this been a one- or three-sheet poster, it would have sold higher in the price range. In 1986, a collector could have bought this window card for under $200.

VERONICA LAKE

Photo courtesy of Camden House, Los Angeles, CA

Veronica Lake, 1946, French stone lithographed poster, Soubie art, very famous poster, 22″ × 24″, Camden House, May 1989, $450. $300–$500

Larceny, Inc., 1942, WB, Edward G. Robinson, Jane Wyman, scene card, Guernsey's, April 1989, $25. $100–$125

La Ronde, 1964, Jane Fonda, 60″ × 48″ French poster, Camden House, May 1989, $125. $150–$200

Last Outpost, The, 1935, PAR, Cary Grant, Claude Rains, window card, good, Guernsey's, April 1989, $70. $150–$200

Lawless Code, 1949, MON, Jimmy Wakely, three-sheet, good, Poster Mail Auction Co., February 1989, $16. $35–$45

Leave Her to Heaven, 1945, 20th, Gene Tierney, Cornel Wilde, one-sheet, Guernsey's, April 1989, $650.   *$900–$1000*

Let It Be, 1970, UA, the Beatles, six-sheet (folded), excellent, Phillips, December 1988, $500.   *$500–$700*

Let's Dance, 1950, PAR, Fred Astaire, Betty Hutton, half-sheet, very good, Guernsey's, April 1989, $80.   *$100–$150*

Let's Make Love, 1960, 20th, Marilyn Monroe, Yves Montand, three-sheet, fair, Camden House, May 1989, $175. *$250–$300*

Letter From an Unknown Woman, 1948, UNIV, Joan Fontaine, Louis Jourdan, 47″ × 63″ French poster, designed by Belin, linen-backed, Guernsey's, April 1989, $225.   *$300–$400*

Life of Riley, The, 1949, UNIV, William Bendix, James Gleason, title card and six scene cards, Guernsey's, April 1989, $25.
          $75–$100

Little Colonel, The, 1935, FOX, Shirley Temple, Lionel Barrymore, Bill Robinson, one-sheet, French, linen-backed, excellent, Phillips, December 1988, $250.   *$250–$500*

Littlest Rebel, The, 1935, 20th, Shirley Temple, window card, Guernsey's, April 1989, $150.   *$300–$500*

NOTE: *Wide price range for this window card but, despite some water damage that did not affect the poster's image, the buyer received a bargain.*

Live and Let Die, 1973, UA, Roger Moore, Jane Seymour, three-sheet, good, Wex Rex Records & Collectibles, May 1989, $35.
          $35–$60

NOTE: *The first James Bond film starring Roger Moore as 007, who replaced Sean Connery. Moore went on to film six more Bond movies.*

Lolita, 1962, MGM, Peter Sellers, James Mason, Sue Lyon, Shelly Winters, 63" × 47" Roger Soubie poster, mint, Poster Mail Auction Co., February 1989, $2500.   *$800–$1200*

NOTE: Considering that this poster was designed in 1962, it was very erotic for its time. Originally banned in Paris, Lolita was controversial almost everywhere it played. It was based on the novel by Vladimir Nabokov and directed by Stanley Kubrick.

Lolita, 1962, complete set of lobby cards, Guernsey's, April 1989, $100.   *$100–$200*

Lone Ranger, The, 1956, WB, Clayton Moore, Jay Silverheels, half-sheet, Guernsey's, April 1989, $100.   *$150–$200*

Louisa, 1950, UNIV, Ronald Reagan, Ruth Hussey, one-sheet, excellent, Phillips, December 1988, $100.   *$150–$200*

Love Is a Many-Splendored Thing, 1955, 20th, William Holden, Jennifer Jones, title card, Poster Mail Auction Co., February 1989, $12.   *$10–$20*

NOTE: Jones received her fifth Academy Award nomination for this film, which won the Oscar for best song and best original music score. The actress won her own Oscar for The Song of Bernadette *(1943).*

Love Me Tender, 1956, 20th, Elvis Presley, Debra Paget, Richard Egan, one-sheet, Camden House, May 1989, $225.

$150–$200

Loves of Sunya, The, 1927, UA, Gloria Swanson, John Boles, insert, Christie's East, June 1989, $880.   *$500–$700*

NOTE: *This insert was a profile portrait of Swanson and co-star, John Boles, over a bubble on a rainbow background. The movie was the first that Swanson made as an independent producer with her own production company, Gloria Swanson, Inc. It released its films through UA and was financed by Joseph P. Kennedy (father of John and Bobby), who was la Swanson's lover and mentor at the time.*

Lucky Devils, 1940, UNIV, Richard Arlen, Andy Devine, title card, very good, Paper Collectibles & Memorabilia Show, May 1989, $10.   *$10–$25*

Lucky Stiff, The, 1949, UA, Dorothy Lamour, Brian Donlevy, scene card, Poster Mail Auction Co., February 1989, $6.

          $5–$12

NOTE: *There was nothing "lucky" about this dreadful movie. The "sarong" girl of PAR (1936–1947), Lamour had gone independent in 1948 but chose one clinker after another. This was one of them.*

Madame Mystery, 1926, Pathe, Theda Bara, Tyler Brooke, complete set of black and white lobby cards, Guernsey's, April 1989, $300.   *$300–$500*

NOTE: *Theda had been the screen's first film vamp at FOX (1914–1919). This comedy by Hal Roach was supposed to be a spoof of her vamp image but unfortunately it didn't turn out that way. Oliver Hardy played the role of Captain Schmaltz, and that just about sums up* Madame Mystery—*schmaltzy.*

Photo courtesy of Camden House, Los Angeles, CA

Maltese Falcon, The, 1941, WB, Humphrey Bogart, Mary Astor, Peter Lorre, Sydney Greenstreet, 63″ × 47″ French poster, linen-backed, Camden House, May 1989, $1400.   *$300–$400*

NOTE: *Brilliant poster. One of the best for a great movie. Title is in French but the actors' names are in English.*

Man From Colorado, The, 1948, COL, William Holden, Glenn Ford, title card, Poster Mail Auction Co., February 1989, $10.

$8–$15

Manhattan Melodrama, 1934, MGM, Clark Gable, Myrna Loy, William Powell, half-sheet, excellent, Guernsey's, April 1989, $1800. $2000–$2500

Mansfield, Jayne, circa 1955, "door poster," 22″ × 62″, rare, Guernsey's, April 1989, $125. $200–$300

★

NOTE: *Mansfield has become a hot commodity in the movie memorabilia marketplace. This poster is of a life-sized Jayne dressed in a bikini.*

★

Mantan Runs for Mayor, 1946, Goldmark Productions, Mantan Moreland, and *Look-Out Sister,* 1946, Astor Pictures, Louis "Two Gun" Jordan, Suzette Harbin, two broadsides, fair, Richard Opfer, February 1989, $65. $60–$80

★

NOTE: *Both posters are damaged; had they been in better condition, the price range would have been higher. "Race" movies appeal to collectors of both movie and black memorabilia.*

Mantan Moreland appeared in some 300 movies and is best remembered as the chauffeur in the Charlie Chan mystery series. Mantan Runs for Mayor *was one of his best comedy "race" movies. He was a gifted comedian who mastered the doubletake in perfect time and was able to run in place. He also made comedy albums for the "race" market.*

Louis Jordan was a jazz star who played in Chick Webb's orchestra, circa 1936, and performed vocals with Ella Fitzgerald. He recorded duets with Bing Crosby and Louis Armstrong before forming his own group in 1938. Jordan was a major influence on rhythm-and-blues artists such as Chuck Berry, Ray Charles, and Little Richard in the 1950s. Besides Look-Out Sister, *he appeared in* Beware *(1946),* Caldonia *(1945), and* Reet, Petite and Gone *(1947).*

★

Marrying Kind, The, 1952, COL, Judy Holliday, Aldo Ray, title card, Poster Mail Auction Co., February 1989, $10. $5–$15

★

NOTE: *Holliday won the best actress Academy Award for her role of the not-so-dumb blonde in 1950s* Born Yesterday.

★

Mary Poppins, 1964, Walt Disney Productions, complete set of lobby cards, original envelope, mint, Collectors' Showcase, November 1988, $148. *$75–$100*

Maynard, Ken, 1940, Cole Brothers Circus, Erie Lithograph & Printing Co., half-sheet, Greenwich Auction Room, June 1989, $125.. *$150–$200*

Meet John Doe, 1941, WB, Gary Cooper, Barbara Stanwyck, scene card, fine, Collectors' Showcase, November 1988, $48.
$40–$60

Melody Time, 1948, RKO, Walt Disney Productions, Roy Rogers, Dennis Day, Frances Langford, the Andrews Sisters, animated feature, one-sheet, Collectors' Showcase, December 1988, $100. *$150–$200*

Men in White, 1934, MGM, Clark Gable, Myrna Loy, half-sheet, mint, Guernsey's, April 1989, $800. *$2000–$2500*

Menace of the Mystery Metal, 1951, COL (Captain Video), Chapter Ten: "Master of the Stratosphere," scene card, very good, Poster Mail Auction Co., February 1989, $25. *$25–$35*

Midsummer Night's Dream, A, 1935, WB, James Cagney, Olivia de Havilland, Mickey Rooney, window card, fine, Guernsey's, April 1989, $125. *$200–$250*

Mighty Joe Young, 1949, RKO, Terry Moore, Ben Johnson, one-sheet, good, Collectors' Showcase, December 1988, $292.
$150–$200

Miracle on 34th Street, 1947, 20th, John Payne, Maureen O'Hara, Edmund Gwenn, Natalie Wood, one-sheet, rare, Guernsey's, April 1989, $425. *$600–$800*

Misleading Lady, The, 1932, PAR, Claudette Colbert, Edmund Lowe, half-sheet, mint, Guernsey's, April 1989, $2500.
$700–$900

★

NOTE: *Beautiful design on this poster. Rare to find in such top-notch condition.*

Modern Times, 1936, UA, Charles Chaplin, Paulette Goddard, window card, Guernsey's, April 1989, $2250.   *$2000–$2500*

Monroe, Marilyn, 1972, pair of promotional posters, 18 ″ × 24 ″, Camden House, May 1989, $175.   *$75–$100*

Monsieur Verdoux, 1947, UA, Charles Chaplin, Martha Raye, 40 ″ × 30 ″ British Quad, Guernsey's, April 1989, $150.

$200–$300

Montana Incident, 1952, MON, Whip Wilson, Rand Brooks, three-sheet, excellent, Poster Mail Auction Co., February 1989, $20.   *$40–$60*

Moon's Our Home, The, 1936, PAR, Margaret Sullivan, Henry Fonda, one-sheet, excellent, Guernsey's, April 1989, $400.

$300–$400

Mother Wore Tights, 1947, 20th, Betty Grable, Dan Dailey, title card and six scene cards, Guernsey's, April 1989, $35.

$125–$175

Mr. Blandings Builds His Dream House, 1948, Selznick, Myrna Loy, Cary Grant, complete set of lobby cards (eight), Guernsey's, April 1989, $70.   *$75–$125*

Mr. Smith Goes to Washington, 1939, COL, James Stewart, Jean Arthur, Claude Rains, scene card, Paper Collectables & Memorabilia Show, November 1988, $200.   *$175–$250*

Mummy, The, 1932, UNIV, Boris Karloff, Zita Johann, title card, very fine, Collectors' Showcase, October 1988, $8784.

$2000–?

★

NOTE: *Despite a pinhole in the mummy's forehead, this title card could, according to Collectors' Showcase, be the finest title card in existence. Highly sought after by collectors.*

★

My American Wife, 1923, PAR, Gloria Swanson, Antonio Moreno, half-sheet, very fine, Collectors' Showcase, January 1989, $400.   *$500–$700*

Mysterious Mr. Wong, The, 1935, MON, Bela Lugosi, scene card, fine, Collectors' Showcase, March 1989, $121.   *$95–$125*

Nabonga ("Gorilla"), 1944, PRC, Buster Crabbe, Fifi D'Orsay, one-sheet, Camden House, May 1989, $100.   *$100–$150*

NOTE: *Singer and actress Julie London debuted in this film.*

Naughty Marietta, 1935, MGM, Jeanette MacDonald, Nelson Eddy, window card, Guernsey's, April 1989, $175.   *$150–$250*

Night and the City, 1950, 20th, Richard Widmark, Gene Tierney, complete set of lobby cards (eight), Guernsey's, April 1989, $70.   *$150–$200*

Night at the Opera, A, 1948 (re-release), MGM, the Marx Brothers, three-sheet, linen-backed, fair, Camden House, May 1989, $375.   *$250–$300*

Nightmare Alley, 1947, 20th, Tyrone Power, Joan Blondell, insert, Guernsey's, April 1989, $100.   *$200–$300*

Nob Hill, 1945, 20th, George Raft, Joan Bennett, complete set of lobby cards, Guernsey's, April 1989, $25.   *$150–$200*

NOTE: *The buyer received a bargain.*

No Man of Her Own, 1932, Clark Gable, Carole Lombard, Dorothy Mackaill, 33″ × 25″ French stone lithographed poster, linen-backed, Camden House, May 1989, $800.   *$800-$1000*

None But the Brave, 1965, WB, Frank Sinatra, Clint Walker, Tommy Sands, scene card, fair, Jerry Ohlinger's Movie Material Store, October 1988, $15.   *$8-$12*

North by Northwest, 1959, MGM, Cary Grant, Eve Marie Saint, James Mason, scene card, fine, Collectors' Showcase, September 1988, $72.   *$45-$60*

NOTE: *This lobby card depicts the actor Cary Grant stalked by a crop-dusting plane in one of the movie's most famous scenes. The entire sequence, which takes place in an Indiana cornfield, runs over nine minutes and forty seconds and comprised some 131 camera shots.*

Now Voyager, 1942, WB, Bette Davis, Paul Henreid, 63″ × 47″ French stone lithographed poster, linen-backed, Camden House, May 1989, $475.   *$900-$1200*

O. Henry's Full House, 1952, 20th, Marilyn Monroe, David Wayne, Charles Laughton, one-sheet, Guernsey's, April 1989, $70.   *$200-$300*

On the Waterfront, 1954, COL, Marlon Brando, Eve Marie Saint, Rod Steiger, Lee J. Cobb, half-sheet, framed, Camden House, May 1989, $300.   *$300-$500*

On the Waterfront, 1954, one-sheet, framed, Camden House, May 1989, $250.   *$300–$400*

Photo courtesy of Camden House, Los Angeles, CA

Original Katzenjammer Kids, The, early cartoon comedy, one-sheet, rare, Camden House, May 1989, $400.   *$500–$600*

Outlaw, The, 1943, RKO, Jane Russell, Jack Buetel, Walter Huston, 13″ × 20″ original issue Italian poster (1949), scarce, very good, Poster Mail Auction Co., February 1989, $128.

$100–$150

NOTE: This movie has a history almost as long and complicated as Gone With the Wind. Suffice it to say that it has never been proved that Howard Hughes really discovered Jane Russell, as the director, Howard Hawks, was supposedly the recipient of that honor. Russell, who was a receptionist in a dentist's office before she was "discovered," was signed to do The Outlaw *in the fall of 1940. The picture ran into Hughes and didn't complete production until the fall of 1941. There was a massive publicity campaign before, during, and after the picture was shot, including a run-in with the Hays Office which insisted the movie had to be re-edited.* The Outlaw *had its world premiere in San Francisco in February 1943. It caused such a ruckus that it was pulled from the theater within a few weeks (although the movie was panned, the public turned out in droves). It wasn't seen again until 1946, when it was again pulled from distribution. It resurfaced for another go-round in September 1949, but by then nobody was really interested anymore.*

Outlaw Roundup, 1944, PRC, Dave O'Brien, Jim Newill, one-sheet, excellent, Poster Mail Auction Co., February 1989, $27.

$50–$75

Palm Beach Story, The, 1942, PAR, Claudette Colbert, Joel McCrea, Mary Astor, Rudy Vallee, three-sheet, linen-backed, excellent, Phillips, December 1988, $1000.   *$1000–$2000*

NOTE: Joel McCrea signed the poster.

Photo courtesy of Camden House, Los Angeles, CA

Pals of the Saddle, 1938, REP, John Wayne, Ray "Crash" Corrigan, three-sheet, linen-backed, Camden House, May 1989, $1250.   *$1200–$1400*

Paris Blues, 1961, UA, Paul Newman, Joanne Woodward, one-sheet, very good, Poster Mail Auction Co., February 1989, $10.
                                                                $35–$40

Paris Honeymoon, 1939, PAR, Bing Crosby, three-sheet, linen-backed, Camden House, May 1989, $325.   *$200–$300*

Paris Interlude, 1934, MGM, Robert Young, Madge Evans, half-sheet, excellent, Guernsey's, April 1989, $200.   *$200–$300*

Pat and Mike, 1952, MGM, Spencer Tracy, Katharine Hepburn, Aldo Ray, three-sheet, linen-backed, Camden House, May 1989, $175.   *$250–$350*

Pay Day, 1922, FN, Charlie Chaplin, half-sheet, linen-backed, very rare, Guernsey's, April 1989, $2500.   *$3000–$3500*

Pearl of Death, The, 1944, UNIV, Basil Rathbone, Nigel Bruce, Evelyn Ankers, complete set of lobby cards, excellent, Phillips, December 1988, $600.   *$1000–$1500*

Perils of Pauline, The, 1914, Pathe, Pearl White, one-sheet, linen-backed, Guernsey's, April 1989, $8500.   *$3500–$4000*

NOTE: *Born in 1889, Pearl White began her career with a small company of touring players before appearing in silent films, initially with Powers Film Co., and then with the Lubin Co. before working briefly at Pathe. She became a major comedy actress with the Crystal Film Co., circa 1911–14, and in 1914 returned to Pathe to work on the first of her famous serials. Produced with financial backing by William Randolph Hearst, who also had a hand in naming the series, the pictures were immensely popular with World War I audiences. The actress also made a few features for both Pathe and FOX before retiring in the mid-1920s. She died in 1938 without ever having set foot in California, as all her movies were filmed in New York.*

Picnic, 1955, COL, William Holden, Kim Novak, Rosalind Russell, Cliff Robertson, one-sheet, framed, Camden House, May 1989, $200.   *$200–$250*

Picnic, 1955, insert, Collectors' Showcase, December 1988, $68.   *$75–$100*

NOTE: *Kim Novak was the last of the "manufactured" stars. She was signed by Harry Cohn of COL to put the heat on the troublesome Rita Hayworth. She soon eclipsed Hayworth in audience popularity.* Picnic *made Novak a star and she is at her loveliest in this film.*

Pinky, 1949, 20th, Jeanne Crain, William Lundigan, Ethel Waters, title card and six scene cards, Guernsey's, April 1989, $35.
                                                $100–$150

NOTE: *Controversial for its time with its theme of miscegenation. Crain was nominated for an Academy Award for her role in this movie—the best of her career.*

Pinocchio, 1945, RKO (Walt Disney Productions), reissue, one-sheet, animated feature, Guernsey's, April 1989, $475.

$300–$400

★

NOTE: *What collectors will pay for Disney reissues!*

★

Possessed, 1947, WB, Joan Crawford, Van Heflin, Raymond Massey, scene card, fine, Paper Collectables & Memorabilia Show, November 1988, $10.   *$10–$20*

Postman Always Rings Twice, The, 1946, MGM, John Garfield, Lana Turner, one-sheet, framed, Camden House, May 1989, $700.   *$750–$1000*

★

NOTE: *This was the original version of the racy James M. Cain novel translated to the screen. Still the best, too.*

★

Prairie Raiders, 1947, COL, Charles Starrett, Smiley Burnette, one-sheet, very good, Poster Mail Auction Co., February 1989, $15.   *$50–$65*

Prince and the Showgirl, The, 1957, WB, Marilyn Monroe, Laurence Olivier, scene card, good, Collectors' Showcase, November 1988, $99.   *$75–$95*

Princess and the Pirate, The, 1944, RKO, Bob Hope, Virginia Mayo, one-sheet, fine, Collectors' Showcase, November 1988, $80.   *$75–$95*

Prisoner of Zenda, The, 1952, MGM, Stewart Granger, Deborah Kerr, complete set of lobby cards, Guernsey's, April 1989, $25.
$100–$150

Private Lives of Elizabeth and Essex, 1939, WB, Bette Davis, Errol Flynn, Olivia de Havilland, 63″ × 47″ French stone lithographed poster, linen-backed, Camden House, May 1989, $425.   *$1000–$1200*

NOTE: *Poster features Errol Flynn but neither of his co-stars. Had Ms. Davis been present, the purchase price would have been higher. The price range is actually quite liberal given only Flynn's appearance on the poster.*

Pygmy Island, 1950, COL, Johnny Weissmuller, title card, Poster Mail Auction Co., February 1989, $11.   *$25–$35*

Rancho Notorious, 1952, RKO, Marlene Dietrich, Mel Ferrer, Arthur Kennedy, half-sheet, Guernsey's, April 1989, $70.
$100–$200

Ranger of Cherokee Strip, 1949, REP, Monte Hale, three-sheet, good, Poster Mail Auction Co., February 1989, $12.   *$40–$65*

JAMES DEAN "REBEL WITHOUT A CAUSE"
CinemaScope and WarnerColor

Photo courtesy of Camden House, Los Angeles, CA

Rebel Without a Cause, 1955, WB, James Dean, Sal Mineo, Natalie Wood, four lobby cards, Camden House, May 1989, $400.
$350–$400

NOTE: *The picture that influenced a nation of rebellious teenagers. A classic!*

Reckless, 1935, MGM, Jean Harlow, William Powell, window card, Guernsey's, April 1989, $400. $900–$1200

NOTE: *Water damage and pinholes lessened the price this particular poster would ordinarily achieve. Price range is really for a poster in excellent condition.*

Red River Robin, 1942, RKO, Tim Holt, one-sheet, good, Poster Mail Auction Co., February 1989, $25. $50–$75

Red Shoes, The, 1948, Eagle-Lion, Moira Shearer, one-sheet, rare, Guernsey's, April 1989, $500.   *$300–$500*

Remember the Day, 1941, 20th, Claudette Colbert, John Payne, scene card, Poster Mail Auction Co., February 1989, $25.

$35–$50

Revenge of Frankenstein, 1958, COL, Peter Cushing, Eunice Grayson, complete set of lobby cards, very good, Black Mountain Antique Center, June 1988, $125.   *$90–$150*

NOTE: *Eunice Grayson turned up as James Bond's girlfriend in* Dr. No *(1962) and* From Russia With Love *(1963).*

Revenge of the Creature, 1955, UNIV, John Agar, Lori Nelson, scene card, framed, Guernsey's, April 1989, $70.   *$75–$125*

NOTE: *The card pictures the creature taking a swim.*

Riders of the Deadline, 1943, UA, William Boyd as Hopalong Cassidy, one-sheet, Camden House, May 1989, $200.

$150–$200

Riffraff, 1936, MGM, Jean Harlow, Spencer Tracy, one-sheet of Jean Harlow, Guernsey's, April 1989, $450.   *$800–$1000*

Rio Grande, 1950, REP, John Wayne, Maureen O'Hara, Ben Johnson, 63″ × 47″ French stone lithographed poster, linen-backed, Camden House, May 1989, $300.   *$400–$500*

NOTE: *Graphic design on this poster by Cartier Dargouge.*

River of No Return, 1954, 20th, Marilyn Monroe, Robert Mitchum, Rory Calhoun, title card and two scene cards, all featuring Monroe, taped on back, Camden House, May 1989, $50.

$75–$100

Road to Bali, 1952, PAR, Bing Crosby, Bob Hope, Dorothy Lamour, half-sheet, very good, Collectors' Showcase, December 1988, $93. $50–$70

★

NOTE: Road to Bali *was the last of the "Road" pictures at PAR with Crosby, Hope, and Lamour* (Road to Hong Kong *in 1962 was released by UA, but Lamour only had a guest appearance in the movie).*

★

Road to Morocco, 1942, PAR, Crosby, Hope, and Lamour, scene card showing Lamour in a harem, fine, Collectors' Showcase, February 1989, $33. $40–$50

Road to Rio, 1947, PAR, Crosby, Hope, and Lamour, scene card, Guernsey's, April 1989, $25. $40–$50

Road to Utopia, 1945, PAR, Crosby, Hope, and Lamour, scene card, Poster Mail Auction Co., February 1989, $25. $40–$55

Roaring Westward, 1949, MON, Jimmy Wakely, one-sheet, very good, Poster Mail Auction Co., February 1989, $16. $35–$45

Rocky, 1976, UA, Sylvester Stallone, Talia Shire, Burgess Meredith, one-sheet fight poster, black and white, mounted, framed under glass, good, Collectors' Showcase, November 1988, $82.
$100–$150

★

NOTE: Rumored to be an exclusive poster, the only one known to exist. Thank goodness!

★

Roman Spring of Mrs. Stone, The, 1961, WB, Warren Beatty, Vivien Leigh, 40″ × 60″ poster, Camden House, May 1989, $50. $50–$75

Romance in Manhattan, 1934, RKO, Ginger Rogers, Francis Lederer, window card, excellent, Guernsey's, April 1989, $250.
$200–$400

NOTE: *The poster design is of Ginger surrounded by a bevy of men's faces.*

Romeo and Juliet, 1936, MGM, Norma Shearer, Leslie Howard, John Barrymore, mini-window card (8″ × 12″), rare, very fine, Collectors' Showcase, December 1988, $155.   *$80–$100*

Rough House, The, 1917, PAR (produced by the Comique Film Corporation), Roscoe "Fatty" Arbuckle, Buster Keaton, Alice Lake, sepia scene card, very good, Collectors' Showcasae, February 1989, $94.   *$50–$100*

NOTE: The Rough House *was filmed at the Norma Talmadge Film Corporation studios at 318 East 48th Street, New York.*

Rustlers on Horseback, 1950, REP, Allan "Rocky" Lane, one-sheet, good, Poster Mail Auction Co., February 1989, $16.
$35–$50

Rustler's Roundup, The, 1933, FOX, Tom Mix and his pony, Tony, Jr., half-sheet, good, Guernsey's, April 1989, $125.
$200–$300

Saigon, 1948, PAR, Alan Ladd, Veronica Lake, one-sheet, Guernsey's, April 1989, $125.   *$150–$200*

NOTE: *Alan Ladd and Veronica Lake appeared together in three other PAR movies including* This Gun For Hire *and* The Glass Key *(1942), and* The Blue Dahlia *(1946).*

Salty O'Rourke, 1945, PAR, Alan Ladd, Gail Russell, one-sheet, fine, Collectors' Showcase, January 1989, $59.   *$60–$90*

Samson and Delilah, 1949, Victor Mature, Hedy Lamarr (the DeMille epic), one-sheet, Guernsey's, April 1989, $225.

$250–$300

San Antonio, 1945, WB, Errol Flynn, Alexis Smith, one-sheet, Camden House, May 1989, $225. $300–$400

Santa Fe Passage, 1955, REP, John Payne, Faith Domergue, Rod Cameron, title card, Poster Auction Mail Co., February 1989, $10. $8–$12

Scarlet Empress, 1934, PAR, Marlene Dietrich, Louise Dresser, John Lodge, Belgian electrotype poster, 33½" × 24", linen-backed, beautifully colored, Camden House, May 1989, $1500.

$1500–$2000

NOTE: Dietrich's daughter, Maria, made her screen debut in this movie, playing the role of Sophia Frederica. This is also the film in which Dietrich, dressed in military dress, rode a white charger up the steps of Peterhof Palace.

Scarlet Letter, The, 1926, MGM, Lillian Gish, Lars Hanson, full-color window card, Collectors' Showcase, March 1989, $330. $75–$125

Sea Chase, The, 1955, WB, John Wayne, Lana Turner, scene card, fine, Collectors' Showcase, October 1988, $31. $25–$30

Sea Hawk, The, 1940, WB, Errol Flynn, Brenda Marshall, Claude Rains, 63" × 47" French stone lithographed poster, linen-backed, Camden House, May 1989, $300. $800–$1000

Searchers, The, 1956, WB, John Wayne, Jeffrey Hunter, Vera Miles, 19" × 14" Belgian poster, linen-backed, Camden House, May 1989, $100. $150–$250

Sea Squawk, The, 1925, Pathe (Mack Sennett), Harry Langdon, one-sheet, Guernsey's, April 1989, $1000. $1000–$1200

Second Chance, 1953, RKO, Robert Mitchum, Linda Darnell, Jack Palance, insert, excellent, Simpson's, February 1989, $250. $25–$75

NOTE: *Somebody in Texas must really love Linda Darnell or Robert Mitchum to pay so much for this "B" insert. Movie was filmed in 3-D.*

Seven Year Itch, The, 1955, 20th, Marilyn Monroe, Tom Ewell, three-sheet, linen-backed, Guernsey's, April 1989, $250.

$400–$500

Seven Year Itch, The, 1955, title card, fine, Collectors' Showcase, September 1988, $188. $125–$225

NOTE: *Both the three-sheet and the title card show Marilyn with her skirt billowing. A classic scene.*

Shall We Dance, 1937, RKO, Fred Astaire, Ginger Rogers, one-sheet, rare, linen-backed, Guernsey's, April 1989, $3250.

$3500–$4000

NOTE: *Astaire and Rogers' posters from their 1930s musicals at RKO are highly desirable. Most of the couple's musical movie paper is rich in Art Deco design which makes them all the more sought after. They are very expensive, as the price paid and the price range will attest. And they keep increasing in value.*

Sheik, The, 1921, PAR, Rudolph Valentino, Agnes Ayres, insert, sepia, linen-backed, Guernsey's, April 1989, $600.

$1500–$2000

Shine on Harvest Moon, 1938, REP, Roy Rogers, Mary Hart, and Trigger (Rogers' horse), one title card and three scene cards, full-color, title card pictures Roy, Mary, and Trigger, scene cards picture Roy on Trigger, very good, Hake's, February 1989, $134.   *$75–$100*

NOTE: *Mary Hart also acted under the screen name Lynn Roberts.*

Since You Went Away, 1944, UA, Claudette Colbert, Joseph Cotten, Shirley Temple, Monty Wooley, Jennifer Jones, complete set of lobby cards, Guernsey's, April 1989, $250.
                                                                $150–$250

Singing Fool, The, 1928, WB, Al Jolson, Betty Bronson, window card, Guernsey's, April 1989, $250.   *$400–$600*

Singin' in the Rain, 1952, MGM, Gene Kelly, Debbie Reynolds, Donald O'Connor, half-sheet, framed, Camden House, May 1989, $200.   *$200–$300*

Singin' in the Rain, 1952, window card, excellent, rare, Poster Mail Auction Co., February 1989, $50.   *$50–$75*

Smilin' Through, 1941, MGM, Jeanette MacDonald, Brian Aherne, one-sheet, Guernsey's, April 1989, $180.   *$150–$250*

Snow White and the Seven Dwarfs, 1937, RKO, animated feature, scene card, Guernsey's, April 1989, $275.   *$250–$350*

Snow White and the Seven Dwarfs, 1937, one-sheet, excellent, Guernsey's, April 1989, $800.   *$900–$1200*

NOTE: *Disneyana movie paper is extremely desirable. This one-sheet is the original RKO style "A" poster.*

Some Like it Hot, 1959, UA, Marilyn Monroe, Tony Curtis, Jack Lemmon, three-sheet, Camden House, May 1989, $375.
$200–$300

NOTE: *Marilyn Monroe posters usually don't bring the high prices that signed movie memorabilia of the actress does. However, in December 1988, Christie's South Kensington Auction Gallery in London auctioned off a similar poster of Monroe in this Billy Wilder classic comedy, and the hammer price was an astounding £.2860, which translates to about $5150 in American dollars. Even more astonishing is that the price range was between £50–£100. Obviously, the bidder was either obsessed with Monroe or a fool, or maybe a bit of both.*

Somewhere in the Night, 1945, 20th, John Hodiak, Nancy Guild, title card and five scene cards, Guernsey's, April 1989, $70.
$100–$125

Son of Dracula, 1943, UNIV, Lon Chaney, Jr., scene card, shows Chaney rising from his casket, linen-backed, good, Collectors' Showcase, March 1989, $104.
$140–$160

Son of Frankenstein, 1939, UNIV, Boris Karloff, Basil Rathbone, Beli Lugosi, 18″ × 14″ Belgian poster, linen-backed, Camden House, May 1989, $175.
$100–$150

Song of the Open Road, 1944, UA, Edgar Bergen, Charlie McCarthy, Bonita Granville, W.C. Fields, three-sheet, good, Poster Mail Auction Co., $55.
$200–$300

NOTE: *Jane Powell was introduced in this movie.*

South Pacific Trail, 1952, REP, Rex Allen, one-sheet, excellent, Hake's, June 1989, $44.
$25–$50

Spawn of the North, 1938, PAR, George Raft, Henry Fonda, Dorothy Lamour, one-sheet, Guernsey's, April 1989, $150.
$150–$250

Spellbound, 1945, RKO, Ingrid Bergman, Gregory Peck, half-sheet, fine, Collectors' Showcase, November 1988, $275.
$200–$300

Spook Chasers, 1957, AA, Huntz Hall, the Bowery Boys, three-sheet, excellent, Poster Mail Auction Co., February 1989, $25.
$35–$55

Stagecoach, 1939, UA, Claire Trevor, John Wayne, Thomas Mitchell, 18″ × 14″ Belgian poster, linen-backed, Camden House, May 1989, $250. $450–$550

Stage Door Canteen, 1943, UA, all-star cast including Harpo Marx, Tallulah Bankhead, Katharine Hepburn, Mary Pickford, Johnny Weissmuller, insert, Guernsey's, April 1989, $100.
$200–$250

Stage Door Canteen, 1943, half-sheet, Guernsey's, April 1989, $50. $100–$150

Stanley and Livingston, 1939, 20th, Spencer Tracy, Nancy Kelly, Richard Greene, window card, Guernsey's, April 1989, $100.
$150–$200

Star Is Born, A, 1937, UA, Janet Gaynor, Fredric March, scene card, Collectors' Showcase, October 1988, $51. $60–$90

Star Is Born, A, 1954, WB, Judy Garland, James Mason, one-sheet, Camden House, May 1989, $850. $300–$400

State Fair, 1945, 20th, Jeanne Crain, Dana Andrews, title card, very good, Collectors' Showcase, November 1988, $30.
$30–$40

Stolen Life, A, 1946, WB, Bette Davis, Dane Clark, insert, Guernsey's, April 1989, $60. $100–$150

Story of Dr. Wassel, The, 1944, PAR, Gary Cooper, Signe Hasso, one-sheet, Camden House, May 1989, $175. $100–$200

Strawberry Blonde, The, 1941, WB, James Cagney, Rita Hayworth, Olivia de Havilland, one-sheet, Camden House, May 1989, $300. $400–$500

Suddenly It's Spring, 1946, PAR, Paulette Goddard, Fred MacMurray, one-sheet, fine, Collectors' Showcase, October 1988, $61. $95–$125

★

NOTE: *The art on this poster was drawn by Varga.*

★

Suddenly Last Summer, 1959, COL, Elizabeth Taylor, Katharine Hepburn, Montgomery Clift, six-sheet, Camden House, May 1989, $275. *$100–$250*

★

NOTE: This poster displays the famous shot of Taylor in a white swimming suit.

★

Superman, 1948, COL, original advance two-color poster for the Kirk Alyn 15-chapter serial, trimmed, rare, fair, Collectors' Showcase, November 1988, $972. *$100–$200*

★

NOTE: Superman movie memorabilia is very collectible and usually relatively expensive. Apparently a collector wanted this particular poster badly enough to shell out almost a thousand dollars. The price range is low because the poster had much wear, tape, and soiling.

★

Surrender, 1950, REP, Vera Hruba Ralston, Walter Brennan, John Carroll, title card, Poster Mail Auction Co., February 1989, $5. *$4–$10*

★

NOTE: Ralston was the wife of Herbert J. Yates (President of REP).

★

Suzy, 1936, MGM, Jean Harlow, Cary Grant, Franchot Tone, scene card, mint, Collectors' Showcase, December 1988, $257. *$125–$150*

Sweet Bird of Youth, 1962, MGM, Paul Newman, Geraldine Page, Shirley Knight, one-sheet, Camden House, May 1989, $100. *$40–$60*

Swing Time, 1936, RKO, Fred Astaire, Ginger Rogers, scene card, mint, Collectors' Showcase, October 1988, $662. *$200–$250*

Talk of the Town, The, 1942, RKO, Gary Grant, Jean Arthur, Ronald Coleman, insert, linen-backed, Guernsey's, April 1989, $175. *$200–$250*

Tarzan Finds a Son, 1939, MGM, Johnny Weissmuller, Maureen O'Sullivan, Johnny Sheffield, lobby scene card, matted, framed, Guernsey's, April 1989, $60. *$150–$250*

Tea and Sympathy, 1956, MGM, Deborah Kerr, John Kerr, one-sheet, Camden House, May 1989, $75. *$50–$100*

Ten North Frederick, 1958, 20th, Gary Cooper, Suzy Parker, Diane Varsi, title card, Poster Mail Auction Co., April 1989, $10. *$8–$20*

Tender Is the Night, 1961, 20th, Jennifer Jones, Jason Robards, Jr., Joan Fontaine, scene card, Paper Collectables & Memorabilia Show, January 1989, $3. *$3–$10*

NOTE: *Based on F. Scott Fitzgerald's last complete novel written in his lifetime.*

Thank Your Lucky Stars, 1943, WB, Bette Davis, Humphrey Bogart, Errol Flynn, John Garfield, complete set of lobby cards, Guernsey's, April 1989, $90. *$200–$300*

That's the Way It Is, 1970, MGM, Elvis Presley documentary, three-sheet, Camden House, May 1989, $75. *$100–$150*

Them, 1954, WB, Edmund Gwenn, Joan Weldon, James Arness, scene card, Paper Collectables & Memorabilia Show, June 1989, $20. *$10–$25*

NOTE: *Scene card does not picture the ants. Price range and seller price would be higher for movie paper picturing the ants.*

This Above All, 1942, 20th, Tyrone Power, Joan Fontaine, one-sheet, excellent, Guernsey's, April 1989, $750. *$500–$700*

This Above All, 1942, insert, Guernsey's, April 1989, $200. *$200–$250*

Three for Bedroom C, 1952, WB, Gloria Swanson, complete set of lobby cards, Guernsey's, April 1989, $25. *$50–$75*

Three Caballeros, The, 1944, RKO (Walt Disney Productions), Donald Duck, Joe Carioca, animated film, one-sheet, Guernsey's, April 1989, $275.   *$300–$400*

Three Musketeers, The, 1948, MGM, Gene Kelly, Lana Turner, Van Heflin, insert, Guernsey's, April 1989, $70.   *$150–$200*

Time Machine, The, 1960, MGM, Rod Taylor, Yvette Mimieux, scene card, Poster Mail Auction Co., February 1989, $25.
                                                     $20–$30

To Be or Not To Be, 1942, UA, Carole Lombard, Jack Benny, 63″ × 47″ French stone lithographed poster, featuring Duccio Marvasi art, linen-backed, Camden House, May 1989, $325.
                                                     $300–$500

To Have and Have Not, 1944, WB, Humphrey Bogart, Lauren Bacall, three-sheet, linen-backed, Guernsey's, April 1989, $1500.   *$700–$900*

Tom Jones, 1963, UA, Albert Finney, Dame Edith Evans, Hugh Griffith, one-sheet, framed, Camden House, May 1989, $50.
                                                     $100–$150

Tonight and Every Night, 1945, COL, Rita Hayworth, Lee Bowman, Janet Blair, one-sheet, Guernsey's, April 1989, $175.
                                                     $200–$250

Tortilla Flat, 1942, MGM, Spencer Tracy, Hedy Lamarr, John Garfield, half-sheet, Guernsey's, April 1989, $160.
                                                     $200–$300

Toy Wife, The, 1938, MGM, Luise Rainer, Robert Young, complete set of lobby cards, excellent, Phillips, December 1988, $250.   *$200–$300*

Trail's End, 1949, MON, Johnny Mack Brown, Max Terhune, three-sheet, very good, Poster Mail Auction Co., February 1989, $25.   *$50–$75*

Treasure Island, 1934, MGM, Wallace Beery, Jackie Cooper, half-sheet, fine, Guernsey's, April 1989, $125.   *$200–$300*

Treasure Island, 1950, Walt Disney Productions, title card and five scene cards, Guernsey's, April 1989, $25.   *$50–$100*

Treasure of the Sierra Madre, 1948, WB, Humphrey Bogart, Walter Huston, Tim Holt, 63″ × 47″ French stone lithographed poster, Rene Paron artwork, linen-backed, Camden House, May 1989, $400.   *$500–$700*

Triple Justice, 1940, RKO, one-sheet, George O'Brien, one-sheet, Poster Mail Auction Co., February 1989, $25.   *$40–$65*

Two-Faced Woman, 1941, MGM, Greta Garbo, Melvyn Douglas, Constance Bennett, half-sheet, Guernsey's, April 1989, $250.   *$200–$300*

NOTE: Garbo's image is very prominent on this poster. This was her last film.

Unholy Three, The, 1925, MGM, Lon Chaney, window card, scarce, Guernsey's, April 1989, $150.   *$300–$500*

Union Pacific, 1939, PAR, Barbara Stanwyck, Joel McCrea, Robert Preston, four scene cards, Guernsey's, April 1989, $30.
                                                    $200–$300

Utah Wagon Train, 1951, REP, Rex Allen, one-sheet, very good, Poster Mail Auction Co., February 1989, $15.   *$25–$45*

Vertigo, 1958, PAR, James Stewart, Kim Novak, Barbara Bel Geddes, one-sheet, Camden House, May 1989, $325.
                                                    $200–$250

NOTE: Saul Bass designed the artwork for this arresting poster with its compelling graphics. Alfred Hitchcock directed the movie.

Very Honorable Guy, A, 1934, FN, Joe E. Brown, Alice White, half-sheet, Guernsey's, April 1989, $375.   *$200–$300*

NOTE: Joe E. Brown was the comedian with the outsized mouth. He was under contract to WB/FN in the late 1920s–early 1930s.

Vigil in the Night, 1940, RKO, Carole Lombard, Brian Aherne, Anne Shirley, half-sheet, Guernsey's, April 1989, $80.

$150–$200

Village Vampire, The, 1918, Triangle, Fred Mace, one-sheet, linen-backed, excellent, Guernsey's, April 1989, $650.

$500–$700

Voodoo Island, 1957, UNIV, Boris Karloff, Beverly Garland, Murvyn Vye, title card, Poster Mail Auction Co., February 1989, $15.   *$15–$30*

NOTE: *Horror movies of the late 1950s are becoming very collectible movie paper. Prices are increasing as more collectors discover the genre.*

Washington Masquerade, The, 1932, Lionel Barrymore, half-sheet, mint, Guernsey's, April 1989, $350.   *$300–$500*

Way of All Flesh, The, 1927, PAR, Emil Jannings, scene card, very fine, Collectors' Showcase, October 1988, $102.

$100–$150

NOTE: *Jannings won the first Academy Award for best actor for his performance in this film, and also for* The Last Command *(PAR, 1928).*

West of the Pecos, 1945, RKO, Robert Mitchum, Barbara Hale, complete set of lobby cards, Guernsey's, April 1989, $40.

$75–$100

Westerner, The, 1940, UA, Gary Cooper, Walter Brennan, Doris Davenport, title card and six scene cards, Guernsey's, April 1989, $100.   *$400–$600*

NOTE: *Walter Brennan won his third Academy Award for best supporting actor for his role in this movie. His other wins included* Come and Get It *(1936),* the picture that also introduced Frances Farmer, *and* Kentucky *(1938).*

When Ladies Meet, 1941, MGM, Joan Crawford, Robert Taylor, Greer Garson, one-sheet, linen-backed, Guernsey's, April 1989, $150. *$200–$300*

When Worlds Collide, 1951, PAR, Richard Derr, Barbara Rush, three-sheet, rare, linen-backed, Guernsey's, April 1989, $600.
$1000–$1500

★

NOTE: *Extremely collectible poster.*

★

Whirlwind, 1933, COL, Tim McCoy, one-sheet, linen-backed, Camden House, May 1989, $125. *$150–$200*

Whispering Smith, 1949, PAR, one-sheet, framed, Camden House, May 1989, $150. *$50–$100*

Whistle Stop, 1945, UA, George Raft, Ava Gardner, scene card, Poster Mail Auction Co., February 1989, $15. *$10–$25*

White Christmas, 1954, PAR, Bing Crosby, Danny Kaye, Rosemary Clooney, Vera Ellen, seven scene cards, Guernsey's, April 1989, $35. *$100–$150*

White Christmas, 1954, one-sheet, Guernsey's, April 1989, $60.
$100–$200

★

NOTE: *This movie was released in VistaVision.*

★

White Heat, 1949, WB, James Cagney, Virginia Mayo, half-sheet, Guernsey's, April 1989, $175. *$200–$300*

Wild Orchids, 1929, MGM, Greta Garbo, Nils Asher, window card, Guernsey's, April 1989, $600. *$800–$1000*

Will Success Spoil Rock Hunter, 1958, 20th, Jayne Mansfield, Tony Randall, scene card, Paper Collectables & Memorabilia Show, February 1989, $10. *$10–$20*

Wine of Youth, 1924, MGM, Eleanor Boardman, William Haines, window card, excellent, Poster Mail Auction Co., February 1989, $50.   *$60–$80*

Wilson, 1944, 20th, Alexander Knox, Geraldine Fitzgerald, Vincent Price, Charles Coburn, complete set of lobby cards, Guernsey's, April 1989, $25.   *$75–$100*

NOTE: *Darryl F. Zanuck had great hopes for this movie, which was billed as "The Most Important Event in 50 Years of Motion Picture Entertainment!" Unfortunately, his dream turned into a nightmare. The movie bombed with a very loud bang.*

Wiser Sex, The, 1932, PAR, Claudette Colbert, Melvyn Douglas, half-sheet, excellent, Guernsey's, April 1989, $425.   *$400–$600*

Wizard of Oz, The, 1939, MGM, Judy Garland, Jack Haley, Bert Lahr, Ray Bolger, Margaret Hamilton, Frank Morgan, Billie Burke, scene card picturing Dorothy, the Wizard, the Tin Man, Lion, and the Straw Man, Guernsey's, April 1989, $2750.   *$2200–$2500*

Wizard of Oz, The, 1939, scene card (Oz saying farewell), Camden House, May 1989, $2700.   *$2000–$3000*

NOTE: *And these are only scene cards!*

Wizard of Oz, The, 1939, 47″ × 63″ Grinsson poster for the original French release, picturing Dorothy and the boys with Toto, linen-backed, Guernsey's, April 1989, $4750.

$4000–$5000

Woman in the Window, The, 1944, UNIV, Edward G. Robinson, Joan Bennett, one-sheet, Guernsey's, April 1989, $150.
                                                                    $200–$300

★

NOTE: *Classic film noir directed by Fritz Lang.*

★

Woman in White, 1948, WB, Eleanor Parker, Alexis Smith, Sydney Greenstreet, one-sheet, Guernsey's, April 1989, $50.
                                                                    $100–$150

Woman of Paris, A, 1923, UA, Edna Purviance, full-color scene card, Collectors' Showcase, December 1988, $86.   *$125–$150*

NOTE: *Purviance was Chaplin's leading lady in several of his silent film comedies. Paris was her first serious attempt at dramatic acting. Chaplin directed the movie with a heavy hand (he reputedly shot one scene over 200 times), and refused to let the movie be reshown until the last year of his life. It was the first movie he directed and distributed through UA, which he had formed in 1919 with Douglas Fairbanks, D.W. Griffith, and Mary Pickford.*

Women, The, 1939, MGM, Norma Shearer, Joan Crawford, Rosalind Russell, Paulette Goddard, Joan Fontaine, scene card, framed, Guernsey's, April 1989, $450.   *$300–$400*

World in My Corner, 1956, UNIV, Audie Murphy, Barbara Rush, title card, Poster Mail Auction Co., February 1989, $28.
$30–$40

Wyoming Mail, 1950, UNIV, Stephen McNally, Alexis Smith, title card, very good, Roger's Comics, April 1989, $2.   *$2–$12*

Yank in the R.A.F., The, 1941, 20th, Tyrone Power, Betty Grable, five scene cards, Guernsey's, April 1989, $400.   *$200–$300*

Yank in the R.A.F., The, 1941, half-sheet, damaged, Guernsey's, April 1989, $200.   *$300–$400*

Yank in the R.A.F., The, 1941, insert, excellent, Guernsey's, April 1989, $550.   *$600–$800*

Yellow Sky, 1949, 20th, Gregory Peck, Anne Baxter, Richard Widmark, one-sheet, Guernsey's, April 1989, $125.   *$150–$200*

Yellowstone Kelly, 1959, WB, Clint Walker, Ed "Cookie" Byrnes, scene card, Jerry Ohlinger's Movie Material Store, $10.
$10–$20

Yolanda, 1924, Marion Davies, window card, very good, Poster Mail Auction Co., February 1989, $65.   *$125–$175*

Yolanda and the Thief, 1945, MGM, Fred Astaire, Lucille Bremer, one-sheet, Guernsey's, April 1989, $350.   *$250–$350*

You'll Find Out, 1940, RKO, Boris Karloff, Peter Lorre, one-sheet, fair, Collectors' Showcase, March 1989, $90.   *$95–$125*

You Only Live Twice, 1967, UA, Sean Connery as James Bond, Donald Pleasance, Ariko Wakabayashi, three-sheet, fair, Camden House, May 1989, $200.   *$100–$150*

★

NOTE: *The above poster included a portrait poster of Sean Connery.*

★

Zander the Great, 1925, MGM, Marion Davies, title card, Guernsey's, April, 1989, $150.   *$100–$150*

★

NOTE: *Davies was William Randolph Hearst's mistress.*

★

Ziegfeld Follies, 1945, MGM, William Powell, Fred Astaire, insert, very good, Collectors' Showcase, March 1989, $218.

$75–$150

PHOTOGRAPHS, PORTRAITS, STILLS

INTRODUCTION

According to *Webster's Dictionary*, a photograph is a picture or likeness obtained by photography; a portrait is a pictorial representation (as in a painting) of a person, usually showing his face; and a still is a static photograph of actors or scenes of a motion picture for publicity or documentary purposes.

All three sum up photography and its importance to a movie star and a motion picture studio. But of the three types of photography mentioned, it is perhaps the portrait that is the most desirable to collectors of movie memorabilia. Usually the higher prices are paid for portraits of movie stars of films that have been photographed by leading studio photographers who are much in demand by collectors. Such photographers included Clarence Sinclair Bull, George Hurrell, and Ruth Harriet Louise, as three of the major talents, and there are many more who worked at the major film studios.

Portraits are particularly valuable if the pose is a full-length shot of a movie star, and the more rare or scarce the movie star's material, the more valuable finding a portrait will be. Greta Garbo, Jean Harlow, Marlene Dietrich, Louise Brooks, Bette Davis, Claudette Colbert, and Marilyn Monroe are particularly sought after by collectors.

Female star portraits are more desirable to collectors simply because most collectors of movie memorabilia happen to be men, and male collectors into movies love the female movie stars much more than their male counterparts. Collectors also prefer portraits that are unframed and unmounted (they can display them better), and black and white portraits usually outrank color portraits unless they are of someone like Marilyn Monroe.

Portraits tend to yellow, as do photographs, and this can be a drawback in their collectibility.

All this is not to say that photographs and stills are not desirable to collectors because if they are striking shots of movie stars, and the stills are original, then their prices can match their beauty and/or rarity.

Photographs were usually shot in a photographer's studio or right on a film set. They can show not only a movie star but an entire soundstage or part of a film set. Photographs are taken of film directors, producers, and studio heads, as well as movie stars. But since most collectors tend to collect by stars, it is these photographs or stills that are more valuable. But stills of scenes from movies also sell well, although not usually at the high prices that star stills do.

An important word about stills. There are many reproductions selling at movie memorabilia shows and through dealers which usually range in price from $2.50 to $5, depending on the show, dealer or region of the country. These stills were reprinted from the original negative and there are literally thousands of them floating around for sale. Prices of reproduced stills will increase, however, if the shot is of an unusual scene or a particularly provocative or glamorous movie star pose. Stills that are clearer in image, with sharp black and white overtones, are also likely to be higher in price. And with some dealers it depends on the customer who walks into their store.

I spoke to a dealer on the West Coast who sold me a particularly provocative pose of a movie star for $5. She might have sold it for less to another person, but from what we discussed I received the impression that more often she sold such a still for a much higher price. She even mentioned that if a particularly knowledgeable or desperate collector walked into her store from another West Coast city (that shall stay unnamed) and had the money, she would consider charging anywhere from $5 to $10 more for the still. Such are the vagaries of the movie memorabilia marketplace.

The following lists of photographs, portraits, and stills are alphabetically arranged by type of photography, i.e., photographs first, and then by title of movie or star, year of photograph, portrait or still, film title information such as star, director, etc.

(but not in all cases), description of the piece of photography, if the portrait or photograph was stamped (meaning name embossed by the photographer either on front or back of the photography), caption (words written either by the studio or film star, usually on the reverse), conditions, sizes, seller, month sold, and prices.

PHOTOGRAPHS LISTING

Bride of Frankenstein, February 1935, lab scene shot with partial view of studio soundstage in background, very fine, 8″ × 10″, Collectors' Showcase, January 1989, $49. $30–$40

Maria Callas, 1970, five color photos of the opera star in *Medea*, only film appearance (documented), Mario Tursi, photographer, 9″ × 12″ each, Camden House, May 1989, $100. $100–$200

Charles Chaplin, 1925, printed between 1950–60 by Edward Steichen, photographer, Swann Gallery, April 1989, $5500.

Charles Chaplin, young and dressed in a business suit, 5″ × 7″, William A. Fox Auction Gallery, March 1989, $200.
$175–$250

Come on Cowboy, "race" movie, also *Chicago After Dark* and *The Dreamer*, lobby photos, glossy, good, Richard Opfer, February 1989, $80. $60–$90

Joan Crawford, circa 1930s, black and white, hand-colored, glass mounted, framed, 4″ × 3″, Camden House, May 1989, $150.
$100–$150

Bette Davis, circa 1931, ingenue at UNIV, Ray Jones, photographer, caption on reverse, mint, 11″ × 14″, Collectors' Showcase, January 1989, $321. $100–$150

Greta Garbo, circa 1941, silverprint photo of the actress on pair of skis from *Two Faced Woman*, 1941, MGM, C.E. Guarino, October 1988, $20. $20–$35

Judy Garland, February 11, 1941, photo of Garland reflected in two mirrors, studio caption, quality paper, 8″ × 10″, Collectors' Showcase, February 1989, $33.   *$50–$75*

William S. Hart, photo from movie *The Gold Deck*, 8″ × 10″, C.E. Guarino, October 1988, $30.   *$25–$40*

Alfred Hitchcock, 1948, candid shot of Hitchcock on set of *Rope* with a few stars of the picture, 8″ × 10″, Collectors' Showcase, February 1989, $82.   *$25–$35*

Boris Karloff, 1932, very rare photo of the actor as Im-Ho-Tep, original title for *The Mummy*, caption, stamp, Freulich, photographer, 11″ × 114″, Collectors' Showcase, March 1989, $1000.   *$300–$350*

Buster Keaton, 1927, silverprint photo depicting the actor atop a railroad car from *The General*, 1927, UA, Museum of Modern Art backstamp, C.E. Guarino, October 1988, $15.   *$15–$30*

King Kong, 1933, RKO, original publicity photo of Kong on top of Empire State Building, plane in paw, caption, stamp, Ernest A. Bachrach, photographer, fine, 10½″ × 13½″, Collectors' Showcase, March 1989, $961.   *$200–$400*

Jayne Mansfield, 1957, calendar photo, glossy, stiff paper, posed in white swimsuit, very fine, 11″ × 23″, Hake's, November 1988, $16.   *$25–$50*

Marilyn Monroe, early nude double-exposure photo, framed, 10″ × 14″, Camden House, May 1989, $125.   *$50–$100*

Marilyn Monroe, circa 1954, original photo of Monroe taking off a sheer negligee, 8″ × 10″, Collectors' Showcase, December 1988, $36.   *$15–$20*

Marilyn Monroe, six-foot long frame of five black and white photographs in consecutive manner to create a Cinemascope portrait session presentation, 12″ × 16″ each photo, Camden House, May 1989, $1000.   *$1250–$1500*

Phantom of the Opera, 1925, original photo of Lon Chaney, unmasked, with co-star Mary Philbin in the catacombs, cream-type paper, very fine, 11″ × 14″, Collectors' Showcase, December 1988, $331.   *$75–$100*

Photo courtesy of Camden House, Los Angeles, CA

Photo courtesy of Camden House, Los Angeles, CA

Photo courtesy of Camden House, Los Angeles, CA

Photo courtesy of Camden House, Los Angeles, CA

Photo courtesy of Camden House, Los Angeles, CA

Publicity Photographs, movie stars placing their hand and shoe imprints in the forecourt cement at Grauman's Chinese Theater, including Marilyn Monroe, John Wayne, Rock Hudson, Jack Lemmon, and Elizabeth Taylor, among others, 28 black and white photos, all rare, each mounted and 11″ × 14″, Camden House, May 1989, $1500 (see photo on previous page).

$600–$800

Ernest Schoedsack, 1931, director of *King Kong*, photo of Schoedsack on a film set, 8″ × 10″, Collectors' Showcase, February 1989, $55. $60–$75

Squaw Man, The, 1913, Dustin Farnum, Cecil B. DeMille, and Dick La Reno in a saloon scene, DeMille is a faro dealer, 14″ × 19″, Christie's East, October 1988, $275. $150–$200

NOTE: *First film produced by the Jesse Lasky Feature Play Co. Photograph from the estate of Cecil B. DeMille.*

Steamboat Willie, 1928, Walt Disney, photo of Mickey Mouse at the wheel of the boat, with negative, two contact prints, Museum of Modern Art stamp, C.E. Guarino, October 1988, $40.

$35–$60

Three Stooges, circa 1938, giveaway photo with movie projector, fine, 5″ × 8″, Collectors' Showcase, December 1988, $199.

$20–$30

NOTE: *Three Stooges material always brings high prices at auctions and through dealers. Very popular comedians with collectors, in the same league with Abbott and Costello and Laurel and Hardy.*

Elizabeth Taylor, circa 1940, first photo session at UNIV, sixth photo shot of a very young Elizabeth, "proof only" stamp, fine, 8″ × 10″, Collectors' Showcase, September 1988, $90.

$50–$75

Shirley Temple and Bill Robinson, 1935, photo of both stars who appeared together in *The Little Colonel* at 20th, matted, framed, 10½" × 12½", Richard Opfer, February 1989, $110.

$90–$125

★

NOTE: *This photo came from an auction of black memorabilia.*

★

Rudolph Valentino, 1921, photo of the actor in a tango scene from *The Four Men of the Apocalypse*, MGM, silverprint, Museum of Modern Art backstamp, 8" × 10", C.E. Guarino, October 1988, $10. $10–$20

Walt Disney, circa 1938, stuffed Mickey Mouse and Donald Duck photo with conductor in front of a mike, 8" × 10", Collectors' Showcase, September 1988, $220. $25–$35

Johnny Weissmuller and Margaret O'Sullivan, circa 1937, two photos, stiff paper, matte sepia Weissmuller photo with actor dressed as Tarzan, O'Sullivan in street clothes, matte black and white O'Sullivan photo, both have facsimile signatures, mailing envelopes, fine, 5½" × 7½" each, Hake's, November 1988, $96. $75–$100

PORTRAITS LISTING

Judith Anderson, two black and white portraits, textured paper, Carl Van Vechten, photographer, stamp, Phillips, December 1988, $100. $200–$300

Ingrid Bergman, black and white portrait from *Casablanca*, 1943, WB, framed, 20" × 16", Camden House, May 1989, $125.

$50–$75

Clara Bow, circa 1928, the "It" girl and her dog, Otto Dyar, photographer, stamp, very fine, 11" × 14", Collectors' Showcase, October 1988, $107. $150–$175

Clara Bow, circa 1929, full-color portrait of actress in bathing suit, 8" × 10", Collectors' Showcase, October 1988, $29.

$20–$30

Louise Brooks, circa 1927, Nishiyama of New York, photographer, 11″ × 14¼″, Collectors' Showcase, January 1989, $385.

$225–$275

Louise Brooks, 1927, full-length studio keybook, linen-backed portrait, Brooks in black ballet costume with black shoes, 8″ × 10″, Collectors' Showcase, February 1989, $205. $150–$250

Louise Brooks, circa 1928, original PAR portrait, Richee, photographer, very fine, 8″ × 10″, Collectors' Showcase, December 1988, $300. $95–$125

Louise Brooks, circa 1929, Hommel, photographer, his name embossed on front of portrait, very fine, 8″ × 10″, Collectors' Showcase, September 1988, $170. $75–$100

Louise Brooks, circa 1929, museum quality, Art Deco, portrait of a mysterious Brooks, quality paper, Hommel, photographer, name embossed on front, very fine, 11″ × 14″, $485.

$200–$300

Louise Brooks, 1929, portrait of the star in *The Canary Murder Case*, PAR, as the follies Canary dancer, Hommel, photographer, name embossed, front, very fine, 11″ × 14″, Collectors' Showcase, March 1989, $435. $250 $350

NOTE: As I mentioned in the introduction, Louise Brooks is one of those stars who developed a "cult" following and whose memorabilia, especially portraits and signed material, bring strong collector interest and high prices. As with the later PAR contract star, Frances Farmer, she was very unconventional in her behavior towards stardom and Hollywood.

Lon Chaney, circa 1920s, smiling portrait, unusual, Collectors' Showcase, September 1988, $27. $35–$50

Claudette Colbert, circa 1933, very fine, Collectors' Showcase, September 1988, $96. $35–$50

Joan Crawford, 1926, in role for *The Unknown*, MGM, as Estrellita (Lon Chaney movie), studio caption, very fine, 8″ × 10″, Collectors' Showcase, January 1989, $44.   *$50–$75*

Joan Crawford, circa 1931, yellowed, George Hurrell, photographer, name embossed, front, 10″ × 13″, Collectors' Showcase, March 1989, $137.   *$150–$200*

Joan Crawford, 1931, original photographic portrait, Hurrell, photographer, name embossed, 13″ × 10″, Camden House, May 1989, $300.   *$200–$300*

Joan Crawford, black and white portrait, board mounted, 20″ × 16″, Camden House, May 1989, $75.   *$50–$100*

Marion Davies, 1929, Ruth Harriet Louise, photographer, name embossed, very fine, Collectors' Showcase, September 1988, $30.   *$25–$40*

Bette Davis, sepia portrait of Davis in *All About Eve*, 20th, and one black and white portrait from *The Private Lifes of Elizabeth and Essex*, 1939, WB, both framed, both 20″ × 16″, Camden House, May 1989, $125.   *$75–$125*

Dolores Del Rio, circa 1931, 11″ × 14″, Collectors' Showcase, October 1988, $104.   *$150–$200*

Cecil B. DeMille, circa 1930, George Hurrell, photographer, name embossed, bit yellowed, 11″ × 14″, Collectors' Showcase, February 1989, $66.   *$100–$150*

Marlene Dietrich, circa 1931, portrait with religious theme, quite stunning, Richee, photographer, 8″ × 10″, Collectors' Showcase, December 1988, $330.   *$60–$75*

Greta Garbo, circa 1940, Clarence Sinclair Bull, photographer, name embossed, stamped, very fine, 10″ × 13″, Collectors' Showcase, January 1989, $238.   *$150–$250*

Ava Gardner, sepia, from *The Snows of Kilimanjaro*, 1952, 20th, 20″ × 16″, Camden House, May 1989, $100.   *$50–$100*

Janet Gaynor, circa 1926, very early portrait of this FOX/20th star, quality paper, Autrey, photographer, 8″ × 10″, Collectors' Showcase, December 1988, $25.   *$30–$40*

NOTE: Gaynor was the first actress to win an Academy Award for Seventh Heaven, Street Angel, *and* Sunrise *(1927–28). Unfortunately, her memorabilia has not appreciated on the same level as contemporaries such as Louise Brooks, Claudette Colbert, or Marlene Dietrich. Part of the problem might be that Gaynor was a sweet, girl-next-door type without any tragic overtones.*

★

Jean Harlow, circa 1931, Clarence Sinclair Bull, photographer, 3-D-like portrait, 8″ × 10″, Collectors' Showcase, January 1989, $121.   *$95–$125*

Jean Harlow,.1935, portrait of the star in a gown by Gilbert Adrian, fine, Collectors' Showcase, September 1988, $72.

$40–$60

Jean Harlow, sepia, board mounted, 20″ × 16″, Camden House, May 1989, $300.   *$75–$125*

Rita Hayworth, 1941, sepia portrait from *Blood and Sand*, 20th, framed, 20″ × 16″, Camden House, May 1989, $125.

$50–$100

Boris Karloff, 1932, as Im-Ho-Tep character in *The Mummy*, UNIV, portrait of the actor in full makeup, Freulich, photographer, caption, very fine, 11″ × 14″, Collectors' Showcase, October 1988, $847.   *$275–$375*

Boris Karloff, 1940, linen-backed paper portrait, keybook, from *Devil's Island*, WB, very fine, 8″ × 10″, Collectors' Showcase, January 1989, $21.   *$40–$50*

Buster Keaton, 1927, *The General*, FN, the actor in Civil War clothes, Melbourne Spurr, photographer, embossed, intense portrait, 10½″ × 13½″, Collectors' Showcase, March 1989, $492.   *$150–$300*

Veronica Lake, black and white portrait, board mounted, 20″ × 16″, Camden House, May 1989, $25.   *$50–$100*

Carole Lombard, 1929, slightly blurry portrait, might be intentional, William E. Thomas, photographer, caption (with name spelled Carol), glue traces, 11″ × 14″, Collectors' Showcase, May 1989, $314.   *$200–$300*

Carole Lombard, 1930, *Safety in Numbers*, PAR, Gene Robert Richee, photographer, 8″ × 10″, Collectors' Showcase, October 1988, $66.   *$40–$50*

NOTE: *This was Carole's first picture at PAR (her home studio throughout the 1930s). After appearing in this film with Charles Buddy Rogers (later married to Mary Pickford), she was signed to a seven-year contract at $350 per week.*

Carole Lombard, 1931, November 7, portrait taken at her Beverly Hills house, very fine, Collectors' Showcase, September 1988, $118.   *$50–$75*

Carole Lombard, circa 1932, PAR portrait, very beautiful, mint, 8″ × 10″, Collectors' Showcase, December 1988, $116.
                                                         $60–$75

Myrna Loy, circa 1929, exotic, Preston Duncan, WB photographer, very fine, 8″ × 10″, Collectors' Showcase, September 1988, $48.   *$40–$60*

Myrna Loy, 1930, portrait of Loy in *Renegades*, FOX, as a spy, mint, Autrey, photographer, 8″ × 10″, Collectors' Showcase, December 1988, $44.   *$40–$60*

Madam Satan, 1930, MGM, Cecil B. DeMille, director, full-length (3/4) exotic portrait of Reginald Denny and Kay Johnson, Manatt, photographer, caption, 10″ × 12″, Collectors' Showcase, October 1988, $27.   *$95–$125*

Marilyn Monroe, 1952, sepia portrait, *Don't Bother to Knock*, 20th, framed, 20″ × 16″, Camden House, May 1989, $100
                                                        $50–$100

Marilyn Monroe, 1953, black and white portrait, *Niagara*, 20th, framed, 20″ × 16″, Camden House, May 1989, $100. *$25–$50*

Marilyn Monroe, 1953, sepia portrait, *Gentlemen Prefer Blondes*, 20th, framed, 29″ × 16″, Camden House, May 1989, $115.
$50–$100

Marilyn Monroe, 1954, sepia portrait, *There's No Business Like Show Business*, 20th, framed, 29″ × 16″, Camden House, May 1989, $50.
$50–$100

Marilyn Monroe, 1955, sepia portrait, *The Seven Year Itch*, 20th, framed, 15½″ × 16″, Camden House, May 1989, $100.
$50–$100

Marilyn Monroe, 1955, sepia portrait, *The Seven Year Itch*, 20th, framed, 15¼″ × 15½″, Camden House, May 1989, $75.
$50–$100

Photo courtesy of Camden House, Los Angeles, CA

Marilyn Monroe, 1956, sepia portrait, *Bus Stop*, 20th, framed, 20″ × 16″, Camden House, May 1989, $225.
$50–$100

Marilyn Monroe, 1957, sepia portrait, *The Prince and the Show-girl*, WB, framed, 20″ × 16″, Camden House, May 1989, $75.

$50–$100

Photo courtesy of Camden House, Los Angeles, CA

Marilyn Monroe, circa 1962, color photograph portrait, famous "last sitting," Bert Stern, photographer, framed, 15¼″ × 15½″, Camden House, May 1989, $1500. $1000–$1500

Marilyn Monroe, circa 1962, color photograph portrait, famous "last sitting," Bert Stern, photographer, framed, 15½″ × 16″, Camden House, May 1989, $1750. $1000–$1500

Laurence Olivier and Greer Garson, 1940 (March 8), paper portrait, *Pride and Prejudice*, MGM, Clarence Sinclair Bull, photographer, caption, very fine, 8″ × 10″, Collectors' Showcase, March 1989, $30. $40–$50

Mary Pickford, 1925, production print portrait, *Little Annie Rooney*, UA, K.O. Rahm, photographer, caption, 8″ × 10″, Collectors' Showcase, October 1988, $44.   *$25–$30*

Norma Shearer, circa 1930, MGM portrait, fine, 8″ × 10″, Collectors' Showcase, October 1988, $70.   *$30–$40*

Norma Shearer, 1931, George Hurrell, photographer, mint, 8″ × 10″, Collectors' Showcase, January 1989, $57.   *$75–$125*

Norma Shearer, 1932, photographic portrait, George Hurrell, photographer, signed, embossed, 13″ × 10″, Camden House, May 1989, $250.   *$250–$350*

Norma Talmadge, circa 1919, Lumiere Studios (New York), early glamour portrait, 8″ × 10″, Collectors' Showcase, October 1988, $12.   *$30–$40*

NOTE: Of the three Talmadge sisters, Norma was the most famous. She began her career in 1910 at Vitagraph in The Household Pest, *and appeared in over 250 productions for that studio, the most famous being* A Tale of Two Cities *opposite Maurice Costello in 1911. In 1915, she signed with FN, later married its president, Joseph Schenck, and went on to rival Mary Pickford as the first lady of the silent screen. Her sister, Constance, made her mark as a silent film comedienne, and Natalie, the youngest sister, acted briefly in films before retiring to marry the comedian Buster Keaton. Norma wisely retired a very wealthy woman in 1930 after two talkies (her Brooklyn accent would have done her in eventually).*

Shirley Temple, 1936, linen-paper, *Captain January*, 20th, mint, 8″ × 10″, Collectors' Showcase, January 1989, $21.   *$30–$40*

Spencer Tracy, January 4, 1937, quality paper portrait, informally posed, Clarence Bull Sinclair, photographer, MGM stamp, Collectors' Showcase, February 1989, $11.   *$40–$50*

Lupe Velez, 1929, oriental-looking Velez portrait, *Where East Is East*, MGM (opposite Lon Chaney), glue spots, caption, 19½" × 13¼", Collectors' Showcase, March 1989, $104.

$100–$150

Lupe Velez, circa 1931, Clarence Sinclair Bull, photographer, fine, Collectors' Showcase, September 1988, $45.   *$50–$75*

STILLS LISTING

John Barrymore, black and white original stills from *Beau Brummel*, 1926, WB, and *Bulldog Drummond's Peril*, 1938, PAR, also studio keybook stills, 8" × 10" each, Camden House, May 1989, $75.   *$100–$200*

Batman, 1943, COL, serial still, black and white, glossy, depicting Lewis Wilson as Batman and Douglas Croft as Robin (at building rooftop with several city buildings in background), very good, 8" × 10", Hake's, February 1989, $42.   *$25–$50*

Batman, 1943, COL, serial still, black and white, glossy, Batman and Robin in an underground cave with tiger gargoyles and Japanese soldiers in background, very fine, 8" × 10", Hake's, February 1989, $42.   *$25–$50*

Citizen Kane, 1941, RKO, seven black and white scene stills, 8" × 10" each, Camden House, May 1989, $50.   *$100–$200*

Cowboy Movie Stills, glossy stills, 1930s, printed titles with stars' names, including Buster Crabbe, "Wild Bill" Elliott, Johnny Mack Brown, Lash La Rue, Randolph Scott, and Charles Starrett, others, 10½" × 8½" each, John Wade, February 1989, $40.

$35–$45

Marlene Dietrich, circa 1930s, provocative black and white still of the actress dressed in a tuxedo, top hat, and putting a cigarette into her mouth, very suggestive, 10″ × 8″, Memory Shop West, June 1989, $5. $5–$20

Greta Garbo and Charles Bickford, 1930, silverprint still of the actors in scene from *Anna Christie*, MGM, Museum of Modern Art backstamp, C.E. Guarino, October 1988, $25. $20–$30

Gone With the Wind, 30 original stills from the personal publicity collection at Selznick Studios, 20 linen-backed, captions, presentation file, rare, Phillips, December 1088, $600.

$600–$1000

Iron Mask, The, 1929, UA, Douglas Fairbanks, five original black and white scene stills, linen-backed, 8″ × 10″ each, Camden House, May 1989, $50.   *$50–$100*

Phantom of the Opera, The, 1925, MGM, five original black and white stills including one of the actor Lon Chaney raising his arm in triumph at the organ, mint, 8″ × 10″, Collectors' Showcase, January 1989, $233.   *$150–$200*

Shirley Temple, 19 original studio black and white keybook stills from *Bright Eyes*, 1934, FOX, 8″ × 10″ each, Camden House, May 1989, $275.   *$150–$250*

Rudolph Valentino, 1921, *The Four Horsemen of the Apocalypse*, MGM, Alice Terry, Alan Hale, original black and white film still, very fine, 8″ × 10″, Collectors' Showcase, December 1988, $42.   *$30–$35*

Rudolph Valentino, 1924, *Monsieur Beaucaire*, PAR, Bebe Daniels, Lowell Sherman, original black and white film still, 8″ × 10″, Collectors' Showcase, December 1988, $31. *$40–$45*

Rudolph Valentino, 1925, *The Eagle*, UA, Vilma Banky, Louise Dresser, original black and white film scene still, very fine, 8″ × 10″, Collectors' Showcase, December 1988, $42.

$30–$35

Clint Walker, 1965, *None But the Brave*, WB, Frank Sinatra star and director, black and white scene still, 10″ × 8″, Hollywood Poster Exchange, August 1988, $3.   *$2.50–$50*

Walt Disney, 1939, scene still from *Three Little Pigs*, 1933, mint, Collectors' Showcase, October 1988, $22.   *$15–$20*

Walt Disney, 1939, scene still from *The Hockey Champ*, mint, Collectors' Showcase, October 1988, $44.   *$40–$50*

Walt Disney, 1939, *Pinocchio*, RKO, Walt Disney Productions, scene still, stamp, caption, very fine + , 9″ × 7″, Collectors' Showcase, October 1988, $37.   *$10–$20*

Wizard of Oz, The, 1939, MGM, six black and white stills from 1938 depicting wardrobe tests for Buddy Ebsen, Jack Haley, Sara Padden, and Ray Bolger, plus a scene still with Bolger, Haley, and Bert Lahr, extremely rare, 8″ × 10″ each, Camden House, May 1989, $400.   *$400–$500*

PRESSBOOKS

INTRODUCTION

Pressbooks contain information for advertising of films either in release or about to be released for the use of the newspaper and, less frequently, magazine medias. The books offer tips to theater managers as to expanding their customer patronage plus more general information about the film that has been, or will be, booked into their theater.

Pressbooks were coordinated and published from the early days of silent films through the present, but were most popular during the golden age of movies, roughly 1910 until the 1950s. They were utilized by all the major studios.

A typical pressbook would include newspaper ads, theater ads, canned stories, photographs or stills, advance newspaper stories complete with cast, and a synopsis of the film, as well as other promotion pieces. The majority of the pages were in black and white, although many were in full color. Some pressbooks also included posters for the film that was being publicized. Pressbooks were also referred to as "Exhibitor's Campaign Books," and often were presented in deluxe presentation formats, i.e., elaborate covers, gold-tooled pages, and leather bindings.

There were also pressbooks published for the reissue of a certain film. These were called reissue pressbooks.

The whole idea behind pressbooks was to make an impression on theater owners, editors, reporters, and other people who could benefit from the publicity of a particular film.

Pressbooks are enjoying a vogue among collectors of movie memorabilia, but they are becoming scarce and truly fine examples are hard to find.

In the following listings, pressbooks are noted by film, year of release, featured players, description, page length, and size, followed by the seller, month sold, and prices.

PRESSBOOKS LISTING

Abbott and Costello Meet Frankenstein, 1948, UNIV, Bud Abbott, Lou Costello, Bela Lugosi, Lon Chaney, 12 pages, fine, 12″ × 16″, Collectors' Showcase, September 1988, $592.

$100–$200

Abbott and Costello Meet Frankenstein, 1948, UNIV, another copy, unfolded, Collectors' Showcase, January 1989, $195.

$150–$200

NOTE: Notice the difference in prices paid from September of 1988 through January of 1989—a difference of almost $400—which only proves that if there is a collector willing to pay the price, the item will sell. Abbot and Costello are very popular, and expensive, movie memorabilia.

Abraham Lincoln, 1930, UA, Walter Huston, Una Merkel, 22 pages, 12″ × 17½″, Collectors' Showcase, January 1989, $38.

$75–$150

Alexander's Ragtime Band, 1938, 20th, Tyrone Power, Alice Faye, Don Ameche, Ethel Merman, Jack Haley, full-color theater posters on back cover, 28 pages, 17″ × 22″, Collectors' Showcase, October 1988, $214.

$95–$125

NOTE: Lon Chaney, Jr., played a bit in this movie as a photographer.

★

Arizona Bound, 1927, *Beau Sabreur*, 1928, and *The First Kiss*, 1928, three Gary Cooper pressbooks, 28 pages total, fragile, good, 11″ × 17″, Collectors' Showcase, March 1989, $51. $125–$150

★

NOTE: Arizona Bound was Cooper's second male leading role in silent films.

Baby Doll, 1956, WB, Carroll Baker, Eli Wallach, Karl Malden, Mildred Dunnock, and the townspeople of Benoit, Mississippi, 24 pages, 11″ × 17″, Collectors' Showcase, December 1988, $30.
$40–$50

NOTE: *Based on a play by Tennessee Williams, this steamy movie was one of the most controversial movies of the 1950s, although today it would be considered extremely tame. It was condemned by the Roman Catholic Church for its lewd depiction of a thumb-sucking, child-bride who is seduced by a macho Sicilian. Baker was nominated for an Academy Award for what was considered her finest performance.*

Beat the Devil, 1954, UA, Humphrey Bogart, Gina Lollobrigida, Jennifer Jones, Peter Lorre, Robert Morley, 20 pages, 17″ × 11″, Collectors' Showcase, January 1989, $75. $40–$60

NOTE: *Written by Truman Capote and directed by John Huston, this satire didn't do very well at the box office, but the movie was adored by college kids in revivals.*

Becky Sharp, 1935, RKO, Miriam Hopkins, Frances Dee, Cedric Hardwick, first complete technicolor movie made in Hollywood, 39 pages, 12″ × 18″, Collectors' Showcase, March 1989, $46.
$100–$150

Buck Jones in the Roaring West, 1935, UNIV, five-chapter serial, 8 pages, fine, 14″ × 21″, Collectors' Showcase, January 1989, $53. $60–$75

Bulldog Drummond, 1929, UA, Ronald Colman, Joan Bennett, Lilyan Tashman, 22 pages, fine, 11½″ × 17½″, Collectors' Showcase, January 1989, $165. $75–$100

NOTE: *Colman's first talking picture and considered the first quality talking picture, although horribly dated today.*

Conquest of Space, 1955, PAR, Eric Fleming, directed by George Pal, 20 pages, fine, 12″ × 15″, Collectors' Showcase, March 1989, $135. $50–$60

Creature From the Black Lagoon, The, 1954, UNIV, Richard Carlson, Julia Adams, folded, 16 pages, very good, 12″ × 18″, Collectors' Showcase, March 1989, $121. $90–$125

Damsel in Distress, A, 1937, RKO, Fred Astaire, Joan Fontaine, Burns and Allen, 44 pages, 12″ × 18″, Collectors' Showcase, March 1989, $92. $100–$125

Dawn Rider, The, 1935, *The Oregon Trail*, 1936, *The Star Packer*, 1934, and *Rainbow Valley*, 1935, four John Wayne pressbooks from the actor's early career, very good, Camden House, May 1989, $150. $100–$150

Don Q., Son of Zorro, 1925, UA, Douglas Fairbanks, softcover, "Exhibitor's Campaign Book," 14 glossy pages, illustrated, photos, 10″ × 13″, Hake's, February 1989, $76. $75–$100

Fort Dobbs, 1958, WB, Clint Walker, Virginia Mayo, Brian Keith, 12″ × 18″, Jerry Ohlinger's Movie Material Store, October 1988, $25. $20–$30

Help, 1965, UA, the Beatles, illustrations and poster included, fine, 18″ × 14″, Poster Mail Auction Co., February 1989, $60.
$50–$70

Invasion of the Body Snatchers, 1955, AA, Kevin McCarthy, Dana Wynter, Carolyn Jones, four-page insert tabloid, 18 pages, 12″ × 18″, Collectors' Showcase, February 1989, $77.
$100–$150

King of the Zombies, 1941, MON, Mantan Moreland, Joan Woodbury, 8 pages, very fine, 12″ × 18″, Collectors' Showcase, September 1988, $22. $40–$50

Photo courtesy of Camden House, Los Angeles, CA

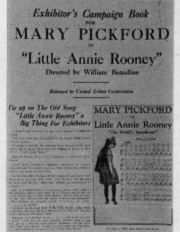

Photo courtesy of Camden House, Los Angeles, CA

Photo courtesy of Camden House, Los Angeles, CA

Little Annie Rooney, 1925, UA, Mary Pickford, 12 pages, fine, 10″ × 13″, Hake's, February 1989, $12. $25–$75

★

NOTE: *During the filming of this movie there was what turned out to be an unsuccessful kidnap plot against Ms. Pickford.*

★

Littlest Rebel, The, 1935, Shirley Temple, John Boles, Jack Holt, 24 pages, fine, 16″ × 22″, Collectors' Showcase, March 1989, $112. *$100–$150*

Lottery Bride, 1930, UA, Jeanette MacDonald, Joe E. Brown, holes on left side from binding removal, 20 pages, good, 12″ × 17½″, Collectors' Showcase, January 1989, $45. *$70–$100*

Heroes of the Flames, 1931, Tim McCoy serial, 12 chapters about firefighters, 4 pages, 11½″ × 18″, Collectors' Showcase, October 1988, $42. *$50–$75*

Men, The, 1950, UA, Marlon Brando, Teresa Wright, Jack Webb, 28 pages, fine, 11″ × 17½″, Collectors' Showcase, January 1989, $29. *$65–$75*

Misfits, The, 1961, UA, Clark Gable, Marilyn Monroe, Montgomery Clift, Thelma Ritter, Eli Wallach, 12 pages, fine, 13″ × 18″, Collectors' Showcase, January 1989, $250. *$75–$100*

★

NOTE: *Very desirable pressbook.*

★

Mr. Deeds Goes to Town, 1936, COL, Gary Cooper, Jean Arthur, 24 pages, fine, 12″ × 18″, Collectors' Showcase, January 1989, $38. *$50–$75*

Raffles, 1930, UA, Ronald Colman, Kay Francis, Alison Skipworth, with comic strip, 12 pages, fine, 12″ × 18″, Collectors' Showcase, January 1989, $46. *$75–$95*

Return of the Ape Man, 1944, MON, Bela Lugosi, 8 pages, 10½″ × 17½″, Collectors' Showcase, January 1989, $49.
$75–$95

Revenge of the Creature, 1955, UNIV, John Agar, Lori Nelson, 2nd in series, 16 pages, very fine, 12″ × 18″, Collectors' Showcase, March 1989, $41. *$75–$100*

Sally of the Sawdust, 1925, PAR, W.C. Fields, Carol Dempster, 16 pages, very good, 10″ × 13″, Hake's, February 1989, $108.
$75–$100

NOTE: *This screenplay was based on the Broadway musical "Poppy," which had starred Fields in 1923. His role in this movie defined the actor's image in all his subsequent movies as that of a scheming but pleasant juggler.*

Scared to Death, 1947, MON, Bela Lugosi, George Zucco, Lugosi's only color film, 12 pages, fine, 17″ × 11″, Collectors' Showcase, January 1989, $38.
$60–$90

She, 1935, RKO, Helen Gahagan, Melvyn Douglas, much color publicity material, 24 pages, very good +, 12″ × 32″, Collectors' Showcase, October 1988, $427.
$200–$300

NOTE: *Walt Disney used* She *as his inspiration for the wicked witch in* Snow White and the Seven Dwarfs.

Song of the South, 1956, Walt Disney Productions, reissue for 1946 RKO film, 18 pages, fine, 12″ × 18″, Collectors' Showcase, November 1988, $45.
$25–$50

Stage Door, 1937, RKO, Katharine Hepburn, Ginger Rogers, Lucille Ball, Eve Arden, Andrea Leeds, Jack Carson, 44 pages, fine, 12″ × 18″, Collectors' Showcase, March 1989, $660.
$100–$150

Star Is Born, A 1954, WB, Judy Garland, James Mason, Charles Bickford, Jack Carson, 28 pages, fine, 18″ × 12″, Collectors' Showcase, November 1988, $94.
$75–$100

Strange Woman, The, 1946, UA, Hedy Lamarr, George Sanders, Louis Hayward, unfolded, 34 pages, Collectors' Showcase, January 1989, $21.
$30–$40

Sullivan's Travels, 1941, *Easy Living*, 1937, *The Palm Beach Story*, 1942, *The Great Moment*, 1944, plus one other, five Preston Sturgess original pressbooks, PAR, fine, Phillips, December 1988, $250.   *$300–$400*

*Woman Like Satan, A,*1959, Brigitte Bardot, original pressbook, 12 pages, fine, 11″ × 17″, Collectors' Showcase, December 1988, $20.   *$35–$40*

Yellow Submarine, 1968, UA, 20 pop-out art decorations, Beatles animated film, full-color illustrations, heavy paper, 10 pages, mint, 9½″ × 15″, Collectors' Showcase, March 1989, $79.
                                                                   $50–$60

Yellow Submarine, 1968, UA, complete, uncut, very good, 18″ × 14″, Poster Mail Auction Co., February 1989, $35.
                                                                   $40–$60

SCRIPTS

INTRODUCTION

Scripts are probably the most important element in the making of a motion picture because if there wasn't a writer there wouldn't be a script, and if there wasn't a script, there wouldn't be a movie. Screenwriters, perhaps the most valuable people in movies, are, unfortunately, the least appreciated or revered.

The following list of scripts are all original (copies of scripts are available in the marketplace but they cannot compare with original scripts for collector status), typed, and almost all presented in binders. There are dialogue and continuity scripts, plus scripts that are revised originals, mimeographed, carbon, draft, shooting, xerox, and leather bound. Many scripts have rewriting on their pages or annotations, but the one thing they all have in common is that they are typed. Imagine being an actor or actress and trying to follow a scriptwriter's handwritten notes! Scripts might be handwritten initially, but once they reach the sound-stage they had better be typed.

Scripts contain every shot in a motion picture, they have instructions that detail camera angles, spoken dialogue by the actors, and technical information necessary for the production of a movie.

Scripts are the actual documents in filming a movie. They are generally 90–120 pages long, some shorter, many longer (see *Citizen Kane* scripts). Traditionally, each page is a minute of screen time—30 minutes for the first act, 60 minutes for the second act, and another 30 minutes for the third act, a total of two hours, which is the running time of most movies. But pages do run over.

Scripts are protected by copyright so they cannot be reproduced. However, reprints and copies are published for study purposes by film students and the general public. Collectors, however, stick with the originals. Some scripts are very desirable. The *Citizen Kane* scripts that sold at Christie's East in June 1989 for $231,000 set a world record at auction. Most scripts have more down-to-earth prices.

Scripts are listed here by film title, date of script, movie title and major stars, description of script type, page number, size, seller, month sold, and prices. Script description varies from listing to listing.

SCRIPTS LISTING

Abbott and Costello Meet the Invisible Man, February 22, 1951, original continuity and dialogue script with rare seven-page trailer script, 135 pages, 8½″ × 11″, Collectors' Showcase, January 1989, $135. *$125–$175*

Abraham Lincoln, 1930, dialogue and continuity script, 60 pages, fine, 8″ × 11½″, Collectors' Showcase, January 1989, $275. *$125–$150*

All About Eve, April 5, 1950, original revised final script, 180 pages, fine, Collectors' Showcase, October 1988, $266.
$150–$200

Captain Blood, 1935, WB, three mimeographed scripts, one a dialogue continuity script, one a continuity and titles script, and one a foreign feature version script, loose sheets, rare, Pepper & Stern, April 1989, $550. *$500–$600*

★

NOTE: This was the film that made Errol Flynn an "overnight" star.

Citizen Kane, 1940, two carbon scripts bound as one volume, stamped *Citizen Kane* and Herman J. Mankiewicz, gilt-stamped cover of Morocco-backed maroon cloth, 11″ × 8½″, Christie's East, June 1989, $231,000.   *$70,000–$90,000*

NOTE: *Herman J. Mankiewicz, older brother of screenwriter and director Joseph Mankiewicz (A Letter to Three Wives, All About Eve), wrote this script with Orson Welles, although film historians dispute just how much Welles actually contributed to the script. The* Citizen Kane *script has annotations by the lawyers for William Randolph Hearst, publisher, who served as the model for Charles Kane. It ran 169 pages and is almost a final shooting script. The American script is a first or second carbon, dated April 16, 1940, and marked "first rough draft," with 268 pages. Both scripts were sold with three others, plus some ephemera including a typed letter by John Houseman of the Mercury Theater.*

Claudius, 1937, original complete preproduction script for the uncompleted Josef Von Sternberg film based on the books of the famous Roman emperor by Robert Graves and starring Charles Laughton, Merle Oberon, 78 pages, rare, 8″ × 13″, Collectors' Showcase, October 1988, $884.   *$150–$200*

Creature From the Black Lagoon, The, 1954, leather-bound script including revision pages, original notes, stills, and a lobby card, property of screenwriter Harry Essex, Camden House, May 1989, $700.   *$300–$400*

Creature Walks Among Us, The, February 17, 1956, dialogue and continuity script, very fine, Collectors' Showcase, December 1988, $43.   *$50–$60*

Desire, 1936, PAR, original working script, November 2, 1935, called "The Pearl Necklace," Marlene Deitrich and Gary Cooper film, 8½″ × 14″, Collectors' Showcase, October 1988, $82.
                    $150–$200

Desperate, 1947, *The Frightened City*, 1950, *The Sons of Katie Elder*, 1965, *He Walked by Night*, 1948, leather-bound scripts of Harry Essex, screenwriter, Camden House, May 1989, $200.
                    $200–$300

Dirty Harry, 1971, *Shane*, 1953, original studio scripts, Camden House, May 1989, $350.   *$200–$300*

Easter Parade, 1948, MGM, original script dated November 26, 1947, about 100 pages with colored changes, very fine, 8½″ × 11″, Collectors' Showcase, December 1988, $99.   *$150–$200*

Forsaking All Others, 1934, MGM, *The Gorgeous Hussy*, 1936, MGM, both with Joan Crawford, original studio scripts, Camden House, May 1989, $175.   *$150–$200*

Foxes of Harrow, The, 1947, 20th, Rex Harrison, Maureen O'Hara, original 1947 shooting script, leather bound, embossed with producer's name, Phillips, December 1988, $170.
                                                          $150–$250

Hello Cheyenne; A Horseman of the Plains, two Tom Mix original, typed carbon scripts, 1927, very good, 9″ × 14″, Collectors' Showcase, September 1988, $127.   *$150–$200*

Help, 1965, shooting script, many rewrite pages, ink annotations, original wrappers, 122 pages, very rare, Pepper & Stern, Apil 1989, $1500.

Horse Feathers, 1932, PAR, original script dated March 7, 1932, for this Marx Brothers film, 76 pages, 8½″ × 14″, Collectors' Showcase, September 1988, $292.   *$150–$200*

How Green Was My Valley, 1941, 20th, Walter Pidgeon, Maureen O'Hara, Donald Crisp, final script dated April 18, 1941, copy #2, Philip Dunne, screenwriter, Collectors' Showcase, October 1988, $282.   *$150–$200*

★

NOTE: *This picture won five Academy Awards including best picture, best supporting actor (Donald Crisp), and best director (John Ford). It was Ford's third Oscar in the directing category.*

Invisible Man, The, 1933, UNIV, Claude Rains, Gloria Stuart, original script dated June 12, 1933, directed by James Whale, 125 pages, Collectors' Showcase, February 1989, $893.

$150–$250

NOTE: *Anything that touches this movie is gold to collectors.*

It Ain't No Sin (Belle of the Nineties), 1934, PAR, Mae West, original first script that was a working script for *Belle*, 80 pages, 8½″ × 14″, Collectors' Showcase, February 1989, $121.

$150–$200

NOTE: *Mae West wrote the story and screenplay.*

It Came From Outer Space, 1953, UNIV, Richard Carlson, Barbara Rush, Harry Essex's script, includes stills, revision pages, and map of the film's locale, leather bound, Camden House, May 1989, $200.

$300–$400

Laura, 1944, 20th, Gene Tierney, Dana Andrews, Clifton Webb, and *Farewell My Lovely*, 1944, RKO, Dick Powell, Claire Trevor, Anne Shirley, original studio scripts, Camden House, May 1989, $700.

$100–$200

NOTE: *Movie memorabilia of these two films is scarce, and of the two films, material on* Laura *(one of this author's favorite films), is more sought after by collectors.*

Let's Make Love, 1960, 20th, Marilyn Monroe, Yves Montand, original shooting script, dated December 30, 1959, final copy #7, 162 pages, rare, 9″ × 11½″, Collectors' Showcase, January 1989, $165.

$150–$250

Photo courtesy of Hake's Americana, York, PA

Maltese Falcon, The, 1941, WB, Humphrey Bogart, Mary Astor, Sydney Greenstreet, Peter Lorre, xeroxed final script by John Huston (from the Dashiell Hammett novel), dated May 26, 1941, bound, reprint, 8½″ × 11″, Limelight Books, August 1988, $20.   *$15–$20*

NOTE: One of a series of modern xeroxed reprint copy scripts that are sold in movie memorabilia shops and mail-order concerns primarily on the East and West Coasts.

Man Made Monster, 1941, UNIV, Lon Chaney, Jr., Lionel Atwill, original script with treatment, and a draft from *The Electric Man*, original title for film, still of Chaney included, Camden House, May 1989, $100.   *$50–$100*

Meet Me in St. Louis, 1944, MGM, Judy Garland, Margaret O'Brien, original studio typed carbon, dated May 7; 1942, 186 pages, very fine, 8½″ × 11″, Collectors' Showcase, September 1988, $293.   *$200–$250*

Mildred Pierce, 1945, WB, Joan Crawford (Academy Award for best actress), Ann Blyth, Zachary Scott, Jack Carson, original script, 1944, Camden House, May 1989, $550.   *$200–$300*

Mummy's Curse, The, 1944, UNIV, Lon Chaney, Jr., Virginia Christine, original script dated July 18, 1944, 94 pages, fine, Collectors' Showcase, February 1989, $298.   *$150–$250*

Night of January 16th, The, 1941, PAR, Ellen Drew, Robert Preston, dialogue movie script, dated May 29, 1941, based on an Ayn Rand play, 90 pages, fine + , 8 1/2 " × 14 ", Collectors' Showcase, November 1988, $102.   *$100–$150*

Nob Hill, 1945, 20th, George Raft, Joan Bennett, final shooting script, dated July 25, 1944, Jerry Ohlinger's, Fall 1988, $75.
$60–$100

Old-Fashioned Way, The, 1934, PAR, W.C. Fields, original working script, annotated, typed, dated April 13, 1934, one-of-a-kind, Collectors' Showcase, February 1989, $308. *$200–$300*

Ox-Bow Incident, The, 1943, 20th, Henry Fonda, Dana Andrews, dialogue and continuity script, dated November 17, 1942, Jerry Ohlinger's, Fall 1988, $100.   *$80–$125*

Panic in the Streets, 1950, 20th, Richard Widmark, Paul Douglas, dialogue and continuity script, dated June 6, 1950, Jerry Ohlinger's, Fall 1988, $100.   *$80–$125*

Poor Little Rich Girl, 1936, 20th, Shirley Temple, Alice Faye, Gloria Stuart, Jack Haley, final script, dated June 17, 1936, Jerry Ohlinger's, Fall 1988, $275   *$225–$325*

Rio Rita, 1942, MGM, Bud Abbott, Lou Costello, Kathryn Grayson, original working script, typed changes, annotations, 129 pages, fine, Collectors' Showcase, December 1988, $302.
$125–$150

Rocky Horror Picture Show, The, 1975, Tim Curry, Susan Sarandon, original continuity and dialogue script, complete post-production, around 175 pages, 8 1/4 " × 13 1/2 ", Collectors' Showcase, October 1988, $205.   *$150–$200*

Roxie Hart, 1942, 20th, Ginger Rogers, George Montgomery, dialogue and continuity script, dated January 22, 1942, Jerry Ohlinger's, Fall 1988, $100.   *$75–$100*

Santa Fe Trail, 1940, WB, Errol Flynn, Olivia de Havilland, Ronald Reagan, original and final script, parts one and two, treatment script with typed carbon letter discussing "perfect casting" of Flynn, 67 pages, Collectors' Showcase, January 1989, $100.   *$150–$200*

Second Fiddle, 1939, 20th, Tyrone Power, Sonja Henie, Rudy Vallee, dialogue and continuity script, dated June 30, 1939, Jerry Ohlinger's, Fall 1988, $75.   *$60–$100*

Secret Agent X-9, 1945, original script for complete 13-chapter serial with original pressbook, 9 pages, script 400 pages, very fine, Collectors' Showcase, October 1988, $99.   *$150–$200*

Should Married Men Go Home, 1928, MGM (Hal Roach), Laurel and Hardy, original continuity script, stamped "vault copy," wrappers, fine, Pepper & Stern, April 1989, $125.   *$100–$150*

Song of Bernadette, The, 1943, 20th, Jennifer Jones, Charles Bickford, Anne Revere, Gladys Cooper, revised final script, dated March 8, 1943, Jerry Ohlinger's, Fall 1988, $100.   *$75–$125*

Song of the Thin Man, 1947, MGM, William Powell, Myrna Loy, Gloria Grahame, Keenan Wynn, Dean Stockwell, Patricia Morrison, original script, dated January 2, 1947, 124 pages, Collectors' Showcase, December 1988, $75.   *$100–$150*

NOTE: *This was the last installment of the* Thin Man *series. There were six movies in all from 1934–1947.*

This Gun For Hire, 1942, PAR, Veronica Lake, Brian Donlevy, Alan Ladd, original script, dated 1941, 143 pages, fine, Collectors' Showcase, October 1988, $141.   *$100–$150*

Undying Monster, The, 1942, 20th, James Ellison, John Howard, original shooting script, dated July 16, 1942, 109 pages, Collectors' Showcase, December 1988, $200.   *$75–$125*

War of the Worlds, The, 1952, Gene Barry, Ann Robinson, revised final mimeographed script, dated January 11, 1952, Jerry Ohlinger's, Fall 1988, $150.   *$125–$175*

Wizard of Oz, The, 1939, MGM, Judy Garland, Ray Bolger, Jack Haley, Bert Lahr, Margaret Hamilton, original script, dated July 5, 1938, 126 pages, Camden House, May 1989, $15,000.
$15,000–$25,000

NOTE: *This is considered the rarest of all movie scripts because cast and crew received only typed pages for the next day's shooting as filming progressed, and then at the end of the day, all the pages were collected. None of the actors were given complete scripts. Scriptwriters were Florence Ryerson and Edgar Allan Woolf who were brought on after writer Noel Langley left the picture.*

★

Young Frankenstein, 1974, 20th, Gene Wilder, Madeline Kahn, Peter Boyle, fourth draft script, dated February 7, 1974, Jerry Ohlinger's, Fall 1988, $75.
$65–$85

SHEET MUSIC

INTRODUCTION

Sheet music collectors have a variety of categories or themes in which to specialize. Considering that sheet music is only one area of movie memorabilia, there exist hundreds of examples of music covers that can stand apart on their own merit as collectibles. Because sheet music is a prime crossover collectible, there is a broad spectrum of themes to choose from. For example, a piece of sheet music that pictures a famous actress disembarking from a train could appeal to both a collector of movie memorabilia and a collector of railroadiana. Frustration occurs when the collector has trouble deciding in which category to place the music.

Themes that are popular with collectors include star covers; composers and lyricists; film genres such as musicals, film noir, comedies, military, or animated cartoons; an article of clothing or jewelry worn by a particular actor or actress; or even a certain word that appears over and over again in certain song titles.

In researching this chapter, I found that some of the best examples of sheet music—those pieces that are rare or scarce— seldom appear in the marketplace because, as one prominent sheet music dealer hypothesized, the best examples are kept out of circulation to preserve their value over the years by keeping collector demand high. Trying to break down dealers' resistance in supplying me with such uncommon pieces of sheet music was very difficult, and most of what follow are songs that are fairly popular and found in large quantities at collectible shows and directly through dealers. They are priced in the low to medium price ranges, say anywhere from $1 to $25. The rare and scarce examples of sheet music are usually sold through mail/phone order auctions run by such dealers as John Aaron and Wayland

Bunnell (see reference chapter for addresses), and Beverly Hamer of East Derry, New Hampshire. John Van Doren, also listed in the reference chapter, sells fine examples of sheet music to collectors who are willing to pay high prices for uncommon music in the best possible condition.

Most sheet music produced after World War I was 9″ × 12″ in size; prior to the war, sheet music was 9″ × 14″ in size. Examples from the 1920s through 1940s are more popular with collectors than music from the 1950s on, although music from the early '50s is also sought after. Sheet music that was printed in the 1950s and later had the price printed into the cover, usually in the lower right-hand corner.

Sheet music should be stored in poly bags with acid-free cardboard backing. The bags should be left open so the music can breathe. Never affix scotch tape to close a poly bag, as it can tear off some of the cover art when the music is removed. Torn, soiled, dirty covers are not appreciated by collectors; neither are covers with ink signatures and loose spines. Think excellent condition when buying sheet music.

Sheet music is listed here by song title, date, movie title, major stars, cover description, lyricist/composer, condition, seller, month sold, price, and price range.

SHEET MUSIC LISTINGS

"*Again*," 1948, *Road House*, ink signature, very good, Music Between the Sheets, December 1988, $3.50.   *$3–$6*

"*All I Do is Dream of You*," 1934, *Sadie McKee*, Joan Crawford, words by Arthur Freed, music by Herb Brown, fine, Antique Prints & Paper (Triple Pier Expo), November 1988, $6. *$5–$10*

"*Alone*," 1935, *A Night at the Opera*, Allan Jones and Kitty Carlisle, partial spine separate, good, Music Between the Sheets, December 1988, $2.   *$2–$5*

"*Alone in the Rain*," 1929, *The Grand Parade*, Helen Twelvetrees, good, Music Between the Sheets, December 1988, $4.
                                                             $4–$8

"Always and Always," 1937, *Mannequin*, Joan Crawford, words by Bob Wright and Chet Forrest, music by Edward Ward, very fine, Paper Collectables & Memorabilia Show, September 1988, $5.   *$4–$9*

"An Earful of Music," 1934, *Kid Millions*, Eddie Cantor, words by Gus Kahn, music by Walter Donaldson, The Attic, July 1988, $2.   *$2–$8*

"Angela Mia (My Angel)," 1928, *Street Angel*, Charles Farrell and Janet Gaynor, words by Lew Pollack, music by Erno Rapee, fine, The Attic, September 1988, $2.   *$2–$5*

"Animal Crackers in Soup," 1935, *Curly Top*, Shirley Temple, soiled, Schoyer's Books, February 1989, $10.   *$9–$15*

"Anne of the Green Gables," 1919, Barbelle color cover, Mary Miles Minter (inset), Schoyer's Books, February 1989, $10.

$8–$12

NOTE: *Mary Miles Minter was a silent film actress whose career was blacklisted because of her involvement in the "murder" of Hollywood director William Desmond Taylor in 1922.*

"As Time Goes By," 1931, *Casablanca*, 1942, Humphrey Bogart, Ingrid Bergman, Paul Henried, fine +, Collectors' Showcase, December 1988, $61.   *$8–$40*

"Baby, It's Cold Outside," 1949, *Neptune's Daughter*, Esther Williams, Red Skelton, light crease mark, good, Music Between the Sheets, December 1988, $3.25.   *$2–$5*

"Blondy," 1929, *Marianne*, Marion Davies, illustrated color cover by John Held, Jr., Schoyer's Books, February 1989, $9.

$7–$13

"Blue Shadows on the Trail," 1948, *Melody Time*, very good, Collectors' Showcase, September 1988, $22.   *$10–$20*

"Boulevard of Broken Dreams," 1933, *Moulin Rouge*, Constance Bennett, words by Harry Dubin, music by Harry Warren, Schoyer's Books, February 1989, $7.   *$5–$10*

"*But Beautiful,*" 1947, *Road to Rio*, Bing Crosby, Bob Hope, Dorothy Lamour (three actors on a mule), inset of Andrew Sisters, Schoyer's Books, February 1989, $6. *$5–$8*

"*Buttons and Bows,*" 1948, *The Paleface*, Bob Hope, Jane Russell, words and music by Jay Livingston and Ray Evans, "special picture release," The Attic, June 1988, $3. *$3–$15*

★

NOTE: *This song won the Academy Award in best song category.*

★

"*By a Waterfall,*" 1933, *Footlight Parade*, words by Sammy Fain, music by Irving Kahal, illustrated cover of Busby Berkeley production number with James Cagney, Joan Blondell, Ruby Keeler, and Dick Powell in star insets, Schoyer's Books, February 1989, $8. *$7–$10*

"*Charming, 1929,*" *Devil May Care*, Ramon Navarro, words by C. Grey, music by H. Stothart, Schoyer's Books, February 1989, $7. *$2–$7*

"*Chatterbox,*" 1920, *Way Down East*, Lillian Gish, Schoyer's Books, February 1989, $10. *$8–$12*

"*College Rhythm,*" 1934, same, Joe Penner, Lanny Ross, Jack Oakie, Helen Mack, back cover montage ad for film, words and music by Mack Gordon and Harry Rovel, Schoyer's Books, February 1989, $10. *$8–$12*

"*Come to Me,*" 1931, *Indiscreet*, Gloria Swanson, words and music by Lew Brown, G.G. DeSylva, and Ray Henderson, very good, Music Between the Sheets, December 1988, $2.50.

$2.50–$7

"*Continental, The (You Kiss While You're Dancing),*" 1934, *The Gay Divorcee*, Fred Astaire and Ginger Rogers (dancing), words by Con Conrad, music by Herb Magidson, Schoyer's Books, February 1989, $10. *$7–$12*

★

NOTE: *Winner of the first Academy Award for best song.*

★

"Daddy Long Legs," 1919, Mary Pickford, Schoyer's Books, February 1989, $12.   *$9–$15*

"Der Fuehrer's Face," 1943, Disney cartoon, good, Collectors' Showcase, November 1988, $138.   *$25–$35*

"Diamonds Are Forever," 1971, Sean Connery, Jill St. John, words and music, Don Black, fine, Eugenia's Place (Atlanta Flea Market and Antiques Center), June 1988, $8.   *$6–$10*

"Did I Remember," 1936, *Suzy*, Jean Harlow, Cary Grant, Franchot Tone, "dedicated to Jean Harlow," words by Harold Adamson, music by Walter Donaldson, very fine, Antique Prints & Paper (Triple Pier Expo), November 1988, $10.   *$10–$25*

"Did I Remember," 1936, *Suzy*, very good, Collectors' Showcase, December 1988, $16.   *$8–$25*

"Dinner at Eight," 1933, illustrated cover features eight major stars from film including John and Lionel Barrymore, Wallace Beery, Marie Dressler, and Jean Harlow, Schoyer's Books, February 1989, $7.   *$6–$9*

"Don't Fence Me In," Hollywood Canteen, 1944, Joan Crawford, Barbara Stanwyck, Jane Wyman, and John Garfield, words and music by Cole Porter, fine, The Attic, June 1988, $3.

                                                                 $2–$6

"Ev'ryone Says 'I Love You,' " 1932, *Horsefeathers*, the Marx Brothers, Schoyer's Books, February 1989, $15.   *$12–$22*

"Everything's Been Done Before," 1935, *Reckless*, Jean Harlow, inset of William Powell (based on Libby Holman scandal), Schoyer's Books, February 1989, $8.   *$6–$10*

"Fallin' in Love Again," 1930, *The Blue Angel*, Emil Jannings, Marlene Dietrich, words and music by Frederich Hollander, very fine, Antique Prints & Paper (Triple Pier Expo), November 1988, $13.   *$12–$50*

"Fascination," 1922, *Mae Murray*, illustrated color cover by artist, Wohlman, fine, Schoyer's Books, February 1989, $8. *$7–$12*

"A Foggy Day," 1937, *A Damsel in Distress,* Fred Astaire, Joan Fontaine, George Burns, Gracie Allen, words by George Gershwin, music by Ira Gershwin, Schoyer's Books, February 1989, $7.   *$5–$10*

"For Heaven's Sake," 1926, title song, Harold Lloyd, Collectors' Showcase, October 1988, $29.   *$20–$30*

"Frankie and Johnny," 1933, *She Done Him Wrong,* Mae West, very provocative cover, words and music by Ralph Rainger, Collectors' Showcase, November 1988, $58.   *$12–$20*

"Freshies," 1925, *The Freshman* (The New Collegiate Fox Trot), inset of Lloyd in illustrated color cover with, in the center of a football, Fred Waring and his Pennsylvanians, fine, Schoyer's Books, February 1989, $12.   *$10–$15*

"Glad Rag Doll," 1929, same, Dolores Costello, illustrated color cover by the artist, Barbelle, Schoyer's Books, February 1989, $8.   *$6–$9*

NOTE: *Dolores Costello was the daughter of Maurice and sister of Helene Costello. Dolores was a silent film actress who married John Barrymore in the late 1920s. She was his third wife. Her best known post-silent film role was probably in* The Magnificent Ambersons *in 1942.*

"Goodbye, Little Darlin', Goodbye," 1940, *South of the Border,* Gene Autrey bluetone photo with gun, saddle, very fine, Hake's, November 1988, $23.   *$10–$25*

"Good Morning," 1939, *Babes in Arms,* Mickey Rooney, Judy Garland, Schoyer's Books, February 1989, $6.   *$4–$8*

"Have You Got Any Castles, Baby?," 1937, *Varsity Show,* small insets of stars including Dick Powell, illustrated color cover, Schoyer's Books, February 1989, $7.   *$5–$7*

"Heigh Ho!," 1937, *Snow White and the Seven Dwarfs,* Snow White and Dwarfs, fine, Cobweb Collectibles, September 1988, $8.   *$8–$33*

"Hello Baby," 1929, *The Forward Pass*, Douglas Fairbanks, Jr., Loretta Young, words and music by Herb Magidson, Ned Washington, and M.H. Cleary, Schoyer's Books, February 1989, $10.   *$8–$10*

"Here It Is Monday," 1944, *Song of the Road*, Sammy Kaye, Edgar Bergen, Charlie McCarthy, and W.C. Fields, others, Schoyer's Books, February 1989, $8.   *$6–$9*

"Hold My Hand," 1950, *Susan Slept Here*, Dick Powell, Debbie Reynolds, good, Music Between the Sheets, December 1988, $2.   *$2–$4*

"Hold Your Man," 1933, Jean Harlow, Clark Gable, words by Arthur Freed, music by Nacio Herb Brown, fine, Collectors' Showcase, October 1988, $82.   *$10–$40*

"How About You," 1941, *Babes on Broadway*, Mickey Rooney, Judy Garland, Schoyer's Books, February 1989, $8.   *$6–$10*

"How Little We Know," 1945, *To Have and Have Not*, Humphrey Bogart, Lauren Bacall, very good, Collectors' Showcase, November 1988, $45.   *$4–$25*

NOTE: *This was the film in which Lauren Bacall made her screen debut.*

"How Long Will It Last," 1931, *Possessed*, Joan Crawford, Clark Cable, words by Max Lief, music by Joseph Meyer, very good, Paper Collectables & Memorabilia Show, November 1988, $3.
                    $3–$7

"How Ya' Gonna Keep 'Em Down on the Farm?," 1942, *For Me and My Gal*, Judy Garland, Schoyer's Books, February 1989, $6.
                    $5–$7

NOTE: *Gene Kelly made his screen debut in this movie.*

"Humoresque," 1946, from the movie of the same name, Joan Crawford, John Garfield, mint, John Van Doren, December 1988, $12.   *$10–$14*

NOTE: *Isaac Stern dubbed the violin solo for actor John Garfield. So it would look authentic that Garfield was playing the violin, a large hole was cut into the elbow of Garfield's coat so a real violinist's hand could do the fingering, while a second violinist, standing directly behind the actor, moved the bow.*

"I Can't Escape From You," 1936, *Rhythm on the Range*, Bing Crosby, Francis Farmer, Schoyer's Books, February 1989, $6.
                    $4–$7

"I Have to Have You," 1929, *Pointed Heels*, Helen Kane, inset of Skeets Gallagher, Schoyer's Books, February 1989, $7.
                    $4–$8

"I Love You Then (As I Love You Now)," 1928, *Our Dancing Daughters*, Joan Crawford, very good, Music Between the Sheets, December 1988, $1.50.   *$1.50–$4*

"I Want You, I Need You," 1933, *I'm No Angel*, Mae West, Wohlman cover, West biography on back cover, words and music by Harvey Brooks, Gladys de Boise, and Ben Ellison, Schoyer's Books, February 1989, $12.   *$10–$16*

"I Wished on the Moon," 1935, *Big Broadcast of 1935*, Bing Crosby, very good, Music Between the Sheets, December 1988, $4.   *$3–$5*

"I'd Know You Anywhere," 1940, *You'll Find Out*, Boris Karloff, Peter Lorre, Bela Lugosi, Helen Parrish, Kay Keyser, words by Johnny Mercer, music by Jimmy McHugh, very good, Schoyer's Books, March 1989, $7.   *$7–$10*

Photo courtesy of Hake's Americana, York, PA

"If I Had My Way," 1929, *The Flying Circus*, William Boyd, Marie Prevost, purpletone photo, very good condition of this early aviation sheet music, Hake's, April 1989, $20.   *$10–$20*

"*If You Please*," 1943, *Dixie*, Bing Crosby, Dorothy Lamour, words and music by Johnny Burke and Jimmy Van Heusen, fine, The Attic, June 1988, $3. $2–$5

"*I'll Sing a Thousand Love Songs*," 1936, *Cain and Mabel*, Clark Gable, Marion Davies (two production numbers), Schoyer's Books, February 1989, $8. $6–$10

"*I'll String Along With You*," 1934, *20 Million Sweethearts*, Dick Powell, Ginger Rogers, words by Al Dubin, music by Harry Warren, Cobweb Collectibles, September 1988, $3. $2–$6

"*I'm Goin' to Break That Mason Dixon Line (Until I Get to That Gal of Mine)*," 1919, Priscilla Dean, Ghurston Hall, Natwick (artist) cover, very good, Music Between the Sheets, December 1988, $4. $4–$6

"*I'm in Heaven When I See You Smile, Diane*," 1927, *Seventh Heaven*, Janet Gaynor, this is the love waltz from *Seventh Heaven*, very good, La Belle Boutique, August 1988, $4. $3–$5

"*I'm the Last of the Red Hot Mammas*," 1929, *Honky Tonk*, Sophie Tucker, Barbelle illustrated color cover, Schoyer's Books, February 1989, $8. $7–$9

NOTE: First feature film of this vaudeville star.

"*I'm Nobody's Baby*," 1940, *Andy Hardy Meets Debutante*, copyrighted music 1921, Judy Garland, Mickey Rooney, words and music by Benny Davis, Milton Ager, Lester Santly, very fine, Cobweb Collectibles, September 1988, $20. $5–$30

NOTE: This is one of those pieces of sheet music where, depending on the buyer, the seller, and the region of the country, the prices can go haywire. In New Jersey, the price was $20, in New York the same piece in a little less fine condition went for $5, at auction on the West Coast it went for $30, and at auction in the Northeast it went for $15. Interesting, too, is that the song was copyrighted in 1921 and is not original to the Andy Hardy movie. But the cover is wonderful with a beautiful shot of Rooney and Garland with big happy smiles on their faces. This is an ideal case of what the buyer will pay, and what the seller will charge.

"In Old Kentucky," 1919, Anita Stewart, Louis B. Mayer (director), horse on cover, good, Music Between the Sheets, December 1988, $4.   *$3–$6*

"Isn't This a Lovely Day," 1935, *Top Hat*, Fred Astaire, Ginger Rogers, words and music by Irving Berlin, music store stamp, very good, Music Between the Sheets, December 1988, $8.

$6–$12

"It Can't Be Wrong," 1942, *Now Voyager*, Bette Davis, very fine, Cobweb Collectibles, September 1988, $8.   *$6–$15*

NOTE: *This was the movie with the immortal Davis line: "Let's not ask for the moon, when we have the stars," at the same time that Paul Henreid lights two cigarettes and hands one to Davis. The line might work today but the audience would be up in arms over the cigarettes. Irene Dunne was originally slated for Davis' role.*

"I've Got a Feelin' You're Foolin'," 1936, *Broadway Melody of 1936*, nine actors depicted on cover including Jack Benny, Robert Taylor, Buddy Ebsen, Eleanor Powell, Schoyer's Books, February 1989, $8.   *$6–$11*

"I've Got to Sing a Torch Song," 1933, *Gold Diggers of 1933*, Ginger Rogers, words by Al Dubin, music by Harry Warren, fine, Schoyer's Books, February 1989, $10.   *$8–$14*

"I've Lost You So Why Should I Care," 1916, no specific movie title tie-in, Theda Bara (first film vamp) large inset, illustrated color cover, Schoyer's Books, February 1989, $12.   *$10–$15*

"I've Got a Pocketful of Dreams," 1938, *Sing You Sinners*, Bing Crosby, Fred MacMurray, Donald O'Connor, and a horse, The Attic, June 1988, $3.   *$3–$5*

"*Jitterbug, The,*" 1939, *The Wizard of Oz*, Judy Garland, Ray Bolger, Jack Haley, Bert Lahr, Frank Morgan, words by E.Y. Harburg, music by Harold Arlen, fine, Paper Collectables & Memorabilia Show, April 1989, $15.   *$10–$22*

"*Just an Old Love Song,*" 1922, *Robin Hood*, theme song, Douglas Fairbanks, Schoyer's Books, February 1989, $10.   *$8–$12*

"*Laugh Clown Laugh,*" 1928, Lon Chaney, worn cover, good, Collectors' Showcase, January 1989, $5.   *$5–$8*

NOTE: *Average price range for a good copy. A better copy would bring anywhere from $10–$20 and higher if bought through a mail-order auction.*

"Let's Begin," 1935, *Roberta*, Irene Dunne, Fred Astaire, Ginger Rogers (Dunne is most prominently photographed on cover), music by Jerome Kern, very good, Collectors' Showcase, January 1989, $10. *$8–$14*

★

NOTE: *If this song had featured only Fred Astaire and Ginger Rogers, with perhaps Irene Dunne in a small inset, then the sheet music would be more desirable to a collector, unless that collector is assembling material on Irene Dunne exclusively. Astaire and Rogers on almost any form of movie memorabilia is very collectible and usually expensive.*

★

"Little Annie Rooney," 1925 (only authorized edition), Mary Pickford, Schoyer's Books, February 1989, $12. *$10–$15*

"Little Colonel," 1935, Shirley Temple and dedicated to her, good, Schoyer's Books, February 1989, $10. *$10–$14*

"Lonely Gal, Lonely Guy," 1961, *The George Raft Story*, Jayne Mansfield, Ray Danton, Barrie Chase, words and music by Jeff Alexander, mint, John Van Doren, February 1989, $25.

$20–$30

"Long Ago and Far Away," 1944, *Cover Girl*, Rita Hayworth, words by Ira Gershwin and Jerome Kern, Schoyer's Books, February 1989, $6. $5–$8

"Louise," 1929, *Innocents of Paris*, Maurice Chevalier (his first talkie film), Schoyer's Books, February 1989, $6. $6–$8

"Love in Bloom," 1934, *She Loves Me Not*, words and music by Leo Robin and Ralph Rainger, Bing Crosby on cover playing guitar, Paper Collectables & Memorabilia Show, June 1988, $3. $3–$6

NOTE: *Very common title—one sees it at every collectible show, usually in the above price range.*

"Love Is Here to Stay," 1938, *The Goldwyn Follies*, the Ritz Brothers, Edgar Bergen and Charlie McCarthy, words by George Gershwin, Schoyer's Books, February 1989, $10. $7–$10

"Lovely to Look At," 1935, *Roberta*, Fred Astaire, Ginger Rogers, large inset of Irene Dunne, soiled, Jerome Kern music, Schoyer's Books, February 1989, $7. $5–$10

"Love Me Tender," 1956, same, Elvis Presley, fine, Black Mountain Antique Center, June 1988, $10. $10–$20

"Lullaby Time," 1919, Mabel Norman full-cover photo, pencil signature, very good, Music Between the Sheets, December 1988, $6. $5–$9

NOTE: *Mabel Norman was involved in the William Desmond Taylor scandal in 1922 and her films were blacklisted as a result. She was a famous silent screen comedienne who began her career circa 1910 at Biograph before teaming up with Mack Sennett in 1912. She went on to become one of the silent film era's most famous stars. A drug addict, she died in 1930.*

"Magic Is the Moonlight," 1944, *Bathing Beauty*, Esther Williams, Red Skelton, Xavier Cugat, Harry James, montage cover, Schoyer's Books, February 1989, $7. $5–$8

"*Marie,*" 1928, *The Awakening,* theme song with center inset of Vilma Banky, words and music by Irving Berlin, Schoyer's Books, February 1989, $8.   *$6–$9*

NOTE: *Vilma Banky was Ronald Colman's vis à vis in several romantic melodramas produced by Samuel Goldwyn in the mid to late 1920s. When sound came in, Banky went out—her voice, with its heavy Hungarian accent, couldn't make the transition to talkies.*

"*Maybe It's Love,*" 1930, large photo of Tim Moynihan from Notre Dame, Ray Montgomery from Pitt, and Howard Harpster from Carnegie Tech (the All-American Football Team), plus insets of Joan Bennett and Joe E. Brown, Schoyer's Books, February 1989, $12.   *$10–$16*

"*Mickey,*" 1917, Mabel Normand, dedicated to her, this title includes four different sheet music covers of Mickey including two Barbelle covers, one Pfeiffer cover (war-time small edition), one other, Normand on all covers, words and music by Williams and Moret, Schoyer's Books, February 1989, $25.   *$22–$30*

"*Moon Is Low, The,*" 1930, *Montana Moon,* Joan Crawford inset, illustrated color cover of cowboy and cowgirl, Schoyer's Books, February 1989, $8.   *$6–$8*

"*Moon of Manakoora, The,*" 1937, *The Hurricane,* Dorothy Lamour, Jon Hall, in a South Seas island setting, words by Frank Loesser, music by Alfred Newman, Schoyer's Books, February 1989, $7.   *$4–$8*

"*Moon River,*" 1961, *Breakfast at Tiffany's,* Audrey Hepburn, words and music by Henri Mancini, Johnny Mercer, very good, Music Between the Sheets, December 1988, $2.   *$2–$4*

NOTE: *Based on the Truman Capote novel.*

"*Moonburn,*" 1936, *Anything Goes,* Bing Crosby, Ethel Merman, montage cover, words by Edward Heyman and Hoagy Carmichael, music by Cole Porter(?), Schoyer's Books, February 1989, $7.   *$5–$8*

"Moonlight Becomes You," 1942, *Road to Morocco*, Bob Hope, Bing Crosby, Dorothy Lamour (in costume), words by Johnny Burke, music by Jimmy Van Heusen, Schoyer's Books, February 1989, $5.   *$3–$6*

"Mother of Mine, I Still Have You," 1927, *The Jazz Singer*, Al Jolson, Schoyer's Books, February 1989, $6.   *$4–$6*

"Mr. and Mrs. Is the Name," 1934, *Flirtation Walk*, Dick Powell, Ruby Keeler, Schoyer's Books, February 1989, $6.   *$5–$7*

"My Baby Just Cares for Me," 1930, *Whoopee*, Eddie Cantor, illustrated color cover by Manning, Schoyer's Books, February 1989, $7.   *$5–$8*

"My Mother's Eyes," 1928, *Lucky Boy*, George Jessel, Schoyer's Books, February 1989, $8.   *$6–$8*

"My Old Flame," 1934, *Belle of the Nineties*, Mae West, minor wear, fine, Collectors' Showcase, October 1988, $49.   *$12–$20*

NOTE: *Collectors' Showcase had an estimate of $25–$30 for this sheet music title, but a more conservative price range would be closer to the above.*

"My Own True Love," 1938, *Gone With the Wind*, illustrated cover of buildings and characters from film, very fine, Willow Valley Collectibles, March 1989, $18.   *$13–$22*

"Night Is Young, The," 1935, Ramon Navarro, Evelyn Laye, words by Oscar Hammerstein II, music by Sigmund Romberg, fine, Paper Collectables & Memorabilia Show, February 1989, $7.   *$0–$8*

"Oh Helen!," 1918, comedian Fatty Arbuckle on cover, dedicated to the silent film comedian, bit wear, fine, Collectors' Showcase, October 1988, $30.   *$25–$35*

On the Atchison, Topeka and the Santa Fe," 1945, *The Harvey Girls*, Judy Garland, words by Harry Warren, music by Johnny Mercer, Schoyer's Books, February 1989, $6.   *$3–$7*

★

NOTE: *This song won the Academy Award in 1946.*

★

"On the Boardwalk (in Atlantic City)," 1946, *Three Little Girls in Blue*, June Haver, George Montgomery, Vera Ellen, Vivian Blaine, Frank Latimore, words by Mack Gordon, music by Josef Myrow, The Attic, September 1988, $1.   *$1–$3*

"On the Good Ship Lollipop," 1934, *Bright Eyes*, Shirley Temple (her most famous song), spine end off, soiled, good, words by Sidney Claire, music by Richard Whiting, Collectors' Showcase, October 1988, $31.   *$15–$25*

★

NOTE: *Above price range is for a fine copy of this sheet music. It is amazing that a collector would pay $31 for a soiled copy with a part of the spine end off. West Coast movie memorabilia collectors tend to spend more money for collectibles than East Coast collectors, many times disregarding the condition of a particular item for sale.*

★

"On the Sentimental Side," 1938, *Doctor Rhythm*, Bing Crosby, Mary Carlisle, Schoyer's Books, February 1989, $6.   *$4–$7*

"Once and For Always," 1948, *A Connecticut Yankee in King Arthur's Court*, Bing Crosby, Rhonda Fleming, Schoyer's Books, February 1989, $7.   *$4–$7*

"One Little Drink," 1930, *Song of the Flame*, Bernice Claire, Alexander Gray, Schoyer's Books, February 1989, $7.   *$6–$8*

"One in a Million," 1936, same, Sonja Henie (on skates, natch), insets of stars and chorus line around Henie center photo, Schoyer's Books, February 1989, $8.   *$5–$8*

"Orchids in the Moonlight," 1933, *Flying Down to Rio*, Fred Astaire, Dolores Del Rio, words by Gus Kahn, Edward Eliscu, music by Vincent Youmans, good, Music Between the Sheets, December 1988, $4.   *$4–$7*

"*Out of the Dawn,*" 1928, *Warming Up*, Richard Dix, Schoyer's Books, February 1989, $8.   *$6-$8*

"*Over the Rainbow,*" 1939, *The Wizard of Oz*, Judy Garland, Ray Bolger, Jack Haley, Bert Lahr, Frank Morgan, words by E.Y. Harburg, music by Harold Arlen, cover wear, good, Collectors' Showcase, November 1988, $42.   *$12-$75*

"*Over the Rainbow,*" 1939, *The Wizard of Oz*, same except fine, Collectors' Showcase, December 1988, $79.   *$12-$75*

"*Over the Rainbow,*" 1939, *The Wizard of Oz*, same except fine, Schoyer's Books, February 1989, $15.   *$12-$75*

"*Over the Rainbow,*" 1939, *The Wizard of Oz*, same except very fine, Hake's, April 1989, $60.   *$12-$75*

NOTE: I have listed four different sellers for "Over the Rainbow" to show how one piece of sheet music in various conditions can sell to collectors at the price they want to pay. The lowest price I have seen this title go for is $12, the highest $65, but I am adding another $10 to the price range because I'm sure somewhere it has been marked for that price, and in all probability, even higher. Notice again that the West Coast buyer paid $42 for a copy of sheet music with cover wear and only in good condition, as opposed to Schoyer's in Pennsylvania with a price of $15 and Hake's, also in Pennsylvania, with a final bid of $60, but for a very fine example.

"*Pagan Love Song,*" 1930, *The Pagan*, Ramon Navarro, very good, La Belle Boutique, August 1988, $5.   *$3-$8*

"*Personality,*" 1945, *The Road to Utopia*, Bob Hope, Bing Crosby, Dorothy Lamour, words by Johnny Burke, music by Jimm Van Heusen, Schoyer's Books, February 1989, $5.   *$3-$7*

"Pettin' in the Park," 1933, *Gold Diggers of 1933*, Warren William, Joan Blondell, Ginger Rogers, Ruby Keeler, Dick Powell, words by Al Dubin, music by Harry Warren, very good, Music Between the Sheets, December 1988, $3.50.   *$3–$5*

"Poor Pauline," 1914, *The Perils of Pauline*, Pearl White, cover detached, but cleanly, Schoyer's Books, February 1989, $12.
          $10–$15

"A Precious Little Thing Called Love," 1928, *The Shopworn Angel*, Gary Cooper, Nancy Carroll inset, Schoyer's Books, February 1989, $8.   *$6–$10*

"Raftero," 1934, *Bolero*, George Raft, Carole Lombard in a very provocative cover pose photo, plus smaller inset photos of the stars, words and music by Ralph Rainger, very good, Papermania, January 1989, $10.   *$8–$12*

"Reaching For the Moon," 1939, Douglas Fairbanks, Bebe Daniels, lightly faded, good, Music Between the Sheets, December 1988, $6.   *$5–$8*

"Reckless," 1935, Jean Harlow, center crease, very good, Collectors' Showcase, October 1988, $50.   *$25–$30*

"Reckless," 1935, same, but in very fine condition, Collectors' Showcase, January 1989, $38.   *$35–$40*

★

NOTE: *It is interesting that the collector who bought the sheet music in the first mail-order auction paid $50 for a creased good copy, while the second collector paid $38 for a copy in very fine condition.*

"Red Lantern, The," 1919, Alla Nazimova, Schoyer's Books, February 1989, $7.   *$5–$9*

"*Re-Enlistment Blues,*" 1953, *From Here to Eternity*, Burt Lancaster, Montgomery Clift, Deborah Kerr, Donna Reed, Frank Sinatra, words and music by James Jones (author of the book on which film was based), Robert Wells, Fred Karger, near mint, John Van Doren, February 1989, $15. $10–$20

"*San Francisco,*" 1936, Clark Gable, Jeanette MacDonald in a clinch on the cover, words and music by Gus Kahn, B. Kaper, W. Jurmann, very good, La Belle Boutique, August 1988, $10. $8–$12

"*School Days,*" 1922, song copyright 1907, Wesley Barry, inset photo thereof, words and music by Gus Edwards, Music Between the Sheets, December 1988, $3.   *$3–$5*

NOTE: *Wesley Barry was a child actor under contract to WB in the very, very early days of the studio. He was a forerunner of the Jackie Cooper-Roddy McDowall-type child actor.*

"*She Doesn't,*" 1925, *Go West,* Buster Keaton and a cow in a cover illustration by Barbelle and dedicated to Keaton and "His Beautiful Baby Cow 'Brown Eyes'," words by Walter Winchell, music by Jimmy Durante, Schoyer's Books, February 1989, $15.   *$12–$20*

"*Sing Baby Sing,*" 1936, Alice Faye, the Ritz Brothers, Adolph Menjou, in front of a microphone, words by Jack Yellen, music by Lew Pollack, very fine, Paper Collectables & Memorabilia Show, September 1988, $6.   *$4–$8*

"*Singin' in the Rain,*" 1929, *Hollywood Revue of 1929,* various actors on cover including Joan Crawford in star inserts, words by Arthur Freed, music by Nacio Herb Brown, La Belle Boutique, August 1988, $10.   *$8–$15*

"*Siren's Song,*" 1919, *The Siren's Song,* Theda Bara, good, Collectors' Showcase, January 1989, $9.   *$8–$15*

"*Someday, I'll Meet You Again,*" 1944, *Passage to Marseille,* black and white photo of Humphrey Bogart and Michele Moran, and pinktone montage of scenes from film, words by Ned Washington, music by Max Steiner, fine, Hake's, November 1988, $30.   *$25–$30*

"*Someday, I'll Meet You Again,*" 1944, *Passage to Marseille,* same as above, but very fine, Collectors' Showcase, October 1988, $57. $10–$25

NOTE: *This is another example of sheet music selling for a much higher price than it deserves. The first copy, although listed as fine, had some flaking off the black portion of the suit Bogart is wearing on the cover. This piece was bought by yours truly before he knew what he knows now, so I only have myself to blame. The second piece went for almost double the price I paid, and in just very fine condition. Both pieces were overpriced for what professional sheet music dealers consider just a standard song title. However, owing to the Bogart craze among collectors, this sheet music will probably go on selling way above its price range (which is also on the high side), particularly at mail-order auctions. Actual price range is closer to $1–$20.*

"*Some Sunday Morning,*" 1945, *San Antonio,* Errol Flynn, Alexis Smith, dancing in western clothes, Schoyer's Books, February 1989, $6. $5–$7

"*Song of the Big Trail,*" title song, 1930, John Wayne (very young looking), Willow Valley Collectibles, June 1989, $18.   *$15–$25*

"*Speedy Boy,*" 1928, *Speedy*, Harold Lloyd, Schoyer's Books, February 1989, $12.   *$10–$16*

"*Suddenly It's Spring,*" 1944, *Lady in the Dark*, Ginger Rogers, Schoyer's, February 1989, $5.   *$2–$6*

"*Tara's Theme,*" 1939, *Gone With the Wind*, Clark Gable, Vivien Leigh, and Tara on cover, name sticker (1954 issue), corner crease, very good, Music Between the Sheets, December 1988, $15.   *$12–$18*

"*That's Amore,*" 1953, *The Caddy*, Dean Martin, Jerry Lewis, Donna Reed, Lewis looking forlornly at Martin and Reed while a golf beg leans against him, words by Jack Brooks, music by Harry Warren, Paper Collectables & Memorabilia Show, September 1988, $4.   *$4–$8*

"*That Wonderful Something,*" 1929, *Untamed*, Joan Crawford, dancing on illustrated cover (Crawford's first talking film), Schoyer's Books, February 1989, $12.   *$7–$15*

"*There's a New Star in Heaven To-Night,*" 1926, Rudolph Valentino, very good, Collectors' Showcase, March 1989, $32.
                                                            $25–$35

"*There's Something in the Air,*" 1936, *Banjo on My Knee*, Barbara Stanwyck, Anthony Martin, plus smaller photos of Joel McCrea and Buddy Ebsen, Schoyer's Books, February 1989, $7.   *$5–$8*

"*They Can't Take That Away From Me,*" 1937, *Shall We Dance*, Fred Astaire, Ginger Rogers, plus two dogs, words by Ira Gershwin, music by George Gershwin, Schoyer's Books, February 1989, $8.   *$8–$15*

"*Third Man Theme, The,*" 1949, Joseph Cotton, Orson Welles, Valli, Schoyer's Books, February 1989, $5.   *$5–$12*

"*Third Man Theme, The,*" 1949, same and identical to above but with minor creases, very good, Collectors' Showcase, November 1988, $28.   *$5–$12*

"This Year's Kisses," 1937, *On the Avenue*, Alice Faye, Dick Powell, both in cameo shot on cover in bluetone, head shots of the Ritz Brothers, scenes from film in pinktone, words and music by Irving Berlin, fine, Paper Collectables & Memorabilia Show, September 1988, $4.   *$4–$9*

"Three Dreams," 1942, *The Powers Girl*, George Murphy and Anne Shirley, inset of Benny Goodman, Schoyer's, February 1989, $7.   *$5–$8*

"Three Little Words," 1930, *Check and Double Check*, Amos 'N' Andy, pinktone and black and white, words, music, and story by Bert Kalmar and Harry Ruby, very fine, Paper Collectables & Memorabilia Show, May 1989, $15.   *$15–$40*

★

NOTE: *This was the only film appearance of the popular radio entertainers Amos 'N' Andy.*

★

"True Confession," 1937, Carole Lombard, Fred MacMurry, Russ Morgan, band leader, biography on back cover, Schoyer's Books, February 1989, $7.   *$6–$10*

"Two Sleepy People," 1938, *Thanks for the Memory*, Bob Hope, Shirley Ross, Artie Shaw, bandleader, biography on back cover, Schoyer's Books, February 1989, $6.   *$4–$7*

"Wait and See," 1919, Constance Talmadge photo on cover, Joe Sherman inset, ink signature, good, Music Between the Sheets, December 1988, $3.   *$3–$5*

★

NOTE: *Constance Talmadge was the middle sister of the famous Talmadge girls of the silent screen. Constance was the happy-go-lucky comedienne of the trio. She retired from films in 1928.*

★

"Waiting at the End of the Road," 1929, *Hallelujah*, spine is partially split, good, Music Between the Sheets, December 1988, $6.   *$5–$6*

"Was It Rain," 1937, *The Hit Parade*, Francis Langford, Phil Regan, words by Walter Hirsch, music by Lou Handman, very good, La Belle Boutique, August 1988, $3.   *$2–$4*

"*Way You Look Tonight, The,*" 1936, *Swing Time*, Fred Astaire and Ginger Rogers dancing, words by Dorothy Fields, music by Jerome Kern, Schoyer's Books, February 1989, $10.   *$8–$15*

NOTE: *Winner of the Academy Award for best song in 1936.*

"*Weary River,*" 1929, Richard Barthelmess in center inset, Schoyer's Books, February 1989, $6.   *$5–$7*

"*Wedding of the Painted Doll, The,*" 1929, *The Broadway Melody*, center inset of Geraldine and Anne Beaumont, child stars, in an illustrated color cartoon cover by the artist, Griffith, Schoyer's Books, February 1989, $10.   *$8–$12*

"*We'll Make Hay While the Sun Shines,*" 1933, *Going Hollywood*, Marion Davies, Bing Crosby, Schoyer's Books, February 1989, $8.   *$6–$9*

"*When I Grow Too Old to Dream,*" 1935, *The Night is Young*, Ramon Navarro, Evelyn Laye, words by Oscar Hammerstein, music by Sigmund Romberg, fine, The Attic, September 1988, $1.   *$3–$6*

"*When the Real Thing Comes Your Way,*" 1929, *Illusion*, Nancy Carroll, Buddy Rogers, insets on illustrated color cover, Schoyer's Books, February 1989, $8.   *$6–$10*

"*When You Wish Upon a Star,*" 1940, *Pinocchio*, Walt Disney Productions, fine, Collectors' Showcase, January 1989, $18.   *$15–$30*

NOTE: *Disney sheet music tends to have cycles as regards prices a collector will pay. The above is a conservative price range, which some dealers might think is too steep, but prices for this particular song title, and others in Disney movies, tend to be standard within the last 13 months.*

"*Where Is the Song of Songs For Me,*" 1929, *Lady of the Pavements*, inset of Lupe Velez, ink signature, edge wear, good, words and music by Irving Berlin, Music Between the Sheets, December 1988, $2.50.   *$2.50–$8*

"Whispers in the Dark," 1937, *Artists & Models*, Jack Benny cover in which the actor is working on a large painting, Schoyer's Books, February 1989, $7.   *$5–$9*

"Who's Afraid of the Big Bad Wolf," 1939, *Three Little Pigs*, Silly Symphony music, words and music by Irving Berlin, very good, Collectors' Showcase, November 1988, $57.   *$25–$35*

"Who's Afraid of the Big Bad Wolf," 1939, *Three Little Pigs*, same as above except for fine condition, Paper Collectables & Memorabilia Show, November 1988, $7.   *$6–$35*

NOTE: *See reference for "When You Wish Upon a Star."*

"Why Didn't You Leave Me Years Ago Instead of Leaving Me Now," 1920, Mabel Normand on cover, words and music by Mitchell and Clarke, light crease, very good, Music Between the sheets, December 1988, $7.50.   *$7.50–$10*

"Why Do I Dream Those Dreams," 1934, *Wonder Bar*, Al Jolson, Dolores Del Rio, Kay Francis, Dick Powell, and Ricardo Cortez, ink signature, light surface wear, good, Music Between the Sheets, December 1988, $3.50.   *$3.50–$8*

NOTE: *This was the quintessential WB musical of the 1930s.*

"With Plenty of Money and You," 1936, *Gold Diggers of 1937*, Berkley chorus line montage, photo of Dick Powell and Joan Blondell, also Blondell in a large central photo, words by Al Dubin, music by Harry Warren, Schoyer's Books, February 1989, $8.   *$6–$9*

"You Brought a New Kind of Love to Me," 1930, *The Big Pond*, Maurice Chevalier, Claudette Colbert, Schoyer's Books, February 1989, $8.   *$7–$9*

"You Gave Me Your Heart (So I Give You Mine)," 1922, *Blood and Sand* (suggestion), color cover with Rudolph Valentino in center photo, Schoyer's Books, February 1989, $10.   *$10–$18*

"You'll Never Know," 1943, *Hello, Frisco, Hello,* Alice Faye, John Payne, Jack Oakie, Lynn Bari in center photo, pinktone border, words and music by Mack Gordon and Harry Warren, fine, Black Mountain Antique Center, June 1988, $1.   *$1–$5*

"You're Getting to be a Habit With Me," 1933, *42nd Street,* Bebe Daniels, Dick Powell, Ginger Rogers, others on cover, words by Al Dubin, music by Harry Warren, good, Paper Collectables & Memorabilia Show, September 1988, $4.   *$3–$7*

"Your Mother and Mine," 1929, *Hollywood Revue of 1929,* cover shows Bessie Love, Buster Keaton, Jack Benny, Marion Davies, Charles King, Joan Crawford, William Haines, and others in star-shaped insets, words by Arthur Freed, music by Nacio Herb Brown, edge wear, very good, Music Between the Sheets, December 1988, $4.50.   *$3–$8*

SONG FOLIOS LISTING

Gene Autry Song Folio, circa 1930s (early), Book #2, 28 western songs, authored entirely or partly by Autry, 64 pages, very good, 9″ × 12″, Hake's, February 1989, $70.   *$25–$40*

Chitty Chitty Bang Bang, vocal selections from movie (songs, action photos, biography), Paper Collectables & Memorabilia Show, January 1989, $4.   *$5–$12*

Hollywood Song Folio, 1939, with 12 stars on the cover including Judy Garland, Bing Crosby, Alice Faye, 66 pages, fine, Collectors' Showcase, January 1989, $10.   *$12–$25*

Tex Ritter Song Folio, 1941, softbound, words and music of western songs, Ritter on cover, biography included, also montage on last page of black and white film scenes from Ritter's movies, 96 pages, fine, 9″ × 12″, Hake's, November 1988, $14.   *$10–$20*

This Is the Army, souvenir album from WB film, 1943, complete words and music by Irving Berlin, many photos, 36 pages, fine, Schoyer's Books, February 1989, $15.   *$15–$20*

Thunderball, 1965, souvenir song album, photos of James Bond, 34 pages, fine, 8½″ × 11″, Collectors' Showcase, October 1988, $25. — $18–$30

Photo courtesy of Hake's Americana, York, PA

Tom Mix Western Songs Folio, softcover, words and music to 46 western and cowboy songs, black and white photo of Mix on cover and four pages in center with photos and a biography, undated but new songs have 1935 copyright, 66 pages, very fine, 9″ × 12″, Hake's, April 1989, $22. $20–$40

Warner Brothers Song Folio, volume #1, full-page portraits of Errol Flynn, Bette Davis, plus photos of Flynn filming *Robin Hood*, music, 50 pages, Collectors' Showcase, November 1988, $35. $25–$35

Wizard of Oz, The, souvenir music album, 1939, Judy Garland, Ray Bolger, Jack Haley, Bert Lahr, and Frank Morgan on cover, contains all the songs from the movie, words by E.Y. Harburg, music by Harold Arlen, later edition, very fine, Papermania, January 1989, $35. $30–$40

SOUVENIR PROGRAMS

INTRODUCTION

Souvenir programs were distributed to moviegoers at theaters where a particular film was being shown. The programs were usually about 20 pages long and included black and white and/or color photographs, plus a text describing the film and its stars. The Disney souvenir program for *Fantasia* was produced in full color.

Souvenir programs were produced from the early days of silent films through the present time, although most "programs" received in theaters these days are really one- or two-page flyers listing the cast and technical credits of a film.

Many souvenir programs were given out at the important Hollywood premieres, such as at Grauman's Chinese Theater. Important illustrators and artists were sometimes commissioned to design the cover of a particular souvenir program; these programs are more valuable to collectors and bring higher prices.

The following list of souvenir programs is arranged by movie title, release date, studio, major stars, program description, condition, size, seller, month sold, and prices.

SOUVENIR PROGRAMS LISTING

All This and Heaven Too, 1940, WB, Bette Davis, Charles Boyer, Barbara O'Neil, 20 pages, fine, 9″ × 12″, Collectors' Showcase, January 1989, $220.   *$100–$150*

Beau Geste, 1926, PAR, Ronald Colman, 20 pages, 9″ × 12″, Collectors' Showcase, January 1989, $22.   *$20–$25*

★

NOTE: Remade in 1939 with Gary Cooper in Colman's role.

★

Ben Hur, 1927, MGM, Ramon Navarro, May McAvoy, Francis X. Bushman, 20 pages, fair, Collectors' Showcase, January 1989, $14.   *$20–$25*

Big Parade, The, 1925, MGM, John Gilbert, Renee Adoree, silent film war epic, cover loose, 16 pages, very good +, 9″ × 12″, Collectors' Showcase, December 1988, $44.   *$35–$45*

Birth of a Nation, The, 1915, Biography, directed by D.W. Griffith, 24 pages, Guernsey's, April 1989, $90.   *$100–$200*

Circus, The, 1928, UA, Charles Chaplin, souvenir program for the opening at Grauman's Chinese Theater in Hollywood, rare, Camden House, May 1989, $100.   *$50–$75*

Cyrano De Bergerác, 1950, UA, Jose Ferrer (Academy Award for best actor), Mala Powers, 20 pages, very good, 9″ × 12″, Collectors' Showcase, January 1989, $27.   *$30–$40*

Fantasia, 1940, RKO, Walt Disney Productions, all color program, 32 pages, fine, 9½″ × 12½″, Collectors' Showcase, September 1988, $111.   *$40–$60*

Fantasia, 1940, RKO, Walt Disney Productions, same as above, Collectors' Showcase, December 1988, $85.   *$40–$60*

★

NOTE: This is one of the most beautiful souvenir programs that was produced by a studio. Although fairly common, it is very much sought after by collectors who will pay X amount of dollars for a copy.

★

For Whom the Bell Tolls, 1943, PAR, Gary Cooper, Ingrid Berg-man, Katina Paxinou (best supporting actress Oscar), 20 pages, with interior paintings, fine, Collectors' Showcase, $26.

$35–$50

Four Horsemen of the Apocalypse, The, 1921, MGM, Rudolph Valentino, Alice Terry, Alan Hale, 16 pages, 9″ × 12¼″, Hake's, November 1988, $81.

$50–$75

NOTE: *Valentino's first leading role after having played bit parts in silents from 1918–20. This is the picture that began his reputation as "the great lover." Valentino memorabilia is highly sought after by collectors.*

Godfather, The, 1972, PAR, Marlon Brando, Al Pacino, James Caan, Diane Keaton, Robert Duvall, 28 pages, very good, 8½″ × 11″, Collectors' Showcase, September 1988, $14.

$25–$40

Gone With the Wind, 1939, MGM, Clark Gable, Vivien Leigh, Olivia de Havilland, Leslie Howard, 20 pages, 9″ × 12″, good, Collectors' Showcase, February 1989, $86.

$15–$20

Gone With the Wind, 1939, MGM, same as above but fine, Poster Mail Auction Co., February 1989, $40.

$55–$75

Gone With the Wind, 1939, MGM, same as above but "movie" program with 20 pages of information and artwork, Camden House, May 1989, $700.

$200–$400

Hell's Angels, 1930, UA, Jean Harlow, Ben Lyon, James Hall, directed by Howard Hughes through his Caddo Co., gold-leaf finish, 38 pages, 5″ × 7″, Camden House, May 1989, $100.

$50–$100

Hell's Angels, 1930, UA, same as cast as above, but opening night program for world premiere at Grauman's Chinese Theater, program with leather cover, embossed with diving plane, Camden House, May 1989, $400.   *$100–$150*

Henry V, 1945, PAR, Laurence Olivier, 20 pages, fine, Collectors' Showcase, January 1989, $33.   *$35–$40*

House of Rothschild, The, 1934, 20th, George Arliss, Loretta Young, Boris Karloff, Robert Young, 12 pages with four pages of montage black and white film scenes, very good +, 9¼" × 12", Hake's, February 1989, $27.   *$25–$50*

Julius Caesar, 1953, MGM, Marlon Brando, Louis Calhern, Greer Garson, Leo Genn, Deborah Kerr, 24 pages, fine, Collectors' Showcase, January 1989, $39.   *$25–$30*

King of Kings, 1927, UA, H.B. Warner, directed by Cecil B. DeMille, 20 pages, Collectors' Showcase, October 1988, $55.
$10–$25

NOTE: *After DeMille parted company from the Famous Players– Lasky Company in 1925, he established his own production company at the Thomas Ince Studios. After a couple of flops, he produced* King of Kings, *about the life of Christ, which was both his greatest and most successful silent film. After seeing the movie, author John Steinbeck was alleged to have said: "Saw the picture; love the book."*

Lloyds of London, 1936, 20th, Tyrone Power, Madeline Carroll, original Los Angeles program, 32 pages, 8½" × 12", Collectors' Showcase, December 1988, $27.   *$35–$50*

Lodger, The, 1926, Gainsborough, directed by Alfred Hitchcock, ditto screenplay, U.S. title: *The Phantom Fiend*, Ivor Novello, Marie Ault, premiere presentation, London, 8 pages, 6″ × 10″, Collectors' Showcase, March 1989, $81.   *$60–$75*

Lost Horizon, 1937, COL, Ronald Colman, Jane Wyatt, Edward Everett Horton, Sam Jaffe, 20 pages, rare, 9″ × 12″, Collectors" Showcase, November 1988, $104.   *$50–$60*

Metropolis, 1927, English premiere on March 21, 1927, Beninsky (Russian artist responsible for design of program cover), includes book of *Metropolis* by Thea Von Harbou, rare, Christie's East's, June 1989, $1980.   *$2000–$3000*

Moulin Rouge, 1952, UA, Jose Ferrer, Colette Marchand, directed by John Huston, 16 pages, very good, Collectors' Showcase, January 1989, $42.   *$30–$35*

North Star, The, 1943, UA, Samuel Goldwyn, 16 pages, rare, fine, 9 ″ × 12 ″, Collectors' Showcase, January 1989, $82.

$40–$60

Queen Christina, 1933, MGM, Greta Garbo, John Gilbert, rare, 20 pages, 9 ″ × 12 ″, Collectors' Showcase, February 1989, $99.

$75–$100

NOTE: *Garbo insisted that her old friend and co-star, John Gilbert, be her leading man. Gilbert had fallen on hard times since his voice was unsuitable for sound films.*

Quo Vadis, 1951, MGM, Robert Taylor, Deborah Kerr, Peter Ustinov (Oscar for best supporting actor), almost full-color, 20 pages, 9 ″ × 12 ″, Collectors' Showcase, January 1989, $42.

$25–$35

Robe, The, 1953, 20th, Richard Burton, Jean Simmons, 20 pages, good, Collectors' Showcase, January 1989, $40. $20–$25

Romola, 1924, Inspiration, Lillian Gish, Ronald Colman, William Powell, Dorothy Gish, 20 pages, very good, Collectors' Showcase, December 1988, $55. $40–$50

Samson and Delilah, 1949, PAR, Victor Mature, Hedy Lamarr, George Sanders, Angela Lansbury, 16 pages, 9 ″ × 12 ″, Paper Collectables & Memorabilia Show, February 1989, $80.

$40–$60

Photo courtesy of Hake's Americana, York, PA

Since You Went Away, 1944, UA, Claudette Colbert, Joseph Cotten, Shirley Temple, Robert Walker, Monty Wooley, Agnes Moorehead, Jennifer Jones, Lionel Barrymore, produced by David O. Selznick, 20 pages, fine, 9″ × 12″, Hake's, February 1989, $27. $25–$50

NOTE: *Each star is featured in this program with a full-page sepia photo accompanied by a biography on the facing page.*

Solomon and Sheba, 1959, UA, Yul Brynner, Gina Lollobrigida, 20 pages, mint, 9″ × 12″, Collectors' Showcase, September 1988, $15.   *$30–$50*

Song of the South, 1946, RKO, Walt Disney Productions, 20 pages, rare, fine, 10″ × 12″, Collectors' Showcase, December 1988, $181.   *$75–$95*

Student Prince, The, 1927, MGM, Ramon Navarro, Norma Shearer, 20 pages, fine, 9″ × 12″, Collectors' Showcase, December 1988, $66.   *$35–$45*

Ten Commandments, The, 1923, Famous Players–Lasky, directed by Cecil B. DeMille, Theodore Roberts, Estelle Taylor, Charles de Roche, 20 pages, very good, 9″ × 12″, Collectors' Showcase, October 1988, $46.   *$25–$40*

NOTE: *The first DeMille* Ten Commandments; *the second was released in 1956.*

Thief of Bagdad, The, 1924, UA, Douglas Fairbanks, 16 pages, Guernsey's, April 1989, $60.   *$100–$150*

Wizard of Oz, The, 1939, MGM, Judy Garland, Ray Bolger, Jack Haley, Bert Lahr, Margaret Hamilton, world premiere at Grauman's Chinese Theater, rare, Camden House, May 1989, $1400.   *$200–$300*

NOTE: Almost any movie memorabilia associated with this movie brings high bucks from collectors.

Women, The, 1939, MGM, Norma Shearer, Joan Crawford, Rosalind Russell, Paulette Goddard, Joan Fontaine, Phyllis Povah, Mary Boland (l'amour, l'amour), world premiere at Grauman's Chinese Theater, 16 pages, very fine, Collectors' Showcase, December 1988, $45.   *$40–$50*

Yearling, The, 1946, MGM, Gregory Peck, Jane Wyman, Claude Jarman, Jr., world premiere at La Carthay Circle Theater in Hollywood, 22 pages, very good, Collectors' Showcase, January 1989, $95.   *$40–$50*

TOYS

INTRODUCTION

Toys help us to recapture a part of our past. Unfortunately, most of the toys we played with as kids—toys that cost our parents a few dollars—now have grown-up price tags in the hundreds and thousands of dollars.

When Stephen Spielberg paid $60,500 for the rosebud sled from *Citizen Kane* in December of 1987, toy prices hit the roof. At the Allentown Toy Show and Sale in November of 1988, over 400 dealers from the United States, Canada, and Europe exhibited toys that were exceptional in quality and pedigree, and sold for such high figures that most collectors with average bankrolls were shut out from the action and had to settle for overvalued, mass-produced, or simply ordinary examples of toys that the serious collectors with huge bankrolls took one look at and dismissed as inferior.

Popular toy makers include Lehmann, Louis Marx, Chein & Co., Corgi, Buddy "L," Keystone, Hubley, Schuco, Wyandotte, Ohio Art Co., Arcade, and Fisher-Price (especially toys they produced between 1931–1963). Toy condition must be excellent or mint to attract the high rollers. Perfect toys, however, are an exception as a visit to any collectible show, dealer, or auction house will show. The majority of toys have been used and look it. Still, for a collector who simply must have a particular key-wind walker, Charlie Chaplin tin wind-up, or battery-operated robot, price and condition take a back seat.

Toys from the 1940s through the 1970s are very hot now, although the really serious collectors stick with early 20th-century toys. Unfortunately, there weren't many movie toys produced in the first years of this century.

Tin, celluloid, and cast-iron toys are the most popular with collectors; rubber, vinyl, and plastic toys that are in great abundance (usually at flea markets) are not considered very desirable. Cast-iron pistols made up until 1940 are also gaining collector interest. Comic character toys such as Disneyana, Buck Rogers, Flash Gordon, Star Trek, and movies that showed space travel from the 1950s are top collecting categories. Charlie Chaplin, Woody Woodpecker, Bugs Bunny, Porky Pig, Gene Autry, Tom Mix, Roy Rogers, the Lone Ranger, James Bond, and Shirley Temple are others. *Star Wars* and Batman toys will undoubtedly increase in value over the next few years.

Gauging the toy market is extremely difficult since the price for a particular toy might be $500 one week and $1500 the next week. Many factors contribute to this phenomenon. The price that a collector is willing to pay for a toy at a particular time is perhaps the most important criterion to consider, but so is the toy itself, its condition and manufacturer, as well as the region of the country where it is selling. West and East Coast movie toys tend to be higher in price than in other regions of the country, although New England and Pennsylvania are becoming major toy-selling markets.

The price ranges in this chapter reflect the approximate values for the toys that are listed within the last 13 months, but by the time this book is published many prices will have increased considerably. Toys are one of the most collectible areas of movie memorabilia and tend to attract collectors for whom money is just frosting on the cake.

TOYS LISTING

Buck Rogers, battle cruiser construction kit, circa 1934, completed, painted, dark red and green accents, original box, 6½″ long, Christie's East, March 1989, $264.   *$200–$300*

Buck Rogers, battle cruiser wooden construction kit, circa 1934, completed, painted, red and yellow and blue accents, 7″ long, Christie's East, March 1989, $462.   *$200–$300*

Buck Rogers, Venus "Fighting Destroyer" construction kit, circa 1934, completed, painted, red with yellow, blue accents, original box, 7″ long, Christie's East, March 1989, $462.

$200–$300

Buck Rogers, pursuit ship wood construction kit, completed, painted, red with yellow, blue, green accents, fin missing, original box, 7½″ long, Christie's East, March 1989, $242.

$200–$300

Buck Rogers, U-235, atomic pistol, circa 1946, chromed finish, signed, Phil Pederson, original box (yellow), 9″ long, Christie's East, December 1988, $385.

$300–$400

Buck Rogers, U-238, atomic pistol and holster, circa 1948, bronze and gold finish, outer space design stamped on holster, red and white original box, 9″ long, Christie's East, December 1988, $715.

$400–$500

NOTE: *The U-238 was the last of the Buck Rogers guns.*

Buck Rogers, XZ-38, disintegrator pistol, circa 1936, copper finish, leather holster stamped "Buck Rogers 25th Century," various space monsters and ships stamped on belt, Christie's East, December 1988, $440.

$300–$400

Buck Rogers, XZ-44, liquid helium water pistol, circa 1936, tinplate, yellow and red paint, original box, 7″ long, Christie's East, December 1988, $605.

$200–$300

Buck Rogers, XZ-44, liquid helium water pistol, circa 1936, copper finish, original orange box, 7½″ long, Christie's East, December 1988, $605.

$200–$300

Buck Rogers, XZ-44, liquid helium water pistol, red and yellow paint, Christie's East, December 1988, $176.

$150–$200

Buck Rogers, 25th-century rocket football, printed with illustration of Buck Rogers and rocket, silver with red fins, fin cracks, dried out inner lining, rare, 12″ long, Christie's East, December 1988, $660.

$800–$1000

Buck Rogers, XZ-31, rocket pistol, circa 1934, Daisy, plated trim blue steel, Suedine holster, original box (orange, black, and white), 9½" long, Christie's East, December 1988, $286.

$300–$400

Buck Rogers, XZ-35, rocket pistol, circa 1935, Daisy, blued steel finish, XZ-35 smaller version, 7" long, Christie's East, December 1988, $242. $200–$300

Buck Rogers, XZ-35, rocket pistol, circa 1935, Daisy, holster, stamped with Buck Rogers, 7" long, Christie's East, December 1988, $286. $200–$250

Buck Rogers, three Tootsietoy airships, battle cruiser, yellow and blue; battle cruiser, white and gray; Venus Duo-Destroyer, green and gold Venus, paint loss on destroyer, original boxes, 4½" long each, Christie's East, December 1988, $264. $150–$200

Buck Rogers, electric caster set, circa 1935, Rapaport Brothers, complete outfit for casting and coloring Buck Rogers characters, 2500 A.D., original box, glued in for display, box lid with Buck and Wilma in a Dick Calkins illustrated adventure with cast lead ship, instruction book, Christie's East, December 1988, $154.

$200–$300

Bugs Bunny, figure, cloth, dressed as sheriff with hat, holster, six shooter, badge, 26" high, Christie's East, December 1988, $154. $80–$100

Bugs Bunny, *Squeaker Toy*, circa 1940s, soft rubber, Bugs with orange carrot, fine, 7½", Hake's, April 1989, $35. $25–$50

Camera, early 1950s, with 16 individual movie star black and white pictures, including Marilyn Monroe, snap switch, viewer, 2" × 1", Collectors' Showcase, February 1989, $58. $25–$30

Charlie Chaplin Boxer, felt covered with black trunks, maroon shirt, brown gloves, Schuco, 6" high, Christie's East, March 1989, $330. $400–$600

★

NOTE: *Schuco is the manufacturer of this pugilist that shuffles forward when he is wound and then lets out a barrage of left and right hooks.*

★

Charlie Chaplin Keywind Walker, Schuco, shuffles forward when wound, twirls his cane with a jointed arm, celluloid Charlie, walker is 6 1/2 " high, Christie's East, March 1989, $418.

$200–$300

Charlie Chaplin Squeak Toy, circa 1920, composition head, plaster limbs, body has bellows squeaker, painted, 7 1/2 " high, Christie's East, December 1988, $198.   *$200–$300*

Charlie Chaplin Squeak Toy, circa 1930, Japan, composition head, papier-mâché arms and legs, cloth outfit, unpainted face, toy is unsqueakable, 7 1/2 " high, Skinner, November 1988, $100.   *$150–$250*

Charlie Chaplin Tinplate Gravity String Toy, lithographed, driver resembles comedian smoking a cigar and pedaling grooved-wheel bicycle, 8 " long, Christie's East, December 1988, $660.   *$300–$400*

Charlie McCarthy, Marx, tin wind-up toy, very good, has 95% of its paint, Knight's, October 1988, $120.   *$100–$175*

Felix Pencil Case, circa 1930s, American Pencil Co., textured cardboard case with brass snap lid, 1/2 " × 5 " × 8 1/2 ", Hake's, February 1989, $58.   *$50–$75*

Felix Push Toy, wooden, jointed, painted, mounted on two rotating discs with shovel handle, pushes cat to move arms and legs, 13 " high, Christie's East, March 1989, $880.   *$300–$500*

Felix Keywind Walker, tinplate, Felix in half-left profile skips to the side and circles when wound, 6 1/2 ", Christie's East, March 1989, $1760.   *$300–$400*

Felix the Cat Wind-up, circa 1920 (copyright label 1922, 1924 by Pat Sullivan, made in Germany), polychromed tin, Felix with hands behind back, jointed legs, tail detached, some paint loss, Skinner, November 1988, $200.   *$250–$300*

Flash Gordon Arresting Ray Gun, tinplate, grip gun lithographed with Flash, 10 " long, Christie's East, December 1988, $110.   *$80–$100*

Flash Gordon Radio Repeater Click Pistol, 1935, Louis Marx, silver and orange, rare space gun, original box, 9½″ × 4½″, Collectors' Showcase, November 1988, $551.   *$200–$300*

Flash Gordon Signal Pistol, Marx, painted red with green trim, Flash decal, screaming sound, original box with instructions, 6½″ long, Christie's East, December 1988, $418.   *$200–$250*

Flash Gordon Signal Pistol, Marx, painted green with red trim, screaming sound, decal, original box, 5″ long, Christie's East, December 1988, $286.   *$200–$250*

Gene Autry Cap Gun, cast iron, simulated pearl grips, top loading for roll caps, Autry's name in raised letters on gun sides, fine, 8 1/2", Hake's, November 1988, $125. $100–$200

Jackie Coogan Character Rattle, fine, 6" high, Knight's, October 1988, $185. $150–$200

Photo courtesy of Hake's Americana, York, PA

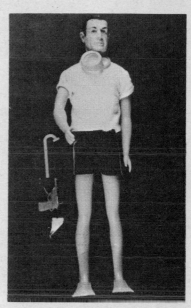

Photo courtesy of Hake's Americana, York, PA

James Bond 007 Action Figure, A.C. Gilbert, 1965 copyright, hard plastic, movable arms and legs, soft realistic vinyl head, movable at neck, orange underwater mask, snorkel, flippers, blue trunks, included a miniature cap-firing pistol, small metal adapter, instruction sheet, 12" figure, fine, box, good, and 2 1/2" × 4 1/4" × 12 1/2" with black and white scenes from *Thunderball*, UA, Hake's, February 1989, $224. $100–$200

James Bond 007 Action Figure, A.C. Gilbert, 1965, everything as above except for scuba outfit with white T-shirt, red trunks, black swim fins, no cap-firing gun, very good, Hake's, April 1989, $135.   *$75–$100*

James Bond 007 Action Toy on Card, 1965, A.C. Gilbert, retail display card with plastic blister for Dr. No's dragon tank with flame-like tongue which shoots out when button is pressed, also Largo's hydrofoil yacht, splits in two parts to become speedy hydrofoil racer, mint, Hake's, February 1989, $62.   *$25–$50*

NOTE: Dr. No *was the first James Bond feature starring Sean Connery and Ursula Andress, and co-starring Joseph Wiseman as Dr. No. The movie was released by UA in 1962. Largo's yacht belonged to the villain of* Thunderball, *1965, also UA. The Italian actor, Adolfi Celi, played Largo.*

James Bond Aston-Martin Super Spy Car, 1965, Aurora, complete set with instructions, car has working parts and ejection seat, twin machine guns, front and rear rammers, revolving license plates, tire cutters, bullet-proof shield, oil spreaders, smoke jets, boxed, 7″ × 13″ × 2¼″, Hake's, February 1989, $301.
                                                         $75–$200

NOTE: *As of December 1987, the most expensive film prop sold at auction was the actual Aston-Martin Super Spy Car used in* Goldfinger, *1964, UA, and driven by Sean Connery in the movie. It sold to Anthony V. Pugliese III, the president of Filmtrek Pictures, for $275,000.*

Photo courtesy of Hake's Americana, York, PA

James Bond 007 Electric Drawing Set, 1966, Lakeside Toys, drawing desk, black plastic, white glass frame on stand, illuminated by 15-watt bulb, desk has "007" insignia with complete set of guide sheets for creating "Spy-O-Graph" enemy agents' faces, full-figure character images, Bond equipment pieces for action scene drawings, 10" × 14 1/2", box is 4" × 10" × 15", Hake's, April 1989, $115. $50–$70

James Bond 007 Shoes, shoebox with unused pair of 007 shoes, grained black leather, lined in gold fabric with 007 symbols, gun design in the "7," size 6 1/2-D, "007" insignia sticker (inside heel of right shoe), mint, Hake's, November 1988, $200. *$100–$200*

James Bond 007 Child's Costume, full-length, printed chest design on jacket with James Bond "007" name and insignia, printed shoulder holster set, very fine, 42" length, Hake's, April 1989, $48. $50–$75

James Bond (Roger Moore) Film Glass, 1981, Danjaq S.A., beverage glass with illustration, inscription on side: "For Your Eyes Only," UA, "007 Collector's Series," very fine, 4", Hake's, April 1989, $30. *$15–$25*

James Bond 007 Moonraker Corgi Replica Toy, 1979, Mettoy Co. (England), cast metal, authentically produced, Bond space shuttle with scaled satellite, hinged solar panels, Moonraker ship has retractable undercarriage with large top hatches opening outward, white with yellow shuttle, black accent, 6″ long, mint, box with independent display on top edge, very fine, 3½″ × 4½″ × 6″, Hake's, April 1989, $72.   *$25–$50*

Photo courtesy of Hake's Americana, York, PA

James Bond "007" Multi-Weapon Attaché Case, 1966, Multiple Toymakers, black plastic, carrying handle, raised "007" crest, "JB" insignia, rocket launcher, pistol rockets, palm gun, pistol, crest insignia releases dart from each side of case when pushed, set works, fine, 2″ × 14″ × 10″, Hake's, November 1988, $265.
          $200–$400

James Bond 007 "Oddjob" Action Figure, 1965, A.C. Gilbert, jointed, hard plastic, soft vinyl head, white fabric karate jacket, black cord belt, black stretch karate knee tights, gold neckerchief, red fabric sweatband, black plastic derby, instruction sheet details how the derby moves through the air and also how the figure's right hand deals a karate blow, mint, 10 1/2 " tall, box is fine and 4 1/2 " × 4 1/2 " × 12 1/2 ", Hake's, November 1988, $260.
$75–$200

NOTE: *Oddjob was played by the actor Harold Sakata in* Goldfinger, *1964, UA.*

Krazy Kat on Scooter, Chein, lithographed in different colors, atop push-drive three-wheeled scooter with green wheels (replaced front wheel), 7" long, Christie's East, March 1989, $242.
$200–$300

Movie Komics Film Projector, shaped like top of double spool movie camera, lithographed with comic characters, original box, 6 1/4 " long, Christie's East, December 1988, $44.
$100–$150

Movie Projector Gun, 1937, metal gun shoots "140 rapid fire films," filmstrips, paper screen, 16" × 10" box, Collectors' Showcase, October 1988, $258.
$100–$125

Pathe News Car, Louis Marx, roof-mounted tripod movie camera with Pathe news, light pressed-steel sedan, red paint, 9" long, Christie's East, December 1988, $528.
$400–$600

Popeye Express "Sky Hawk" Airplane Go-round, lithographed base, tower balancing two planes, Popeye and Olive Oyl each in a plane, 9" high, Christie's East, March 1989, $770.
$400–$600

Popeye Express Keywind "Blow Me Down Airport," Louis Marx, lithographed base with various characters, Popeye flies above a circling train, original box, Christie's East, December 1988, $880.   *$500–$600*

Popeye Boom-Boom Pull Toy, Fisher-Price, Popeye with Swea' Pea, lithographed paper on wood playing a drum, wheeled base, 7 1/2″ long, Christie's East, March 1989, $385.   *$300–$400*

Popeye the Champ, keywind, circa 1935, Louis Marx, celluloid Popeye and Bluto slug it out in a boxing ring, lithographed, partial box, 7″ × 7″ × 7″, Christie's East, March 1989, $3520.
                                                   $1800–$2200

Popeye Express Keywind Walker, Popeye pushing a wheelbarrow with steamer trunk inside and a pop-up parrot, 8 1/4 ″, Christie's East, December 1988, $418.   *$300–$400*

Popeye Transit Company Moving Van, Linemar, lithographed Popeye with crew members, friction drive, 14″ long, Christie's East, March 1989, $330.   *$100–$150*

Porky Pig "Soaky" Container, circa 1960s, molded vinyl plastic body, hard plastic movable head, fine, Hake's, February 1989, $8.   *$25–$35*

Porky Pig Wind-up, 1939, Louis Marx (and Leon Schlesinger) copyright, lithographed, full-dimensional metal toy with Porky twirling a red and white-striped parasol, 7 1/2 ″, Hake's, April 1989, $280.   *$100–$300*

Quo Vadis Chariot Set, Johillio, with chariot, two-horse team, driver, two-foot gladiators, label illustration on original box with photographs from 1951 MGM film, box stains, Phillips, June 1988, $275.   *$125–$150*

Photo courtesy of Hake's Americana, York, PA

Robby the Robot, battery operated, very large, black body with red feet, red and silver arm sections that contain a pair of three-pronged black rubber hands on the end, movable to various positions, painted, four small metal pistons under dome move up and down while plastic base shines with pink color, two wire atennae on robot's head spin rapidly as robot walks, very fine, 5″ × 6″ × 13″ tall, Hake's, February 1989, $1700. *$1500–?*

Photo courtesy of Hake's Americana, York, PA

Scrappy Paint and Crayon Set, American Toy Works (licensed by COL), #4001, Hake's, November 1988, $58.   *$50–$75*

Scrappy and Margy Pull String Toy, lithographed paper on wood figures, wheeled metal base, Scrappy plays xylophone as Margy dances when toy rolls, based on COL characters, 13¾", Christie's East, December 1988, $220.   *$300–$400*

Shirley Temple, chalkware string holder, "Atlantique City" Collectibles Market, March 1989, $395.

Photo courtesy of Hake's Americana, York, PA

Photo courtesy of Hake's Americana, York, PA

Shirley Temple, magnetic TV theater, 1958, Amsco Toys, TV plays "The Three Bears," "Red Riding Hood," "Sleeping Beauty," magnet moves fairytale characters within a simulated TV screen, fine, box has split corners, toy missing hardware (nuts, bolts, etc.), 12″ × 19″ × 2″, Hake's, February 1989, $75.

$75–$100

Shirley Temple, mirror, blue, small (for the hand), re: Little Princess, J. Goldsmith Antiques, August 1988, $18.   *$14–$22*

Star Trek Action Figure, 1979, Mego Corp., retail display box, colorful Decker from *Star Trek* cast, insignia of *Star Trek* on chest of figure's clothes, 12″, box, 2″ × 9″ × 13½″, Hake's, February 1989, $15.   *$25–$50*

Superman Krypto Raygun Pocket Projector, Daisy, blued steel, raised flying Superman with arm outstretched on pistol, 16mm film, original box, 6¾″, Christie's East, December 1988, $528.

$300–$400

Woody's Cafe Alarm Clock, circa 1959, Time Products, animated, metal wind-up clock with illustrated dial of Woody Woodpecker as chef, full-color menu design, Plexiglas crystal, solid ivory enamel base, 1½″ × 4½″, Hake's, February 1989, $180.   *$100–$200*

Photo courtesy of Hake's Americana, York, PA   *Photo courtesy of Hake's Americana, York, PA*

Yellow Submarine Replica Toy, 1968, Corgi (King Features/Subafilms Ltd. copyright), wide-window display box, colored, with die-cast metal, detailed replica of yellow submarine (1968 Beatles animated film), with four yellow periscopes that revolve as toy is pushed, tiny replica figures of Beatles in submarine seats, yellow with white, red, and blue accents, boxed, very fine, 2½" × 3½" × 6½", Hake's, February 1989, $271.

$100–$200

Zorro Cup, print transfer on white color, J. Goldsmith Antiques, August 1988, $9.50. $8–$12

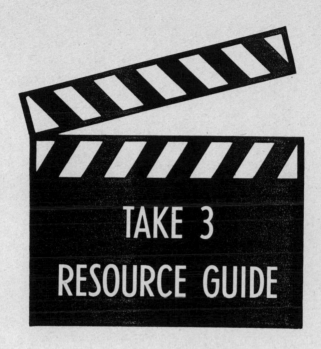

TAKE 3
RESOURCE GUIDE

AUCTION HOUSES

Camden House
10921 Wilshire Boulevard
Suite 808
Los Angeles, California
    90024
213-476-1628
Specialty: Movie
    memorabilia; 10% buyer's
    premium included on all
    lots but not included in
    final prices listed
    throughout price guide.

Caropreso Gallery
136 High Street
Lee, Massachusetts 01238
413-243-3424
Specialty: Disneyana, movie
    collectibles, toys; 10%
    buyer's premium included
    on all lots.

Christie's East
219 East 67th Street
New York, New York 10021
212-000-0543
Specialty: Animation art and
all types of movie
memorabilia except sheet
music, magazines, movie
tearsheet ads; 10% buyer's
premium included on all
lots.

*Christie's South Kensington
    Auction Gallery*
85 Old Brompton Road
London, England, SW7
581-7611 (preceded by
    overseas code)
Specialty: Most types of
    movie memorabilia; 10%
    buyer's premium included
    on all lots.

Collectors' Showcase
(Discontinued mail/phone
    auctions)
1708 N. Vine Street
Hollywood, California 90028
213-467-3296
Specialty: All types of movie
    memorabilia.

Herman Darvick Autograph Auctions
P.O. Box 467
Rockville Centre, New York
   11571-0467
516-766-0289
516-766-7456 (fax)
Specialty: Major autograph
   house which features
   about six sales a year,
   usually in February, April,
   June, August, September,
   and November;
   autographs and
   autographed books.

William Doyle Galleries
175 East 87th Street
New York, New York 10128
212-427-2730
Specialty: Primarily
   autographs and books, but
   also handles estate sales of
   celebrities such as Rock
   Hudson.

William Fox Auctions
676 Morris Avenue
Springfield, New Jersey
   07081
201-467-2366
Specialty: Autographs and
   selected movie
   memorabilia.

Greenwich Auction Room Ltd.
110 East 15th Street
New York, New York 10003
212-533-5550

Specialty: Primarily an
   antique and collectible
   auction house, but they
   occasionally have auctions
   of puppets, figures, dolls,
   and posters.

C.E. Guarino
Box 49
Denmark, Maine 04022
207-452-2123
Specialty: Film ephemera,
   photographs, portraits,
   and stills.

Guernsey's
136 East 73rd Street
New York, New York 10021
212-794-2280
Specialty: Lobby cards,
   posters, souvenir
   programs.

Hake's Americana & Collectibles (mail/phone
   order auctions)
P.O. Box 1444
York, Pennsylvania 17405
717-848-1333
Specialty: All types of movie
   memorabilia.

Knight's (Bruce and Vivalyn
   Knight)
2109 Olympic Street
Springfield, Ohio 45503
513-399-4321
Specialty: Selected movie
   memorabilia including
   toys.

Howard Lowery
3818 W. Magnolia
  Boulevard
Burbank, California 91507
818-972-9080
Specialty: Animation art and
  related movie memorabilia
  items.

NASCA (Division of R.M.
  Smythe & Co., Inc.)
26 Broadway
New York, New York 10004
800-622-1880
Specialty: Autographs; 10%
  buyer's premium on all
  lots.

*Richard Opfer
  Auctioneering, Inc.*
1919 Greenspring Drive
Timonium, Maryland 21093
301-252-5035
Specialty: Toys; 10% buyer's
  premium on all lots.

Phillips
406 East 79th Street
New York, New York 10021
212-570-4830
Specialty: Most types of
  movie memorabilia; 10%
  buyer's premium on all
  lots but not included in
  prices used in the price
  guide.

Note: In the Autograph
  chapter, reference was
  made to the name Neales,

which is actually the
London division of
Phillips. For further
information contact the
above number or Phillips,
West 2, 10 Salem Road,
London W2 4BU,
011-441-723-2647. Ask for
Paul Gillan. The correct
name is Phillip Neale &
Son.

Poster Mail Auction Co.
  (Elaine and R. Neil
  Reynolds)
Box M-133
2 Patrick Street
Waterford, Virginia 22190
703-882-3574
Specialty: Posters and lobby
  cards, magazines, pin-up
  art; 10% buyer's premium
  on all lots for this mail/
  phone order auction
  house.

Skinner (Skinner, Inc.)
357 Main Street
Bolton, Massachusetts 01740
508-779-6241

Skinner (Skinner, Inc.)
2 Newbury Street
Boston, Massachusetts 02116
617-236-1700
Specialty: Disneyana,
  musical instruments, paper
  dolls, puppets, toys; 10%
  buyer's premium on all
  lots.

Sotheby's
1334 York Avenue
New York, New York 10021
212-606-7424
Specialty: Selected movie
  memorabilia; 10% buyer's
  premium on all lots but
  not included in prices used
  in the price guide.

Swann Galleries
104 East 25th Street
New York, New York 10010
212-254-4710
Specialty: Autographs,
  books, posters, lobby
  cards, photographs.

Theriault
2148 Renard Court
Annapolis, Maryland 21401
Specialty: Dolls; 10%
  buyer's premium on all
  lots.

MOVIE MEMORABILIA DEALERS

Abbey Book Shop (out of business)

Alexander Gallery (Alexander Acevedo)
996 Madison Avenue
New York, New York 10021
212-472-1636
Specialty: Animation cels, Disneyana, toys.

Antique Prints and Papers
9 South Adelaide Avenue
Highland Park, New Jersey 08904
201-545-5223
Specialty: Sheet music, magazines.

Artis Books
410 N. Second
Alpena, Michigan 49707
517-354-3401
Specialty: Books.

A & S Book Company
304 West 40th Street
New York, New York 10018
212-714-2712
Specialty: Magazines, stills, stock photos, trade publications.

The Attic
415 Westfield Avenue
Westfield, New Jersey 07090
201-233-1954
Specialty: Figures, sheet music; also does appraisals and house sales in which movie memorabilia is sometimes included.

Auston Books
P.O. Box 512
Fredonia, New York 10463
Specialty: Books.

Autographics
P.O. Box 210061
Dallas, Texas
214-298-5896
Specialty: Autographs.

Blue Bird Books (David Stalzer)
31 Rhinecliff Road
Rhinebeck, New York
Specialty: Books.

Wayland Bunnell
199 Tarrytown Road
Manchester, New Hampshire
   03103
603-668-5466
Specialty: Sheet music for
   direct sale and also via
   mail/phone order auctions;
   buys, sells, trades,
   consigns.

Calico Cat Antiques
Route 8, Box 3070
Rapid City, South Dakota
   57702
605-343-4162
Specialty: Dolls, figures,
   toys.

Mario Carrandi, Jr.
122 Monroe Avenue
Belle Mead, New Jersey
   08502
201-874-0630
Specialty: Autographs,
   movie books (signed and
   unsigned).

Cinema Collectors
1507 Wilcox Avenue
Hollywood, California 90028
1-213-451-6516
Specialty: Posters, books,
   and photographs.

*Cobweb Collectibles &
   Ephemera (Sheldon
   Halper)*
9 Walnut Avenue
Cranford, New Jersey 07016

201-272-5777
Specialty: Autographs,
   postcards, sheet music,
   toys.

Collectors Bookstore
1708 N. Vine Street
Hollywood, California 90028
213-467-3296
Specialty: All types of movie
   memorabilia except toys.

Jim Collins
201 North Palisades Drive
Signal Mountain, Tennessee
   37377
615-886-3340
Specialty: Artwork.

*Cover to Cover (Mark
   Schuman)*
Box 687
Chapel Hill, North Carolina
   27514
919-967-1032
Specialty: Books.

Dell's Book Outlet
1018 Windsor Street
P.O. Box 13156
Reading, Pennsylvania 19612
Specialty: Autographs,
   books.

Sherry Dempsey
P.O. Box 29
Cemerton, New York 12415
Specialty: Film ephemera,
   toys.

DeVolder Antiques
17494 Meadow Lake Circle
Fort Myers, Florida 33912
813-267-7571
Specialty: Magazines, film
  ephemera.

John C. Van Doren
35 Hart Avenue
Hopewell, New Jersey 08525
1-609-466-2196
Specialty: Posters, lobby
  cards, stills, pressbooks,
  autographs, souvenir
  programs, books,
  soundtracks, sheet music,
  celebrity coloring books,
  paper dolls; buys, sells,
  and trades.

Larry Edmunds Bookstore
6658 Hollywood Boulevard
Hollywood, California 90028
1-213-463-3273
Specialty: Famous bookstore
  selling scripts, books,
  pressbooks, posters, and
  related movie
  memorabilia.

Eugenia's Place
Booths 14, 15, 35
Atlanta Flea Market &
  Antique Center
5360 Peachtree Ind.
  Boulevard
Chamblee, Georgia 30341
Specialty: Sheet music,
  assorted movie
  memorabilia.

*Family Publications (Bill
  Cartmel)*
P.O. Box 463
Auburn, Maine 04210
207-738-1378
Specialty: Magazines, film
  ephemera, books.

Ghost to Ghost Antiques
188 West Middle Turnpike
Manchester, Connecticut
  06040
203-643-7295
Specialty: Magazines, film
  ephemera.

*J. Goldsmith Antiques
  (Judith Goldsmith-
  Carrasco)*
1924 Polk Street
San Francisco, California
415-771-4055
Specialty: Disneyana, Big
  Little Books, toys,
  magazines, sheet music.

*Jerry Granat and Herman
  Darvick*
P.O. Box 92
Woodmere, New York 11598
516-374-7809
Specialty: Autographs and
  autographed books

Happier Days (Dan Daniel)
Atlanta Flea Market
5360 Peachtree Ind.
  Boulevard
Chamblee, Georgia 30341
404-451-1725
Specialty: Film collectibles,
  specializes in *Life* magazine.

Hollywood Poster Exchange (Bob Colman)
965 North La Cienega Boulevard
Los Angeles, California 90069
213-657-2461
Specialty: Posters, lobby cards, appraisals.

Hughes Papers
10194 Eden Church Road
St. Louisville, Ohio 43071
617-745-2503
Specialty: Magazines, film ephemera, books.

Illustrator's Collector's News
P.O. Box 1958
Sequim, Washington 98382
206-683-2559
Specialty: Magazines, film ephemera.

Brian Kathenes
P.O. Box 77296
West Trenton, New Jersey 08628
609-530-1350
Specialty: Autographs.

La Belle Antiques and Collectibles (Joan Blair, Kelly Butenhoff)
2047 Polk Street
San Francisco, California 94109
415-673-1181
Specialty: Sheet music.

Alan Levine
P.O. Box 1577
Bloomfield, New Jersey 07003
201-743-5288
Specialty: Cigarette cards, books, other movie memorabilia.

Limelight Film & Theater Bookstore (Ken Bullock, Roy Johnson)
1803 Market Street
San Francisco, California 94103
415-864-2265
Specialty: Books, scripts, photographs, portraits.

William Linehan Autographs
Box 1203
7 Summer Street
Concord, New Hampshire 03301
603-224-7226
Specialty: Autographs.

Memory Shop West
3460 16th Street
San Francisco, California 94114
415-626-4873
Specialty: Lobby cards, posters, stills, photographs, related movie memorabilia.

Mode Moderne
1029 Pine Street
Philadelphia, Pennsylvania
19107
215-627-0299
Specialty: Lunch boxes, toys,
movie memorabilia-related
items.

*The Mouse Man Ink (Robert
Crooker)*
103 Salem Street
Wakefield, Massachusetts
01880
1-617-246-3876
Specialty: Disneyana;
accepts consignments.

Constance Nadig
215 Green Lane
Philadelphia, Pennsylvania
19128
215-482-8113
Specialty: Glass lantern
slides, film ephemera.

W.M. Nussbaum
29 10 137th Street
Flushing, New York 11354
718-886-0558
Specialty: Film ephemera,
girlie magazines, books.

Oceanside Books
173A Woodfield Road
West Hempstead, New York
11552
516-565-4710
Specialty: Mystery film-
related books.

*Jerry Ohlinger's Movie
Material Store, Inc.*
242 West 14th Street
New York, New York 10011
212-674-8474/212-989-0869
Specialty: Posters, lobby
cards, stills, photographs,
magazines, other movie
memorabilia.

Oregon State Autograph Co.
P.O. Box 1
Umpqua, Oregon 97486
800-544-3836
Specialty: Autographs.

Paper Chase Antiques
P.O. Box 145, Route 37
North Bridgeton, Maine
04057
207-647-2230
Specialty: Books, film
ephemera.

*People's Magazine Service
(Ron Dashiell,
Al Joseph III)*
701 Seventh Avenue
Suite 9 West
New York, New York 10036
212-757-3995
Specialty: Magazines from
1930s–1980s including *Life*
and *Playboy*, buy
magazines and estates,
magazine search.

Pepper & Stern
P.O. Box 2711
Santa Barbara, California
    93120
805-569-0735
Specialty: First editions of
    movie books, photographs,
    autographs, contracts,
    related movie
    memorabilia.

P.M. Antiques &
    Collectables
    (Phil A. Grundy)
P.O. Box 224
Coffeyville, Kansas 67337
316-251-5308 (evenings)
Specialty: Artwork,
    autographs, film
    ephemera; accepts lay-
    away orders.

Pomander Bookshop
955 West End Avenue
New York, New York 10025
212-866-1777
Specialty: Books on film
    topics.

Cordelia Price Platt and
    Thomas E. Platt, Jr.
1598 River Road
Belle Mead, New Jersey
    08502
201-359-7959
Specialty: Autographs,
    buying and selling.

Kenneth W. Rendell Gallery
Place des Antiquaires
125 East 57th Street
New York, New York 10022
212-935-6767
Specialty: Autographs.

RNL Books
Boulevard Drive
Tallapoosa, Georgia 30176
Specialty: Books, magazines.

Roger's Comics
525 Sixth Avenue
New York, New York 10014
212-691-0380
Specialty: Posters, lobby cards,
    records, books, *Playboy* and
    Life magazines, movie
    magazines, Disneyana,
    film books, sheet music,
    trade publications.

Schoyer's Books
    (Marc Selvaggio)
1404 South Negley Avenue
Pittsburgh, Pennsylvania
    15217
412-521-8464
Specialty: Sheet music,
    movie magazines.

Sekino & Gray
    (Leonard J. Gray)
Two Grove Street
New York, New York 10014
212-255-8714
Specialty: Games, related
    movie memorabilia.

Henry Sundvik
306 Valley Brook Avenue
Lyndhurst, New Jersey
  07071
201-933-4499
Specialty: Books.

True Value Books
1110 Borbeck Avenue
Philadelphia, Pennsylvania
  19111
215-547-5530
Specialty: Books.

Twentieth Century Nostalgia
Ninth Avenue and 19th
  Street
New York, New York 10011
Specialty: Various categories
  of movie memorabilia.

Urban Archaeology Ltd.
285 Lafayette Street
New York, New York 10002
212-431-6969
Specialty: Motorcycles, big-
  ticket memorabilia items.

John Wade
P.O. Box 991041
Cincinnati, Ohio 45201
513-661-2890
Specialty: Stills, film
  ephemera.

Waiting for Godot
Cambridge, Massachusetts
  02139
017-001-1824
Specialty: Books.

Willow Valley Collectibles
  (Chuck Barger)
392 Twitchell Road
Mansfield, Ohio 44903
419-529-8710
Specialty: Film ephemera
  including newspapers.

Wex Rex Records &
  Collectibles
  (Gary Sohmers)
P.O. Box 702
65 Main Street
Hudson, Massachusetts
  01749
508-568-0856
Specialty: Records, posters,
  vintage toys, games,
  Disneyana.

Wizard of Os Antiques
  (David J. Oglesby,
  Susan I. Stock)
57 Lake Shore Drive
Marlboro, Massachusetts
  01752
617-481-1087
Specialty: Games.

Richard Wright Antiques
  (Richard Wright and
  Richard Saxman)
Flowing Springs and Hollow
  Roads
Birchrunville, Pennsylvania
  19421
215-827-7442
Specialty: Dolls.

MOVIE MEMORABILIA
COLLECTIBLE SHOWS

Annex Antiques Fair & Flea Market
20th Street and Sixth Avenue
New York City
212-243-5343
Time: Held every Saturday and Sunday throughout the year
  except in inclement weather. Open 9 A.M.–5 P.M.
Specialty: Various categories of movie memorabilia.

"Atlantique City" Indoor Antiques & Collectibles Market
Atlantic City Convention Center
Atlantic City, New Jersey
Time: Held third week in March, this 7 1/2-acre indoor show is
  home to over 500 dealers. Saturday admission is $10;
  Sunday, $7. A two-day admission is $14. Open 9 A.M.–8 P.M.
  on Saturday, 10 A.M.– 6 P.M. on Sunday. Call toll-free
  1-800-526-2724 or write Brimfield Associates, Box 1519,
  Pleasantville, New Jersey 08232

Black Mountain Antique Center
Route 30
off I-91, Exit 2
Brattleboro, Vermont 05301
Time: Dealer booths on one floor. Open year round, 10 A.M.–
  5:00 P.M. daily. Call 1-800-254-3848 for information.
  Managers are Chuck and Betty Anne Stokes. Flea market
  held on the grounds every Sunday.
Specialty: Various categories of movie memorabilia.

Liberty State Park Antiques & Collectibles Expo
Exit 14B of New Jersey Turnpike, on the Hudson River
Jersey City, New Jersey
201-768-2773 (Stella Show)
Time: Dealers display in June and October. Admission $2.50 or
    $2.00 with antique/collectible ads found in collectible
    newspapers such as *The Newtown Bee*, *Maine Antique
    Digest*, *P.A.C.*, and *Antique Digest* (Mid-Atlantic Region).
Specialty: Various categories of movie memorabilia.

Mid-Manhattan Wednesday Book Sales (11:00 A.M.–2:00 P.M.)
Mid-Manhattan Library
Fifth Avenue and 40th Street
New York City
Specialty: Books.

Northeast Collectibles Extravaganza
Bayside Convention Center
Boston, Massachusetts
Time: Held the first weekend in December and in early spring
    at the Northeast Trade Center in Woburn, Massachusetts.
    Produced by Show Promotions, Burlington, Massachusetts;
    call 617-229-2414
Specialty: All categories of movie memorabilia.

Nostalgia Con
Holiday Inn
Exit 138 (west of Garden State Parkway)
Kenilworth, New Jersey
201-677-3878 (ask for George)
Time: Eight shows a year featuring dealers from six states.
    Regular admission is $3; early admission is $20.
Specialty: Movie memorabilia including toys, games,
    premiums, film ephemera.

Paper Collectables & Memorabilia Show
St. Francis Xavier Church (basement)
30 West 16th Street (off Sixth Avenue)
New York City
Time: Held on Saturdays 10 months of the year (except July
    and August) from 10 A.M.–6 P.M. Usually about 25 to 30
    dealers who buy, trade, and sell. Coordinated by the

Gallagher Brothers, Bob and Paul, 72-39 66th Place,
Glendale, New York 11385. Admission is $3 but $2.50 with
mailing list postcard announcing the upcoming show.
Specialty: All categories of movie memorabilia.

Papermania (annual event)
Hartford Civic Center
Hartford, Connecticut
Time: Usually held the first weekend in January. Open 10
A.M.–7 P.M. on Saturday, noon–6 P.M. on Sunday. For
further information call 203-529-6997.
Specialty: Film ephemera collectibles.

Tama Fair
Third Avenue (14th-34th Streets)
New York City
Time: Usually held second Sunday in September. For further
information call 212-684-4077.
Specialty: Various categories of movie memorabilia.

Triple Pier Expo
Manhattan Antiques & Collectibles Show
The New York Passenger Ship Terminals
48th to 55th Streets and 12th Avenue
New York City
Time: Held on three piers, this 600-plus dealer show is one of
the largest in the Northeast. Admission is $12 for Saturday/
Sunday, and $10 for Sunday only. Usually held over
Thanksgiving Day weekend, and also in the winter. For
further information, call Stella Management at 201-388-
1130, or write Box 482, Paramus, New Jersey 07652.
Pier times as follows:
Pier 88:   Saturday—11:00 A.M.–6:00 P.M., Sunday—
            11:00 A.M.–7:00 P.M.
Pier 90:   Saturday—9:00 A.M.–6:00 P.M., Sunday—
            11:00 A.M.–5:00 P.M.
Pier 92:   Saturday—10:00 A.M.–6:00 P.M., Sunday—
            11:00 A.M.–6:00 P.M.
Specialty: As this show includes a heavy emphasis on antiques
and nonrelated movie collectibles, it would be wise to check
ahead of time which pier has the largest concentration of
movie memorabilia dealers. The piers are spread far and

wide, and knowing which pier has what items will cut down considerably on unnecessary walking.

The Mark Twain Library Book Fair
Redding Elementary School
Lonetown Road
Redding, Connecticut 07875
Book Fair Coordinator: Lewis M. Rosen
Time: Held each year for four days over the Labor Day weekend. One of the most famous book shows in the country. Books are double priced on Friday, the day the fair opens; full price on Saturday; half price on Sunday; and sold in box lots on Monday. Plans for the 1990 show are to have two full days of double-priced books beginning on the Thursday preceding the Labor Day weekend.
Specialty: Books, magazines, some film ephemera.

MOVIE MEMORABILIA PUBLICATIONS

The American Collector's Journal
P.O. Box 407
Kewanee, Illinois 61443
1-309-852-2602
Rates: Published bi-monthly in January, March, May, July,
    September, and November. Subscription rates are $4.25 per
    year, or $8 for two years. Single copies are $1.
Specialty: Autographs, auction news, banks, books, costumes,
    dolls, magazines, newspapers, photographs, toys.

Antiquer's Guide
P.O. Box 388
Sidney, New York 13838
Rates: Subscription rates are $12 per year.
Specialty: Primarily devoted to antiques but issues have some
    collectible information on movie memorabilia.

Antiques & Auction News
Route 230 West
P.O. Box 500
Mount Joy, Pennsylvania 17552
1-717-653-9797
Rates: Subscription rates are $15 for one year, sent third class,
    and $60 for one year, sent first class. A six-month
    subscription, sent first class, is $35.
Specialty: Features news articles, publicity, and feature articles

on collectibles, museums, shows, shops, auction results, auctioneers, etc.

The Antique Trade Weekly
Dubuque, Iowa 52001
1-319-588-2073
1-800-334-7165 (toll free)
Rates: A trial subscription of eight weeks costs $5, or $24 for a yearly subscription.
Specialty: Features information on collectibles of interest to movie memorabilia collectors.

Antique Week (Mid-Atlantic Edition)
15 Catoctin Circle, Southeast,
Leesburg, Virginia 22975 or:
Box 5001
Leesburg, Virginia 22975
1-703-771-8558
1-800-428-4156 (toll free)
Rates: Published weekly. Subscription rates as follows: a trial subscription is $1 for one month (four issues), 26 weeks is $10.15, one year is $19.25, two years, $36.70 (all issues except trial subscription issues include the current year's *Mid-Atlantic Antique Shop Guide*).* Readers can also write for a free sample copy.
Specialty: Covers antique and collectible dealers for Delaware, District of Columbia, Eastern Ohio, Maryland, New Jersey, New York, North Carolina, Pennsylvania, South Carolina, Virginia, and West Virginia.
   This is a wonderful antique weekly with loads of information for collectors of movie memorabilia. All varieties of movie memorabilia are covered, but not in each weekly issue. Recent in-depth articles have included information on Big Little Books, Greta Garbo, and James Dean. There is also a weekly column by Harry Rinker, well-known collectibles authority. Lots of book ads and a directory of antique and collectible shops.

---

*Includes dealers and retailers who sell, consign, and buy collectibles with maps of regional areas where shops are located.

Barr's Post Card News
70 South 6th
Lansing, Iowa 52151
1-319-538-4500
Rates: Subscription rates are $25 for one-year subscription.
    Published each Thursday and dated the following Monday.
    Classified ads accepted.
Specialty: Postcards.

Collectrix
389 New York Avenue
Huntington, New York 11743
516-424-6479
Rates: Subscription rates are $7.50 for one year (three issues a
    year).
Specialty: Antiques, collectibles.

Comics Buyer's Guide
Department CX
Iola, Wisconsin 54990
Specialty: Classifieds list dealers of Disneyana, gum cards,
    movie magazines, James Bond collectibles, rare character
    collectibles, Big Little Books, and related film collectibles.

Maine Antique Digest
P.O. Box 645
Waldoboro, Maine 04572
Rates: Subscription rates are $29 for one year, and $50 for two
    years.
Specialty: Primarily a monthly newspaper for antiques, but
    also has extensive coverage of major movie memorabilia
    auctions such as Sotheby's and Christie's East.

Old Toy Soldier Newsletter
209 North Lombard
Oak Park, Illinois 60302
Rates: Subscription rates are $25 for first class (United States or
    Canada), or $15 for bulk-rate postage.
Specialty: Twelve-year-old bi-monthly newsletter which
    features articles on companies that manufacture military
    figures as well as civilian lines.

P.A.C. (The Paper and Advertising Collector)
Official publication of The National Association of Paper &
   Advertising Collectors
P.O. Box 500
Mount Joy, Pennsylvania 17552
1-717-653-8240
Rates: Subscription rates are $12 per calendar year, which
   includes membership in NAPAC. A membership card is sent
   with each subscription.
Specialty: Film ephemera. Articles and photographs on all
   paper and advertising collectibles, and each issue features
   dealer ads for film ephemera.

Paper Collector's Marketplace
P.O. Box 127
Scandinavia, Wisconsin 54977
Rates: Subscription rates are $15.95 for one year; $28.95 for two
   years; and $39.95 for three years (each yearly subscription
   entitles the subscriber to place one free classified ad).
Specialty: Primarily film ephemera. A good source for movie
   collectibles, as most issues feature some information on
   various categories of memorabilia such as Shirley Temple,
   Popeye, Disneyana, etc.

Paper Pile Quarterly
Box 337
San Anselmo, California 94960
1-415-454-5552
Rates: Subscription rates are $10 for one year (four issues).
   Published in January, April, July, and October. Issues come
   in a vinyl binder for easy reference. Ads accepted from
   collectors to buy, sell, or trade paper memorabilia. After
   payment of an ad that runs three times, the fourth ad
   insertion is free. Business card display ads also accepted at $8
   per single business card insertion.
Specialty: Film ephemera.

The Postcard History Society
c/o John H. McClintock
P.O. Box 1765
Manassas, Virginia 22110
1-703-368-2757

Rates: Annual dues are $5, which includes four annual newsletters. This is the major deltiological publication in the country. A roster of over 250 postcard dealers is available to members free (include 39¢, #10 self-addressed, stamped envelope). Back issues of *The Postcard Dealer and Collector Magazine*, which was published from 1978 to 1985, cost $12.50 postpaid and include a 32-page dissertation on "How to Price Old Picture Postcards" and a postcard encyclopedia.
Specialty: Postcards.

Remember That Song
5821 North 67th Avenue
Suite 103-306
Glendale, Arizona 85301
Lois Cordrey, Editor
Rates: Subscription rate is $14 for 12 issues. Annual membership includes a 40-word ad. Add $8 for first-class mailing to the above price. Otherwise, subscriptions are sent bulk mail.
Specialty: Sheet music.

Toy Shop
Circulation Department
700 E. State Street
Iola, Wisconsin 54990
1-715-445-22114
Rates: Subscription rates are $37.75 for one year, first class, and $15.95 for one year, third class. Subscription rates include a free 25-word classified ad.
Specialty: Dolls, toys. This is an indexed toy publication for buying or selling toys. Hundreds of classified ads plus full-page display and dealer ads.

MOVIE MEMORABILIA CLUBS, MUSEUMS, AND FAN PUBLICATIONS

Rex Allen Day's, Inc.
Rex Allen Cowboy Museum, Inc.
Sherriff Posse Arena
Willcox, Arizona 85643
602-384-3183
Specialty: A 2800-square-foot museum in Rex Allen's
   hometown. Allen made his debut in *The Arizona Cowboy* in
   1950. A theater is located next to the museum and shows
   first-run movies and cowboy serials featuring Allen and other
   cowboy stars.

American Museum of the Moving Image
35th Avenue and 36th Street
Astoria, New York 11106
Rates: Membership categories run from $35 for an individual
   to $1000 for "Director's Circle." These are yearly
   membership fees; for a two-year membership double all fees.
   Membership includes a quarterly newsletter and a calendar
   of events bulletin, plus other amenities depending on the
   price of membership.
Specialty: The American Museum of the Moving Image is the
   first museum in the United States to devote itself to the
   history of exhibiting, producing, and promoting motion
   pictures, television, and video art. There are 60,000 objects

in the museum's collection including early movie cameras.
The museum is adjacent to the Astoria Studios complex,
which dates from the silent film era.

Beatlefan
P.O. Box 33515
Decatur, Georgia 30033
Rates: Yearly subscription to this newsletter is $12 for six issues
  ($15 for express delivery and first-class mailings to Canada
  and Mexico). Subscription rate for England, Europe, and
  Latin America is $21 per year.
Specialty: Issues feature interviews with friends and relatives of
  the Beatles, plus features on their films, Beatle artwork, and
  articles on the group's music career.

The Big Little Book Collector's Club of America
P.O. Box 1242
Danville, California 94526
Rates: The $10 yearly membership fee includes a membership
  card, bi-monthly publication (*The Big Little Times*) with
  articles, interviews, and classified ads for selling, trading,
  and buying Big Little Books. A free classified ad is included
  with a membership. The club has over 400 members.

The Ephemera Society of America
124 Elm Street
Bennington, Vermont 05021
Rates: Yearly dues are $20.

Gone With the Wind Collector's Club (founded in 1979)
P.O. Box 503
Walkersville, Maryland 21793
1-301-254-2461
Rates: Membership fee is $12 per year (first class) and $18 (for
  special mailing class). Club publication is called the *GWTW
  Collector's Club Newsletter*. The club has over 400 members
  and an annual budget of $50,000–$100,000. Marlene
  Ridzenous is the corresponding secretary.

The James Bond 007 Fan Club
P.O. Box 414
Bronxville, New York 10708-0414

Rates: Membership dues are $15 for United States and Canada, $17 for Europe and South America, and $20 for the Far East and Africa. Membership includes several thousand people in 30 different countries—this is the biggest and longest established James Bond Fan Club in existence. Acknowledged by Eon Productions.

Membership includes an official membership card, two issues of *Bondage*, the club magazine, two issues of *Bondage Quarterly Club Newsletter*, four 8″ × 10″ glossy photo portraits including one each of Ian Fleming, Sean Connery, Roger Moore, and Timothy Dalton. Also exclusive membership priviliges which include free offers and special merchandise/memorabilia offerings. Club publications include rare stills, inside information on Bond films, interviews with stars and film makers, and unpublished writings by Bond creator, Ian Fleming.

James Bond Fan Club
Dr. No.
2269 Chestnut Street, #438
San Francisco, California 14123
Rates: Membership includes a quarterly newsletter and photographs for $5.

The James Dean Gallery
425 Main Street
Fairmount, Indiana 46928
317-948-3326
Specialty: Opened on September 22, 1988, with a diverse collection of Deanology—the largest such collection in the United States. James Dean died in September 1955.

The London Toy & Model Museum
21/23 Craven Hill
London W2 EN
01-262-7905
Time: Founded by collector Allen Levy. Open Tuesday through Saturday from 10 A.M. to 5:30 P.M., and on Sundays, from 11 A.M. to 5:30 P.M.

The Marx Brotherhood
The Freedonia Gazette
Darien 28
New Hope, Pennsylvania 18938-1224
Rates: $4 for sample issue, for free information send a self-addressed, stamped envelope (two first-class stamps).
Specialty: Magazine and original Marx memorabilia including posters, photos, records—all for sale.

Tom Mix Museum
Dewey, Oklahoma

Playing Card Collectibles Association, Inc.
Miss Elsie Fiebrich
3621 Douglas Avenue
Apartment 524
Racine, Wisconsin 53402

Chicago Playing Card Collectors, Inc.
1559 West Platt Boulevard
Chicago, Illinois 60620

Roy Rogers–Dale Evans Collectors Association
PACE
P.O. Box 1166
Portsmouth, Ohio 45662
Attn: LaRue Horsley
Rates: Membership is $15 per year and includes bi-monthly newsletter, one 8″ × 10″ black and white autographed photograph of Roy Rogers and Dale Evans, a membership card, and a 16-page booklet with 24 photos, which is called *Roy Rogers Homecoming, 1982.*
    Portsmouth, Ohio, is the boyhood home of Roy Rogers. His home is open to visitors on selected occasions.

Studio Collectors Club
P.O. Box 1566
Apple Valley, California 92307
Specialty: Movie personalities and movie memorabilia.

The Shirley Temple Club
c/o Rita Dubas
8811 Colonial Road
Brooklyn, New York 11209
1-718-745-7532
Rates: Membership is $15 per year (first class), and includes
The Shirley Temple Collector News, which features
photographs of Ms. Temple, both past and present, loads of
gossip about the actress, letters from readers, a classified
section, and an "In the Media" section, which describes
interesting tidbits about Shirley Temple that have appeared,
and continue to appear, in newspapers and magazines
worldwide.

Universal Autograph Collectors Club
P.O. Box 6181
Washington, D.C. 20044-6181
Bob Erickson, Secretary
Rates: One year membership is $18, regular, and $15, student.
A lifetime membership costs $275.
The Pen and Quill is the club's publication and a member
may list up to three different collecting areas which will then
be published in *The Pen and Quill*. Sample copies are $3.50
in the United States, Canada, Mexico, and other areas with
zip codes, or $5 elsewhere.
Specialty: UACC was founded in 1965 and boasts over 2000
members in the United States, Canada, England, and 30
other countries on six continents.

MAJOR ACADEMY AWARD WINNERS (1927/28–1989)

1927/28

Picture .... *Wings* (PAR)
Actor .... Emil Jannings, *The Way of All Flesh* (PAR); *The Last Command* (PAR)
Actress .... Janet Gaynor, *Seventh Heaven* (FOX); *Street Angel* (FOX); *Sunrise* (FOX)
Director .... Frank Borzage, *Seventh Heaven* (FOX)

1928/29

Picture .... *Broadway Melody* (MGM)
Actor .... Warner Baxter, *In Old Arizona* (FOX)
Actress .... Mary Pickford, *Coquette* (Pickford, UA)
Director .... Frank Lloyd, *The Divine Lady* (FN); *Weary River* (FN); *Drag* (FN)

1929/30

Picture .... *All Quiet on the Western Front* (UNIV)
Actor .... George Arliss, *Disraeli* (WB)
Actress .... Norma Shearer, *The Divorcee* (MGM)
Director .... Lewis Milestone, *All Quiet on the Western Front* (UNIV)

1930/31

Picture......................*Cimarron* (RKO)
Actor.......................Lionel Barrymore, *A Free Soul* (MGM)
Actress....................Marie Dressler, *Min and Bill* (MGM)
Director ....Norman Taurog, *Skippy* (PAR)

1931/32

Picture....................*Grand Hotel* (MGM)
Actor.......................Wallace Beery, *The Champ* (MGM)
                           Fredric March, *Dr. Jekyll and Mr. Hyde* (PAR)
Actress....................Helen Hayes, *The Sin of Madelon Claudet* (MGM)
Director ....Frank Borzage, *Bad Girl* (FOX)

1932/33

Picture....................*Cavalcade* (FOX)
Actor.......................Charles Laughton, *The Private Life of Henry VIII* (London Films, UA)
Actress....................Katharine Hepburn, *Morning Glory* (RKO)
Director ....Frank Lloyd, *Cavalcade* (FOX)

1934

Picture....................*It Happened One Night* (COL)
Actor.......................Clark Gable, *It Happened One Night* (COL)
Actress....................Claudette Colbert, *It Happened One Night* (COL)
Director ....Frank Capra, *It Happened One Night* (COL)

1935

Picture....................*Mutiny on the Bounty* (MGM)
Actor.......................Victor McLaglen, *The Informer* (RKO)
Actress....................Bette Davis, *Dangerous* (WB)
Director ....John Ford, *The Informer* (RKO)

1936

Picture .... *The Great Ziegfeld* (MGM)
Actor .... Paul Muni, *The Story of Louis Pasteur* (WB)
Actress .... Luise Rainer, *The Great Ziegfeld* (MGM)
Supporting Actor .... Walter Brennan, *Come and Get It* (Goldwyn, UA)
Supporting Actress ...... Gale Sondergaard, *Anthony Adverse* (WB)
Director .... Frank Capra, *Mr. Deeds Goes to Town* (COL)

1937

Picture .... *The Life of Emile Zola* (WB)
Actor .... Spencer Tracy, *Captain Courageous* (MGM)
Actress .... Luise Rainer, *The Good Earth* (MGM)
Supporting Actor .... Joseph Schildkraut, *The Life of Emile Zola* (WB)
Supporting Actress ...... Alice Brady, *In Old Chicago* (20th)
Director .... Leo McCarey, *The Awful Truth* (COL)

1938

Picture .... *You Can't Take It With You* (COL)
Actor .... Spencer Tracy, *Boy's Town* (MGM)
Actress .... Bette Davis, *Jezebel* (WB)
Supporting Actor .... Walter Brennan, *Kentucky* (20th)
Supporting Actress ...... Fay Bainter, *Jezebel* (WB)
Director .... Frank Capra, *You Can't Take It With You* (COL)

1939

Picture .... *Gone With the Wind* (Selznick, MGM)
Actor .... Robert Donat, *Goodbye Mr. Chips* (MGM)
Actress .... Vivien Leigh, *Gone With the Wind* (Selznick, MGM)

Supporting Actor ....Thomas Mitchell, *Stagecoach* (Wanger, UA)
Supporting Actress ......Hattie McDaniel, *Gone With the Wind* (Selznick, MGM)
Director ....Victor Fleming, *Gone With the Wind* (Selznick, MGM)

1940

Picture......................*Rebecca* (Selznick, UA)
Actor........................James Stewart, *The Philadelphia Story* (MGM)
Actress ....Ginger Rogers, *Kitty Foyle* (RKO)
Supporting Actor ....Walter Brennan, *The Westerner* (Goldwyn, UA)
Supporting Actress ......Jane Darwell, *The Grapes of Wrath* (20th)
Director ....John Ford, *The Grapes of Wrath* (20th)

1941

Picture......................*How Green Was My Valley* (20th)
Actor........................Gary Cooper, *Sergeant York* (WB)
Actress ....Joan Fontaine, *Suspicion* (RKO)
Supporting Actor ....Donald Crisp, *How Green Was My Valley* (20th)
Supporting Actress ......Mary Astor, *The Great Lie* (WB)
Director ....John Ford, *How Green Was My Valley* (20th)

1942

Picture......................*Mrs. Miniver* (MGM)
Actor........................James Cagney, *Yankee Doodle Dandy* (WB)
Actress ....Greer Garson, *Mrs. Miniver* (MGM)
Supporting Actor ....Van Heflin, *Johnny Eager* (MGM)
Supporting Actress ......Teresa Wright, *Mrs. Miniver* (MGM)
Director ....William Wyler, *Mrs. Miniver* (MGM)

1943

Picture	*Casablanca* (WB)
Actor	Paul Lukas, *Watch on the Rhine* (WB)
Actress	Jennifer Jones, *The Song of Bernadette* (20th)
Supporting Actor	Charles Coburn, *The More the Merrier* (COL)
Supporting Actress	Katina Paxinou, *For Whom the Bell Tolls* (PAR)
Director	Michael Curtiz, *Casablanca* (WB)

1944

Picture	*Going My Way* (PAR)
Actor	Bing Crosby, *Going My Way* (PAR)
Actress	Ingrid Bergman, *Gaslight* (MGM)
Supporting Actor	Barry Fitzgerald, *Going My Way* (PAR)
Supporting Actress	Ethel Barrymore, *None But the Lonely Heart* (RKO)
Director	Leo McCarey, *Going My Way* (PAR)

1945

Picture	*The Lost Weekend* (PAR)
Actor	Ray Milland, *The Lost Weekend* (PAR)
Actress	Joan Crawford, *Mildred Pierce* (WB)
Supporting Actor	James Dunn, *A Tree Grows in Brooklyn* (20th)
Supporting Actress	Anne Revere, *National Velvet* (MGM)
Director	Billy Wilder, *The Lost Weekend* (PAR)

1946

Picture	*The Best Years of Our Lives* (Goldwyn, RKO)
Actor	Fredric March, *The Best Years of Our Lives* (Goldwyn, RKO)
Actress	Olivia de Havilland, *To Each His Own* (PAR)
Supporting Actor	Harold Russell, *The Best Years of Our Lives* (Goldwyn, RKO)

Supporting Actress ......Anne Baxter, *The Razor's Edge* (20th)
Director ....William Wyler, *The Best Years of Our Lives* (Goldwyn, RKO)

1947

Picture.....................*Gentleman's Agreement* (20th)
Actor.......................Ronald Colman, *A Double Life* (Universal-International)
Actress ....Loretta Young, *The Farmer's Daughter* (RKO)
Supporting Actor ....Edmund Gwenn, *Miracle on 34th Street* (20th)
Supporting Actress ......Celeste Holm, *Gentleman's Agreement* (20th)
Director ....Elia Kazan, *Gentlemen's Agreement* (20th)

1948

Picture.....................*Hamlet* (Rank-Two Cities, British)
Actor.......................Laurence Olivier, *Hamlet* (Rank-Two Cities, British)
Actress ....Jane Wyman, *Johnny Belinda* (WB)
Supporting Actor ....Walter Huston, *Treasure of Sierra Madre* (WB)
Supporting Actress ......Claire Trevor, *Key Largo* (WB)
Director ....John Huston, *Treasure of Sierra Madre* (WB)

1949

Picture.....................*All the King's Men* (COL)
Actor.......................Broderick Crawford, *All the King's Men* (COL)
Actress ....Olivia de Havilland, *The Heiress* (PAR)
Supporting Actor ....Dean Jagger, *Twelve O'Clock High* (20th)
Supporting Actress ......Mercedes McCambridge, *All the King's Men* (COL)
Director ....Joseph L. Mankiewicz, *A Letter to Three Wives* (20th)

1950

Picture......................*All About Eve* (20th)
Actor.......................Jose Ferrer, *Cyrano de Bergerác* (UA)
Actress.....................Judy Holliday, *Born Yesterday* (COL)
Supporting Actor........George Sanders, *All About Eve* (20th)
Supporting Actress......Josephine Hull, *Harvey* (Universal-
                        International)
Director....................Joseph L. Mankiewicz, *All About Eve*
                        (20th)

1951

Picture......................*An American in Paris* (MGM)
Actor.......................Humphrey Bogart, *The African Queen*
                        (UA)
Actress.....................Vivien Leigh, *A Streetcar Named
                        Desire* (WB)
Supporting Actor........Karl Malden, *A Streetcar Named
                        Desire* (WB)
Supporting Actress......Kim Hunter, *A Streetcar Named Desire*
                        (WB)
Director....................George Stevens, *A Place in the Sun*
                        (PAR)

1952

Picture......................*The Greatest Show on Earth* (PAR)
Actor.......................Gary Cooper, *High Noon* (UA)
Actress.....................Shirley Booth, *Come Back, Little
                        Sheba* (PAR)
Supporting Actor........Anthony Quinn, *Viva Zapata!* (20th)
Supporting Actress......Gloria Grahame, *The Bad and the
                        Beautiful* (MGM)
Director....................John Ford, *The Quiet Man* (REP)

1953

Picture......................*From Here to Eternity* (COL)
Actor.......................William Holden, *Stalag 17* (PAR)
Actress.....................Audrey Hepburn, *Roman Holiday*
                        (PAR)

Supporting Actor ....Frank Sinatra, *From Here to Eternity* (COL)

Supporting Actress ......Donna Reed, *From Here to Eternity* (COL)

Director ....Fred Zinnemann, *From Here to Eternity* (COL)

1954

Picture.....................*On the Waterfront* (COL)

Actor.......................Marlon Brando, *On the Waterfront* (COL)

Actress....................Grace Kelly, *The Country Girl* (PAR)

Supporting Actor ....Edmund O'Brien, *The Barefoot Contessa* (UA)

Supporting Actress ......Eve Marie Saint, *On the Waterfront* (COL)

Director ....Elia Kazan, *On the Waterfront* (COL)

1955

Picture.....................*Marty* (UA)

Actor.......................Ernest Borginine, *Marty* (UA)

Actress....................Anna Magnani, *The Rose Tattoo* (PAR)

Supporting Actor ....Jack Lemmon, *Mister Roberts* (WB)

Supporting Actress ......Jo Van Fleet, *East of Eden* (WB)

Director ....Delbert Mann, *Marty* (UA)

1956

Picture.....................*Around the World in 80 Days* (Todd, UA)

Actor.......................Yul Brynner, *The King and I* (20th)

Actress....................Ingrid Bergman, *Anastasia* (20th)

Supporting Actor ....Anthony Quinn, *Lust for Life* (MGM)

Supporting Actress ......Dorothy Malone, *Written on the Wind* (Universal-International)

Director ....George Stevens, *Giant* (WB)

1957

Picture.....................*The Bridge on the River Kwai* (COL)

Actor.......................Alex Guiness, *The Bridge on the River Kwai* (COL)

Actress .... Joanne Woodward, *The Three Faces of Eve* (20th)
Supporting Actor .... Red Buttons, *Sayonara* (WB)
Supporting Actress ...... Miyoshi Umeki, *Sayonara* (WB)
Director .... David Lean, *The Bridge on the River Kwai* (COL)

1958

Picture .... *Gigi* (MGM)
Actor .... David Niven, *Separate Tables* (UA)
Actress .... Susan Hayward, *I Want to Live* (UA)
Supporting Actor .... Burl Ives, *The Big Country* (UA)
Supporting Actress ...... Wendy Hiller, *Separate Tables* (UA)
Director .... Vincente Minnelli, *Gigi* (MGM)

1959

Picture .... *Ben-Hur* (MGM)
Actor .... Charlton Heston, *Ben-Hur* (MGM)
Actress .... Simone Signoret, *Room at the Top* (Romulus, Continental)
Supporting Actor .... Hugh Griffith, *Ben-Hur* (MGM)
Supporting Actress ...... Shelly Winters, *The Diary of Anne Frank* (20th)
Director .... William Wyler, *Ben-Hur* (MGM)

1960

Picture .... *The Apartment* (UA)
Actor .... Burt Lancaster, *Elmer Gantry* (UA)
Actress .... Elizabeth Taylor, *Butterfield Eight* (MGM)
Supporting Actor .... Peter Ustinov, *Spartacus* (Universal-International)
Supporting Actress ...... Shirley Jones, *Elmer Gantry* (UA)
Director .... Billy Wilder, *The Apartment* (UA)

1961

Picture .... *West Side Story* (UA)
Actor .... Maximilian Schell, *Judgement at Nuremberg* (UA)

Actress .... Sophia Loren, *Two Women* (Ponti, Embassy-Italian)
Supporting Actor .... George Chakiris, *West Side Story* (UA)
Supporting Actress ...... Rita Moreno, *West Side Story* (UA)
Director .... Robert Wise and Jerome Robbins, *West Side Story* (UA)

1962

Picture .... *Lawrence of Arabia* (COL)
Actor .... Gregory Peck, *To Kill a Mockingbird* (Universal-International)
Actress .... Anne Bancroft, *The Miracle Worker* (UA)
Supporting Actor .... Ed Begley, *Sweet Bird of Youth* (MGM)
Supporting Actress ...... Patty Duke, *The Miracle Worker* (UA)
Director .... David Lean, *Lawrence of Arabia* (COL)

1963

Picture .... *Tom Jones* (Woodfall, UA-Lopert, British)
Actor .... Sidney Poitier, *Lilies of the Field* (UA)
Actress .... Patricia Neal, *Hud* (PAR)
Supporting Actor .... Melvyn Douglas, *Hud* (PAR)
Supporting Actress ...... Margaret Rutherford, *The V.I.P.'s* (MGM)
Director .... Tony Richardson, *Tom Jones* (Woodfall, UA-Lopert, British)

1964

Picture .... *My Fair Lady* (WB)
Actor .... Rex Harrison, *My Fair Lady* (WB)
Actress .... Julie Andrews, *Mary Poppins* (Disney, Buena Vista)
Supporting Actor .... Peter Ustinov, *Topkapi* (UA)
Supporting Actress ...... Lila Kedrova, *Zorba the Greek* (20th)
Director .... George Cukor, *My Fair Lady* (WB)

1965

Picture......................*The Sound of Music* (20th)
Actor........................Lee Marvin, *Cat Ballou* (COL)
Actress......................Julie Christie, *Darling* (Anglo-
               Amalgamated, Embassy)
Supporting Actor.........Martin Balsam, *A Thousand Clowns*
               (UA)
Supporting Actress......Shelley Winters, *A Patch of Blue*
               (MGM)
Director....................Robert Wise, *The Sound of Music*
               (20th)

1966

Picture......................*A Man for All Seasons* (COL)
Actor........................Paul Scofield, *A Man for All Seasons*
               (COL)
Actress......................Elizabeth Taylor, *Who's Afraid of
               Virginia Woolf?* (WB)
Supporting Actor.........Walter Matthau, *The Fortune Cookie*
               (UA)
Supporting Actress......Sandy Dennis, *Who's Afraid of
               Virginia Woolf?* (WB)
Director....................Fred Zinnemann, *A Man For All
               Seasons* (COL)

1967

Picture......................*In the Heat of the Night* (UA)
Actor........................Rod Steiger, *In the Heat of the Night*
               (UA)
Actress......................Katharine Hepburn, *Guess Who's
               Coming to Dinner?* (COL)
Supporting Actor.........George Kennedy, *Cool Hand Luke*
               (WB/Seven Arts)
Supporting Actress......Estelle Parsons, *Bonnie and Clyde*
               (WB/Seven Arts)
Director....................Mike Nichols, *The Graduate* (Embassy)

1968

Picture .... *Oliver!* (COL)
Actor .... Cliff Robertson, *Charly* (ABC-Selmur, Cinerama)
Actress .... Katharine Hepburn, *The Lion in Winter* (Avco Embassy)
Actress .... Barbra Streisand, *Funny Girl* (COL)
Supporting Actor .... Jack Albertson, *The Subject Was Roses* (MGM)
Supporting Actress ...... Ruth Gordon, *Rosemary's Baby* (PAR)
Director .... Carol Reed, *Oliver!* (COL)

1969

Picture .... *Midnight Cowboy* (UA)
Actor .... John Wayne, *True Grit* (PAR)
Actress .... Maggie Smith, *The Prime of Miss Jean Brodie* (20th)
Supporting Actor .... Gig Young, *They Shoot Horses, Don't They?* (ABC Pictures, Cinerama)
Supporting Actress ...... Goldie Hawn, *Cactus Flower* (COL)
Director .... John Schlesinger, *Midnight Cowboy* (UA)

1970

Picture .... *Patton* (20th)
Actor .... George C. Scott, *Patton* (20th)
Actress .... Glenda Jackson, *Women in Love* (UA)
Supporting Actor .... John Mills, *Ryan's Daughter* (MGM)
Supporting Actress ...... Helen Hayes, *Airport* (UNIV)
Director .... Franklin J. Schaffner, *Patton* (20th)

1971

Picture .... *The French Connection* (20th)
Actor .... Gene Hackmann, *The French Connection* (20th)
Actress .... Jane Fonda, *Klute* (WB)
Supporting Actor .... Ben Johnson, *The Last Picture Show* (COL)

Supporting Actress ......Cloris Leachman, *The Last Picture Show* (COL)
Director ....William Friedkin, *The French Connection* (20th)

1972

Picture ....*The Godfather* (PAR)
Actor ....Marlon Brando, *The Godfather* (PAR)
Actress ....Liza Minnelli, *Cabaret* (ABC Pictures, AA)
Supporting Actor ....Joel Grey, *Cabaret* (ABC Pictures, AA)
Supporting Actress ......Eileen Heckart, *Butterflies Are Free* (COL)

1973

Picture ....*The Sting* (UNIV)
Actor ....Jack Lemmon, *Save the Tiger* (PAR)
Actress ....Glenda Jackson, *A Touch of Class* (Avco Embassy)
Supporting Actor ....John Houseman, *The Paper Chase* (20th)
Supporting Actress ......Tatum O'Neal, *Paper Moon* (PAR)
Director ....George Roy Hill, *The Sting* (UNIV)

1974

Picture ....*The Godfather, Part II* (PAR)
Actor ....Art Carney, *Harry and Tonto* (20th)
Actress ....Ellen Burstyn, *Alice Doesn't Live Here Anymore* (WB)
Supporting Actor ....Robert De Niro, *The Godfather, Part II* (PAR)
Supporting Actress ......Ingrid Bergman, *Murder on the Orient Express* (PAR)
Director ....Francis Ford Coppola, *The Godfather, Part II* (PAR)

1975

Picture ....*One Flew Over the Cuckoo's Nest* (Fantasy Films, UA)

Actor........................Jack Nicholson, *One Flew Over the*
                          Cuckoo's Nest (Fantasy Films, UA)
Actress.....................Louise Fletcher, *One Flew Over the*
                          Cuckoo's Nest (Fantasy Films, UA)
Supporting Actor.........George Burns, *The Sunshine Boys*
                          (MGM)
Supporting Actress......Lee Grant, *Shampoo* (COL)
Director...................Milos Forman, *One Flew Over the*
                          Cuckoo's Nest (Fantasy Films, UA)

1976

Picture......................*Rocky* (UA)
Actor........................Peter Finch, *Network* (MGM/UA)
Actress.....................Faye Dunaway, *Network* (MGM/UA)
Supporting Actor.........Jason Robards, *All the President's Men*
                          (WB)
Supporting Actress......Beatrice Straight, *Network* (MGM/UA)
Director...................John G. Avildsen, *Rocky* (UA)

1977

Picture......................*Annie Hall* (UA)
Actor........................Richard Dreyfuss, *The Goodbye Girl*
                          (WB)
Actress.....................Diane Keaton, *Annie Hall* (UA)
Supporting Actor.........Jason Robards, *Julia* (20th)
Supporting Actress......Vanessa Redgrave, *Julia* (20th)
Director...................Woody Allen, *Annie Hall* (UA)

1978

Picture......................*The Deer Hunter* (UNIV)
Actor........................Jon Voight, *Coming Home* (UA)
Actress.....................Jane Fonda, *Coming Home* (UA)
Supporting Actor.........Christopher Walken, *The Deer Hunter*
                          (UNIV)
Supporting Actress......Maggie Smith, *California Suite* (COL)
Director...................Michael Cimino, *The Deer Hunter*
                          (UNIV)

1979

Picture	Kramer Vs. Kramer (COL)
Actor	Dustin Hoffman, Kramer Vs. Kramer (COL)
Actress	Sally Field, Norma Rae (20th)
Supporting Actor	Melvyn Douglas, Being There (Lorimar Film/UA)
Supporting Actress	Meryl Streep, Kramer Vs. Kramer (COL)
Director	Robert Benton, Kramer Vs. Kramer (COL)

1980

Picture	Ordinary People (PAR)
Actor	Robert De Niro, Raging Bull (UA)
Actress	Sissy Spacek, Coal Miner's Daughter (UNIV)
Supporting Actor	Timothy Hutton, Ordinary People (PAR)
Supporting Actress	Mary Steenburgen, Melvin and Howard (UNIV)
Director	Robert Redford, Ordinary People (PAR)

1981

Picture	Chariots of Fire (The Ladd Company/WB)
Actor	Henry Fonda, On Golden Pond (UNIV)
Actress	Katharine Hepburn, On Golden Pond (UNIV)
Supporting Actor	John Gielgud, Arthur (Orion)
Supporting Actress	Maureen Stapleton, Reds (PAR)
Director	Warren Beatty, Reds (PAR)

1982

Picture	Ghandhi (COL)
Actor	Ben Kingsley, Ghandi (COL)

Actress ....Meryl Streep, *Sophie's Choice* (UNIV)
Supporting Actor ....Louis Gossett, Jr., *An Officer and a Gentleman* (PAR)
Supporting Actress ......Jessica Lange, *Tootsie* (COL)
Director ....Richard Attenborough, *Ghandi* (COL)

1983

Picture ....*Terms of Endearment* (PAR)
Actor ....Robert Duvall, *Tender Mercies* (UNIV)
Actress ....Shirley MacLaine, *Terms of Endearment* (PAR)
Supporting Actor ....Jack Nicholson, *Terms of Endearment* (PAR)
Supporting Actress .....Linda Hunt, *The Year of Living Dangerously* (MGM/UA)
Director ....James L. Brooks, *Terms of Endearment* (PAR)

1984

Picture ....*Amadeus* (Orion)
Actor ....F. Murray Abraham, *Amadeus* (Orion)
Actress ....Sally Field, *Places in the Heart* (Tri-Star)
Supporting Actor ....Haing S. Ngor, *The Killing Fields* (WB)
Supporting Actress ......Peggy Ashcroft, *A Passage to India* (COL)
Director ....Milos Forman, *Amadeus* (Orion)

1985

Picture ....*Out of Africa* (UNIV)
Actor ....William Hurt, *Kiss of the Spider Woman* (H.B. Filmes/Sugarloaf Films, Island Alive)
Actress ....Geraldine Page, *The Trip to Bountiful* (Bountiful, Island)
Supporting Actor ....Don Ameche, *Cocoon* (20th)

Supporting Actress ......Anjelica Huston, *Prizzi's Honor* (ABC
                              Motion Pictures, 20th)
Director ....Sydney Pollack, *Out of Africa* (UNIV)

1986

Picture.....................*Platoon* (Hemdale, Orion)
Actor.......................Paul Newman, *The Color of Money*
                              (Touchstone, Buena Vista)
Actress ....Marlee Matlin, *Children of a Lesser
                              God* (PAR)
Supporting Actor ....Michael Caine, *Hannah and Her Sisters*
                              (Orion)
Supporting Actress ......Dianne Weist, *Hannah and Her Sisters*
                              (Orion)
Director ....Oliver Stone, *Platoon* (Orion)

1987

Picture.....................*The Last Emperor* (Hemdale, COL)
Actor.......................Michael Douglas, *Wall Street* (20th)
Actress ....Cher, *Moonstruck* (MGM)
Supporting Actor ....Sean Connery, *The Untouchables*
                              (PAR)
Supporting Actress ......Olympia Dukakis, *Moonstruck* (MGM)
Director ....Bernardo Bertolucci, *The Last
                              Emperor* (Hemdale, COL)

1988

Picture.....................*Rain Man* (MGM/UA)
Actor.......................Dustin Hoffman, *Rain Man* (MGM/UA)
Actress ....Jodie Foster, *The Accused* (PAR)
Supporting Actor ....Kevin Kline, *A Fish Called Wanda*
                              (MGM/UA)
Supporting Actress ......Geena Davis, *The Accidental Tourist*
                              (WB)
Director ....Barry Levinson, *Rain Man* (MGM/UA)

1989

Picture ....*Driving Miss Daisy* (WB, Zanuck Co. Production)

Actor ....Daniel Day-Lewis, *My Left Foot* (Miramax, Ferndale/Granada Production)

Actress ....Jessica Tandy, *Driving Miss Daisy* (WB, Zanuck Co. Production)

Supporting Actor ....Denzel Washington, *Glory* (Tri-Star)

Supporting Actress ......Brenda Ficker, *My Left Foot* (Miramax, Ferndale/Granada Production)

Director ....Oliver Stone, *Born on the Fourth of July* (UNIV)

INDEX

YOU'VE GOT THE LOOK!

...And *The Official® Identification and Price Guide to Costume Jewelry* is the ideal reference, to find out why your "junk" jewelry has gone to collector status!

Expert HARRICE SIMONS MILLER, dealer *and* designer of costume jewelry, holds us spellbound as she takes us from the twenties to the eighties, spanning all the name designers *and* their costume jewelry through each decade. From Chanel to Dior, Hobé to Kenneth Jay Lane, we take a fascinating journey into fashion history, where every phase, fad, and style is encountered!

◆ Over 250 photos...eight pages of glorious color...fully indexed!

THIS GUIDE HAS BEEN ENDORSED BY *VOGUE* AND *GLAMOUR* AS A MUCH-NEEDED REFERENCE!

AN ENCYCLOPEDIA TO FASHION!

From bustles to minis, *The Official® Identification and Price Guide to Vintage Clothing* takes us through the extraordinary fashion revolutions between 1890 and 1970.

Expert CYNTHIA GILES dresses this book with exciting, informative tips on building and maintaining a collection and much more!

☆Wonderful photos and illustrations...eight pages of dramatic color...fully indexed!

THIS BOOK SHEDS THE LIGHT ON VINTAGE FASHION COLLECTIBLES!